Regulatory and Economic Challenges in the Postal and Delivery Sector

Topics in Regulatory Economics and Policy Series

Michael A. Crew, Editor

Center for Research in Regulated Industries
Graduate School of Management, Rutgers University
Newark, New Jersey, U.S.A.

Previously published books in the series:

Crew, M.A. and Kleindorfer, P. R.:
Emerging Competition in Postal and Delivery Services
Cherry, B.A.:
The Crisis in Telecommunications Carrier Liability: Historical Regulatory Flaws and Recommended Reform
Loomis, D.G. and Taylor, L. D.:
The Future of the Telecommunications Industry: Forecasting and Demand Analysis
Alleman, J. and Noam, E.:
The New Investment Theory of Real Options and its Implications for Telecommunications Economics
Crew, M. and Kleindorfer, P. R:
Current Directions in Postal Reform
Faruqui, A. and Eakin, K.
Pricing in Competitive Electricity Markets
Lehman, D. E. and Weisman, D. L.
The Telecommunications Act of 1996: The "Costs" of Managed Competition
Crew, Michael A.
Expanding Competition in Regulated Industries
Crew, M. A. and Kleindorfer, P. R.:
Future Directions in Postal Reform
Loomis, D.G. and Taylor, L.D.
Forecasting the Internet: Understanding the Explosive Growth of Data
Crew, M. A. and Schuh, J. C.
Markets, Pricing, and Deregulation of Utilities
Crew, M.A. and Kleindorfer, P.R.
Postal and Delivery Services: Pricing, Productivity, Regulation and Strategy
Faruqui, A. and Eakin, K.
Electricity Pricing in Transition
Lehr, W. H. and Pupillo, L. M.
Cyber Policy and Economics in an Internet Age
Crew, M. A. and Kleindorfer, P. R.
Postal and Delivery Services: Delivering on Competition
Grace, M. F., Klein, R. W., Kleindorfer, P. R., and Murray, M. R.
Catastrophe Insurance: Consumer Demand, Markets and Regulation
Crew, M. A. and Kleindorfer, P. R.
Competitive Transformation of the Postal and Delivery Sector
Crew, M. A. and Spiegel, M.
Obtaining the Best from Regulation and Competition

Regulatory and Economic Challenges in the Postal and Delivery Sector

edited by

Michael A. Crew
Center for Research in Regulated Industries
Graduate School of Management
Rutgers University
Newark, New Jersey, U.S.A.

and

Paul R. Kleindorfer
Risk Management and Decision Process Center
The Wharton School
University of Pennsylvania
Philadelphia, Pennsylvania, U.S.A.

Kluwer Academic Publishers

Library of Congress Cataloging-in-Publication Data

A C.I.P. Catalogue record for this book is available
from the Library of Congress.

ISBN 1-4020-7972-9 e-ISBN 0-387-23637-6 Printed on acid-free paper.

Printed in the United States of America.

9 8 7 6 5 4 3 2 1 SPIN 11054962

springeronline.com

CONTENTS

CONTENTS

AUTHORS

Daniel Bahar, Associate, Sidley Austin Brown and Wood LLP

Etienne Billette de Villemeur, Associate Professor, GREMAQ and IDEI, University of Toulouse

Philippe De Donder, Professor, GREMAQ and IDEI, University of Toulouse

Geoff Bickerton, Research Director, Canadian Union of Postal Workers

Reto Bleisch, Economist, Regulatory Affairs, Swiss Post

Lynn Bue, 1st National Vice President, Canadian Union of Postal Workers

Catherine Cazals, Researcher, GREMAQ and IDEI, University of Toulouse

Robert H. Cohen, Director, Rates Analysis & Planning, U.S. Postal Rate Commission

João Confraria, Professor, Faculdade de Ciências Económicas e Empresariais, Universidade Católica Portuguesa

Helmuth Cremer, Professor of Economics, GREMAQ and IDEI, University of Toulouse

Michael A. Crew, Professor of Economics and Director—Center for Research and Regulated Industries, Rutgers Business School, Rutgers University

Helmut M. Dietl, Professor and Chair of Services and Operations Management, Universität Zürich

Paul Dudley, Head of Regulatory Economic Analysis, Royal Mail Group

Philippe De Donder, Professor of Economics, IDEI, University of Toulouse

Kari Elkelä, Development Manager, Finland Post Corp

Frédérique Feve, Researcher, GREMAQ and IDEI, University of Toulouse

Jean-Pierre Florens, Director of Research, GREMAQ and IDEI, University of Toulouse

Mary Ann Gibbons, Senior Vice President and General Counsel, United States Postal Service

Roger Hill, Business Modeller, Royal Mail Group

Helen Jenkins, Director, Oxera

Paul R. Kleindorfer, Anheuser–Busch Professor of Management Science and Economics, Wharton School, University of Pennsylvania

Joy M. Leong, Partner, Sidley Austin Brown & Wood LLP

David M. Levy, Partner, Sidley Austin Brown & Wood LLP

Leonardo Mautino, Senior Consultant, Oxera

Richard Moriarty, Director – Competition and Regulation, Postal Services Commission

Dimosthenis Papakrivopoulos, Associate, Sidley Austin Brown & Wood LLP

Edward S. Pearsall, Consultant, U.S. Postal Rate Commission

Sophie Richard, Senior Economist, Royal Mail Group

D. Rijnders, Senior Consultant, Nolan, Norton & Co.

Matthew Robinson, Postal Rate and Classification Specialist, U.S. Postal Rate Commission

Richard Robinson, Senior Business Modeller, Royal Mail Group

Frank Rodriguez, Head of Economics, Royal Mail Group

Bernard Roy, Head – Department of Regulatory Economics, La Poste

Thomas M. Sharkey, Director – Strategic Planning and Performance Reporting, United States Postal Service Office of Inspector General

Renee Sheehy, Analyst, U.S. Postal Rate Commission

Paul Smith, Deputy Director – Retail, Postal Services Commission

Soteri Soterios, Royal Mail Group

J. Strikwerda, Professor University of Amsterdam

Joëlle Toledano, Director, European and National Regulation, La Poste

Urs Trinkner, Economist, Corporate Development Postmail, Swiss Post

Mark van der Horst, Chair - European Express Association, UPS

John Waller, Assistant Director, Rates Analysis & Planning, U.S. Postal Rate Commission

David C. Williams, Inspector General, United States Postal Service Office of Inspector General

Spyros Xenakis, Economist, U.S. Postal Rate Commission

SPONSORS

Rutgers University, Rutgers Business School, CRRI—Center for Research in Regulated Industries
University of Pennsylvania, Wharton School,Risk Management and Decision Processes Center
Royal Mail Group
Deutsche Post World Net
United States Postal Service
Canada Post Corporation
FedEx
La Poste
La Poste / De Post
R.R. Donnelley & Sons Company
UPS
Swiss Post
CTT Correios
IBM Business Consulting Services
Pitney Bowes
Postcomm – Postal Services Commission
Siemens Dematic Postal Automation
United States Postal Rate Commission
Posten AB
Finland Post Corporation
Anacom
An Post
A.T. Kearney GmbH
Correos y Telégrafos
Poste Italiane
TPG Post
Canadian Union of Postal Workers
Sidley Austin Brown and Wood LLP
Frontier Economics
Envelope Manufactures Association
London Economics
National Association of Letter Carriers
New Zealand Post
Oxera
Venable LLP
Association for Postal Commerce
Haldi Associates

PREFACE AND ACKNOWLEDGEMENTS

This book arises out of the Twelfth Conference on Postal and Delivery Economics held in Cork, Ireland, June 2-5, 2003. Leading practitioners, postal administrations, and the courier industry, as well as a number of regulators, academic economists, mailers, consultants, technology suppliers, and lawyers came together to examine some of the major policy and regulatory issues facing the industry. Issues addressed included international postal policy, strategies for the postal sector, the universal service obligation, regulation, competition, entry, cost and productivity, interaction of law and economics, and future technologies.

The conference and the book follow our earlier conferences. In 1990, the first Conference on Postal and Delivery Economics (CPDE) was held at Coton House, Rugby, England, July 22-25, 1990, in honor of the one hundred and fiftieth anniversary of the Penny Post and the contributions of Sir Rowland Hill. The ensuing book, *Competition and Innovation in Postal Services*, was published by Kluwer Academic Publishers in 1991. In 1992 2nd CPDE was held at Village PTT, La Londe les Maures, France, on March 18-21, 1992. This conference resulted in *Regulation and the Nature of Postal and Delivery Services,* published by Kluwer Academic Publisher in 1993. Both conferences were recognized by the European Express Organization with the Hermes Award 1992 at its annual award dinner in Munich on June 22, 1992. The first workshop, The Workshop on Postal and Delivery Economics, was held June 23-26, 1993 in Daun, Germany. In 1994 the 3rd CPDE was held in Stockholm, Sweden, May 18-21,1994, and a workshop, in Hakone, Japan, June 1-4, 1994 combined to produce the volume *Commercialization of Postal and Delivery Services,* published by Kluwer Academic Publisher in 1995. A workshop was held in Naantali, Finland, June 7-10, 1995. The 4th CPDE was held in Monterey, California, May 22-25, 1996, and resulted in the book *Managing Change in The Postal and Delivery Industries,* published by Kluwer Academic Publisher in 1996. The next book, *Emerging Competition in Postal and Delivery Services* was a direct result of the 5th and 6th CPDEs the former was held in Helsingor, Denmark, June 11-14, 1997; and the latter held in Montreux, Switzerland, June 17-20, 1998. . The 7th CPDE was held in Sintra, Portugal, June 23-26, 1999, which resulted in the book *Current Directions in Postal Reform*, published by Kluwer Academic Publishers in 2000. The 8th CPDE, was held in Vancouver, Canada, June 7-10, 2000, resulting in the book *Future Directions in Postal Reform*, published by Kluwer Academic Publishers in 2001. The 9th CPDE was held in Sorrento, Italy, June 6-9, 2001, and the book *Postal and Delivery Services: Pricing, Productivity, Regulation and Strategy*, was published by Kluwer Academic Publishers in 2001. The 10th

CPDE was held in Potsdam, Germany, June 5-8, 2002, and the resulting book, *Postal and Delivery Services: Pricing, Delivering on Competition,* was published by Kluwer Academic Publishers in 2002. The 11th CPDE was held in Toledo, Spain, June 4-7, 2003, and the resulting book, *Competitive Tranformation of the Postal and Delivery Sector*, was published by Kluwer Academic Publishers in 2004.

The 2004 conference was made possible by the support of the following organizations: CRRI—Center for Research in Regulated Industries, Rutgers Business School, Rutgers University; University of Pennsylvania, Wharton School, Risk Management and Decision Processes Center; Royal Mail Group; Deutsche Post World Net; United States Postal Service; Canada Post Corporation ; FedEx; La Poste; La Poste / De Post; R.R. Donnelley & Sons Company; Swiss Post; United Parcel Service; CTT Correios; IBM Business Consulting Services; Pitney Bowes; Postcomm – Postal Services Commission; Siemens Dematic Postal Automation; United States Postal Rate Commission; Posten AB ; Finland Post Corporation; Anacom; An Post; A.T. Kearney GmbH; Correos y Telégrafos; Poste Italiane; TPG Post; Sidley Austin Brown and Wood LLP; Frontier Economics; Canadian Union of Postal Workers; Envelope Manufactures Association; London Economics; National Association of Letter Carriers; New Zealand Post; Oxera; Venable LLP; Association for Postal Commerce; and Haldi Associates

We would like to thank sponsors not only for financial support, but also for their advice and encouragement, and for serving on the organizing committee. In particular, we would like to thank Stephen Agar, John Allen, Anthony Alverno, Gary Battaglia, Maynard Benjamin, Geoff Bickerton, Marion Brouwer, Philip Burns, Maria Carmo Seabra, Ralph Carter, Robert Cohen, Jeff Colvin, Robert Curry, Gonzales d'Alcantara, Gene Del Polito, Charles Fattore, Stephen Ferguson, Nick Fincham, Rutger Goethart, Stefano Gori, John Haldi, George Houpis, Helen Jenkins, Luis Jimenez, Daniel Krähenbühl, Anton van der Lande, Joy Leong, David M. Levy, José Maria Marcos, Walter Maschke, Richard Moriarty, Heikki Nikali, Louis O'Brien, George Omas, Wolfgang Pickave, Wolfgang Pordzik, Alberto Pimenta, Leon Pintsov, Sarah Prosser, Ian Reay, Frank Rodriguez, Jim Sauber, David Spence, Gregory Swinand, Joëlle Toledano, David Treworgy, Mark van der Horst, Anton van der Lande, Lars Vesterlund, Ian Volner, Sture Wallander, and Ingo Willems.

The host country plays an important role in these conferences. This year's conference, the *Twelfth Conference on Postal and Delivery Economics*, benefited greatly from the efforts of our host, An Post. Their representative Stephen Ferguson was a gracious host. He provided not only advice and assistance on numerous occasions but also wrote a brief history of An Post available on www.crri.rutgers.edu/post.

We would like to thank our distinguished dinner speakers, Donal Curtin, John Nolan, and Michael J. Critelli. In the tradition of these conferences we very much enjoyed the speech by Donal Curtin, Chief Executive, An Post. His keynote speech at the Conference provided an outlook on the future of postal and delivery networks from the unique perspective of An Post. John Nolan, Deputy Postmaster General, United States Postal Service, presented a speech, which gave an interesting perspective from the point of view of a PO in midst of reform. Michael J. Critelli, Chairman and Chief Executive Officer, Pitney Bowes, provided commentary on the role of a leading technology provider in the future of the mail.

Finally, we would like to thank Andrew Mearman of the University of the West of England and Jeremy T. Guenter for their assistance. Andrew provided editorial assistance, which added considerably to the clarity and readability of this volume. We are especially appreciative of the efforts of Jeremy T. Guenter, Senior Administrative Assistant in the Center for Research in Regulated Industries, for his efforts in making this book possible. We would like to thank him not only as editors but also on behalf of the authors to whom he provided considerable assistance. He continues to develop a research tool available to all through the CRRI web site providing access to the many references used in this and other postal books in the series as well as regulatory economics more generally. The database now has over 9000 entries; it is updated continuously. Visit us on the web at http://crri.rutgers.edu.

The usual disclaimers are applicable. In particular, the views expressed are the views of the authors and are not necessarily those of the sponsors.

Michael A. Crew
Paul R. Kleindorfer

Chapter 1

Competition, Universal Service and the Graveyard Spiral*

Michael A. Crew and Paul R. Kleindorfer
Rutgers University and University of Pennsylvania

1. INTRODUCTION

This paper provides another examination of the issue of competition and universal service in the postal sector. While there has been much interest in the issue, most of the debate so far has had the effect of generating more heat than light. This paper, while having lofty objectives, is unlikely to prove an exception. There have been two main camps. The one camp argues that further competitive entry will have a deleterious effect on a PO's ability to remain financially viable. The other argues that competitive entry conveys so many benefits in terms of increased efficiency that the risks of undermining the financial viability of the POs are very small compared to these benefits and should be ignored. The two camps agree on one thing: that the universal service obligation (USO) should remain. There may be some willingness to allow the USO to be relaxed, but this has proved difficult for POs to achieve in practice, as public outcry is the usual response to proposals to shut down post offices or relax the USO in other ways. The protagonists of liberalization usually cite the successful experience of New Zealand and Sweden. The problem is that both sides make powerful

* We are grateful for the programming assistance of Ralph Ahn for the simulation modeling results presented in Section 2. We also acknowledge helpful comments from Ian Reay and Frank Rodriguez on an earlier draft, and the support of Royal Mail and the Russell L. Ackoff Endowment for this research.

opposing arguments and there seems little prospect of any meeting of minds. Moreover, neither side has yet been able to show convincingly the superiority of one policy over the other. This arises primarily because of the rather complex nature of the issues involved.

This paper aims to inform the debate by providing a model of entry and access that integrates earlier contributions and provides some perspectives on the factors underlying the financial viability of a PO with a USO and facing various forms of competitive entry. Section 2 will review the debate so far on entry and access with a USO. It will relate the situation in posts with that in other industries, for example, telecommunications where these types of issues are also currently being addressed. This section notes factors identified in earlier papers that have been argued to affect the viability of a PO under entry. Section 3 will provide the motivation, underlying assumptions and a discussion of the principal results of a simulation model developed to study the issues. The intended contribution of the model is to synthesize a number of approaches and attempt to throw additional light on the impact of entry on POs facing a USO. Section 4 will be by way of conclusions and implications for entry and access policy. The Appendix sets out the analytical model underlying the simulations of Section.

2. THE DEBATE ON ENTRY

The USO drives the debate on entry. It provides the basis of a credible case against unrestricted entry. The USO is the obligation to deliver letters and parcels ubiquitously and, in the case of letters, at a uniform price. In addition, there is an obligation to provide some uniformity in service quality. While outlying areas get lower quality service, the general consensus is that delivery standards should not be drastically different from those of accessible areas. To meet these obligations POs have typically been granted a reserved area, a weight or price limit, where they are the only legal providers. Absent the obligation of the uniform price and some service uniformity, the ubiquity requirement could be satisfied without a reserved area. The question is then if a USO is to continue whether a reserved area is required. Crew and Kleindorfer (2000, 2001) have argued that a meaningful USO is unlikely to be feasible absent a reserved area or some other method of funding. This argument is further elaborated in Crew and Kleindorfer (2004) to accommodate economies of scope between letters and parcels. However, even with revenues derived from significantly increased parcel volumes, it seems unlikely for most countries that the lettermail USO can be supported without a reserved area, unless service standards are relaxed. Entrants would price below the incumbent in the low cost markets. The incumbent would raise its (uniform) prices making a larger market more attractive to the entrants. The process may result in a graveyard spiral of increasing prices and continuing losses.

The graveyard spiral is a dynamic process. Entry is allowed and entrants take some of the incumbent's most profitable business. The uniform price is then raised further with the result that previously unprofitable traffic now becomes profitable for entrants. This in turn attracts more entry as the increase in the uniform price again fails to raise sufficient revenue to break even. This process continues through more iterations, with the PO continuing to fail to break even, until cumulative losses eventually lead to the financial collapse of the PO.

Although this is a rather complex dynamic process, it can be illustrated by a simple numerical example. Consider a PO with two types of letter, urban and rural. Urban costs 4 to deliver and rural costs 12. Fixed costs are 50. The demand for urban and rural respectively is 10 and 5. At a uniform price of 10 the PO breaks even, since 50 = 10x15 – 4x10 – 12x5. However, if entry is allowed, the urban mail is lost to entrants and, assuming an elasticity of demand of zero, the PO now breaks even by charging a uniform price of 22, since 50 = 22x5 – 12x5. However, if demand is not completely inelastic, there may be no price that will yield the necessary revenue to cover costs, thus forcing the PO out of business, thereby ending or curtailing service to rural areas, or requiring a direct subsidy.

Although this is the essence of the concern about the effect of entry, the process in reality is much more complicated than this. Indeed, it is the complexity of the problem that makes consensus on entry policy difficult to achieve. While protagonists on either side agree on many of the pieces of what is quite a complicated puzzle, they find it hard to agree on a policy on entry because of the complexities involved. Some of these major complexities are now examined briefly.

The first issue concerns whether there should be a USO or not, and here there is probably the greatest agreement. Very few economists argue against a USO with the possible exception of Geddes (2003) who argues that inefficiencies implied by the USO outweigh the benefits it provides. While this is distinctly a minority view, there is a broader debate as to what form the USO should take. A number of proponents of entry, notably Cohen et al. (2000), have argued that relaxation of some of the requirements of the USO in outlying areas might be considered as part of a strategy for financial viability under entry. These could include reducing the frequency of delivery to five days a week or less for remote areas. However, reducing the obligations of the USO amounts to reducing benefits for fairly large groups of postal customers and this is politically not readily achievable. This is illustrated by the European Postal Directive, which has increased obligations in some instances. So even on the nature and extent of the USO there does not appear to be agreement. A further issue is whether reducing the obligations in an acceptable manner would result in sufficient cost reductions to enable POs to stay viable under various entry policies, let alone what these changes should be.

A second issue concerns the extent of liberalization. Should the entire market be opened up and the incumbent PO still face a USO? If this were the case, would the PO be required to provide access to its networks to entrants? Presumably, deregulation would imply that POs would only be required to provide access on a freely negotiated basis and would not be compelled by a regulator or the government to provide access. More likely, even if a PO's reserved area were eliminated it might be required to provide access through an access tariff or otherwise be subject to regulation of access. An alternative might be to provide a small reserved area and tariffed access. Yet another would be not to have a reserved area in terms of weight or price but to provide a PO with a delivery-only monopoly below a certain price or weight limit but require access to be provided based on a published tariff. In some respects this resembles an extension of the situation faced by USPS, which allows more downstream access than any other major PO.

A third issue affecting financial viability under liberalization is the pricing and product flexibility offered to a PO. If a PO finds that price flexibility is denied by regulation and product introductions are significantly delayed through lengthy regulatory proceedings, then financial viability will be more difficult to achieve under entry (see De Donder et al. (2002) for a discussion of pricing flexibility and the USO). However, a system of regulation in the form of price caps, allowing a PO more pricing flexibility, might enable it to be more effective in competing both in price, quality and variety.

A fourth issue is the nature and extent of contestability. Following Baumol et al. (1988), contestability of particular customers or mail volumes means that even though the incumbent may be serving these customers/volumes now, these could be subject to capture by entrants under entry. Contestability of particular customers or volumes depends on many factors, including underlying switching costs and brand loyalty to the incumbent, service quality and scope of product line. The term contestability is used broadly to mean the vulnerability of an incumbent to losses in revenue or volume from a specific customer segment to entrants, which is similar to the usage by other authors in addressing competition and the USO. There is considerable agreement that contestability plays a major role in determining whether a PO can remain viable in the face of entry. The disagreement is over its nature and extent. The more of its mail that is non-contestable, the more likely it is that a PO will be financially viable after entry. There is no disagreement about this. At one extreme all the mail may be contestable. At another almost none would be. Cohen et al. (2004) view a large percentage of the mail being non-contestable while d'Alcantara and Amerlynck (2004) argue the opposite for the case of Belgian Post. Other possibilities include mail in the low-cost delivery areas being contestable but that in the high cost areas being non-contestable. The latter would leave the incumbent PO with the high cost mail and make financial viability more difficult to achieve. The model and simulations developed in this paper attempt to address the issues of contestability in a more general manner that enables the views of Cohen et al. and d'Alcantara and Amerlynck to be addressed and their impact on the graveyard spiral evaluated.

An overarching issue is that once entry is allowed, traditional ways of viewing the problem no longer apply. In simplistic terms, this might be thought of as going from "monopoly" thinking to "competitive" thinking. This means that traditional approaches to problems have to be re-evaluated. As noted by Cohen et al. (2004), some routes are profitable while some are unprofitable at the uniform prices charged by the PO. It seems reasonable to believe that the profitable routes will be lost to entrants leaving the PO with the unprofitable routes. However, this notion is an oversimplification. As argued in Crew and Kleindorfer (2001), competitors are going to compete directly for customers and only indirectly for routes. In particular, the USO will require that the PO continue to deliver some mail to all routes, whether or not they are profitable. What this means is that traditional concepts of route profitability might not be very helpful in analyzing overall financial viability of the PO in the face of entry. Unless profits are rather uniform for routes, it is very difficult to conclude what route profitability implies for the likelihood of a graveyard spiral, as route profitability curves are only meaningful *ceteris paribus*.

The matter of route profitability is illustrated in Figure 1. The curve shows gross profits (excluding non-route-specific fixed costs) from routes ranked in order beginning on the left with least profitable with the break even point shown at A. The original route profit curve is shown by curve ABC. As a result of entry, some revenues are lost to entrants and the PO raises the uniform price to achieve breakeven operations. Many cases are possible, and we show only one of these in Figure 1, with a new route-profit curve A'B'C'. In the instance illustrated in Figure 1, the PO's initial gross contribution to cover its non-route-specific fixed costs F, including those associated with the USO, are F = G – L, where G = BCD are the gross profits from profitable routes (those to the right of route r_0) and L = AB0 are the losses from unprofitable routes (those to the left of r_0). After entry and the price increase, gross profits from profitable routes are G' = B'C'D and losses from unprofitable routes (those to the left of r_e), L' = A'B'0. If the

PO, as illustrated in Figure 1, fails to achieve financial viability with the initial price increase (i.e., if F > G' – L'), which is clearly the case in Figure 1, then the PO would have to raise its uniform price again, and if this resulted in continuing losses, the PO would be on the way to a graveyard spiral.

Figure 1: Route Gross Profits Pre-Entry and Post-Entry

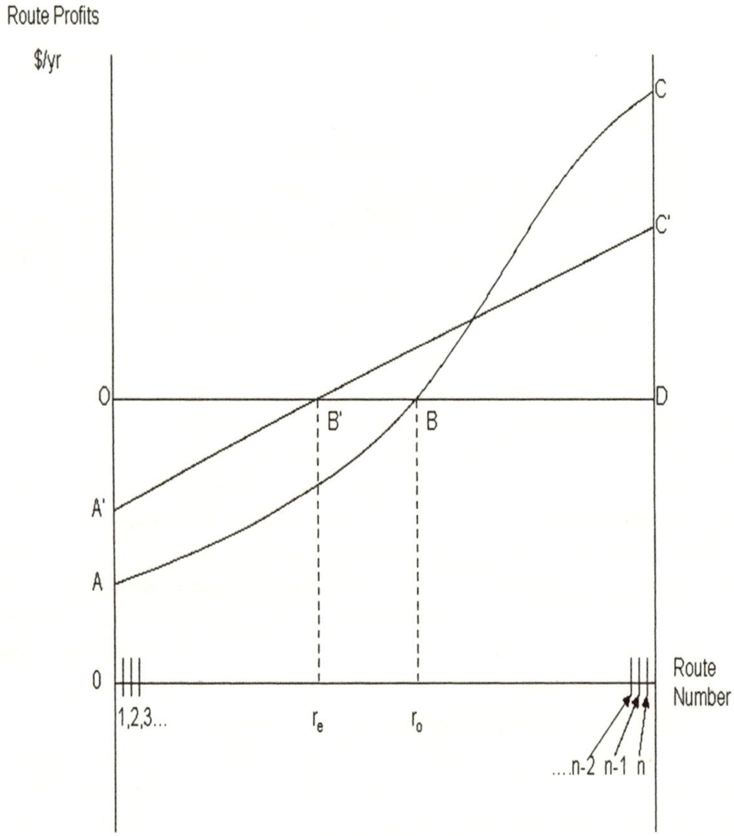

The consequences for route profitability from entry may be more complicated than as represented in Figure 1 (which already entail problems of forecasting demand responses and competitive reactions). Indeed, the curve A'B'C' need not even have the same ordering as the curve ABC;[1] the

---

[1] Although generally it seems reasonable to expect that the loss area, A'B'O and the profit area, B'C'D will both be smaller than the corresponding pre-entry loss and profit areas, the number of routes that are profitable may be greater or less. (In Figure 1, there are

magnitude of losses arising from entry for specific routes might be considerably greater than for other routes; and issues of brand loyalty and pricing may further complicate the matter. Thus, historic route profitability is only one indicator of the ability of a PO to sustain the USO post-entry, and it is likely not to be a very good indicator. Indeed, it seems highly likely that route profitability will change dramatically in the face of entry.

It is not easy to provide a graph that represents clearly the situation in which the PO retains all its routes but finds that its route profitability changes with entry as a result of raising the uniform price.[2] What is likely to happen is that the high cost routes actually lose less with the increase in the uniform price but the formerly profitable routes either become less profitable or even unprofitable. The shape of the profit curve would change but the area representing profits to the right may still be still less than the losses to the left. Raising the uniform price further may not eliminate the losses and may exacerbate the problem as more entry is generated. How to address these issues is complicated. This is particularly true when it comes to addressing dynamic effects, and graphical analysis is limited in its ability to illustrate such effects.

Since competitors will compete for customers, not routes, they will compete initially for large mailers. How profitable a customer will be will depend on the percentage of the customer's mail the entrant delivers. The entrant has the option of delivering the mail himself or handing it to the PO. Absent any special access pricing regime the entrant will hand all mail that he does not deliver to the PO at either the single-piece rate or a presort rate or quantity discounted rate. Depending on the pricing regime of the PO, different outcomes can occur for the entrant and for the PO. All cases have a different impact on a PO's ability to fund its USO. In all cases, only letters and not parcels are considered. Some possibilities include the following where entrants deliver some of the mail themselves and use PO facilities for the rest.

(a) PO Charges Single-Piece Rate Only

All mailers pay the single-piece rate and there are no discounts of any kind. If a competitor uses PO facilities it can only access them at the single piece rate. This has the effect of encouraging the competitor to deliver as

actually fewer routes incurring losses, and a greater number of routes making profits, post entry.) Note also that the routes are ordered in terms of initial profitability so that the curve through ABC is necessarily monotonic increasing. The same need not be the case for the post-entry curve A'B'C' though we show it as monotonic for graphical clarity in Figure 1.

2 Although not modeled here, there is likely to be a loss of scale economies on profitable routes.

much as possible even when its cost are higher than those of the PO. It also means that it has to be more selective of customers. A large customer with a significant portion of mail for delivery by the PO may not be very attractive, as the competitor has to absorb the entire costs of handing the mail over to the PO and has no discounts to defray such costs. Under this arrangement the entrant's own delivery will be inefficiently large. Several effects are at work in conflicting directions. Failure to compete may cause loss of business but making entrants' access to its network costly works in the other direction.[3]

(b) PO Offers Presort and Possibly Quantity Discounts but no Downstream Access Rates

The competitor has a reduced incentive to develop excessive delivery facilities but may find more customers attractive relative to (a) in that he now has a discount to help defray the costs of handing mail to the PO.

(c) PO Offers Discounts in (b) plus Downstream Access Rates

In principle, this option seems to offer the greatest promise of economic efficiency. It has the potential to retain scale and scope economics in that it will result in the most efficient supplier delivering the mail if prices are set efficiently. Additionally, it gives the PO the greatest opportunity to compete successfully and to explore whether, indeed, it is financially able to provide a USO under entry. Here downstream access rate are assumed to be set at least approximating efficient prices, along the lines, for example, of delivery access pricing (DAP) developed by Crew and Kleindorfer (2002) In principle, this arrangement provides the potential for access rates to be set efficiently. Of course, if access rate are set too low there will be an economically inefficiently large amount of access provided by the PO and vice versa if they are set too high.

While (c) has the greatest potential for economic efficiency and financial viability it does not necessarily guarantee financial viability any more than

---

[3] We do not consider this case further in the rest of the paper. At least for telecommunications in the U.S., it is of potential interest. The Regional Bell Operating Companies (RBOCs), the owners of the local networks, have resisted offering access to their networks to competitors at the rates set by regulators and have recently won a significant victory in the case United State Telephone Association vs. Federal Communications Commission , decided by U.S. Circuit Court of Appeals of the District of Columbia, March 2, 2004. The approach puts considerable pressure on competitors to build their own facilities, the so-called "facility-based entry".

(a) and (b) do. In terms of achieving financial viability, (a) has some benefits at deterring entry and promoting PO profitability. However, the PO does not provide entrants with opportunities to build up traffic on a route to a level where it could deliver directly, so there is a potential loss in welfare resulting from decreased scope of product offerings. It is not possible *a priori* to provide an answer to the question of which of the above alternatives best promotes the dual objective of maximizing total welfare subject to maintaining a viable USO. Indeed, our simulation results show that there is no general answer to this question; the outcome depends on the parameters of the context in question.

The model in the Appendix and the simulations in Section 3 will attempt to address these kinds of issues. Some important issues can only be addressed indirectly. In particular, dynamic issues are address when examining conditions that result in a graveyard spiral. Another issue is the current situation of declining demand facing postal service. This may mean that entry has fewer benefits than might be expected. It is salutary to note that even in telecommunications, where demand and technologic change were growing strongly, a serious meltdown has nonetheless occurred[4]. In the postal sector there are fewer potential gains given declining demand and minimal technological change. As we will see in the next section, this implies increased risk from entry for the viability of the incumbent. Such issues will be addressed again in the concluding discussion of Section 4.

3. DISCUSSION OF THE RESULTS OF THE SIMULATION MODEL

The purpose of the simulations, whose results are reported and discussed here, is to throw light on the effects of entry generally and to explore the issue of the graveyard spiral in particular. The analysis makes it possible to examine not only the directions that entry policy might take but makes it possible to compare the approaches to entry being considered by various countries. TPG, for example, is opposed to mandating access, while Postcomm, the UK regulator and Royal Mail are putting in place comprehensive mandatory access offerings. In the US highly developed upstream access arrangements have been available for many years and downstream access policies are being introduced.

The technical details of the analysis are explained in the Appendix. The idea is to produce a model incorporating incumbent's and entrants' demand

---

4 "Meltdown" here refers to the bankruptcy of MCI WorldCom and the huge loss in asset values across the telecom sector.

and cost structures that is sufficiently simple to interpret but at the same time captures the essential aspects of the problem. For example, the model should allow for cases where the PO provides downstream access to its network and instances when it does not. Inevitably, given the complexity of the problem, such an approach can never be completely successful.

The model we propose to analyze these issues has an incumbent PO and a competitive fringe.[5] There are two mail products, residential mail and business mail where class of mail is identified by the originator. Residential mail is assumed to be completely non-contestable in that the entrant does not enter that market. For business mail, the demands for the PO's mail and the entrants demand are not only functions of each other's prices but also incorporate "loyalty". The term should not be interpreted literally. The idea of "brand loyalty" or "switching costs" captures the effect of a consumer's cost of switching to another supplier, and incorporates both elements of familiarity and knowledge of purchasing arrangements as well as relationship-specific investments by customers in working with a particular supplier. In the literature on the graveyard spiral, the effects of loyalty were incorporated by d'Alcantara and Amerlynck (2004); their notion of loyalty is essentially what is used here. Namely loyalty (to the incumbent) is represented as the level of price discount that must be offered by entrants to compete on an even footing with the incumbent. Such loyalty effects will, of course, depend on the customer segment, and on the delivery zone of mail arising from this segment, and is taken account of the model. The technical representation of loyalty in the demand equations has the same effect as quality of the incumbent's service being better perceived relative to entrants. In practice, brand loyalty to the incumbent is therefore related to the notion of contestability of a particular product. For example, the ubiquity and the brand name of a PO may mean that it can charge a somewhat higher price than an entrant without suffering significant demand erosion, and the loyalty variable is intended to capture such effects. Over time such advantages may diminish, especially for business customers, and loyalty parameters could be adjusted accordingly.

The cost structure of entrants and the incumbent are likely to be different. The incumbent is expected to have higher costs because of the USO and these are incorporated through higher fixed costs. In addition, the incumbent may have labor agreements that result in higher costs. Putting this together it seems likely that the incumbent will have a cost advantage in the high cost routes because of ubiquity and the entrant on the low cost routes because of his ability to employ lower priced labor. We use a cubic cost structure to represent the high likelihood that there will be significant departures from

---

[5] A competitive fringe is a simpler alternative to a Cournot or Bertrand approach. See De Donder et al (2001) for a discussion of alternative models of competition.

average costs in both the low-cost and high-cost areas. While the same cubic cost structure employed is employed for both the PO and for entrants, it can be readily adjusted to take into account such differences in costs by adjusting the parameters of the general cost function in the appropriate manner. To allow for zonal cost differences, we assume 10 zones, with the highest cost zone being 10 and the lowest 1. The details of the parameter values and the cost structure can be found in the Appendix.

Pricing decisions are made within the framework of these demand and cost structures. Three pricing approaches are used. Avoided Cost/ECPR (ACE), Approximate Delivery-Zone Access Prices (DAP) with Limited Information and Approximate Delivery-Zone Access Prices with Full Information (DAPFI). The first two are recognized in the literature and in the case of the first in practice, as ACE is actually employed by some POs in some form. ACE is a close approximation to DAP as indicated by Crew and Kleindorfer (2002). ACE is defined in the usual manner and is sometimes referred to as top down efficient component pricing. It is the single-piece price less the value of the cost savings of the incumbent as a result of the entrant performing upstream work (typically collection, barcoding and presortation). One problem with ACE is that it assumes implicitly that the top down price is close to economic cost. Given that the single piece uniform price is too high in the low cost areas and too low in the high cost areas, ACE is going to perpetuate these inefficiencies. Take the case of a high cost area costing 50 cents a letter but the uniform price is 30 cents and the presort discount 10 cents. To charge an access price of 30 minus 10 = 20 cents would exacerbate the funding problem. The correct (DAP) price would be 40 cents but the entrant would not pay this, as the single piece price is 30 cents. So DAP takes the cost of delivery in the area concerned and deducts any presort discount as long as the resulting access price is 30 cents or less. Otherwise the access price is the single piece price of 30 cents. It is based, in effect, on the value of the work still required when the letter enters the mail stream. DAPFI is an extension of DAP in the sense that it assumes perfect knowledge of the costs of the competitive fringe. Thus, it takes entrants' costs into account and adjusts access prices accordingly. DAPFI enables the PO to compete more effectively and therefore provide more funding for the USO. As perfect information about entrants' costs is not available DAPFI cannot be employed in practice. However, it does indicate that there may be some potential benefit to an incumbent in making an estimate of entrants' cost justifying some departure from simple DAP.

The base case employs the values of the cost function provided in the Appendix. The assumptions are intended to be rather conservative. The PO is assumed to set prices to break even. The entrant has a significant advantage in the lowest cost area, namely Zone 1, relative to the incumbent.

As the zones get higher cost the advantage to the PO increases. So in Zone 10 the entrant has a cost of 83.2 cents and the incumbent has a cost of 64.3 cents, whereas in Zone 1 the situation is reversed at 7.6 cents and 11.2 cents respectively. The parameter values are set so as to imply moderate loyalty to the incumbent in the low cost zones, growing to significant loyalty to the incumbent in high-cost areas.

Consider Table 1, where four variations of the base case are examined. Case 1: Pure Monopoly is a case that rarely exists anymore. It is the case where entrants have nothing to do with mail. The PO has the entire vertically integrated value chain. The entrants produce nothing at all. This is modeled in our simulations by making loyalty to the incumbent absolute. Case 2: Upstream Access is where the entrant is permitted to enter mail upstream as in the case of collection and presort. This case corresponds to the current situation in many countries, and we refer to this "partial liberalization" case as our Base Case (using ACE as the access pricing method). Case 3: Downstream Entry allows the entrant not only to feed mail into the PO stream at any stage but also to bypass it completely. Case 3 (full liberalization) will attract most attention in the discussion of outcomes since it represents the most liberalized view of entry policy and is at the heart of the current debate on entry and the USO. Finally, in Case 3GS, we show the level of fixed costs F for the incumbent that give rise to a graveyard spiral for our base case under full liberalization. In what follows, we will not compute all graveyard spirals to their conclusion, but will truncate the process whenever the required price for breakeven either does not exist or is in excess of 100c.

Table 1 shows the single-piece price, fixed costs for I, the ratio of these fixed costs to total costs (or total revenue since breakeven operations are maintained), I's market share (measured as the ratio of I's revenue to total revenue of both I and E), and total welfare for the three cases (with welfare measured in the standard fashion as the sum of consumer surplus plus total profits). It is interesting to note that welfare actually decreases under full liberalization relative to the Base Case (upstream entry and worksharing only). This reflects the fact that the incumbent PO has to increase substantially under full liberalization because of loss of revenues from the low-cost zones. This substantial increase in price is not made up by the decreased cost of delivery occasioned by entry, with the result that welfare is slightly decreased.

Table 1: Outcomes of the Model for Three Entry Scenarios and Graveyard Spiral

	Case 1	Case 2 (ACE)	Case 3 (ACE)	Case 3 (ACE/GS)
Single-Piece Price	47.6c	49.6c	64.1c	>100c
Incumbent's Fixed Costs (F)	30,000	30,000	30,000	41,700
F/(Incumbent's Revenue)	0.246	0.368	0.412	NA
Incumbent's Market Share	100%	66.7%	59.3%	0%
Total Welfare	609,169	699,113	698,619	NA

Case 1 might be considered the case that some really old timers still dream about. Here there is effectively absolute loyalty to the incumbent in that the PO literally handles all the mail from each end of the value chain, collection, processing, transportation and delivery. Interestingly, upstream entry in Case 2 results in a lower single piece price and higher welfare. Complete freedom of entry in Case 3 results in a much higher single-piece price. If fixed costs increase significantly (from 30,000 to 41,700), a graveyard spiral results.

Comparing access pricing methodologies, these have two effects. One is to increase welfare in going from ACE to DAP to DAPFI. The other is to increase the viability (or survivability) of the incumbent. Tables 2 and 3 present compare the outcomes of the three access pricing methods for the Base Case (upstream entry only) and for Full Liberalization (end-to-end service by entrants is possible as well as upstream entry and use of I's delivery services). As expected based upon Crew and Kleindorfer (2002) DAP offers only a small gain over ACE, but DAPFI offers a significant gain. Again this is not very surprising. The benefits of competitive intelligence are usually considered to be significant.

Let us now investigate the graphically the various factors that might influence the occurrence of a graveyard spiral. Comparing Tables 2 and 3, just for the level of fixed cost at which a graveyard spiral is induced, we see that the PO has considerable leeway when only upstream entry is allowed (Table 2) versus full liberalization.[6] The contrasting levels of fixed cost necessary to induce a graveyard spiral under these two regimes are, respectively, 70,800 and 41,700. Given this relative robustness of the PO under the Base Case, we will be primarily focused on the results of Full Liberalization. We will also consider only the DAP method of access pricing, as it is clearly feasible and slightly more efficient than the ACE approach.

---

6 Note that DAP and DAPFI give identical results in this case since no benefit arises to the Incumbent from knowledge of the entrants' delivery cost, since entrants do not deliver in the Base Case.

Table 2: Outcomes of the Model for Three Access Pricing Methods[7] (Base Case)

	Case 2 (ACE)	Case 2 (DAP)	Case 3 (DAPFI)
Single-Piece Price	49.6c	49.2c	49.2c
Incumbent's Fixed Costs (F)	30,000	30,000	30,000
F/(Incumbent's Revenue)	0.368	0.367	0.367
Incumbent's Market Share	66.7%	66.9%	66.9%
Total Welfare	699,113	699,294	699,294
Fixed Cost (F) at which Graveyard Spiral is Induced	70,800	70,800	70,800

Table 3: Outcomes of the Model for Three Access Pricing Methods (Full Liberalization)

	Case 3 (ACE)	Case 3 (DAP)	Case 3 (DAPFI)
Single-Piece Price	64.1c	63.8c	61.8c
Incumbent's Fixed Costs (F)	30,000	30,000	30,000
F/(Incumbent's Revenue)	0.412	0.411	0.409
Incumbent's Market Share	59.3%	59.5%	59.8%
Total Welfare	698,619	699,039	701,574
Fixed Cost (F) at which Graveyard Spiral is Induced	41,700	41,700	43,900

Several factors could affect the existence of a graveyard spiral, and we illustrate the effects of several of these for our Base Case data. In each of the Figures 2-5 below, we graph on the X-axis a particular variable of interest, and show its effects on two sets of outcomes. On the left Y-axis, we show the effects of the variable on the incumbent's and entrants' prices. In the case of the incumbent, this is just the single-piece price. In the case of the entrants, as their price varies from zone to zone, we compute a quantity-weighted average price. On the right Y-axis we show the effects of the variable on I's market share. In each instance, a graveyard spiral is shown as a price in excess of 100. When a graveyard spiral occurs, I ceases to be viable and its market share becomes zero. Although the chaos that would

[7] While our Base Case results show no increase in the sustainable level of fixed costs F at which the Graveyard Spiral is induced between ACE and DAP pricing, in general DAP will provide additional protection, especially under Full Liberalization. Indeed, as the formulae in the Appendix make clear, DAP access prices in any zone *k* will be higher than ACE prices precisely when $C_{IU} + C_{ID}(k) > P_I$, i.e., whenever end-to-end unit costs for I exceed the single-piece rate. For very high fixed costs *F*, the single-piece rate needs to be very high so that $C_{IU} + C_{ID}(k) \leq P_I$ will hold for *F* (or P_I) sufficiently high. Thus, as graveyard spiral conditions approach, there is no difference between ACE and DAP under Partial Liberalization.

develop when the incumbent PO becomes non-viable would be significant, we continue to show the entrants' weighted price, though entrants may serve high-cost zones only at very high prices when a graveyard spiral occurs. This price is cost driven and not demand driven, of course, as we assume that the entrants form a competitive fringe. However, entrants' price is somewhat affected by the increasing price of the incumbent via access prices that are driven, in part, by the single-piece price.

Figure 2 (see also Tables 1-3) shows that an increase in fixed cost of about 20% will induce a graveyard spiral under DAP and full liberalization. It is to be expected, of course, that the magnitude of fixed costs will be a fundamental factor underlying whether or not a graveyard spiral will result from entry. Other determinants include factors thc level of demand, which is facing absolutes declines in most developed countries.

Figure 2: The Effects of Fixed Cost (*F*) on Price and Marketshare (Full Liberalization)

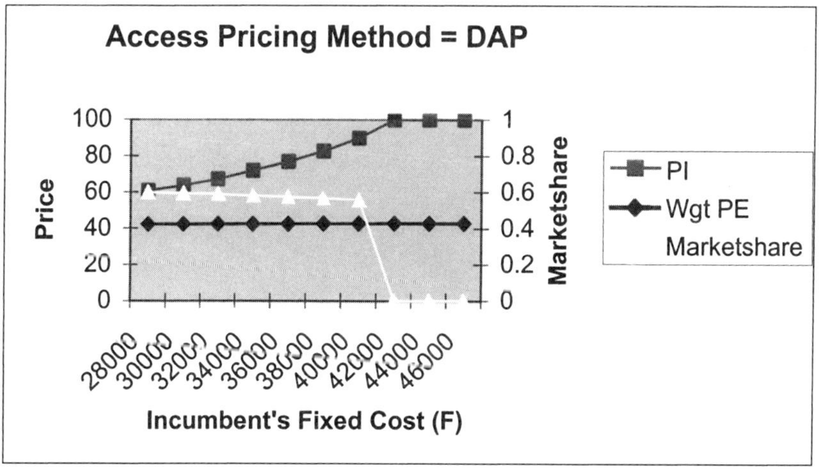

We show in Figure 3 the consequences of demand decline by manipulating the multiplicative constant H(B, k) in the demand equation for the business segment, which accounts for about 80% of the incumbent's revenues (see the Appendix for details on the structure of demand). Figure 3 shows that about a 25% decline in business sector demand is enough to send the PO into a graveyard spiral under our Base Case conditions.

Figure 3: The Effects of Level of Business Segment's Demand on Price and Marketshare (Full Liberalization)
Results obtained by varying X_B, where $H(B, k) = X_B - kY_B$ ($Y_B = 2000$)

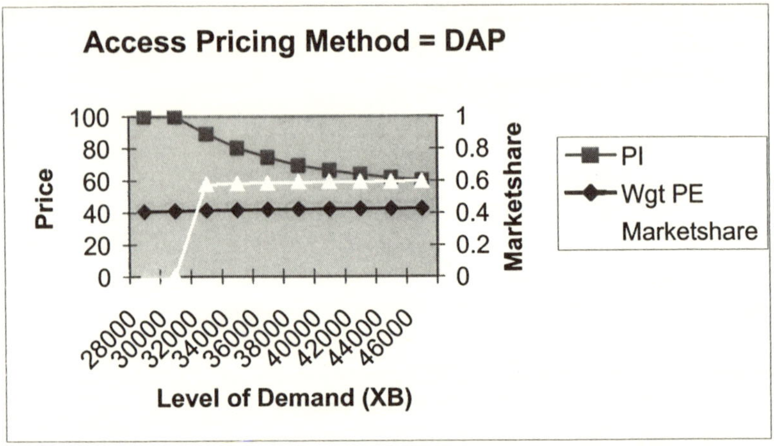

Other factors that could clearly impact on the existence of a graveyard spiral include underlying cost differences between the incumbent and entrants, as well as the contestability of customer mail destined for various zones (especially the low-cost, profitable zones). On the former issue, we show in Figure 4 the effects of entrants' upstream cost on prices and market share. As expected, competing against higher cost entrants leads to a greater incumbent market share and a lower single-piece price (although the effect is not dramatic).

Figure 4: The Effects of Entrants' Upstream Cost (C_{EU}) on Price and Market share (Full Liberalization)

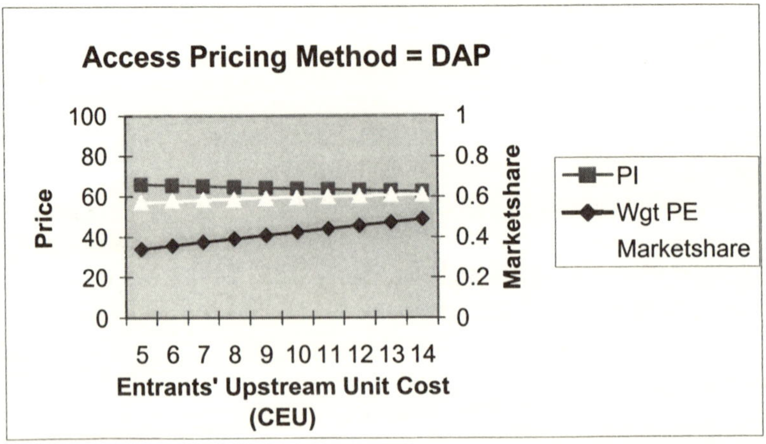

An interesting factor underlying demand is brand loyalty, which may be thought of as a central driver of contestability. If the market is more contestable, then a graveyard spiral could be induced more readily. To illustrate this, we show in Table 4 below the consequences of eroding loyalty for prices and market shares, again for the full liberalization case under DAP access pricing. Recall that the Base Case assumes a slight loyalty advantage for the incumbent, with a loyalty premium of about 10% in the low-cost zone 1, growing to 40% in zone 10. To see the effects of brand loyalty, we show what would happen if the incumbent's brand loyalty were significantly reduced, namely to the case where entrants now enjoy a 10% loyalty premium in the low-cost areas eroding to a 10% loyalty premium for the incumbent in the high cost zone. Clearly, brand loyalty is a major determinant of contestability and survivability of the PO.

Table 4: The Effects of Incumbent Brand Loyalty (L(k)) on Price and Marketshare (Full Liberalization)

	Base Case (More Loyal to Incumbent)									
Zone k	1	2	3	4	5	6	7	8	9	10
L(k)	1.11	1.14	1.16	1.19	1.22	1.25	1.28	1.32	1.35	1.39
P_I	63.8	63.8	63.8	63.8	63.8	63.8	63.8	63.8	63.8	63.8
$P_E(k)$	24.6	34.2	40.3	44.8	49.3	55.4	65.0	79.5	92.1	103.3
	Alternative Case (Less Loyal to Incumbent)									
Zone k	1	2	3	4	5	6	7	8	9	10
L(k)	0.91	0.93	0.94	0.96	0.98	1.00	1.02	1.04	1.06	1.09
P_I	72.8	72.8	72.8	72.8	72.8	72.8	72.8	72.8	72.8	72.8
$P_E(k)$	24.6	34.2	40.3	44.8	49.3	55.4	65.0	79.5	100.8	106.8

Perhaps the most critical element of this analysis is the complex interdependency of all of the factors underlying the sustainability of the PO and the USO under entry.[8] As noted above, these factors include comparative cost advantages, demand characteristics, including brand loyalty, the level of fixed costs, as determined in great degree by the definition of the USO, the pricing flexibility of the PO to respond in a timely fashion to entry before losses accumulate, the structure of revenue and cost determinants across routes and customer segments, and the type of access policy (both in terms of access pricing and the terms of access). Any of these factors, singly or in combination, and statically or dynamically, could provide the essential vulnerability of a PO to entry. To illustrate one set of

[8] We illustrate here only one of the interdependencies, but obviously a number of others could be examined. For example, if incumbent's price elasticity of demand is decreased or if brand loyalty to the incumbent is increased, then a higher level of fixed costs can be supported without giving rise to a graveyard spiral.

interdependencies, we show in Figure 5 below the interaction between sustainable fixed cost for the incumbent and entrants' markup. Intuitively, the larger the entrants' markup (reflecting larger fixed costs for entrants), the less vulnerable the incumbent is to cream skimming from the profitable low-cost areas.

Figure 5: The Effect of Entrants' Required Markup (M_E) on the Value of Incumbent Fixed Cost (F) that can be supported under Full Liberalization (Access Pricing = DAP)

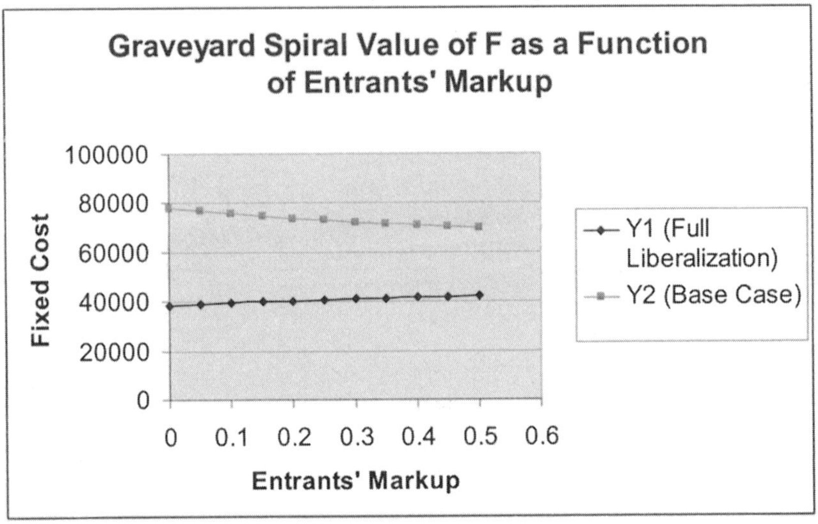

Considering Figure 5, two things are interesting to note. First is how little difference significant changes in entrants' fixed costs (and corresponding markups) makes to the level of sustainable incumbent fixed costs under full liberalization. This is because the largest damage to I's revenues is done in the lowest cost zones, and this remains the case even under significant markups. Second, under the Base Case, where end-to-end delivery is prohibited to entrants, there is actually a decline in sustainable fixed costs for I as E's required markup increases. This is because less efficient upstream operations by E causes I to have to bear a larger portion of the upstream cost and, in addition, there is an overall demand erosion because both I and E, as a result, charge higher prices. Here we see the interaction of entry policy, sustainable fixed cost and entrants' markup policy that indicates one of the several complex interdependencies in this arena.

4. CONCLUDING DISCUSSION

From the results of these simulations, it is clear that a graveyard spiral can be relatively easily induced by a number of factors. The most obvious direct effect would be through an increase in fixed costs. One implication of this is that a graveyard spiral might be avoided if the USO is weakened and fixed costs decreased. Variables driving contestability of demand, especially on currently high-profit routes, are also clearly important. These include brand loyalty to the incumbent (whether driven by perceived quality differences or the ubiquity of the incumbent's service outlets). Thus, as entrants build up their business and brand loyalty, the incumbent PO will face a more difficult problem maintaining the USO and financial viability. With declining demand and eroding brand loyalty, it may take a few years for the graveyard spiral to develop, but once the spiral is entered, it will be difficult if not impossible to reverse the process.

Alternatively, the pressure from entrants may induce the PO to renegotiate more economical labor contracts, become more efficient, and offer more attractive products thereby not losing significant loyalty and perhaps even stimulating new sources of demand with product innovations. However, this does not seem very likely with a public enterprise structure that cannot go bankrupt. This may imply continuing losses. The effects of stagnant or declining volumes, together with increasing price elasticity, clearly make the likelihood of a graveyard spiral greater and further complicate the matter of achieving a smooth downsizing of the incumbent's operations. Of all the access and entry policies examined here, the safest from the point of view of most government-owned POs is partial liberalization (with final delivery retained by the PO), which roughly corresponds to the status quo. POs would retain a statutory monopoly in delivery with entrants performing more and more upstream operations. As we have argued elsewhere, this should be coupled with DAP access pricing to ameliorate subsidization of access to high-cost areas.

Current trends, in the EU particularly, are not going in this direction, but rather towards greater liberalization. Given the actual or anticipated downturn in mail volumes, the results of this paper would suggest that there will be a growing tension to relax the USO or to provide subsidies to support it. The nature of the changes required in the USO is unlikely to be in the form of a trivial adjustment. Indeed, even conceivable changes such as the frequency, uniformity and reliability of delivery, will almost certainly not be enough, absent significant changes in management and labor practices. These concerns about financial viability and the USO are serious, and especially so if their effects arise in a crisis mode and after irreversible choices have been made. If there were the prospect of great benefits in the form of efficiency, innovation and customer satisfaction from liberalization, then perhaps it would be worthwhile to take on the risks arising from the concerns raised here. However, it has yet to be demonstrated that the gains from liberalization in the letter mail area are likely to be significant. Indeed, quite the reverse; letter mail volumes are stagnating or declining the world over, bypassed or substituted by electronic means, and it seems hardly likely that liberalization will bring the sort of innovation that will reverse this. In contrast to the academic world, where small stakes give rise to vitriolic arguments, there may be a case for accepting something close to the current system for letter mail, warts and all, rather than in engaging in chaotic, costly and unnecessary radical surgery.

A. TECHNICAL APPENDIX: MODELING THE GRAVEYARD SPIRAL

General Framework for the Model

There is an incumbent PO (referred to as I) and a set of entrants (referred to as E), both offering postal and delivery services. There are two customer segments, a residential (R) and business (B) segment. I offers two products, end-to-end service, priced uniformly for all delivery zones ($k = 1, \ldots, K$), and an access service for each zone. The access service is offered by I to E for each zone at a price $P_A(k)$, priced separately for each zone k. We assume that there are no differences in upstream collection and processing costs across zones k, but there may be significant differences in delivery costs to different zones.

E only serves the business segment B, leaving R to be served by I. Under full liberalization, E is allowed to provide end-to-end service. Under partial liberalization, E may collect and consolidate upstream mail, receiving a discount from I for so doing, but E must then hand over all mail to I for final delivery.

E is assumed throughout to be a competitive fringe so that pricing across all entrants is equal to the average cost of the service provided, i.e. competition is assumed to drive prices down to the zero profit level. We assume that entrants' fixed costs are recovered through a constant markup over marginal costs. I is assumed to maximize welfare subject to a breakeven constraint. Since significant fixed USO costs will require that the breakeven price is above marginal cost, welfare increases as price decreases, and we will therefore only be looking for the breakeven pricing point, and computing the welfare at this level.

A graveyard spiral will be said to take place when the profit-maximizing price for I (subject to whatever restrictions on entry and access pricing are assumed) is still not sufficient to allow breakeven operations. We will not study the dynamics of the spiral itself here, but only the conditions when the USO is unsustainable.

Cost Specifications

$C_{IU} + C_{ID}(k)$ = unit cost for incumbent PO of servicing mail and delivering it to delivery zone $k = 1, ..., K$, where C_{IU} = cost of upstream collection and sortation by I and $C_{ID}(k)$ = unit cost of downstream delivery by I.

$C_a + C_{ID}(k)$ = unit cost for incumbent PO to service mail destined for delivery zone $k = 1, ..., K$, that has been pre-*sorted* by an entrant and remailed through the PO. We call C_a the acceptance cost (per unit) and it reflects the cost of putting mail collected and presorted by entrants into I's mail stream for delivery. It is assumed that there are some benefits from collection and presortation in that $C_a < C_{IU}$.

F = fixed cost (per period) of the incumbent to maintain the USO

$C_{EU} + C_{ED}(k)$ = unit cost for entrants of servicing mail and delivering it to delivery zone $k = 1, ..., K$, where C_{EU} = cost of upstream collection by E and sorting and $C_{ED}(k)$ = unit cost of downstream delivery by E

M_E = markup above marginal cost, charged by entrants on all products ($M_E \geq 0$).

We assume that unit delivery costs for I and E followed a general structural form given by the following cubic equation:

$$C_{iD}(k) = a_i(k - b_i)^3 + c_i k + d_i, \quad i \in \{I, E\}; \quad k = 1, 2, ..., K$$

where the parameters a_i, b_i, c_i, d_i may be varied to achieve various zonal cost structures. The Base-Case values used in the runs reported here are given in the Table below.

Flow of decisions:

Let P_I = unit price (assumed uniform) for USO-service anywhere. Then the basic timing and sequence of decisions, both in reality and in this model, is as follows.

1. The "regulator" determines the extent of entry (full or partial liberalization) and the method (we consider 3) of pricing access.

2. Incumbent sets uniform price P_I for end-to-end single-piece service.

3. Based on P_I, access prices $P_A(P_I, k)$ for zones k = 1, ..., K are determined according to 1 of 3 methods given below.

4. If partial liberalization only is allowed, then Entrants hand over mail collected upstream and pay an "access fee" to have I deliver this mail.

5. Under full liberalization, Entrants determine for each zone k, which is the cheaper of $P_A(k)$ and $C_{ED}(k)$. They then choose to hand over all mail (serviced by E) destined for zone k to I for delivery if $P_A(k)$ is the cheaper way of doing this and they deliver themselves if $C_{ED}(k)$ is the cheaper way.

6. Entrants prices are assumed to be set, for all zones, as $P_E(k) = (1 + M_E)Cost(k)$, where Cost(k) = full unit cost for the delivery method chosen and $M_E \geq 0$ is the entrants' markup to recover their fixed cost. See (A3) below for the exact pricing expression used for $P_E(k)$.

7. Profits are computed. If P_I is too low for breakeven operations, it is increased. If too high, it is decreased, until ultimately I's profits are zero. If no such breakeven P_I exists (in the sense that even for the profit-maximizing price P_I, negative profits result), then there is no breakeven price and a graveyard spiral would result from attempting to reduce losses through increased prices. Note that binary search can quickly identify the Ramsey-optimal breakeven price P_I by searching between the profit maximizing price P_{Imax} as the upper bound on price and the price $P_{Imin} = MIN\{C_{IU}, C_{EU}\} + MIN\{C_{ID}(k), C_{ED}(k): k = 1, ..., K\}$, as any breakeven price P_I must always exceed P_{Imin}.

8. Finally, welfare is computed for any feasible case (any case in which there is a breakeven price P_I)

Base Case Values for Cost Parameters

Upstream Cost for I (C_{IU})	10
Upstream Cost for E (C_{EU})	10
Adaptation Cost (C_a)	2
USO Fixed Cost (F)	30,000

Zone k	$C_{ID}(k)$	$C_{ED}(k)$
k=1	11.2	7.6
k=2	13.9	14.4
k=3	16.0	18.8
k=4	18.1	22.0
k=5	20.8	25.2
k=6	24.7	29.6
k=7	30.4	36.4
k=8	38.5	46.8
k=9	49.6	62.0
k=10	64.3	83.2

Access Price Rules

Three access-pricing rules will be used, as described in Section 3. The first is the well-known avoided cost or Efficient Component Pricing (ECPR) Rule. The second and third derive from Crew and Kleindorfer (2002, 2004) and our analysis of Delivery-Zone Access Pricing (the DAP Rule).

(1) Avoided Cost/ECPR Rule: Access prices are determined (for all $k = 1, \ldots, K$) by:

$$P_A(k) = P_I - C_{IU} + C_a$$

This amounts to finding the lowest uniform single-piece letter rate P_I for which breakeven operations are possible, with access prices determined by the avoided cost rule.

(2) Approximate Delivery-Zone Access Prices (DAP) with Limited Information: Access prices are set according to the rule (for all $k = 1, \ldots, K$):

$$P_A(k) = Min\left[P_I, Max\left[P_I - C_{IU} + C_a, C_a + C_{ID}(k)\right]\right],$$

This access-pricing rule follows the logic of charging ECPR rates unless these are less than adaptation and delivery costs, in which case the latter will determine access rates. Of course, access cannot be greater than I's end-to-end rates.

(3) Approximate Delivery-Zone Access Prices with Full Information: Access prices are set according to the following (for all $k = 1, \ldots, K$):

$$P_A(k) = Min[P_I, Max(P_I - C_{IU} + C_a, C_a + C_{ID}(k))][1 - h(k)]$$

$$+ Min[P_I, C_{ED}(k) - \tau, Max(P_I - C_{IU} + C_a, C_a + C_{ID}(k))]h(k)$$

where $h(k) = 0$ if $C_{ED}(k)\text{-}C_a\text{-}C_{ID}(k) \leq 0$ and 1 otherwise, and where the tolerance $\tau > 0$ is suitably small (in effect, a tie-breaker). The essence of this summary rule is to separate two cases, one in which the incumbent is more efficient than entrants (the case where $h(C_{DEk} - C_a - C_{DIk}) = 1$) and the case where the entrants are more efficient than the incumbent (the case where $h(C_{DEk} - C_a - C_{DIk}) = 0$). In the former case, this rule assures that access prices will be set so that the more efficient incumbent does final delivery. In the latter case, the rule assures that the access price for zone k is set to provide incentives for the more efficient entrants to deliver mail in zone k (unless the ceiling price of the incumbent's end-to-end service becomes active and entrants then use the PO's services).

Demand Specification

For demand, I gets all residential (R) demand. There is competition for the business (B) demand between I and E.

We assume two products, a product offered by I and an imperfect substitute offered by entrants (E). We use the following model specifications to describe outcomes for market shares and total sales for each product.

Residential Customers (R)

Residential customers use only the incumbent's end-to-end services. We assume underlying preferences for residential customers sending mail to zone k are quasi-linear of the form $U(D, m; R, k) = V(D; R, k) + m$, with the willingness-to-pay $V(D; R, k)$ given by:

$$V(D;R,k) = \frac{D_I(P_I,R,k)}{B_R H(R,k)^{(-1/\varepsilon)}} \left[\frac{\varepsilon}{(\varepsilon - 1) D_I(P_I,R,k)^{(1/\varepsilon)}} - \frac{A_R}{H(R,k)^{(1/\varepsilon)}} \right] \quad \text{(A1)}$$

where $\varepsilon > 1$ is a parameter influencing elasticity (computed explicitly below). The standard demand problem of maximizing $V(D; R, k) - P_I D$ then gives rise to the demand from residential customers for services in zone $k = 1, \ldots, K$ as:

$$D_I(P_I, R, k) = H(R, k)(A_R + B_R P_I)^{-\varepsilon} \qquad \text{(A2)}$$

where A_R and B_R are positive parameters, and $H(R, k) > 0$ is a further set of parameters determining the demand level in zone k. We assume the following:

Base Case Values for R-Demand Parameters

A_R	100
B_R	5
E	1.2
Demand Level H(R, k)	42,000 – 2,000*k

Business Customers (B)

We use the demand model developed in Crew and Kleindorfer (1998) for this case. Business customers use the services of both I and E, which we assume are imperfect substitutes. We assume that entrants can offer different prices for delivery zones and that competition drives these prices down to the zero profit level, so that for each $k = 1, 2, \ldots, K$ entrants' prices are determined as:

$$P_E(k) = (1 + M_E)[C_{EU} + Min[C_{ED}(k), P_A(k)]] \qquad \text{(A3)}$$

Recall that M_E is the entrants' markup to recover fixed costs. We assume underlying preferences for business customers sending mail to zone k are quasi-linear of the form $U(D, m; B, k) = V(D; B, k) + m$, with the WTP function $V(D; B, k)$ given by:

$$V(D_I, D_E; B, k) =$$

$$H(B, k) log_e \left(D_I(P_I, P_E(k), k)^{\alpha} + \frac{D_E(P_I, P_E(k), k)^{\alpha}}{L(k)} \right) \qquad \text{(A4)}$$

where D_I and D_E are, respectively, the demands of business customers for delivery services in zone $k = 1, \ldots, K$ for the products of I and E, and where $H(B, k) > 0$ and $\alpha \in (0, 1)$ are parameters, and where

$L(k)$ = loyalty coefficient, a positive number representing the advantage enjoyed by I relative to E. The effect of $L(k)$ is discussed further below on the basis of the demand curves resulting from (A4).

The demands $D_I(P_I, P_E(k), B, k)$ and $D_E(P_I, P_E(k), B, k)$ are derived from the standard demand problem of maximizing $[V(D_I, D_E; B, k) - P_I D_I - P_E(k) D_E]$ with respect to D_I and D_E and are given by:

$$D_I(P_I, P_E(k), B, k) = \frac{\alpha H(B,k)}{P_I + \left(\frac{P_I}{L(k)}\right)\left(\frac{P_I}{L(k)P_E(k)}\right)^{[\alpha/(1-\alpha)]}} \qquad \text{(A5)}$$

$$D_E(P_I, P_E(k), B, k) = \frac{\alpha H(B,k)\left(\frac{P_I}{L(k)P_E(k)}\right)^{[1/(1-\alpha)]}}{P_I + \left(\frac{P_I}{L(k)}\right)\left(\frac{P_I}{L(k)P_E(k)}\right)^{[\alpha/(1-\alpha)]}} \qquad \text{(A6)}$$

with $P_E(k)$ given by (A1). The reader may verify from (A5)-(A6) that if $P_E(k) = P_I/L(k)$, then $D_I = D_E$ in zone k. Thus, the loyalty coefficient represents the price discount (if $L(k) > 1$) that must be offered by entrants to offset brand loyalty of customers to the incumbent (or the premium the entrant can charge if $L(k) < 1$). Loyalty is therefore zone-dependent (and would more generally be expected to be dependent on customer segments as defined by large and small customers, types of business mail involved and other segmentation drivers). As can be seen from the table just below, we will assume for our base case that the incumbent still enjoys considerable brand loyalty, with the loyalty premium in the lowest cost area being about 11% = (1/0.9) (zone $k = 1$), which grows to a very significant loyalty premium in the higher cost zones, with e.g., $L(10) = 1/(0.72) = 1.39$ in the highest cost zone $k = 10$.

Base Case Values for B-Demand Parameters

A	0.35
Loyalty Coefficients $L(k)$	$1/(s - t^*k)$, s = 0.92; t = .02
Demand Level $H(B, k)$	42,000 – 2,000*k

Price Elasticities

The absolute values of own-price elasticities and cross-elasticities are computed as for each zone k = 1, 2, ..., K as follows:

$$\eta_{IR}(k) = \varepsilon \frac{B_R P_I}{A_R + B_R P_I}$$

$$\eta_{IB}(k) = 1 + \left(\frac{\alpha}{1-\alpha}\right) \frac{\left(\frac{P_I}{L(k)}\right)\left(\frac{P_I}{L(k)P_E(k)}\right)^{[\alpha/(1-\alpha)]}}{P_I + \left(\frac{P_I}{L(k)}\right)\left(\frac{P_I}{L(k)P_E(k)}\right)^{[\alpha/(1-\alpha)]}}$$

$$\eta_{EB}(k) = 1 + \left(\frac{\alpha}{1-\alpha}\right) \frac{P_I}{P_I + \left(\frac{P_I}{L(k)}\right)\left(\frac{P_I}{L(k)P_E(k)}\right)^{[\alpha/(1-\alpha)]}}$$

$$\eta_{IEB}(k) = \frac{\partial D_I}{\partial P_E}\frac{P_E}{D_I} - \left(\frac{\alpha}{1-\alpha}\right) \frac{\left(\frac{P_I}{L(k)}\right)\left(\frac{P_I}{L(k)P_E(k)}\right)^{[\alpha/(1-\alpha)]}}{P_I + \left(\frac{P_I}{L(k)}\right)\left(\frac{P_I}{L(k)P_E(k)}\right)^{[\alpha/(1-\alpha)]}}$$

$$\eta_{EIB}(k) = \frac{\partial D_E}{\partial P_I}\frac{P_I}{D_E} = \left(\frac{\alpha}{1-\alpha}\right) \frac{P_I}{P_I + \left(\frac{P_I}{L(k)}\right)\left(\frac{P_I}{L(k)P_E(k)}\right)^{[\alpha/(1-\alpha)]}}$$

From these expressions, we can see that for our specific demand functions the following two identities hold for sum of the (absolute values of) elasticities and cross-elasticities in zone k:

$$\eta_{EB}(k) + \eta_{IB}(k) = 2 + \frac{\alpha}{1-\alpha}$$

$$\eta_{IEB}(k) + \eta_{EIB}(k) = \frac{\alpha}{1-\alpha}$$

Delivery Volumes for Entrants and the Incumbent

First note that I delivers all of the mail it collects upstream, which includes R mail and all of its own customers' B mail, i.e., I delivers all of $D_I(P, R, k) + D_I(P, B, k)$. Concerning mail collected by entrants, denote by $Q_{IE}(P, k)$ and $Q_{EE}(P, k)$ the quantity of mail collected upstream by entrants and delivered by I and E respectively in zone k. In regimes in which entrants are prohibited from delivering mail, I delivers all mail, whether collected by E or I upstream, so $Q_{IE}(k) = D_E$ in such regimes. We adopt the convention that when regulation prohibits downstream access by E then $C_{ED}(k) = \infty$, so that I will always be used by entrants for downstream delivery. With this convention, we may write:

$$Q_{IE}(P,k) = D_E(P_I, P_E(k), B, k)[1 - h(P_A(k) - C_{ED}(k))]$$

and

$$Q_{EE}(P,k) = D_E(P_I, P_E(k), B, k)[h(P_A(k) - C_{ED}(k))]$$

where the price vector $P = (P_I, P_E(1), \ldots, P_E(K))$ and $h(x) = 1$ if $x > 0$ and 0 else. Note that the effect of the h function above is that E makes downstream delivery in zone k whenever the access price is higher than the entrants' downstream delivery cost.

Incumbent Profits

By construction, E's profits are zero. I's profits are derived from the above Demand and Cost specifications as the sum of zonal profits across zones $k = 1, \ldots, K$, minus USO fixed costs F, i.e.:

$$\Pi_I(P) = \sum_{k=1}^{K} \left[(P_I - C_{IU} - C_{ID}(k)) \left(D_I(P_I, R, k) + D_I(P_I, P_E(k), B, k) \right) \right]$$

$$+ \sum_{k=1}^{K} \left[(P_A(k) - C_a - C_{ID}(k)) Q_{EI}(P, B, k) \right] - F \qquad \text{(A7)}$$

The Welfare Function

Since (in instances in which a feasible breakeven solution exists), the profits of both E and I will be zero, the standard welfare function *W(P)* reduces to net consumer surplus, which from (A1) and (A4) can be written here as:

$$
\begin{aligned}
W(P) = & \sum_{k=1}^{K} V(D_I(P_I, P_E(k), B, k), D_E(P_I, P_E(k), B, k), B, k) \\
& + \sum_{k=1}^{K} V(D_I(P_I, R, k), R, k) \\
& - \sum_{k=1}^{K} P_I \left(D_I(P_I, P_E(k), B, k) + D_I(P_I, R, k)\right) \\
& - \sum_{k=1}^{K} P_E(k) D_E(P_I, P_E(k), B, k)
\end{aligned}
\tag{A8}
$$

In the above, as noted in the "Flow of Decisions", $P_E(k) = P_E(P_I, k)$ is determined from (A3) once P_I and the access pricing methodology is specified. Thus, our problem is complete. We need only specify: (1) The access pricing methodology, and (2) The allowed form of entry (upstream only, or complete liberalization). Thereafter, the Ramsey-optimal price is easily determined by iterating on P_I to determine the breakeven price, if one exists, subject to access pricing and entry policies. If no such price exists (i.e., if for the access and entry policies concerned the profit-maximizing price, P_I, result in negative profits), then a graveyard spiral would be triggered by the given scenario. The discussion in section 3 highlights the many factors that can lead to a graveyard spiral.

REFERENCES

Baumol, William J., John C. Panzar, and Robert D. Willig. 1988. *Contestable Markets and the Theory of Industry Structure.* (Revised Edition), Harcourt, Brace, Jovanovich, New York.

Cohen, Robert H., William W. Ferguson, John D. Waller, and Spyros S. Xenakis. 2000. "Universal Service without a Monopoly." In *Current Directions in Postal Reform*, edited by M.A. Crew and P.R. Kleindorfer. Boston, MA: Kluwer Academic Publishers.

Cohen, Robert H., Matthew Robinson, Renee Sheelhy, John D. Waller, and Spyros S. Xenakis. 2004. "An Empirical Analysis of the Graveyard Spiral." In *Competitive Transformation of the Postal and Delivery Sector*, edited by M.A. Crew and P.R. Kleindorfer. Boston, MA: Kluwer Academic Publishers.

Crew, Michael A., and Paul R. Kleindorfer. 2000. "Liberalization and the Universal Service Obligation in Postal Service." In *Current Directions in Postal Reform*, edited by M.A. Crew and P.R. Kleindorfer. Boston, MA: Kluwer Academic Publishers

Crew, Michael A., and Paul R. Kleindorfer. 2001. "Whither the USO under Competitive Entry: A Microstructure Approach." In *Future Directions in Postal Reform*, edited by M.A. Crew and P.R. Kleindorfer. Boston, MA: Kluwer Academic Publishers.

Crew, Michael A., and Paul R. Kleindorfer. 2002. "Balancing Access and the Universal Service Obligation." In *Postal and Delivery Services: Delivering on Competition*, edited by M.A. Crew and P.R. Kleindorfer. Boston, MA: Kluwer Academic Publishers.

Crew, Michael A. and Paul R. Kleindorfer. 2004. "Access and the USO for Letters and Parcels." In *Competitive Transformation of the Postal and Delivery Sector*, edited by M.A. Crew and P.R. Kleindorfer. Boston, MA: Kluwer Academic Publishers.

d'Alcantara, Gonzales and Bernard Amerlynck, "Financial Viability of the Universal Postal Service Provider Under Uniform Cost-Related Tariffs." In *Competitive Transformation of the Postal and Delivery Sector*, edited by M.A. Crew and P.R. Kleindorfer. Boston, MA: Kluwer Academic Publishers.

De Donder, Philippe, Helmuth Cremer, Jean-Pierre Florens, André Grimaud and Frank Rodriguez. 2001. "Uniform Pricing and Postal Market Liberalization." In *Future Directions in Postal Reform*, edited by M. A. Crew and Paul R. Kleindorfer. Boston, MA: Kluwer Academic Publishers.

De Donder, Philippe, Helmuth Cremer, and Frank Rodriguez. 2002. "Funding the Universal Service Obligation under Liberalisation." In *Postal and Delivery Services: Pricing, Productivity, Regulation and Strategy*, edited by M.A. Crew and P.R. Kleindorfer. Boston, MA: Kluwer Academic Publishers.

Geddes, Rick. 2003. *Saving the Mail: How to Solve the Problems of the U.S. Postal Service.* Washington, DC: AEI Press.

Chapter 2

Will Entrants into a Liberalized Delivery Market Attract Investors*

Robert H. Cohen, Matthew Robinson, Renee Sheehy, John Waller, and Spyros Xenakis
U.S. Postal Rate Commission

1. INTRODUCTION

The purpose of this paper is to examine the question of whether entry into a liberalized letter delivery market would be attractive to venture capital investors. At the outset it should be recognized that such an enterprise would be quite risky. Competition by a startup against an established incumbent who enjoys significant scale economies could be quite difficult. For example, CityMail, an entrant against the incumbent Sweden Post, began operations in 1991 and has twice gone into bankruptcy. It has had several primary shareholders including most recently Norway Post and prior to that Royal Mail. While CityMail is currently profitable, we can say with perfect hindsight that it would not have attracted investors if its original business plan had been analyzed correctly by them.[1,2]

---

* The views expressed in this paper are those of the authors and do not necessarily represent the opinions of the Postal Rate Commission.

1 Publishers Express in the United States is another delivery startup. It had an all star lineup of investors (including Time, Inc., Meredith Corp. American Express and R.R. Donnelly). Publishers Express delivered mail excluded from the letter monopoly for a couple of years before it folded in the mid-nineties.

2 An investment in a business like CityMail might be more attractive after bankruptcy than as a startup. This could happen if at time of bankruptcy the business had built significant scale or the startup losses were wiped off the books.

In this paper we develop a financial model of an entrant into the U.S. letter mail delivery market in order to evaluate the economic feasibility of the required investment. The cream-skimming model from our graveyard spiral paper (Cohen et al. 2004) provides inputs to the financial model. We conduct sensitivity analysis on the variables used in both models to determine their relative importance. We then calculate the internal rate of return (IRR)[3] for specific values of the most important variables. This provides insight into the likely success of an entrant in attracting adequate startup capital, which is a precondition for successful entry.

2. THE SWEDISH EXPERIENCE

Sweden has the only liberalized letter mail market with an entrant that has garnered significant portions of the market. It thus provides the only source of information for a financial analysis of entry into a newly liberalized market. CityMail reports that it was in the black for the first quarter of this year and for the first time it is heading for a positive result for a full calendar year (2004).[4]

Table 1: CityMail Volume and Shares (1992-2003)

Year	Volume (Millions)	Share of Total Swedish Mail Volume	Year	Volume (Millions)	Share of Total Swedish Mail Volume
1992	18	1%	**1998**	152	4%
1993	19	1	**1999**	167	5
1994	29	1	**2000**	148	4
1995	36	1	**2001**	174	5
1996	54	2	**2002**	192	6
1997	116	3	**2003**	216	7

Average Annual Volume Growth	
1992-2003	**25.6%**

Table 1 displays CityMail's growth and market share. Delivery operations began in 1991 with 1992 being the first complete year of operations. CityMail targeted bulk computer-generated mailings destined for the city of Stockholm. In 1996 service expanded to the areas

---

[3] IRR is a standard financial measure used to evaluate investment opportunities. See Section 3.2 for a definition of IRR and Section 5.3 for a discussion of minimum values considered necessary to justify investments.

[4] Email from CityMail, May 12, 2004.

surrounding Stockholm and to Sweden's second and third largest cities, Malmo and Goteborg. In 2000, service began to the surrounding areas of Malmo and Goteborg. A slight dip in volume occurred in 2000 as CityMail scaled back operations while new financing was being obtained. The Swedish postal regulator (PTS) has observed that "CityMail's [recent] increases in volume are from the Malmo and Goteborg areas, while the Stockholm volume is rather stable."[5]

The growth pattern exhibited by CityMail is fairly typical of new companies. It can be characterized by an initial period of slow growth followed by rapid expansion before leveling off as the entrant nears its maximum market share. The annual incremental growth often approximates a normal distribution and the cumulative growth an S-shaped curve. Figure 1 plots both the cumulative and incremental volumes for CityMail and it can be seen that the annual incremental curve has a normal shape and the cumulative curve is S-shaped.

Figure 1: Bass Model S-Curve Fit to CityMail Volume

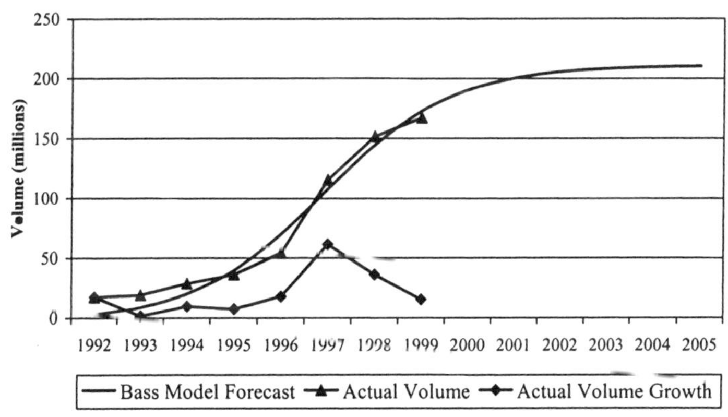

A fit of a Bass business growth model to the initial growth cycle of CityMail in the Stockholm area is included in Figure 1.[6] CityMail estimates that the amount of bulk mail destined for the areas it currently serves is approximately 900 million pieces per year. After more than ten years of operation CityMail has been able to capture 216 million pieces of mail. Based on the Bass Model growth curve, volume for the market currently served should stabilize around 287 million pieces, which is slightly less than

5 Email from Swedish postal regulator, May 14, 2004

6 To model the growth of the entrant, we use the diffusion model proposed by Frank M. Bass (1969). The Bass model describes the growth of new product sales as an S-shaped curve defined by coefficients for innovation, imitation, and total sales potential. See Section 4.6 for a discussion of the application of the Bass model.

30 percent of all bulk mail in the areas served by CityMail.[7] A spokesman from CityMail has observed that capturing "volume in this market is a very slow process. . . . one can expect a lot of conservatism among the customers. This is especially true about administrative mail (bank account statements, invoices, etc.). It takes time to prove your quality."[8]

CityMail currently delivers every third day on a rotating basis over the service area versus five days per week by Sweden Post. CityMail uses carriers that belong to the same union as the incumbent and they receive comparable compensation. Separate contract provisions reportedly allow flexibility to improve efficiency.

Some lessons can be drawn from the CityMail experience. Growth has extended over more than ten years and has reached approximately 24 percent of the bulk mail in its market. An upper bound of its market share is predicted to be about 30 percent. In addition, we can report that Sweden Post has differentiated its bulk mail tariff along geographical lines with lower prices in the cities served by CityMail. It maintains a uniform tariff for First-Class mail. Prices for single-piece letters have approximately doubled, whereas prices for bulk letters have remained roughly constant over the last decade. Sweden Post has reduced its employment by more than 40 percent since it began preparing for competition in 1990.

3. THE MODELS

Figure 2 presents a diagram of the interrelation of the two models and their parametric inputs. The *cream-skimming model* examines the 229,000 USPS delivery routes to determine the ones the entrant could serve profitably. It provides the fixed and variable costs of these routes and the revenue that the entrant would receive from them.[9] The *financial model* lays out a year-by-year projection of route profits/losses over the time period that it will take the entrant to reach its maximum level of profit.

The model includes a parameter (#5) for unprofitable routes because we believe that an entrant would have to serve entire contiguous areas and could not serve only the profitable routes in an area. This is the pattern we observe with CityMail, which serves entire cities. Apparently, CityMail cannot simply serve profitable routes and turn over mail for unprofitable routes to

---

[7] See Section 4.6 for a more detailed description of estimating the ultimate size of CityMail's market size using the Bass model.

[8] Email from CityMail, May 12, 2004.

[9] In this paper we develop prices by upstream and downstream activities and by shape. We assume that all costs of upstream activities (mail processing and transportation) are recovered by upstream prices. See Appendix.

Sweden Post, a model some observers think is feasible for entrants. We believe that several factors would prevent this as discussed in Section 4.5.

It should be noted that the model implicitly assumes that there are only two players in the market: the incumbent and the entrant. If a second entrant were to appear, then the model would overstate the IRR.

Figure 2: Inputs and Outputs of Cream-Skimming and Financial Model

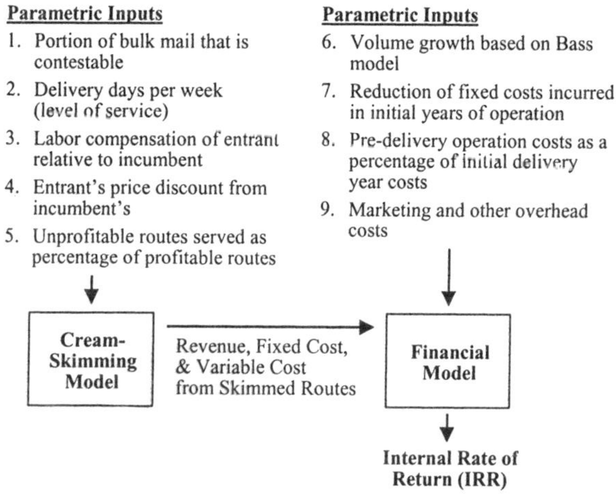

3.1 Cream-Skimming Model

In our Graveyard Spiral paper (Cohen et al. 2004) we presented a model to calculate the total volume that an entrant would expect to skim from the incumbent under the assumptions implied by parametric inputs. The model uses data from U.S. Postal Service delivery operations to identify the routes on which an entrant will be able to price at a given discount from the incumbent's price and be profitable. The model assumes that on those routes the entrant skims all of the contestable mail.[10] The model reduces the incumbent's contribution to overhead by the amount lost due to the skimmed mail and calculates a new breakeven price for the incumbent. The remaining

---

[10] This is a "best possible case" assumption. It is highly favorable to the entrant. Just because an entrant can price its service below the incumbent does not mean that every mailer who sends contestable mail to the recipients on that route will switch. Considerations including the importance of frequency of delivery, dealing with a single vendor, loyalty to a vendor, the need for the entrant to prove quality, and the practical issue of physically transporting mail to the profitable routes from all over the nation make this assumption quite favorable to the entrant.

routes are examined at the new price to see which additional ones can be skimmed. The iterative process continues until equilibrium is achieved.

The entrant captures mail, not routes, from the incumbent. The incumbent is assumed to continue to provide service on all routes and satisfy all universal service obligations. The cream-skimming model can be viewed as an empirical model because it uses actual delivery route data to calculate the maximum possible volume or profit that an entrant could achieve at given values for the input parameters.

Significant improvements have been made in the revised version of the cream-skimming model. Most important is a shape-based delivery charge replacing the content-based charge.[11] See Appendix for further discussion.[12]

3.2 Entrant Financial Model

As with many startup businesses, the entrant can expect to lose money in the first few years of operation before reaching a period of sustained profitability. The viability of the business depends upon the final profit level, the magnitude and duration of unprofitable operations, and the risks involved. To evaluate a business for investment, disciplined investors look at the projected stream of cash flows and apply suitable discount rates to calculate the net present value of the stream, and this accounts for the time value of money.

To analyze the viability of the entrant's business model, we generate estimated cash flows over the life of the firm. Our model calculates revenue based on a constant percentage discount from the incumbent's price. Expenses include the fixed costs for each route served plus the variable costs of delivery (which are determined by the volume captured each year).[13] Expenses also include all capital equipment and space costs, which the model assumes are handled as leases.[14] In addition, an amount is added each year for marketing and administrative expenses equal to a percentage of annual revenue from the volume ultimately captured. The final year's profit, reflecting the ultimate state of the entrant, is valued as a perpetuity. The analysis thus includes the value of expected profits over the life of the firm.

---

[11] Our colleagues at La Poste (Joëlle Toledano, Bernard Roy, Stephane Bernard and others) pointed out the distortions caused by content-based (subclass) pricing differentials, as opposed to cost-based (activity and shape) pricing. We also note that CityMail has a shape-based charge.

[12] Further description of the models including a mathematical presentation and a comparison to our previous paper can be found at www.prc.gov.

[13] At current USPS volume levels about half of route costs are fixed. Fixed cost as a percentage of total cost is inversely related to volume.

[14] We use the depreciation expenses of USPS to approximate the rents paid by the entrant for the lease of equipment and facilities.

Once the future stream of cash flows has been estimated, a metric must be applied to allow comparative analysis among scenarios and with competing investment opportunities. One of the most common methods of valuing a stream of cash flows is Net Present Value (NPV), where a discount rate is used to find the present value of the future cash flows. The appropriate discount rate is the return that investors will demand for their investment in the project, known as the project's *cost of capital.*

Estimating the cost of capital for the entrant presents many difficulties. For a specific project, it is largely determined by prevailing conditions in the capital markets (e.g., interest rates and inflation) combined with the perceived risk of the investment. As we have seen, gaining market share from an entrenched monopoly is difficult. In addition, the regulatory environment of a newly liberalized delivery market is likely to be prone to unforeseeable changes. Finally, given the widespread belief that First-Class mail volume per household in the U.S. has begun a permanent decline, the limited upside potential for long-term growth would also place upward pressure on the return demanded by investors.

Our model calculates the internal rate of return (IRR) of the entrant, which is the discount rate that results in a net present value of zero for a stream of future cash flows.[15] As such, it is the break-even discount rate, the rate at which the present value of cash outflows equals the present value of cash inflows.[16] If the entrant's cost of capital (discount rate) is less than the IRR, then the NPV of the venture is positive. Conversely, if the cost of capital exceeds the IRR then the NPV is negative, and the entrant's business model is not viable. The IRR allows the reader to judge whether the entrant's cost of capital will justify the investments necessary to enter the market. In the discussion of the results in Section 5.3 we will provide some guidance as to a reasonable range for the entrant's cost of capital.

4. PARAMETRIC VARIABLES

Nine variables are used as parametric inputs in the interrelated cream-skimming and financial models. We select a base case value for each input and an optimistic and pessimistic value for use in a sensitivity analysis.

---

15 Since the stream of cash flows in every scenario changes sign only once, a unique IRR can be calculated.

16 The IRR is known by other names such as the Marginal Efficiency of Capital, True Yield, Interest Rate of Return, and Expected Rate of Return.

4.1 Contestable Mail

Single-piece mail is excluded from contestable volume since it would require an entrant to develop and invest in a collection and upstream infrastructure.

In Cohen et al. (2004), we defined as contestable the mail that could be presorted to the carrier route and dropshipped to a delivery unit or a regional sectional center facility (SCF). This corresponds to 30 percent of all bulk-entered mail delivered by the Postal Service in 1999 (Cohen et al. 2004, 126–129). The upstream market is competitive in the U.S. as a result of the Postal Service offering worksharing discounts equal to the costs it avoids. When a mailer or third party can reach the carrier route level of presort and dropship to the local (or regional) level with costs equal to or less than the Postal Service, it does so unless other overriding factors deter it. The most important factor is the need to present whole mailings to USPS in such a way that the delivery window can be estimated with a high degree of confidence. Whatever the reason, the market provides evidence that the volume of mail likely to be contestable for delivery by entrants is less than 30 percent of bulk mail.

The U.S.-based estimate is corroborated by the CityMail experience. CityMail estimates that it could in theory deliver all of the 900 million bulk-entered pieces of mail destined for the areas it serves this year, but experience to date demonstrates that this is not likely to occur. Some mailers may not be able to prepare their mail economically for delivery by an entrant such as CityMail, just as mailers in the U.S. currently do not find it economically feasible to take advantage of discounts for presorting mail to carrier route levels. In the absence of structural knowledge of the Swedish mail market, we estimate the contestable mail volume in the markets served by CityMail to be the maximum volume predicted by the Bass model. It was calculated in Section 2 to be 287 million or slightly less than 30 percent of all bulk mail in the market. This matches our U.S. base case (i.e., 30 percent of all bulk mail is contestable). To explore the sensitivity of the IRR to the amount of contestable mail, we analyze situations where the percentage of bulk mail considered contestable ranges from 15 percent to 100 percent.

4.2 Delivery Days (Level of Service)

The entrant can reduce its fixed costs by reducing the number of days a week on which delivery occurs.[17] The model is designed to allow for any number of delivery days ranging from one to six. The most pessimistic case

---

[17] In the U.S. delivery is six days a week, but many countries deliver only five days per week. Some deliver even fewer times per week to some rural areas.

for the entrant is delivery six days a week, the middle value is every other day (three times a week) and an optimistic value is delivery twice a week. It should be noted that delivery days are related to the amount of contestable mail. Many mailers of bulk mail require next day service or delivery more rapidly than a reduced number of delivery days would allow.[18] Thus, it would seem that the higher the percentages of contestable mail the more frequent the delivery.

4.3 Labor Compensation

The entrant can also reduce costs relative to the incumbent by paying its employees less. It is not obvious that this will occur as Sweden Post and CityMail draw upon labor from the same labor union at similar compensation rates. Likewise, the compensation paid to delivery personnel by UPS and FedEx in the U.S. is not below that paid by the Postal Service. In some countries, such as the United Kingdom, the incumbent already has low compensation rates that may be difficult for an entrant to undercut. Yet, in many countries it is likely that the entrant's labor will be compensated at a rate lower than the incumbent's. For this reason, the model uses entrant labor costs that are 100 percent (pessimistic case), 90 percent (base case) or 80 percent (optimistic case) of the incumbent's labor compensation costs.

4.4 Entrant's Price Discount

The cream-skimming model assumes that the entrant offers delivery services at a discount from the incumbent's uniform price in order to attract customers. Because the entrant follows an umbrella pricing strategy, both the incumbent's and the entrant's prices will increase over time as the entrant skims increasing amounts of mail and forces the incumbent to raise prices in order to break even. This price adjustment occurs on each iteration of the cream-skimming model. In the analysis presented here we examine price discounts of 5, 10, and 15 percent with 10 percent taken as the base discount. The cream-skimming model caps the entrant's final price at twice the initial price. Higher prices would attract additional entrants that would in turn lead to lower prices.

---

[18] Delivery less frequent than every day implies the delivery of some mailings would be staggered, as carriers serve different routes depending on the day of the week. This also would reduce volume, as some mailers require all items to be delivered on the same day.

4.5 Unprofitable Routes

The entrant ideally would like to delivery mail only on routes where it makes a profit. Theoretically, this could be accomplished in two ways. The entrant could accept mail only for recipients on profitable routes in a given contiguous area or it could accept mail for the entire area and turn over mail on unprofitable routes to the incumbent. In reality neither option seems practical, and an entrant would be forced to serve some unprofitable routes. An important concern of many mailers is maintaining the integrity of their product before delivery to ensure a given delivery day or window. Thus, having different delivery providers handle a mailer's product in an area is unlikely. Additionally, neither the mailer nor the entrant could take full advantage of the incumbent's upstream presort discounts if only some of an area's volume was given to the incumbent.[19]

CityMail has employed an area-by-area strategy, first Stockholm, then its suburbs, then the next two largest cities. Area-by-area delivery would also be feasible in the U.S. since large numbers of high-income families, and thus high-volume mail recipients, tend to cluster in and around the major population centers. These areas primarily contain profitable routes on which an entrant could expect to profitably capture contestable mail. These would be the primary service areas for the entrant. It would be advantageous for the entrant to serve areas corresponding to those designated by the five-digit ZIP code, the basis for many presort discounts. Taking all mail for such areas would preserve the upstream presort discounts a mailer could earn.

The cream-skimming model ranks all routes according to profits from the most profitable to the least. The result is the curve displayed in Figure 3 which has a relatively small number of routes with large profits and losses (the tails of the figure) and a broad, flat middle section in which losses are close to zero. The model assumes that the entrant will provide service on a number of unprofitable routes equal to a certain percentage of the number of profitable routes it serves, starting with the least unprofitable routes (i.e., in Figure 3, the routes in the region immediately to the right of the point where the profit curve crosses the horizontal axis). This assumption is quite favorable to the entrant since it implies the entrant will not have to serve highly or even moderately unprofitable routes. The base case assumes that the entrant serves one third as many unprofitable routes as profitable routes. The pessimistic case assumes half as many unprofitable routes as profitable routes, and the optimistic case assumes one fourth as many. To account for the need to provide service on these unprofitable routes, profit is adjusted downwards in the financial model by subtracting the losses generated by serving them.

[19] The level of presort depends on density which in turn is a function of volume.

Figure 3: Routes Ordered by Entrant's Profit (Base Case)

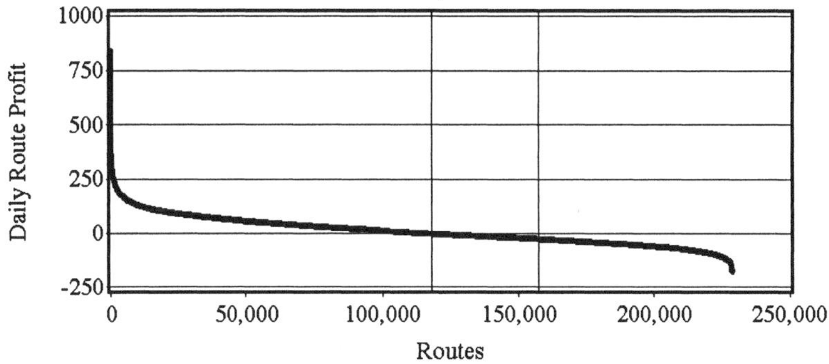

4.6 Volume Growth Based on Bass Model

Based on the experience of CityMail and entrants in other industries, we assume that the entrant's volume growth will follow the Bass model (1969). The annual volume of the entrant is defined as

$$Y(t) = mF(t) = m\left(\left(1 - e^{-(p+q)t}\right)/\left(1 + (q/p)e^{-(p+q)t}\right)\right)$$

where p is the coefficient of innovation, q is the coefficient of imitation, m is the entrant's final volume, and t is the time period.

The values of $p = 0.00981$, $q = 0.71706$, and $m = 210.9$ million[20] are estimated econometrically by fitting the above equation to CityMail's annual volume data from 1992 through 1999. Volumes from 2000 to 2003 are excluded from the estimation process because during this time CityMail underwent changes that affected the pace of its expansion. Including these years would preclude the selection of a single S-curve Bass model to fit the volume growth of CityMail. Figure 1 shows a comparison of the actual and forecast volumes.

In each scenario, the maximum potential volume (MPV) of the entrant is substituted for m, with p and q held constant at their estimated values. The volume forecast by the fitted Bass equation for Year 10 exceeds 95 percent of the final amount captured (i.e., MPV). The financial model assumes that in Year 11 and beyond the entrant fully captures the MPV.

To evaluate the sensitivity of the IRR to the speed with which the entrant captures volume, we also use five and fifteen years to capture 95 percent of the MPV. In the five-year scenario, the value of each t is divided by 0.5, and

---

[20] The estimated maximum volume for CityMail (287 million) cited in Section 2 is calculated by increasing this estimate (211 million) in proportion to the increase since 1999 in households served by CityMail.

in the fifteen-year scenario it is divided by 1.5. This maintains the shape of the S-curve while compressing the growth period to five years or extending it to fifteen years.

4.7 Reduction of Fixed Costs in Initial Years of Operation

If the entrant is assumed to start operations on all routes that eventually will be profitable, the entrant will encounter the same total fixed costs in each year of operation as delivered volume slowly builds. This is the major source of unprofitability in the initial years. Faced with the prospect of large losses for several years, the entrant might find ways to reduce the fixed costs in the early years of operation by altering the route structure. To accommodate these potential adjustments in route structure, we build up the fixed costs in the early years gradually. For the base case, where the period of growth to achieve maximum potential volume is assumed to be ten years, fixed costs for the first, second, third, and fourth years of delivery operations are set at 20, 40, 60, and 80 percent respectively to obtain a reduction. For the five-year growth period, the reduction factor for the first and second years of delivery operations is set at 40 and 80 percent. For the fifteen-year growth period, the initial year factors are set at 20, 30, 40, 50, 60, 70, 80, and 90 percent. For a given growth period, these factors are not varied in the sensitivity analysis.

4.8 Pre-delivery Operation Costs

New business operations do not start instantaneously; they require a pre-operational period. The cost of this would be significant for a postal delivery operation. These costs include marketing and sales, hiring and training a large number of letter carriers, setting up a transportation network, and acquiring facilities and sorting equipment. The model uses 25 percent of the total costs in the initial year of delivery operations as an estimate of pre-operation costs. Fifteen percent and 35 percent are the optimistic and pessimistic values. This variable is strongly attenuated by the *reduction of fixed cost in the initial years of operation*.

4.9 Marketing and Other Overhead Costs

The cream-skimming model uses only the direct and overhead costs associated with delivery to determine whether the entrant will capture the contestable mail on a route. In other words, it assumes bare-bones operations without marketing, administrative, or other non-delivery overhead costs that a business must incur. To make the analysis more realistic, these non-delivery costs, expressed as a percentage of revenue, are included as a parametric input variable in the financial model. The base case value is 10 percent of projected revenue on profitable routes when the entrant's maximum level of volume is achieved. The pessimistic case value is 15 percent and the optimistic value is 5 percent. These costs are reduced in the early years of operation by the same factors applied to fixed delivery costs.

5. RESULTS

5.1 Sensitivity

Above we discussed each variable and its pessimistic, middle, and optimistic value. We designate the middle values as our base case. Table 2 displays these values.

Table 2: Values of the Model Inputs Used in Sensitivity Analysis Variables

	Pessimistic	Base	Optimistic
Contestable Mail (percentage of delivered bulk mail)	15%	30%	65%
Growth Period (years)	15	10	5
Marketing & Other Overhead (percentage of maximum annual revenue)	15%	10%	5%
Delivery Days	6	3	2
Unprofitable Routes (percentage of profitable routes)	50%	33%	25%
Labor Compensation (percentage of incumbent's)	100%	90%	80%
Entrant's Price Discount (percent)	15%	10%	5%
Pre-delivery Operation Costs (percentage of Year 2 costs)	35%	25%	15%

The variables are listed in the order of their impact on the sensitivity of the IRR. Table 3 displays the IRR when an optimistic or pessimistic value for a variable is substituted *ceterus paribus* into the base case (which has an 9.5% IRR).

Contestable volume is the most important variable. The optimistic value causes a more than three-fold increase in the base case IRR. It can be seen that changes in the values of this variable cause decidedly non-linear changes in the IRR.

Growth period is the next most important variable. The IRR doubles in the optimistic case as compared to the base case. Again, the effect on the IRR of changes in the values of this variable is also highly non-linear.

Table 3: Sensitivity of IRR to Changes in the Values of the Inputs Variables[a]

Benchmark	9.5%	
	Pessimistic	Optimistic
Contestable Mail	7.1%	32.1%
Growth Period	6.7	19.1
Marketing & Other Overhead	6.9	12.5
Delivery Days	7.3	12.0
Unprofitable Routes	7.0	10.8
Labor Compensation	8.5	10.7
Entrant Price Discount	8.9	10.1
Pre-delivery Operation Costs	9.5	9.6

[a] The IRR is displayed for a change (from the base case) in a single variable.

The IRR is much less sensitive to changes in the remaining individual variables, but, as is seen in the next section with *delivery days*, there can be significant interaction with the *contestable volume* variable. Thus, estimating the amount of contestable volume and the number of years necessary for the entrant to achieve its maximum volume are most important in evaluating an investment in the venture. A complete sensitivity analysis would examine changes in all combinations of variables, and some variables would exhibit greater variation than shown in Table 3.

5.2 Selected Business Strategies

In this section, the model is used to analyze scenarios of general interest involving various combinations of the input variables. In all cases we assume that the growth period to achieve maximum potential volume in the area served is ten years. We believe shorter time periods are overly optimistic and longer time periods are of little interest to most investors because of the lower IRRs that result. Table 4 presents the results of the model assuming 18 combinations of two significant parameters: the amount of contestable mail and the number of delivery days. The resulting IRRs are also displayed as a surface graph in Figure 4. As the contestable mail increases, the sensitivity of the IRR to the number of delivery days increases as can be seen from the slope of the surface for contestable mail corresponding to percentages of bulk mail greater than 65 percent.[21]

[21] An exception to the monotonic changes in IRR in Figure 4 occurs at the extreme point corresponding to low contestable volume and six-day-a-week delivery. This is due to the fact that in this scenario only routes with extremely high profits are skimmed. When a

Table 4: Internal Rate of Return Resulting from Varying the Level of Contestable Volume and the Number of Delivery Days

Contestable Mail	Delivery Days		
Volume (% of Delv. Bulk)	2	3	6
18 billion (14.7%)	7.6%	7.1%	14.1%
36 billion, benchmark (29.4%)	12.0	9.5	7.3
46 billion (37.6%)	20.8	11.6	8.0
78 billion (64.2%)	41.5	32.1	13.2
102 billion (83.3%)	47.2	38.2	21.6
122 billion (100.0%)	51.0	42.4	26.1

Figure 4: Internal Rate of Return (IRR) Resulting from Varying the Level of Contestable Volume and the Number of Delivery Days

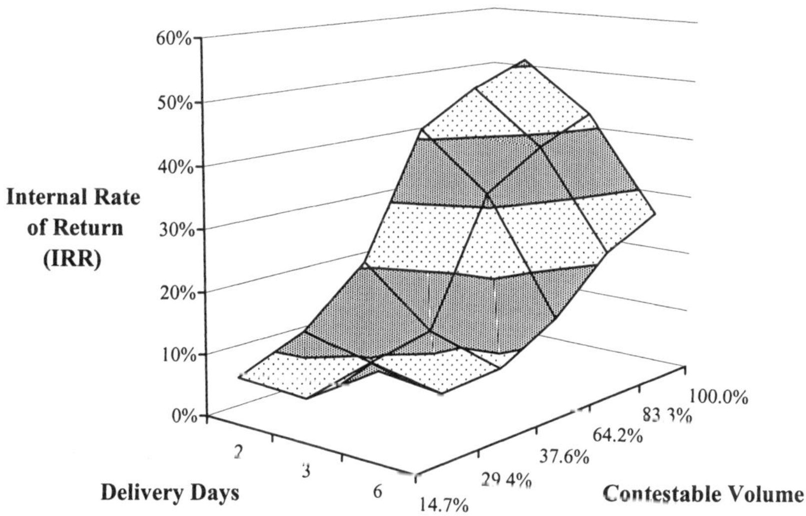

If the amount of contestable mail is greater than 65 percent it is reasonable to expect that the entrant will have to provide a high quality of service and make sizeable expenditures in marketing. To reflect this situation, a stand-alone scenario is modeled where the amount of contestable mail is very optimistic (65 percent of bulk) but other variables assume pessimistic values (6-day delivery, 15 percent price discount, 100 percent of incumbent's labor compensation, 15 percent of revenue allocated to marketing and administration, and first year costs at 35 percent of Year 2 costs). The model produces an IRR of 8.5 percent for this high-volume scenario.

---

profit curve similar to Figure 3 is produced for this case, the entrant captures primarily the vertical part of the curve. The profitability of these routes may be exaggerated due to the use of average costs for the city carrier routes in the cream-skimming model.

On the other hand, a market with low or very low contestable volume suggests a possible niche service in which service quality and marketing costs are less than in the base case. Model inputs reflecting this scenario are contestable mail at 15 percent of bulk volume, 2 delivery days per week, 5 percent price discount, 80 percent of incumbent's labor compensation, low marketing expenses at 5 percent of eventual revenue, and low first year costs at 15 percent of Year 2 costs. This niche market scenario produces an IRR of 11.7 percent.

Interestingly, the large contestable mail and niche market scenarios have similarly low IRR values yet they would require substantially different operations with substantially different capital requirements and profits.

5.3 Assessing Model Results

In order to interpret the results of the models presented here, it is necessary to put the calculated IRRs in context. In each of the scenarios, the entrant experiences losses in the early years of operation before reaching profitability as delivered volume grows. Therefore upfront capital is needed to cover the losses in the early years of the project. This capital may come from a number of potential sources, but regardless of the source, the project must compete for capital resources with other investment opportunities. To successfully attract the necessary capital investment, the entrant must pay an adequate return to the investors. From the entrant's point of view, this is the cost of capital for the project. As discussed in Section 3.2, if the project's IRR exceeds its cost of capital, then it can be considered viable; if not, the returns will not be sufficient to attract investment. In this way, the cost of capital for a project can be viewed as a hurdle rate that must be exceeded by the IRR.

The required rate of return for investment in a project (i.e., the project's cost of capital) compensates the investor not only for inflation and the time value of money, but for the relative risk of the investment as well. As discussed in Section 3.2, an entrant to the postal delivery market would face substantial risks in challenging a well-established monopoly with huge scale economies for a contestable market of unknown size while taking on considerable regulatory risk.

Many startup businesses receive early stage financing from venture capital firms. In consultations with Wall Street venture capital analysts regarding investments in startups, we have been told that the minimum return that would be required (i.e., the entrant's cost of capital) in the current investment environment is 25 percent, and could exceed 40 percent depending on the perceived risk.[22] Greater uncertainty in the estimates of the models' variables implies greater risk, and therefore a higher required rate of return (cost of capital). Business scenarios treating sizeable portions of bulk mail as contestable may produce relatively high IRRs, but the risk is also greater. For instance, experience to date in the U.S. with worksharing discounts provides evidence that the maximum amount of contestable mail for an entrant (i.e., bulk mail that can be economically carrier route presorted and dropshipped regionally) is less than 30 percent of the delivered bulk-entered mail. Assuming a higher percentage would represent a significant risk in the calculation of the IRR.

Based on venture capital market requirements, our models predict that an entrant must have a contestable mail market that is greater than 60 percent of all bulk mail delivered in the geographic area served. Capturing this amount of mail would likely require sizeable startup and marketing costs, with deep discounts, and better service, which implies everyday delivery by skilled staff paid at compensation rates equal to the incumbent's. All these factors contribute to lowering the IRR to 8.5% percent. This is similar to the IRR that a niche market entrant would achieve, but with much higher capital requirements and profits in absolute terms.

While the estimated IRRs demonstrate that it will be very hard for an entrant to attract the necessary capital and thereby limit competition for an incumbent post, liberalization can still affect the postal delivery market in several ways. On the positive side, if competition does develop, even in a limited market, it can lead to innovations in service, giving more choices to customers. More importantly, even the mere threat of competition can lead incumbents to cut costs and to improve efficiency and service. On the other hand, entry will cause a loss of scale economies. The issue is whether the gains in innovation, efficiency, and service quality outweigh the costs of entry.[23]

6. CONCLUSIONS

Based on the results given above, we make the following conclusions concerning the potential for obtaining venture capital for an entrant delivery service.

---

[22] If an entrant were not a startup firm, but a new division of an existing company, its cost of capital would likely be somewhat lower. A well-run firm with experience in the area of entry would have a lower risk and hence a lower cost of capital. However, it is likely that the cost of capital for this type of project would still be high.

[23] For more discussion of the tradeoff in positive and negative impacts of liberalization, see Cohen et al. (2004) and Cohen and Chew (1997).

1. It is unlikely that a realistic business plan will attract capital for an entrant delivery service in a liberalized postal market with characteristics like the U.S. market. Thus, liberalization is unlikely to trigger a graveyard spiral.
2. In order to achieve an IRR sufficient to attract venture capital, about two thirds of bulk mail would have to be contestable. This is highly unlikely.
3. The most significant variables in a business plan are:
   a) the amount of contestable mail in the market served
   b) the rate at which the business grows to its maximum volume
   c) marketing and overhead expenses as a share of revenue
   d) the number of days of delivery per week.

More scenarios can be examined with the models presented here. In addition, the models can be enchanced with new input variables for future research.

A. APPENDIX: THE MODELS[24]

A.1 Cream-Skimming Model

The cream-skimming model used here is a modified version of the model originally presented in Cohen et al. (2004). An important improvement in this version of the cream-skimming model is the use of cost-based prices by activity and shape instead of full-service, content-based subclass prices. This affects the revenue from contestable mail and the loss of delivery profits by the incumbent as a result of cream skimming.

Content-based subclass prices cause the price of contestable mail to be artificially low. By using cost-based prices for delivery of three mail shapes (letters, flats and parcels), we have eliminated the downward distortion in the price of contestable mail caused by subclass prices.

The higher delivery prices for contestable mail enable the entrant to capture more mail. They also increase the delivery profit lost by the incumbent for a given amount of captured volume. The combined effect of the new activity- and shape-based pricing is to make cream skimming more painful for the incumbent. Our conclusions in Cohen et al. (2004) remain largely unaffected.

---

[24] A mathematical description of the cream-skimming model, an interactive version of the financial model, and a comparison to our previous paper (Cohen et al. 2004) is available on www.prc.gov.

A.1.1 Model Overview

1. The model examines individual routes to identify the ones where an entrant can profitably deliver the contestable volume.
2. The incumbent's profit from these routes is reduced by the contribution to overhead from the lost contestable volume.
3. The incumbent's delivery prices are raised to recover the profit lost to cream skimming and the subsequent effect of demand price elasticities.
4. The rise in the incumbent's delivery prices creates additional cream-skimming opportunities for the entrant. The model returns to step 1 until equilibrium is achieved.

A.1.2 Data

U.S. delivery data are from the USPS City Carrier Cost System and the Rural National Mail Count System (USPS-LR-I-448 and USPS-LR-I-474 2000). City carriers make up 72 percent of the routes and rural carriers make up the remainder.[25]

The City Carrier System contains a stratified sample of 8,300 routes and the 1999 Rural National Mail Count System provides data on 39,737 rural routes. These sources provide the subclass volumes delivered on each route. City carrier time is derived from the USPS Cost Segments and Components Report for FY 1999 and the average time is calculated and used for all city carrier routes. Rural carrier time is included in the rural mail count system.

To develop variable and fixed costs, we divide out-of-office delivery costs into activity components using the method developed by USPS (USPS-LR-I-404 2000). Load time is included in the variable costs. For simplicity the variable portion of access and travel to and from the beginning of the route are ignored. Variable costs on a route are estimated by multiplying route volume by average variable costs.[26] The remaining time is fixed and includes the time between stops (route time and the fixed portion of access) and the fixed portion of travel time.

The initial unit prices for the delivery function are calculated to be 19.9 cents per letter, 22.2 cents per flat, and $1.49 per parcel.

---

[25] Approximately 30 percent of rural routes serve non-rural urban suburbs.

[26] For a few high-volume routes, this results in variable costs that exceed the average total route cost. Average costs may not accurately reflect the cost characteristics of these routes.

Table A-2: Summary of Annual Financial Results of Entrant and Internal Rate of Return
(Base Scenario)

Percent of Final Fixed Costs		20%	40%	60%	80%	100%	100%	100%	100%	100%	100%
	Year 1	**Year 2**	**Year 3**	**Year 4**	**Year 5**	**Year 6**	**Year 7**	**Year 8**	**Year 9**	**Year 10**	**Years 11+**
Letter Volume		179,133	533,990	1,207,311	2,386,413	4,187,744	6,437,039	8,632,973	10,317,837	11,387,090	12,605,959
Flat Volume		234,655	699,501	1,581,518	3,126,084	5,485,739	8,432,206	11,308,771	13,515,861	14,916,530	16,513,188
Parcel Volume		481	1,434	3,242	6,409	11,246	17,287	23,184	27,709	30,580	33,853
Total Volume		414,270	1,234,925	2,792,072	5,518,905	9,684,729	14,886,532	19,964,928	23,861,406	26,334,199	29,153,000
Markup factor		0.002	0.007	0.017	0.033	0.058	0.088	0.119	0.142	0.157	0.173
Letter Price		0.180	0.180	0.182	0.185	0.189	0.195	0.200	0.205	0.207	0.210
Flat Price		0.200	0.201	0.203	0.206	0.211	0.217	0.224	0.228	0.231	0.234
Parcel Price		1.344	1.351	1.363	1.385	1.418	1.460	1.500	1.531	1.551	1.573
Letter Revenue		32,162	96,340	219,818	441,429	793,205	1,254,897	1,729,671	2,110,048	2,358,695	2,649,000
Flat Revenue		47,000	140,786	321,232	645,083	1,159,153	1,833,847	2,527,659	3,083,523	3,446,884	3,871,123
Parcel Revenue		647	1,937	4,420	8,876	15,949	25,233	34,779	42,428	47,427	53,265
Total Revenue		79,808	239,063	545,470	1,095,388	1,968,307	3,113,977	4,292,109	5,235,999	5,853,006	6,573,388
Variable Route Costs		24,482	72,980	165,002	326,148	572,333	879,742	1,179,857	1,410,125	1,556,258	1,722,840
Fixed Route Costs		554,732	1,109,464	1,664,195	2,218,927	2,773,659	2,773,659	2,773,659	2,773,659	2,773,659	2,773,659
Total Route Costs		579,214	1,182,443	1,829,197	2,545,075	3,345,992	3,653,400	3,953,516	4,183,784	4,329,917	4,496,499
TOTAL Net Delivery Profit	-	**(499,406)**	**(943,380)**	**(1,283,726)**	**(1,449,687)**	**(1,377,685)**	**(539,423)**	**338,593**	**1,052,215**	**1,523,089**	**2,076,889**
Marketing and Other Overhead		131,468	262,936	394,403	525,871	657,339	657,339	657,339	657,339	657,339	657,339
Total Costs	177,670	710,681	1,445,379	2,223,600	3,070,946	4,003,331	4,310,739	4,610,855	4,841,123	4,987,256	5,153,837
Profit (Loss)	**(177,670)**	**(630,873)**	**(1,206,316)**	**(1,678,130)**	**(1,975,558)**	**(2,035,024)**	**(1,196,762)**	**(318,746)**	**394,876**	**865,750**	**1,419,551**
											Value of Perpetuity
Future Values	(177,670)	(630,873)	(1,206,316)	(1,678,130)	(1,975,558)	(2,035,024)	(1,196,762)	(318,746)	394,876	865,750	14,888,078
Internal Rate of Return (IRR)	**9.5%**										
PV	(162,204)	(525,821)	(917,919)	(1,165,781)	(1,252,936)	(1,178,301)	(632,619)	(153,825)	173,977	348,234	5,467,196
NPV	0										
NPV check	0										
Assumed Discount Rate	9.5%										

Note: Other scenarios available from the authors.

A.2 Financial Model

The financial model spreads over time the entrant's growth in volume, revenue, and costs to calculate annual profits and losses and the IRR from the resulting cash flows. The calculations are performed in a series of Excel worksheets that reflect different parametric values for the input variables. The model for the base case is given in Table A-2. An interactive version of the model is given at www.prc.gov.

REFERENCES

Bass, F.M. 1969. "New Product Growth for Model Consumer Durables." *Management Science* 15(5): 215.

Cohen, Robert H. and Edward H. Chu. 1997. "A Measure of Scale Economies for Postal Systems." In *Managing Change in the Postal and Delivery Industries,* edited by Michael A. Crew and Paul R. Kleindorfer. Boston, MA: Kluwer Academic Publishers.

Cohen, Robert H., Matthew Robinson, Gennaro Scarfiglieri, Renee Sheehy, Vincenzo Visco Comandini, John Waller, and Spyros Xenakis. 2004. "The Role of Scale Economies in the Cost Behavior of Posts" presented at Wissenschaftliches Institut für Kommunikationsdienste (WIK), 8th Köenigswinter, February 16-18, 2004 and to be published by WIK. Copy available at www.prc.gov.

Cohen, Robert H., Matthew Robinson, Renee Sheehy, John Waller, and Spyros Xenakis. 2004. "An Empirical Analysis of the Graveyard Spiral" In *Competitive Transformation of The Postal and Delivery Sector*, edited by Michael A. Crew and Paul R. Kleindorfer. Boston, MA: Kluwer Academic Publishers.

United States Postal Service. 2000. *USPS-LR-I-259, Billing Determinants, Fiscal Year 1999.* Filed in Postal Rate Commission Docket No. R2000-1 (March 31, 2000). Washington, D.C., www.prc.gov.

United States Postal Service. 2000. *USPS-LR-I-404, Order No. 1294/Summary Description of USPS Development of Costs by Segments and Components, FY 1999.* Filed in Postal Rate Commission Docket No. R2000-1 (July 7, 2000). Washington, D.C., www.prc.gov.

United States Postal Service. 2000. *USPS-LR-I-448, FY 1999 City Carrier "Z" File.* Filed in Postal Rate Commission Docket No. R2000-1 (August 7, 2000). Washington, D.C., www.prc.gov.

United States Postal Service. 2000. *USPS-LR-I-474, FY 1999 Rural Carrier "Z" File.* Filed in Postal Rate Commission Docket No. R2000-1 (August 21, 2000). Washington, D.C., www.prc.gov.

Chapter 3

Liberalization and Regulation of the Swiss Letter Market*

Helmut M. Dietl,[1] Urs Trinkner[1,2] and Reto Bleisch[1,2]
University of Zurich[1] and Swiss Post[2]

1. INTRODUCTION

The European Union is gradually opening up its domestic letter markets for competition. Complete liberalization is planned for 2009. In contrast to the European developments, the United States developed worksharing as a means to introduce competition in the postal sector. However, despite the examples of the EU and the U.S., in most countries letter services are still national monopolies.

In Switzerland, the universal service provider (USP) is Swiss Post, which currently enjoys a monopoly on addressed letters up to a weight of 1 kilogram. The Swiss government has the power to open up the letter market if the provision of the universal service obligation (USO) remains guaranteed. Hence, prior to any further market opening, it is crucial to know how competition affects the financial viability of Swiss Post with or without a licensing system. Such a licensing system has been introduced in the recently liberalized parcels market. The regulatory authority PostReg is entitled to collect licensing fees that amount up to 3% on an entrant's turnover to compensate Swiss Post for its universal service provision if needed.

---

* The views expressed in this paper are those of the authors and do not necessarily reflect the opinion of Swiss Post.

Our paper provides insights on the consequences of different kinds of liberalization or regulatory rules of the Swiss letter market. We examine welfare effects and financial consequences for both Swiss Post and potential market entrants. We start with an analysis of what would happen if the current regulation of the parcels market were applied to the letter market.

The paper proceeds as follows. In Section 2, we develop and tailor a game theoretic model to the Swiss postal system. In Section 3, we calibrate the model with Swiss data. Section 4 presents our results on end-to-end competition and compares them with an evaluation of the regulated monopoly of 2003. We show that end-to-end competition results in lower welfare and problems to finance the USO even if a licensing system is introduced. Building on these results, we expand the model in Section 5 and analyze alternative regulatory scenarios. We show that worksharing will increase economic welfare. The last section contains a discussion and our main conclusions.

2. BASIC MODEL AND FORMAL RESULTS

In order to analyze the effects of liberalization in the Swiss letter market, we use a standard game theoretic approach. On the supply side, we let Swiss Post as incumbent *I* compete with a representative entrant *E*. The demand side links the two operators. Customers value the available products with respect to quality and prices. Strategic interaction takes place, where one operator's behavior affects both operators' profits. For example, when the incumbent raises its prices, some consumers will switch to the entrant and boost the entrant's sales.

Technically speaking we use a Dixit-like approach to model price competition with product differentiation and assume that there are no information asymmetries.

2.1 Basic Model

On the *demand side,* we assume a representative sender with quasilinear preferences with respect to money.[1] The quasilinearity implies a cardinal utility measure that enables us to compute and compare overall welfare of

[1] Having in mind that most senders are businesses, quasilinearity is a reasonable assumption in the modeled riskless world. Businesses invest into mail as long as the NPV of an additional mailing is nonnegative, i.e. marginal utility of mail is greater than or equal to 1. Further, in an economy like Switzerland where postal consumption is small compared to total expenditure, postal consumption will be independent of the initial wealth endowment *Y*.

different market structures. To obtain linear demand curves, we assume a quadratic utility function over every quantity of mail q_i^{rs} sent in segment s of region r through the network of operator i. Formally, we follow De Donder et al. (2001) and write total utility U as

$$U(q,m) = m + \sum_r \sum_s \left(a_I^{rs} q_I^{rs} - \frac{b^{rs}}{2} \left(q_I^{rs}\right)^2 + a_E^{rs} q_E^{rs} - \frac{b^{rs}}{2} \left(q_E^{rs}\right)^2 - e b^{rs} q_I^{rs} q_E^{rs} \right),$$

where a, b, $e > 0$ and m is the amount of money spent on other goods. The last term reflects the fact that the mail services offered by the two operators are not perfect substitutes but rather differentiated products. The higher the degree of differentiation, the closer to zero is parameter e. Parameters a and b determine the market size and the slope of the demand curve.

A consequence of this utility specification is that demand in one market does not affect demand in another one. That is, cross-price elasticities between the market segments are zero and operators cannot increase demand in one market segment by serving an additional segment, i.e. no network externalities are directly included.

Utility maximization implies that our representative consumer satisfies with equality the budget constraint $\Sigma\Sigma(p_I^{rs} q_I^{rs} + p_E^{rs} q_E^{rs}) + m \leq Y$, where p_i^{rs} is the price the consumer has to pay to operator $i \in \{I, E\}$ for the mail product s delivered to region r. Y represents the initial wealth endowment of the economy. By computing the first-order conditions of the Lagrange function and solving the resulting equation system, we obtain the demand functions for the incumbent and the competitor as

$$q_i^{rs}(p_i^{rs}, p_j^{rs}) = \frac{1}{b^{rs}(1-e^2)} \left(a_i^{rs} - e a_j^{rs} - p_i^{rs} + e p_j^{rs}\right). \tag{1}$$

The slope of the demand curve in a given market is equal for both operators. Quantities are negatively related to the own price and positively to the price of the competitor ($\partial q_i / \partial p_i < 0$; $\partial q_i / \partial p_j > 0$). Furthermore, quantities increase with a higher degree of product differentiation (i.e., a smaller e).

On the *supply side*, pricing possibilities and cost structures determine profit functions. In the case of unregulated competition, where the incumbent and the entrant face no regulatory restrictions on pricing and production decisions, the operators are able to differentiate prices for every market segment and hence take into account demand properties specified in (1). We assume that there are no economies of scope between products, segments or regions. This assumption allows us to treat the production decision in each market segment independently.

Total costs per segment consist of a fixed and variable part. Entry occurs if entrant E's earnings exceed variable costs cq and fixed costs F. In contrast, the incumbent's fixed costs are sunk and cannot be avoided. The introduction of fixed costs is equivalent to increasing economies of scale, so the market has the property of a natural monopoly especially in those segments where fixed costs are high.

2.2 Regulated Competition with Swiss Licensing System

So far, there was no political or regulatory authority captured in the model. When such authorities set market rules, they usually change the underlying cost structures of the various operators. In Switzerland, the incumbent Swiss Post must provide universal service. This USO contains uniform tariffs across regions and service provision in every market segment. Additionally, the mail section of Swiss Post has to pay a transfer T to cover the deficit in the postal offices. If the incumbent does not break even due to cherry-picking entrants, the regulatory authority is entitled to charge licensing fees. Such fees are collected as a fixed fraction μ of the entrant's turnover. We treat μ as an exogenous parameter. Under such a regulatory regime, the profit functions in a given market segment are

$$\begin{aligned} \pi_I(p_I) &= \sum_r \left[\left(p_I - c_I^r\right) q_I^r(p_I, p_E^r) + \mu \cdot p_E^r q_E^r(p_I, p_E^r) - F_I^r \right] - T, \\ \pi_E(p_E^r) &= \sum_r \max\left\{0, \left(p_E^r(1-\mu) - c_E^r\right) q_E^r(p_I, p_E^r) - F_E^r\right\}. \end{aligned} \tag{2}$$

Profit maximization yields $s(r+1)$ first-order conditions (FOC). Substituting the demand functions (1) into these first-order conditions, we obtain the reaction functions for the two operators. For the case of two regions D (dense) and R (rural), the two reaction functions in a given market segment s are

$$\begin{aligned} p_I(p_E^D, p_E^R) &= \frac{b^R\left[a_I^D - ea_E^D + ep_E^D(1+\mu) + c_I^D\right] + b^D\left[a_I^R - ea_E^R + ep_E^R(1+\mu) + c_I^R\right]}{2(b^D + b^R)}, \\ p_E^r(p_I) &= \tfrac{1}{2}\left(a_E^r - ea_I^r + \tfrac{c_E^r}{(1-\mu)} + ep_I^r\right) \quad r \in \{D, R\}. \end{aligned} \tag{3}$$

The incumbent's reaction function is much more complicated because it must average its price over the two regions. By solving this equation system, we obtain the equilibrium prices for each operator *given that entry occurs,* i.e. the entrant's revenues exceed variable *and* fixed costs:

$$p_I = \frac{b^R\left[c_I^D + a_I^D - ea_E^D + \frac{e(1+\mu)}{2}\left(a_E^D - ea_I^D + \frac{c_E^D}{1-\mu}\right)\right] + b^D\left[c_I^R + a_I^R - ea_E^R + \frac{e(1+\mu)}{2}\left(a_E^R - ea_I^R + \frac{c_E^R}{1-\mu}\right)\right]}{(b^D + b^R)\left(2 - \frac{e^2(1+\mu)}{2}\right)}. \quad (4)$$

Once this price is calculated, we obtain the price of the entrant by appropriately substituting this result into (3). If the entry condition is satisfied, the corresponding quantities can be calculated with the demand functions in (1).

If entry is not profitable at the incumbent's price in (4), the above formulae no longer hold. For example, if the entrant fails to break even in the dense area, the incumbent can improve its profits by increasing the price up to the limit at which the entrant just breaks even.[2] This 'opponent break even price' is limited by the monopoly price p^M. However, because of uniform pricing, any increase in the incumbent's price affects both regions and it is not clear how to balance the two different 'opponent break even prices' in every situation. In our simulation, we solve this problem numerically through appropriate use of the entrant's reaction and profit functions. With the resulting equilibrium prices, quantities and profits we can compute overall welfare by subtracting industry expenses from gross utility. Doing so is equivalent to summing consumer net utility and the operators' profits.

2.3 Licensing fees lead to higher prices

Expressions (3) and (4) yield a first interesting result. Because the first derivative with respect to the licensing rate μ is positive under reasonable calibration, the incumbent will *increase* prices the more the regulator tries to finance the incumbent's USO through the licensing system. Intuitively, one would expect exactly the opposite. To see the intuition behind this result, we first study the impact of an increase in μ on the price of the entrant. To offset the negative effect of higher unit costs, the entrant must respond with an increase in prices; a higher licensing fee reduces the competitiveness of the entrant in equilibrium. Now the incumbent can charge a slightly higher price without losing any volume and thus further increases profits.

The financial effects to the incumbent can be identified by analyzing the marginal effect of μ on its profit function:

---

2 This limit price p^{Limit} can be calculated as follows:
$\pi_E(p_I^{\text{Limit}}, p_E^r(p_I^{\text{Limit}})) = 0 \quad \Leftrightarrow p_I^{\text{Limit}} = a_I^r - \frac{1}{e}a_E^r + \frac{c_E^r}{e(1-\mu)} \pm \frac{2}{e}\sqrt{b^r \frac{1-e^2}{1-\mu} F_E^r}$.

$$\frac{d\pi_I(p_I^*, p_E^*, \mu)}{d\mu} = \frac{\partial \pi_I}{\partial \mu} + \frac{\partial \pi_I}{\partial p_I}\frac{dp_I^*}{d\mu} + \frac{\partial \pi_I}{\partial p_E}\frac{dp_E^*}{d\mu} > 0.$$

The first term is the direct effect and represents the positive impact of the collected licensing fees. This direct effect equals $p_E q_E$ and is positive. The second and third terms represent indirect effects arising from price responses of both operators. The second term is zero at the optimum (because of the FOC). The third term is positive because both parts are positive (prices are strategic complements and both optimal prices increase with the license fee). We can therefore conclude that the incumbent's profits increase with a higher licensing fee. Thus, the licensing fee will help to sustain the USO, but will lead to a higher overall price level.

3. CALIBRATION WITH SWISS DATA

In order to predict price and welfare effects more precisely, we simulate the model using Swiss data. In Switzerland, geographic characteristics have a major impact on the cost structure of services. Differences in delivery time per household between dense and rural areas are significant and vary between delivery offices as much as 1:6. Accordingly, we divide the market into a dense region *D* and a rural region *R*.

To reflect the market structure we segment the market into five basic market segments *s*. The two basic sender groups, "businesses" and "households," can choose between two products "slow mail" and "fast mail." In addition, businesses have the option of mass mail. Crossing regions and segments yields ten submarkets.

To estimate the demand functions (1) for each operator in each submarket, we must calibrate the parameters *a* and *b* with market data from 2003, when Swiss Post was still the only operator in the letter market and charged regulated prices. Rewriting (1) for the case of this regulated monopoly (RM) we get in every segment

$$q_{2003}(p_{2003}) = \frac{a_{RM} - p_{2003}}{b_{RM}} \quad \text{with price elasticity} \quad \varepsilon_{2003} = -\frac{1}{b_{RM}}\frac{p_{2003}}{q_{2003}}. \quad (5)$$

After rearranging (5), we can directly calibrate parameter *b* with prices, quantities and elasticities from 2003.

Parameter a_i influences the size of the market of the two operator's services. By setting $a_I > a_E$, we can include effects like customer inertia, reputation effects, switching costs, or even quality differences like universal service provision that work in favor of the USP. Formally, we define x as the percentage of total demand the incumbent receives if the entrant were to offer the same price for its services. In the remainder of the paper, we will refer to x as "incumbent advantage." For calibration we evaluate demand given in (1) at 2003 prices for both operators and solve the resulting equation system. We obtain

$$a_I = a_{RM}; \quad x = \frac{q_I}{q_I + q_E}; \quad p_I = p_E = p_{2003}$$

$$a_E = \frac{1}{1-e+\frac{e}{x}}\left(a_I(e-1+\tfrac{1}{x}) + p(1-e)(2-\tfrac{1}{x})\right).$$

Table 1 summarizes the major demand characteristics of the model. According to its 2003 annual report, Swiss Post delivered about 2.8 billion pieces of addressed mail, of which we assume 25% was destined to rural areas. The price elasticities are a delicate issue for two reasons. First, econometric studies report significantly different price elasticities. See Cazals and Florens (2002) for an overview and discussion. Second, price elasticities determine the slope of the demand curves; competition would result in larger welfare gains if price elasticities were higher, *ceteris paribus*. The most recent data of Swiss Post 2004 suggests that the values in Table 1 are overestimated. These reflect our assumptions based on estimations from former Swiss data, studies from other countries, and industry experts. However, we expect mail elasticity to grow over time due to an increase of substitutes. Therefore, we stay on the safe side with the overestimation. The main intuition behind the differences between segments are a substantially higher value per sent item for households (so businesses are more price sensitive), and an increasing variety of urgent communication possibilities such as e-mail resulting in a higher elasticity of fast mail compared to slow mail.[3]

The incumbent advantage x is assumed to be higher for households than for businesses because of higher relative switching and information costs. The experiences from other liberalized postal, telecommunications or electricity markets support our assumptions; recent examples in Switzerland include Swiss Post in the parcels market.

[3] This assumption is consistent with recent observations that customers are willing to switch to slow mail products after price increases.

Table 1: Major Demand Characteristics

	Market size 2003	Prices 2003 (in €)	Price elasticity	Incumbent advantage
Fast Mail B	21 %	0.56	-0.5	70 %
Fast Mail HH	6 %	0.60	-0.4	75 %
Slow Mail B	26 %	0.43	-0.4	65 %
Slow Mail HH	6 %	0.47	-0.3	70 %
Mass Mail B	39 %	0.33	-0.4	60 %

For the production side of the economy we estimate variable and fixed costs for collection, processing, delivery and overhead. This detailed attribution is somewhat artificial, as some economies of scale and scope get lost. Such effects could be included numerically, but then we could not compute unique equilibrium formulae anymore.

Table 2 shows how costs differ in the various market segments. In a first step, we map total costs based on data from Swiss Post's 2003 annual report onto processes. Thereby we first corrected total cost by subtracting the € 234 million contribution that the addressed letter products paid last year to finance the postal outlet network's deficit. In line with empirical and technical estimations from comparable countries in Europe, Table 2 shows that delivery accounts for the largest portion of total costs.

In a second step, we attribute these process costs to market segments and regions. The figures are estimates and cannot reflect the economies of scope between the various segments and processes. Implicitly, we assume that collection costs are much higher for households and slightly higher for fast mail segments. Processing is slightly more expensive for fast mail but cheaper for mass mail because of extended presorting possibilities. Delivery costs are mainly determined by the quantity per segment and are slightly more expensive for fast mail and household segments. Overhead spreads equally over all segments.

Table 2: Major cost characteristics

	Collection	Processing	Delivery	Overhead
	10 %	30 %	55 %	5 %
Cost attribution to market segments				
Fast Mail B	15 %	20 %	24 %	20 %
Fast Mail HH	38 %	17 %	8 %	20 %
Slow Mail B	10 %	18 %	26 %	20 %
Slow Mail HH	30 %	16 %	6 %	20 %
Mass Mail B	7 %	29 %	36 %	20 %
	100 %	100 %	100 %	100 %
Fraction of variable costs				
Incumbent	50 %	80 %	40 %	10 %
Entrant	75 %	85 %	50 %	50 %

For the implemented scale effects, the fraction of fixed costs is important. In Switzerland, the number of letters per capita is the second largest in the world. Hence, the total time the mail carriers need to reach the various delivery points is almost fixed and the economies of scale in delivery are large. In accordance with most of the literature, we assume that processing costs are much more elastic. In total, about 50% of the incumbent's total costs are fixed. Compared to the incumbent, whose infrastructure is designed for private customers and more capital intensive (postal outlets, sorting centers, delivery offices), the entrant's percentage of variable costs is higher.

So far, the main difference between the two operators was the entrant's lower fraction of fixed costs. According to current observations in the Swiss parcel market, competitors pay lower wages. As stated by the labor unions, the wage premium is currently around 16% and hits the incumbent especially hard because about 80% of total costs are labor costs. The network design tailored to business customers further reduces the entrant's cost. We assume the upstream efficiency advantage (collection and presorting) of about 30% to reflect the savings realized by computerized sorting in the printing stage. In delivery, this advantage is much smaller (5%). Most business mailings are business-to-consumer. Consequently, one large customer causes a great deal of delivery points. Hence, a delivery network similar to that of the incumbent is needed with limited ways of cost innovation (the work is mainly physical).

4. RESULTS & DISCUSSION

With the calibrated model, we are now able to give some insight into the overall welfare consequences of various regulatory frameworks. In addition, we can perform sensitivity analysis and derive recommendations for postal operators on the strategies they should pursue under specific market rules. We focus on the first question and carry out sensitivity analysis only to judge the robustness of the results. In a first step, we evaluate the regulated monopoly of Swiss Post of 2003. Next, we analyze different forms of end-to-end competition (complete liberalization without access possibilities) and change the introduced model slightly where needed. The monopoly scenarios serve primarily as a benchmark.

The quantitative results presented in this section serve as rough guidelines in which directions the examined regulatory regimes influence the market equilibrium in terms of prices, quantities, surpluses, and profits.

4.1 Monopoly: Positive effects of a price freeze

It is straightforward to evaluate the *regulated monopoly (RM)* of 2003, since the model was calibrated with data of 2003. Swiss post charged uniform prices at an average of 44 cents. With the underlying cost structure, the resulting loss was € 54 million, thus Swiss Post was close to break even despite of the USO. From now on, we will use this scenario as a benchmark reflecting the status quo.[4]

As a second benchmark, we examine the case of an *unregulated monopoly (UM)*. What would happen, if the incumbent charged profit maximizing uniform prices? The results are interesting. The monopolist almost doubles its prices to 82 cents on average and thereby boosts its profit up to € 349 million. Profits are positive in all market segments except fast mail for households in rural areas. However, the higher price level reduces consumer welfare dramatically: despite the high profit, a net welfare decrease of € -497 million results. Table 3 presents the details.

We conclude that Swiss Post did not charge monopoly prices in 2003.[5] For that reason, one could view the legal framework of 2003 as an effective price cap combined with a break-even constraint. However, one does not know whether the regulated monopolist produced efficient.

Table 3: Results monopoly cases

Legal Monopoly	Regulated	Unregulated
Average Price	0.44	0.82
Quantities (in Mio)	2836	1'787
Consumer Surplus	1491	591
Profit after transfer	-54	349
Welfare	1'437	940
Welfare change		-497

4.2 End-to-end Competition: Universal service at risk

In theory, competition leads to positive welfare effects mainly due to marginal cost pricing, improved efficiency, and product innovation. To reflect these potential benefits, we equipped the entrant with a substantial efficiency advantage. Additionally, we assume that the entrant improves product diversification, technically we set $e = 0.75$.[6] However, it is not clear for two main reasons, whether these positive effects lead to an increase in overall welfare. First, economies of scale are sacrificed when entry occurs,

---

4 At this point, we note that there was a price increase in Switzerland in the beginning of 2004 due to the deficit in the postal network.

5 Only if elasticities were assumed to be 3.5 times larger than the values in Table 1, the model would predict monopoly pricing for Swiss Post in 2003.

6 In line with De Donder (2001) and Dietl/Waller (2002).

so the market ends up with larger industry wide production costs. Second, the combination of a relatively inelastic demand with product differentiation possibilities could lead to oligopolistic pricing rather than marginal cost pricing. It will be interesting to see whether the model predicts prices above or below the ones from 2003.

In our first end-to-end competition case, hereafter referred to "Regulated Competition (RC)", there are no restrictions on market entry. The incumbent must fulfill the universal service obligation as presented in Section 2. In return, the entrant must pay a licensing fee of 3% of its turnover.

The model predicts an overall welfare decrease with universal service at risk. Despite an 18% increase in the overall price level, the incumbent's loss rises to about € 189 million. Entry occurs in all three dense business segments. Both operators make substantial profits with single-piece business mail. The incumbent enjoys its highest margins in rural business segments where no economies of scale are lost. The main losses occur in the household segments. The results are straightforward and support similar findings from Panzar (2001, 2002), Crew/Kleindorfer (2002), De Donder (2004) and Dietl/Waller (2002).

Table 4: Results End-to-End Competition

	Regulated (uniform pricing for I)			Unregulated (non uniform pricing)		
Licensing Rate	$\mu = 0\%$	$\mu = 3\%$	$\mu = 20\%$	$\mu = 0\%$	$\mu = 3\%$	$\mu = 20\%$
Average Price (€)						
Incumbent	0.56	0.57	0.48	0.43	0.45	0.50
Entrant*	0.39	0.39	0.43	0.38	0.39	
Average	0.49	0.50	0.48	0.43	0.44	0.50
Quantities (Mio #)						
Incumbent	1'652	1'631	2'408	2'540	2'503	2'571
Entrant	1'176	1'177	350	322	323	-
Total	2'828	2'808	2'759	2'863	2'826	2'571
Welfare (Mio €)						
Consumer Surplus	1'351	1'331	1'356	1'481	1'444	1'246
Profit I after transfer	-217	-196	-27	-124	-97	82
Profit Entrant	168	159	36	41	39	-
Welfare	1'302	1'294	1'365	1'398	1'386	1'328
Welfare change**	-135	-143	-72	-39	-51	-109
Other						
Licensing Fees (€)	-	14	30	-	4	-
Entry in # segments	3	3	1	1	1	-

* The values in this row represent weighted averages in active market segments.

** Values compared to the regulated monopoly case.

The incumbent's main problem arises from the combination of universal service provision and uniform pricing. The entrant is able to undercut the incumbent in the dense segments and "picks the cherries," offered by the incumbent's tariff balancing act between the dense and rural region. This cherry-picking effect is much stronger than the cure for it, the licensing system. The entrant has to pay no more than € 15 million in licensing fees, a sum that represents less than 10% of its profits (and the incumbent's loss).

We observe a lot of price differentiation between the various market segments. Prices for households rise about 50%, whereas the average price in business segments rises about 10%, despite the entrant's cheaper prices.

One promising strategy for the USP against this kind of cherry picking is to abolish the uniform price. In such an Unregulated Competition (UC), the incumbent can differentiate its prices between regions. To implement this regulatory framework into the model, we make appropriate changes to expressions (2), (3) and (4). Doing so results in major change. The USP can now prevent entry in all segments except slow mail business. In the three market segments in which the entrant cannot enter anymore, we observe predatory behavior. The incumbent sets prices below the optimal prices in (4) to turn the entrant's profit into a deficit; the entrant cannot break even anymore and no entry occurs. The incumbent is better off because he defends 100% of the market. From this combination of predatory pricing and price discrimination between regions, consumers gain a € 100 million net surplus; the incumbent's prices are much lower on average, e.g. mass mailers gain about € 70 million net surplus (on the cost of rural regions). Nevertheless, there are also losers, namely the entrant and the less price elastic households in rural areas where tariffs explode by more than 100%.

Compared to the regulated competition, the model predicts an overall welfare gain of € 92 million and a better financial situation for the incumbent. Still, the results are worse than in the case of the regulated monopoly of 2003. Table 4 summarizes the results.

4.3 Ambiguous effects of the licensing rate μ

For the above results, we assumed a licensing rate of 3%. If no licensing fee were collected (μ = 0%), the results would change only slightly. As predicted in section 2.3, both operators offer lower prices. Consequently, the incumbent's loss rises by an additional € 21 million, which is more than the foregone licensing fees (€ 14 million). Thus, the indirect effect of the licensing system is in this case € 7 million (caused by price changes). The lower rate increases the entrant's potential profit margin, weakens the entry barrier function of the licensing system and leads to higher losses for the incumbent.

If the licensing rate is set to 20%, we observe a further important aspect of the licensing system. In the case of RC, we observe now only one market entry instead of three. The licensing system turns into a barrier to entry. In this special case, the entry barrier is desirable because the threat of entry forces the incumbent to charge low prices. As a result, overall welfare increases and the incumbent almost breaks even due to the indirect effect worth € 156 million (direct effect = additional 16 million). These good results are only one side of the coin, as we can see for the case of UC, where the incumbent's prices rise and welfare decreases. If the licensing rate is too high, the threat of entry is too low and the incumbent improves profits at the cost of overall welfare.

Figure 1 gives further insight into the mechanism of the licensing system. Under Regulated Competition, the incumbent breaks even with a licensing rate of 23%. Welfare is maximized at 26%. This is the point at which the entrant has to give up service even in the last segment (slow mail businesses). Still the threat of entry persists and sets the upper bound for the incumbent's prices. Any further rate increase would decrease the threat of entry and the incumbent (now a monopolist) can adjust his prices towards the profit maximizing unregulated monopoly solution.

Figure 1: Impact of the licensing rate on welfare and profits

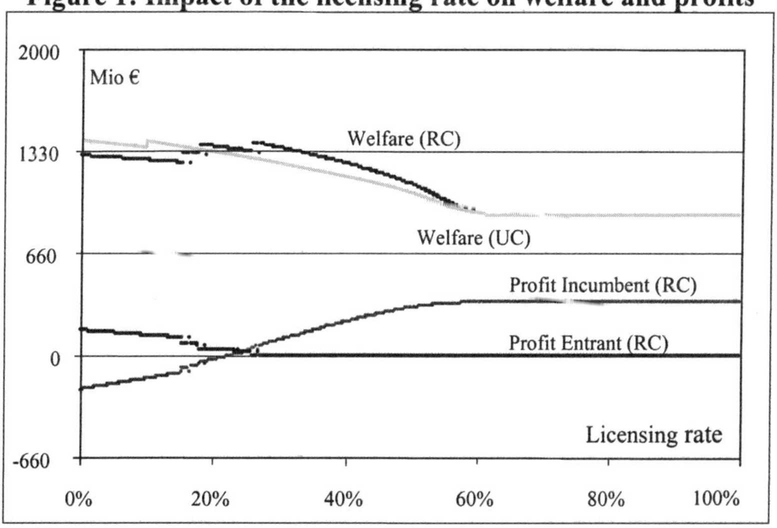

In the case of UC, the optimal licensing rate is 0% where entry occurs in only one market segment. Up to a rate of 10%, the entrant stays in. At 10%, the incumbent is able to push the entrant out of the market by profitable predatory pricing. This discrete drop in prices yields the welfare jump that can be seen in the graph. From now on, any increase of the licensing rate reduces welfare.

4.4 Comparison of the four regulatory regimes and first conclusions

Having calculated overall price levels as well as the welfare of the different market rules, we are now able to make normative statements about which of the four scenarios a welfare-maximizing regulator should prefer. None of the competitive scenarios described above could reach the welfare of the Regulated Monopoly of 2003, even if a regulator maximized welfare with an optimal licensing rate. The model gives the following ordering in terms of welfare[7]: $RM \succ RC_{\mu^*=26\%} \succ UC_{\mu^*=0\%} \succ UM$.

If we apply these results to Switzerland, neither of the discussed competition scenarios is efficient. End-to-end competition does not necessarily lead to lower prices because of strategic interaction and the natural monopoly in delivery. Welfare is likely to decrease, and Swiss Post's ability to fund its universal service obligation is heavily reduced. These conclusions include positive effects of competition, such as higher product choice and a highly more efficient entrant.

In a dynamic context, Regulated "Competition" with a licensing rate between 20% and 25% might still be best because a profit-maximizing incumbent has direct incentives to reduce costs further. Suppose a regime in which the regulator reduces the licensing rate yearly by 1% for ten years. If the incumbent is able to reduce his costs appropriately, it can lower prices further to prevent a competitor's entry and thereby secure a 100% market share for exploiting the scale effects in distribution. From this point of view, a regulatory system similar to the one in Finland is reasonable.

4.5 Other ways for competition

There are various other ways to introduce competition in the letter market. One could relax universal service restrictions further, find other mechanisms for financing the USO (taxes, fixed licensing rates, etc), introduce various forms of access regimes, copy U.S. Worksharing, or combine the discussed competition designs with price cap regulation.

Combining end-to-end competition with some form of downstream access, where entrants can hand over mail to the incumbent's delivery network if wanted, will provide entrants with additional possibilities of cherry picking by focusing on processes (in addition to customers and regions). Crew/Kleindorfer (2004), De Donder (2004) and Panzar (2003)

---

[7] Only if elasticities are assumed at least 50% higher than the ones in Table 1, both competition scenarios turn out to be better than RM. As pointed out in section 3, the most recent market data rejects such high elasticity values.

show that these "bypass possibilities" will have negative effects on welfare and USO provision. We leave the Swiss access issue for further research and focus directly on worksharing as a means to introduce competition in the letter market.

5. WORKSHARING AND PRICE CAP COMPETITION

Worksharing aims to minimize the costs of industry-wide service provision in the U.S. letter market. The incumbent United States Postal Service (USPS) is granted a monopoly in delivery ("downstream monopoly"), whereas competitors can perform upstream services like collection and presorting just as well. For these upstream services, USPS gives "worksharing discounts" on the official retail prices, depending on the value of the competitor's services for USPS. The system makes sense in economic terms if delivery has the property of a natural monopoly and its innovation potential is limited in contrast to upstream services. Worksharing evolved over the last 30 years. Today, about 70% of total U.S. mail volume is workshared and the sum of all worksharing discounts is about US$ 14.

5.1 Modeling Worksharing

To compare Worksharing (WS) with the regulatory frameworks discussed above, some small changes of the model are needed. We change the demand side only to the extent that two calibration values are slightly changed. First, we reduce the incumbent advantage x in all segments by 50% (i.e. $x_{new} = \frac{1}{2}x_{old} + \frac{1}{4}$) because the entrant takes some advantage of the incumbent's downstream reputation and quality. Customers will switch faster to the entrant. Second, product differentiation possibilities are smaller because the entrant cannot deliver anymore. Therefore, we assume the product differentiation factor e to rise to 0.85. In other words, the two services of the two operators are still considered as two different products and demand is still described by (1).

The major changes are on the cost side, as the entrant is legally obliged to buy the downstream services from the incumbent. In return, the entrant receives a discount of δ^s (the "worksharing discount") for his collection and presorting efforts in market segment s.[8] In other words, the entrant pays

8 I.e. the modeled worksharing system is very stylized. In the U.S., there are various classes of worksharing discounts, and private operators need not to do all the upstream work as one block. They can specialize in any single discount.

the access price $A = p_I - \delta$ to the incumbent for final processing and delivery. The entrant's variable costs for its upstream activities are c_{Eu}, whereas the incumbent's variable costs split up in an upstream and downstream part, i.e. $c_I = c_{Iu} + c_{Id}$.

Since the universal service obligation can now be financed by the downstream monopoly, there is no reason for a licensing fee anymore, i.e. $\mu=0$. We thus rewrite the profit functions (2) as follows (for any given market segment):

$$\begin{aligned}\pi_I(p_I,\delta) &= \sum_r \underbrace{\left(p_I - c^r_{Iu} - c^r_{Id}\right) q^r_I(p_I, p^r_E)}_{\text{Incumbent Mail}} + \underbrace{\left(p_I - \delta - c^r_{Id}\right) q^r_E(p_I, p^r_E)}_{\text{Workshared Mail}} - F^r_I - T,\\ \pi_E(p^r_E) &= \sum_r \max\left\{0, \left(p^r_E - c^r_{Eu} - p_I + \delta\right) q^r_E(p_I, p^r_E) - F^r_{Eu}\right\}.\end{aligned} \tag{6}$$

5.2 U.S. Worksharing

In the U.S., both retail prices and worksharing discounts are regulated. The Postal Rate Commission (PRC) is entitled to give its recommendations about pricing issues raised by the USPS. Worksharing discounts are calculated using ECPR, where discounts equal USPS' cost savings for the respective worksharing activity ("avoided costs").

In the model, the incumbent's savings are exactly the upstream variable costs c_{Iu}. We rewrite (6) accordingly and set $c_{Iu} = \delta$ for the worksharing discount and $p_I = p_{2003}$ for the retail prices (i.e. again a price freeze to compare with the other price freeze scenarios). To obtain the profit-maximizing price for the entrant, we compute its first order condition. In equilibrium, optimal prices are

$$\begin{aligned}p_I^* &= p_{2003},\\ p^{r*}_E &= \tfrac{1}{2}\left(a^r_E - ea^r_I + ep_{2003} + c^r_{Eu} + p_{2003} - c^r_{Iu}\right) \quad r \in \{D, R\}.\end{aligned} \tag{7}$$

The results are straightforward. If entry occurs, there is a Pareto improvement compared to the Regulated Monopoly. The incumbent is indifferent whether to workshare or not and is better off if the entrant generates additional volume. Consumers only buy the products of the entrant if they gain net utility. The entrant can only enter if it charges lower prices due to more efficient production and/or it generates additional demand through product differentiation. In both cases, volumes increase when demand is downward sloping as assumed. Empirical findings from Cohen et al. (2002) support this argument.

In line with the theory, the model predicts an increase in overall volume of 2.2%. In total 640 million letters are workshared. The welfare improvement is € 77 million and the sum of worksharing discount totals € 97 million. Entry occurs in 5 segments (all business segments but rural fast mail). We note that these results do not hold anymore if worksharing discounts were set above avoided costs.

It is interesting to observe that the entrant charges a higher price than the incumbent does. Parameter analysis with different values for *e* shows that only for high values of *e* are the entrant's prices lower. I.e., only if the entrant cannot differentiate its products relative to the incumbent's ones, it must charge a lower price. If the entrant reaches to do product innovation, it might benefit from higher prices. In this case, consumers also benefit (their needs are better served) and, of course, so does the incumbent, who gets the additional volume for downstream delivery.

Table 5: Results Worksharing and Price Cap Competition

	U.S. Worksharing		Price Cap Competition		
	$e = 0{,}85$	$e = 0{,}75$	$\mu = 0\%$	$\mu = 3\%$	$\mu = 20\%$
Average Price (€)					
Incumbent	0.44	0.44	0.44	0.44	0.43
Entrant	0.46	0.51	0.35	0.36	0.41
Average	0.45	0.46	0.41	0.41	0.42
Quantities (Millions #)					
Incumbent (*upstream)	2'291*	2'307*	2'073	2'079	2'432
Entrant	640	705	1'016	1'008	538
Total	2'932	3'012	3'090	3'088	2'970
Welfare (Millions €)					
Consumer surplus	1'515	1'533	1'612	1'610	1'560
Profit I after transfer	-22	-1	-300	-287	-165
Profit Entrant	21	48	90	79	21
Welfare	1'514	1'580	1'402	1'402	1'416
Welfare change (RM)	+77	+143	-35	-35	-21
Welfare change (RC)			+100	+108	+51
Other					
Discounts/Fees (Millions €)	97	118	0	10	44
Entry in # segments	5	7	3	3	2

Table 5 presents detailed model results and illustrates the positive welfare and profit effects of a further increase in product differentiation.

The model supports the experience from the U.S.: Successful entry occurs in business segments, the USP gains and can better sustain the USO at low prices. There is only one group, which is worse off, namely the workforce who represents the avoided upstream variable costs. However, they lose much less than in the case of regulated competition.

5.3 Price Cap Competition

The two end-to-end competition cases from section 4 yield much lower overall welfare than worksharing. One reason is the price-driving effect of the licensing system. To offset this price-driving effect, we supplement the RC case with a price freeze.

Table 5 reports the results of such a "Price Cap Competition." The price freeze has a positive effect on overall welfare compared to the Regulated Competition case (but not compared with the Regulated Monopoly) because the overall price level drops. The incumbent is worse off. He has no further possibility of responding competitively and its deficit increases up to € 287 million – the USO burden is not covered at all. Once again, this regulatory regime is not feasible for Switzerland from a legal point of view. Similar to the findings in section 4, only a sufficiently high licensing rate can stabilize the financial situation of the USP. It prevents entry, and if the rate is set accordingly, it gives the incumbent incentives to reduce costs and to avoid potential entry.

5.4 Discussion

Both the regulatory regimes presented in this section did help to improve overall welfare compared to the competition cases examined in section 4. However, Price Cap Competition is desirable for consumers (higher net utility), but not for the ones who must pay the higher burden of the universal service obligation. If this burden would have to be paid by the consumers through a special postal tax, they are again worse off compared to the Regulated Monopoly of Swiss Post in 2003.

In contrast, Worksharing seems to be the only system that can improve economic efficiency in the sector. Worksharing realizes the benefits of competition without sacrificing the economies of scale in delivery and putting universal service at risk.

Empirically, one could try to find out how tariffs and volumes do vary between the different regulatory regimes applied in practice today. The model predicts that the United States should have large volumes per capita ceteris paribus. In liberalized markets, postal operators should have problems sustaining the USO due to smaller volumes. In regulated monopolies (or licensing regimes with very high rates) tariffs and volumes should lie somewhere in between. However, such a comparison is difficult, because demand and supply factors vary heavily across nations.

6. CONCLUSIONS

Like the member states of the European Community, Switzerland is in the process of liberalizing its domestic postal markets. In 2004, a new postal ordinance fully opened the parcels market by introducing end-to-end competition using a licensing system to help the incumbent fund its universal service obligation.

We asked, what would happen if the letter market were liberalized in the same way? To gain deeper insight on this issue, we adapted a price competition framework from De Donder et al. (2001), tailored it to Swiss circumstances and extended it further to include worksharing. The model enables quantitative comparisons between monopoly, competition and worksharing scenarios. Despite the limits of such a quantitative model, we believe that the main results are robust and straightforward.

We identify U.S. Worksharing[9] as a Pareto improvement compared to monopoly regulation. Moreover, our model predicts higher welfare and much better USP stability than various ways of end-to-end competition with different levels of licensing rates. End-to-end competition with its full liberalization of the postal value chain is leading to serious difficulties for the incumbent to sustain the Universal Service requirements. The more restrictions are imposed on the incumbent's pricing flexibility (uniform price, price freeze), the worse becomes the financial situation of the incumbent.

We conclude that Switzerland should be very cautious when copying European plans of end-to-end competition. We believe caution is especially indicated when the assumption of high economies of scale in delivery truly reflects the industry. Our model predicts that complete letter market liberalization will lead to higher prices, to much more price differentiation between regions and customers (in favor of business customers and cities), to an erosion of Universal Service due to Swiss Post's attempts to adapt its business model to the underlying market forces and to continuous financial problems of the incumbent. Some of these problems could be mitigated by combining liberalization with a mandatory access regime under which competitors could use the incumbent's delivery network when needed. However, the financial consequences to the USP will remain serious because the entrant's competitive advantage gets even larger. We leave an evaluation within our model for further research.

The model cannot cope with some dynamic advantages of competition. For example, there were no possibilities for Swiss Post for dynamic efficiency gains over time. If one believes those efficiency potentials to be

---

[9] The Pareto improvement is only achieved if retail prices stay regulated *and* worksharing discounts are equal or less to avoided costs.

large, end-to-end competition could still be a desirable solution. However, postal services already face increasing indirect competition through digital means of written communication. The overall volume in single-piece mail is shrinking in most highly developed countries, including Switzerland despite growing written communication markets. This rapidly evolving "e-competition" threatens the postal services as end-to-end competition does. Regulated "monopolists" and worksharers are "hit" only once, whereas incumbents competing in fully liberalized letter markets are "hit" twice.

REFERENCES

Cazals, Catherine, and Jean-Pierre Florens. 2002. "Econometrics of Mail Demand" In *Postal and Delivery Services: Delivering on Competition*, edited by M.A. Crew and P.R. Kleindorfer. Boston, MA: Kluwer Academic Publishers.

Cohen, Robert H., William W. Ferguson, John D. Waller and Spyros S. Xenakis. 2002. "The Impact of Using Worksharing to Liberalize a Postal Market." In *Liberalisation of Postal Markets*, edited by G. Kulenkampff and H. Smit. Rheinbreitbach: Druckerei Plump KG.

Crew, Michael A., and Paul R. Kleindorfer. 2002. "Putty-Putty, Putty-Clay or Humpty-Dumpty? Universal Service Under Entry." In *Postal and Delivery Services: Pricing, Productivity, Regulation and Strategy*, edited by M.A. Crew and P.R. Kleindorfer. Boston, MA: Kluwer Academic Publishers.

Crew, Michael A., and Paul R. Kleindorfer. 2004. "Access and the USO for Letters and Parcels": In *Competitive Transformation of the Postal and Delivery Sector*, edited by M.A. Crew and P.R. Kleindorfer. Boston, MA: Kluwer Academic Publishers.

Dietl, Helmut M. and Peter Waller. 2002. "Competing with Mr. Postman: Business Strategies, Industry Structure, and Competitive Prices in Liberalized Letter Markets." In *Schmalenbach Business Review* 54: 148 – 170

De Donder, Philippe, Helmuth Cremer and Frank Rodriguez. 2004. "Access Pricing and Uniform Tariff in the Postal Sector." In *Competitive Transformation of the Postal and Delivery Sector*, edited by M.A. Crew and P.R. Kleindorfer. Boston, MA: Kluwer Academic Publishers.

De Donder, Philippe, Helmuth Cremer, Jean-Pierre Florens, André Grimaud and Frank Rodriguez. 2001. "Uniform Pricing and Postal Market Liberalization." In *Future Directions in Postal Reform*, edited by M. A. Crew and P.R. Kleindorfer. Boston, MA: Kluwer Academic Publishers.

Panzar, John C. 2003. *The Economic Effects of Combining Liberalization and Unbundling Policies in Postal Markets*. Third Conference on Regulation, Competition and Universal Service in the Postal Sector, Toulouse.

Panzar, John C. 2002. "Reconciling Competition, Downstream Access, and Universal Service in Postal Markets." In *Postal and Delivery Services: Delivering on Competition*, edited by M.A. Crew and P.R. Kleindorfer. Boston, MA: Kluwer Academic Publishers.

Panzar, John C. 2001. "Funding Universal Service Obligations: The Costs of Liberalization." In *Future Directions in Postal Reform*, edited by M.A. Crew and P.R. Kleindorfer. Boston, MA: Kluwer Academic Publishers.

Chapter 4

The Financial Equilibrium of Universal Service Providers in a Liberalized Postal Market*

Roger Hill, Richard Robinson, and Frank Rodriguez
Royal Mail Group

1. INTRODUCTION

In their paper on liberalization and universal service, Crew and Kleindorfer introduced the concept of a "graveyard spiral" (Crew and Kleindorfer, 2000). Under certain circumstances, liberalization of the postal market could lead, despite successive price increases, to an undermining of the financial equilibrium of a universal service provider (USP). The financial position of the USP could become so adverse that the universal service obligation (USO) would need to be significantly compromised, entry restricted or a subsidy provided. In trying to determine the likelihood of such an outcome, Crew and Kleindorfer conclude their paper by stating that "The sixty four billion dollar question is how big a USO and how much entry? The current state of knowledge is inadequate in answering it".

It is clear that if little entry occurs then a graveyard spiral will not arise. This is the central case developed in Cohen et al (2004, 2005) for the USA. Cohen et al (2004) in their benchmark case estimate that less than 20% of mail is contestable and, unless entrants are assumed to be very much more efficient than USPS, most of the contestable traffic would remain with USPS if delivery were open to competition. Furthermore, limited entry and the implied low level of financial return would make it difficult for entrants to

* We wish to thank the editors, Helmuth Cremer, and Philippe De Donder for valuable comments and suggestions on earlier versions of this paper.

attract funding from capital markets. Earlier work by the USPS suggested that the risk of entry would be higher (Kolin and Smith, 1999). Cohen et al (2004) also examine cases where much more entry is assumed to occur and here find that price increases, in some cases very large ones, would provide sufficient revenue to allow USPS to maintain financial equilibrium after entry. By contrast, Crew and Kleindorfer (2005) and D'Alcantara and Amerlynck (2004) develop models which indicate that a graveyard spiral is possible in the absence of a subsidy or significant relaxation of the USO.

In this paper we examine the prospects for a graveyard spiral in the UK, focusing on the case where the USO remains unchanged so that the key issues involve the second of Crew and Kleindorfer's uncertainties, namely the extent and implications of entry. In this we use Royal Mail data and apply it to a model of competitive entry. We follow a similar approach to that adopted by Cohen et al (2004) and calculate the scale of price increases necessary to offset losses in contribution due to entry where entrants do not react to changes in Royal Mail's prices and the definition of universal service is unaltered. Clearly, there are other ways to try to recover the losses in contribution arising from competitive entry, most notably through improvements in the underlying efficiency and cost level of Royal Mail, and although these are not considered further in the paper they impact on the prospect or otherwise of a graveyard spiral. Royal Mail's prices are subject to price controls on their overall level and at product level through sub-caps. However, the UK regulator's primary duty is to ensure the provision of a universal postal service so we report results in the paper which allow prices to change to required levels irrespective of the terms of the current price control.

The paper is structured as follows. Section 2 outlines our approach and results are reported in section 3. In a final section we draw conclusions and implications from our results regarding the requirements for financial equilibrium of USPs in a liberalized postal market. An appendix sets out a brief statement of the model used to evaluate the prospects for a graveyard spiral.

2. OUTLINE OF APPROACH

With an unchanged USO, liberalization and ensuing entry are likely to lead to a loss of contribution by a USP which is required to meet the fixed costs of universal service provision. How significant this loss of contribution is likely to be is an empirical question. In terms of a forward-looking assessment of whether such a loss is likely to lead to a graveyard spiral, it is necessary as a minimum to formulate and calibrate a quantitative model of entry and to specify clearly the form of liberalization in a well-defined scenario.

In this paper we address this question using Royal Mail's entry pricing model (EPM). A summary of the model is set out in the appendix which contains the technical detail and calibration of the base case underpinning the results presented in the main paper. The EPM models entry to the postal market as being cream-skimming in nature with entrants choosing to enter most where contribution or margins are highest. Such differences in margins are created by a lack of full cost reflectivity in the overall level of prices of Royal Mail products and by various characteristics of the postal market, most notably the existence of uniform (geographically averaged) tariffs for products in the universal service. The EPM incorporates the option of entry through downstream access (DA) to Royal Mail's network both by entrants and by final customers (customer direct access (CDA)). Both the EU Directive and Royal Mail's License mandate access to Royal Mail's network by both types of user.

The model is used to analyze a particular liberalization scenario which is evaluated, first, for the base case calibration values set out in the appendix and then for various sensitivities on these parameters. The scenario examined in the paper is one of full liberalization which allows entrants to offer, if they find it profitable, end to end (E2E) services through their own delivery network (or bypass) to any segment of the market. The prices entrants can charge are not constrained to require uniform pricing. Additionally, entry can occur through DA. As shown in the appendix, the EPM models the impact of variations in access prices and different access prices result in different patterns and levels of entry. For the purpose of the current paper, the scenario adopts the access prices proposed by the UK postal regulator in May 2003 (Postcomm, 2003).[1] Above the basic weight step, these prices were set at approximately avoided cost levels (although well below this at the basic weight step) and nationally averaged. Access at these prices would also have been available to customers meeting the criteria for being able to obtain access as well as to entrants.[2]

Under this liberalization scenario, entry leads to a loss of contribution and this is estimated by the EPM. This loss is calculated on the assumption

1 A different set of access prices would lead to a different outcome in terms of the extent to entry and hence to the possible development of a graveyard spiral. The impact of access prices is a large subject in itself and we do not consider alternative access pricing scenarios in the current paper. For an extensive analysis of the impact of alternative access pricing rules on the financial viability of USPs, welfare impacts and related issues see Crew and Kleindorfer (2004a) and De Donder et al (2004).

2 This set of access prices had been proposed by Postcomm for consultation in response to a request for a determination on access prices by a mail operator. Subsequently, in February 2004, Royal Mail agreed separately an alternative set of access prices with this operator.

that there is no response to entry and, in particular, that prices remain at their pre-entry levels. For simplicity and to gain insights into the likelihood of a graveyard spiral, it is assumed in the modeling that all effects occur instantly as if applied in the base year of the model, FY2001/02. In practice, the impact of liberalization takes time to develop before reaching its full effect. Over this period other factors are likely to change including cost levels; the mix of traffic from public tariff or single piece mail towards presorted mail, which increases the likely extent of entry; a risk of total volumes declining; and potentially also the values of some of the key parameters in the model. Furthermore, the graveyard spiral as originally conceived by Crew and Kleindorfer is a dynamic process where price increases in response to financial losses due to entry lead to further price increases which cumulate into growing and unsustainable losses over time. However, the primary focus of the paper is on the circumstances under which a graveyard spiral might occur and the phasing and precise timepath of such a development is of subsidiary interest. Considering a one year effect in this way provides valuable insights although it is by no means a complete approach for this purpose. In particular, it may provide a good understanding of the possibility of a graveyard spiral in the near term but understate these risks over the long term.

Figure 1: Example of Switching Function

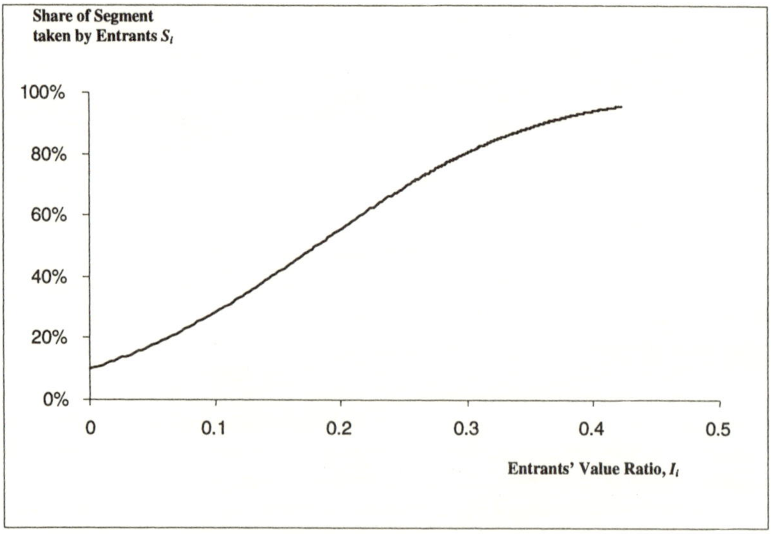

The loss of traffic arising from entry is modeled using switching functions (Robinson and Rodriguez, 2000). A greater share of traffic is taken by entrants when the "value" they offer through their services is higher and this is the basic concept reflected in a switching function. An example is shown in figure 1 and the technical underpinning is set out in the appendix.

The lower the price and/or the higher the quality of service offered by entrants relative to Royal Mail, the higher the "value ratio" of entrants and the greater their share of that segment of traffic. However, because mail services are differentiated services and some customers, at least, are likely to show a considerable amount of inertia or loyalty, entrants will gain less than 100% of the market even if their value ratio is high. This can be mapped through a switching function which is cumulative Normal in form where the precise shape is defined by the mean and variance of the distribution. The calibration of the switching functions varies across segments of traffic and the parameters are set by making assumptions about the amount of traffic switching to entrants at an equal/price quality offering (the point at which the switching function crosses the vertical axis) and the value ratio at which the maximum rate of switching occurs. The loss of traffic by segment due to competitive entry, under the assumption that Royal Mail prices remain unchanged, is used to calculate the loss of revenue, reduction in costs and loss in contribution arising from liberalization[3].

The approach followed is then to seek to recover the loss of contribution arising under this scenario by applying an algorithm in the model which raises prices on all Royal Mail products, initially by an equal percentage amount. The use of equal percentage increases follows the approach adopted by Cohen et al (2004) and applies both to the prices of all E2E services and to access prices. As shown in the appendix, an increase in Royal Mail prices has no impact on prices for postal service offered by entrants through bypass but it raises the prices of entrants using DA as part of their service. Note that the switching functions and elasticities in the model differ across products and this implies that prices reach their contribution-maximizing level at different increases compared with their starting points.

In the algorithm, prices continue to be increased either until the pre-liberalization scenario level of contribution is regained, which indicates that a graveyard spiral will not take hold, or ever increasing price rises cause contribution to fall back, which indicates a turning point in contribution with respect to prices at below the pre-liberalization scenario level. The latter

[3] Note that implicit in the formulation of the switching functions is the assumption that in principle, at least, all mail is contestable. However, in practice, for many types of mail the prices entrants would have to charge would be very high (their value ratio would be very low) while customers would be reluctant to move (the switching function would cut the vertical axis in figure 1 close to the origin and be very flat). For these types of mail, entrants would be modeled to take close to 0% of that segment and hence effectively that mail would not be contestable through a bypass service although the existence of DA implies that entrants have a lower cost alternative to offer service to such segments. This would improve the value they offer but not affect the switching functions.

case implies a graveyard spiral in the specific sense that price increases alone are unable to secure financial equilibrium. Of course, as noted earlier, there may be other, non-price means to try to ensure the cost of continuing to provide the USO is met but these are not considered further here.[4] Additional information on the algorithm is set out in the appendix but the basic methodology is outlined here. Let π^{M} represent Royal Mail's contribution from its postal network pre-entry, π^{RM} represent its contribution after entry at pre-entry prices (implying that $\pi^{RM} < \pi^{M}$) and β_j represent a factor indicating a proportionate increase in the price of product j $(j = 1,....J)$. The algorithm adopted increases β_j for each product in small increments until $\pi^{RM}_{\beta} = \pi^{M}$ so that the pre-entry level of contribution is recovered where:

$$\pi^{RM}_{\beta} = \sum_{j=1}^{J} \pi^{RM}_{j,\beta} = \sum_{j=1}^{J} q^{RM}_{j} \left[p^{RM}_{j} \left(1 + \beta_j\right) - c_j \right] \tag{1}$$

and $\pi^{RM}_{j,\beta}$ is the contribution on product j after the pre-entry price of product j, p^{RM}_{j}, is increased by the proportion β_j; q^{RM}_{j} is the volume of product j after the increase in price; c_j is the unit cost of an item of product j; and the term inside $[\cdot]$ measures the contribution from an item of product j[5]. As noted above, the algorithm does not attempt to model the dynamic timepath of price rises leading to losses which lead to further price rises which then either lead to π^{RM}_{β} regaining the level π^{M} or become ever larger to produce a graveyard spiral. Instead it adopts a sequential approach to identifying the β_j which yield the lowest price increases to recover loss of contribution or those yielding the maximum level of contribution if the loss cannot be recovered in full.

We apply two methods in determining the set of β_j. First, $\beta_j = \beta$ or that all products are increased in price by an equal proportion, β. As prices are increased, contribution per item rises (the term inside $[\cdot]$ increases) but traffic switches to entrants through the switching function (so that volume,

---

4 A fuller discussion of alternative means of funding the USO under liberalization and the wider issues involved in this is contained in De Donder et al (2002a).

5 Expression (1) is a simplified version of π^{RM}_{β} to allow the methodology to be outlined briefly. The algorithm uses a more detailed formulation at the greater level of segmentation which identifies separately entrant access and CDA (expression (14) in the appendix).

q_j^{RM}, declines). Under this approach, when the value of β is sufficiently high the volume effect will begin to dominate and contribution will start to fall on some products. We therefore apply a second approach which differentiates β_j across products. Define β_j^* as the value of β_j which maximizes contribution for product j. Then price increases vary according to the following rule:

$$\beta_j = \begin{cases} \beta_j & \text{if } \dfrac{\partial \pi_j^{RM}}{\partial \beta_j} > 0 \\ \beta_j^* & \text{if } \dfrac{\partial \pi_j^{RM}}{\partial \beta_j} \leq 0 \end{cases} \tag{2}$$

or that β_j is adopted if contribution for product j rises following a small rise in β_j but that if contribution falls for a small rise in β_j, then β_j^* is used instead to calculate that product's price. Given the nature of the profit function in prices,[6] this implies that β_j is given by $\min\{\beta_j, \beta_j^*\}$ so that where price increases can be differentiated across products prices are raised only to their contribution maximizing level[7]. If prices need to be increased further to regain the pre-liberalization level of contribution then these increases are applied only to those products where prices remain below their contribution maximizing level.

As will be seen, the second approach can produce lower average price increases and, indeed, allow a greater level of losses to be recovered. It leads, however, to significant differences in price rises across products and implies that the differences in contribution per item prior to entry can be changed significantly by these price changes.[8] In the paper, an improvement in contribution can be achieved by applying this differentiation at a level that is still highly aggregated and assumes geographically averaged prices. Within the model it would be possible, as a benchmark exercise, to differentiate prices far below this to the level of the individual segment or

[6] This is approximately quadratic in form although because the EPM is an operational model using business data rather than mathematical functions there may be lack of smoothness in some of the outputs from the model.

[7] In the differentiated prices application of the algorithm we do not model potential cross price effects where the change in relative prices might lead to a movement from higher to lower priced products other than the effect of changing the relative price of access and E2E services which is an explicit part of the model. Because the change in E2E relative prices would probably imply some switching from higher to lower contribution products the omission of cross price impacts understates the necessary rise in prices to reach π_β^{RM}, although probably by quite a small amount.

[8] A formal analysis of this subject is contained in De Donder et al (2001).

route to identify, in theory, how much contribution could be recovered through complete differentiation of prices. [9] This would also provide some insights into the extent to which averaging and uniformity of prices leads to higher prices overall given the requirement to achieve financial equilibrium.

3. RESULTS

3.1 Base Case

Results for the base case scenario using the EPM and the methodology outlined in section 2 are summarized in table 1. Volumes, prices and contribution levels are indexed to pre-liberalization scenario values equal to 100 to simplify presentation.[10] For the scenario of full liberalization with access as outlined in the previous section and applying the model and parameter values set out in the appendix, delivered volumes fall by 19% (index at 81). Within this amount, E2E volumes decline further than this from their pre-liberalization scenario base but delivered volumes also include access, either by entrants or CDA, and this reduces the fall in total delivered volume. The decline in contribution is substantially more than the drop in delivered volumes. Partly this is due to access on which the contribution per item is less than for E2E items at the basic weight step, given that this scenario includes the access prices from Postcomm (2003). However, it is due also to the differential entry projected by the EPM across segments of traffic and cream-skimming.

The results reported in table 1 indicate that, for this scenario of bypass and access, if prices were to be increased equally across the board ($\beta_j = \beta$ for all β_j) an average price rise of 50% (index=150) would be required to recover the loss of contribution. Price increases on this scale would cause delivered volumes to halve, partly through switching to entrants but also through price elasticity impacts of higher prices on segments of traffic where entry is unlikely even at these prices. The final row of table 1 also shows that if price increases were to be differentiated $\left(\beta_j = \min\{\beta_j, \beta_j^*\}\right)$ it would be possible to raise prices overall by less than if equal increases were applied. In the scenario evaluated prices would rise on average by 37% rather than 50%. Furthermore, within this average of 37%, the required price increase for every individual product group would be less than the across the board average price rise of 50% using the approach of equal price increases. The reason for this is that products with a higher price elasticity would not have

[9] The complex nature of cross price effects would lead to an exercise of this kind producing results which were only approximate in nature.

[10] That is to the base year (2001/02) values of the model.

their prices raised above their contribution maximizing level for to do so would worsen contribution. Hence the contribution to be raised from other products is less so that price increases on these other products can also be less, a beneficial effect which would be likely to increase with the degree of price differentiation. Delivered volumes, although significantly lower than at unchanged prices, would be higher than in the case where prices rise equally across all products.

Table 1: Liberalization Scenario of Bypass and Access: Base Case

	Index Numbers, Pre-liberalization Case = 100		
	Price[1]	Delivered Volume[2]	Contribution
Pre-liberalization scenario	100	100	100
Following liberalization scenario:			
- at unchanged prices	100	81	68
- recovery of contribution by equal price increases	150	50	100
- recovery of contribution by differentiated price increases	137	61	100

[1.] The index numbers for prices are calculated as 100.(1+β) where post-entry values of β are found using the algorithm described in the paper.
[2.] Delivered volume is the sum of end-to-end items and downstream access. Access prices used are as set out in Postcomm (2003).

The results reported in table 1 do not support the proposition that a graveyard spiral will arise in the base case for the liberalization scenario under review. However, the prospects for entry are inherently uncertain and some of the variables and parameters in the model may change over time. This raises the issue of how sensitive the results in the base case are to the parameter values and under what circumstances a graveyard spiral might arise.

3.2 Sensitivities on switching function

There are a number of elements in the model where sensitivities show a significant range of possible outcomes and we focus, first, on the calibration of the switching functions. For products that are commodities and have low switching costs, a relatively small change in price results in entire volumes switching from one supplier to another so that switching functions are much more like a step function in form. For differentiated products where switching costs are likely to be incurred, such as mail services, an S-shaped formulation is more appropriate but the question remains of how steep or flat the switching functions are in practice. The steeper the switching functions are, the greater the underlying propensity of customers to switch supplier and hence the more likely a graveyard spiral. However, while market research and contingent valuation techniques can provide useful information on this key sensitivity, there is uncertainty about the precise shape of these functions and whether they will change in the future and these will only be confirmed as the impact of liberalization unfolds into the future.

For the purpose of formulating sensitivity testing of the parameters of the switching functions in the EPM, unfortunately it is quite difficult to provide a simple, intuitive summary indicator which reflects fully changes in the shape of the switching functions collectively for all products. However, we have focused on testing the effect of varying the mean of the distribution, at the same time adjusting its standard deviation such that the functions continue to imply approximately the same market share for entrants at an equal price/quality offering as in the base case. In figure 1, this is equivalent to steepening the curve but holding the point where the function cuts the vertical axis constant. A summary of our results is reported in table 2. The first column of the table is a summary indicator of the propensity of customers to switch which is a (volume) weighted average across all products of the price discount relative to RM prices that entrants would require to offer to be able to take 50% of the total market.[11] This does not mean that entrants will take 50% of the market as their prices will almost certainly be higher than this value compared with RM prices. Rather, if customers were to be more responsive to price than in the base case then the percentage discount that would be necessary to gain 50% of the market would be smaller than if they were less responsive to price differences. In the base case, this percentage discount is 37%. Successive rows of table 2 record lower values of the average discount and hence that customers would have a higher propensity to switch than in the base case. In the final row, an average discount of only 21% in entrants' prices relative to RM's prices would be required for 50% of the market to be taken by entrants.

The second and third columns of table 2 report results for the case where prices of all products are raised equally in order to try to recover the loss of contribution due to entry. At higher propensities to switch, summarized through the indicator of a lower discount to RM prices for customers to switch to entrants' services, the average price increases required to recover the loss of contribution rise quite sharply. When this indicator is 32%, the average price rise required would be 120% (index = 220). If customers have a higher propensity to switch than this case, price increases alone would not

[11] This is perhaps the simplest way to interpret the mean of the distribution underpinning the switching function. However, quality enters the value ratio as well as price so that the full interpretation is more complex (see appendix). Note also that this indicator is closely related to price elasticities which would be more intuitive but are complex to extract and summarize across products and segments of traffic.

recover the loss of contribution which given the assumptions in the paper then implies the existence of a graveyard spiral. In the case with the highest switching propensity (indicator at 21%) only about two thirds of contribution would be recoverable. Note also that the contribution maximizing price increase becomes lower at higher switching propensities.[12]

The remaining columns of table 2 report results for the differentiated price increase case, reporting also the highest price increase applied to any product. As in the equal price increase case, the price increases required to recover the loss of contribution due to entry are higher at higher switching propensities.

Table 2: Liberalization Scenario of Bypass and Access: Sensitivity Testing on Parameterization of Switching Function

Summary Indicator of Switching Propensity [1]	Index Numbers, Preliberalization Case = 100				
	Equal Price Increase		Differentiated Price Increase		
	Price [2]	Contribution [3]	Price	Highest Price	Contribution
37	150	100	137	145	100
35	164	100	144	155	100
33	185	100	147	165	100
32	220	100	150	175	100
31	230	98	152	188	100
29	230	92	158	245	100
27	215	85	157	290	93
25	210	79	149	225	85
21	180	68	140	205	73

1. Simplified summary interpretation of mean and variance across switching functions for all products given by percentage average price discount of entrants' prices relative to RM prices required if entrants were to take 50% of the market. Lower value implies higher switching propensity so increasing the possibility of a graveyard spiral.

2. Price (expressed as an index, pre-liberalization price = 100) required to recover loss of contribution due to entry or contribution-maximizing price where full recovery not possible.

3. Contribution at less than 100 indicates that no increase in prices recovers the loss of contribution due to entry and hence that a graveyard spiral would occur without additional means of funding.

However, there are some important differences. First, the average price increase is significantly below that in the equal price increase case. Products with higher than average (absolute) price elasticities have below average contribution maximizing price increases which may indeed imply reductions in prices are necessary to maximize contribution on that product. These products have their prices held at that level so only other products would have increases to their prices. Secondly, the highest price increase on an individual product is still less than the average across all products in the

[12] This is an implication of the demand functions being linear in form (see appendix).

equal price increase case where the loss in contribution can be recovered in full. [13] In this sense, differentiated prices clearly dominate equal price increases because every customer faces a lower price in the price differentiation case. Volume levels, although not reported, are significantly higher as well. Thirdly, the likelihood of a graveyard spiral is reduced and price changes can recover the loss of contribution at a higher underlying propensity to switch. However, if the propensity to switch is high enough differentiated price increases would be unable to recover the loss of contribution in full and a graveyard spiral would occur if there were no alternative or additional means of funding this loss. This is an important result common to both equal and differentiated price increases: a graveyard spiral is possible if customers have a high enough propensity to switch supplier.

3.3 Sensitivities on Entrants' Costs

There are a number of other parameter values which have the potential to impact significantly on the results reported above including non-price factors such as service specification and quality of service. However, we limit sensitivity testing to a second specific area which is a key element of entrants' value, namely entrants' costs and hence prices. Table 3 reports results for the same cases on switching propensities as table 2 but where entrants' costs are 10% lower.[14] The pattern of results is similar to those reported in table 2 but lower entrant costs increase the likelihood of a graveyard spiral. In the equal price increase case the summary indicator of switching propensity (the average discount on RM prices for entrants to gain a market share of 50%) would only need to be above 33%, rather than 31% in table 2, for contribution to be recovered in full. Furthermore, substantially higher price increases would be required so that at the base switching propensity indicator of 37% prices would have to be increased by 77% rather than 50%. At all other values of the switching propensities, the contribution maximizing prices also would be above those reported in table 2, in some cases substantially so. However, despite higher prices less contribution would be recovered at each value of the indicator of switching propensity.

---

[13] The highest increases are on public tariff (single piece) products. Except at the lowest switching propensities other prices would be at their contribution maximizing level so that the column reporting the highest price also represents the path of single piece prices as switching propensities rise.

[14] In terms of figure 1, this is equivalent to entrants having a higher value ratio for a given shape of switching function. The additional gain in entrants' share implied by this varies by product.

A similar pattern of conclusions can be drawn from the case of differentiated price increases where entrants' costs are lower by 10% compared with those reported in table 2. The likelihood of a graveyard spiral would be greater where entrants' costs are lower as this would occur at a lower switching propensity (the value of switching indicator would only be required to be above 31% rather than 27%). Price increases would be significantly higher than in the base case and the maximum amount of contribution that could be recovered would be lower if a graveyard spiral were to develop putting additional demands on alternative forms of recovery. Therefore a relatively small change to a key variable in the model, entrants' costs, produces a significant impact on both the extent of price increases that would be implied if prices alone were used to try to recover the loss of contribution due to competitive entry and the prospects for a graveyard spiral. Relatively modest changes to other key parameters and variables such as non-price factors including service specification and quality would also have a significant impact on the possibility of a graveyard spiral developing.

Table 3: Liberalization Scenario of Bypass and Access: Sensitivity Testing on Parameterization of Switching Function and Entrants' Costs 10% less than in Base Case

	Index Numbers, Pre-liberalization Case = 100				
Summary Indicator of Switching Propensity[1]	Equal Price Increase		Differentiated Price Increase		
	Price[2]	Contribution[3]	Price	Highest Price	Contribution
37	177	100	152	167	100
35	200	100	160	182	100
33	300	97	162	215	100
32	240	93	166	270	100
31	240	90	171	360	99
29	237	84	166	315	92
27	230	77	144	290	82
25	210	71	140	275	75
21	190	60	132	240	63

1. Simplified summary interpretation of mean and variance across switching functions for all products given by percentage average price discount of entrants' prices relative to RM prices required if entrants were to take 50% of the market. Lower value implies higher switching propensity so increasing the possibility of a graveyard spiral.
2. Price (expressed as an index, pre-liberalization price = 100) required to recover loss of contribution due to entry or contribution-maximizing price where full recovery not possible.
3. Contribution at less than 100 indicates that no increase in prices recovers the loss of contribution due to entry and hence that a graveyard spiral would occur without additional means of funding.

4. CONCLUSIONS

In this paper we have examined the prospects for a graveyard spiral in the UK within a fully liberalized postal market. This includes downstream access being available to both entrants and customers as well as the possibility of full end to end competition.[15] We find that a graveyard spiral does not materialize in the base case if prices alone are used to recover the loss of contribution due to competitive entry, although the price increases required would be large (see table 1). The primary duty of the UK postal regulator is to ensure the continuing provision of a universal postal service, so it is assumed that price controls could be relaxed in order to allow sufficient contribution to be retained. Other, non-price measures such as improving efficiency and changing the specification of the universal postal service might also be used to recover some, or all, of the loss of contribution due to competitor entry. However, we have also used our model to consider other plausible sets of assumptions regarding the propensity of customers to switch to entrant services and the implications of lower entrants' costs and prices than in our base case. Where the propensity to switch is higher, we find outcomes where price increases alone would be insufficient to recover the loss of contribution due to entry and in some cases by a significant margin despite large price increases. This result is reinforced in the sensitivity where entrants' costs and prices are lower (see tables 2 and 3). The changes to the base case assumptions required to yield such outcomes are not large and well within the range of what is possible. Further while we have used a single year application of the model, there are changes over time which are likely to increase the possibility of this outcome. The mix of traffic is likely to change towards presort products where entry is likely to be above average and there is a risk that letter volumes, especially single piece items, will decline. It may also be the case that the propensity to switch will rise as entrants' products become better known and come to offset, at least partially, the very high level of preference towards Royal Mail products assumed in the base case parameters. Our overall conclusion, then, is tempered by these results to one which states that a graveyard spiral is perhaps not the most likely outcome in the near term but one that remains a distinct and realistic possibility over the longer term.

In all our results we find that significant price increases result whether or not the outcome is a graveyard spiral if price alone is used to recover contribution. One conclusion that emerges regarding prices, in all cases, is

---

[15] The scenario is applied to a single year (base year data of FY 2001/02) as if all impacts of liberalization come through without delay and uses access prices set out in Postcomm (2003). As noted previously, a different set of prices would produce results that would change quantitatively although possibility less so qualitatively.

that the average price increase to recover or at least minimize the loss of contribution due to competitive entry can be reduced by differentiating the extent of price increases across products. For products where own price elasticities (in absolute terms) and the propensity to switch are higher, restricting prices to the contribution maximizing level is preferable not only for those products but also for others as it lowers the total amount of contribution that needs to be raised from other products. Indeed, as a consequence, raising prices differentially across products leads to price increases which are lower for all customers as well as reducing the likelihood of a graveyard spiral (see tables 2 and 3).[16]

There remains, necessarily, a high level of uncertainty surrounding key parameter values, for example regarding the propensity of customers to switch to entrants' services, and how they may change over time. Although market research and contingent valuation techniques can provide some guidance on this and should be undertaken on a regular basis, ultimately it is what customers do rather than what they say they will do which matters. Given this level of uncertainty and other changes over time, such as the mix of traffic and whether the total size of the mail market will decline, there is a continuing requirement to manage risks to the financial equilibrium of universal service providers in a liberalized environment. The facility to raise and where appropriate lower prices is an important component of this but may not be sufficient on its own.

APPENDIX: ENTRY PRICING MODEL AND ALGORITHM FOR PRICE CHANGES

The results reported in the paper were derived using the 2003 version of Royal Mail's entry pricing model, EPM (2003). An outline of an earlier version of the model was presented in Robinson and Rodriguez (2000). The model has since been developed in a number of ways including changes to modeling of entrant prices and the incorporation of downstream access (DA). This appendix briefly summarizes EPM (2003) with a high level overview of the various choices modeled in EPM (2003) shown in figure 2.

A.1 Segmentation of Volumes and Overall Approach

The starting point for describing the EPM is to view the postal network as a large number of segments of traffic or "routes". These segments are not defined geographically but by six characteristics: product, size, distance

[16] A formal analysis of these issues is contained in De Donder et al (2001, 2002a).

traveled, delivery area, delivery type and weight. An example of a segment of traffic defined in this way is first class stamped letters under 60g, posted and delivered within the same postcode area and delivered to a business address in an urban area. The volume, long run marginal cost (LRMC) and average price are estimated for each of these segments of Royal Mail traffic for a base year. The only costs assigned to routes are on an LRMC basis and costs which do not vary with volume are not allocated arbitrarily to this level.

Figure 2: EPM (2003): Choices Modeled in Evaluating Liberalization Scenarios

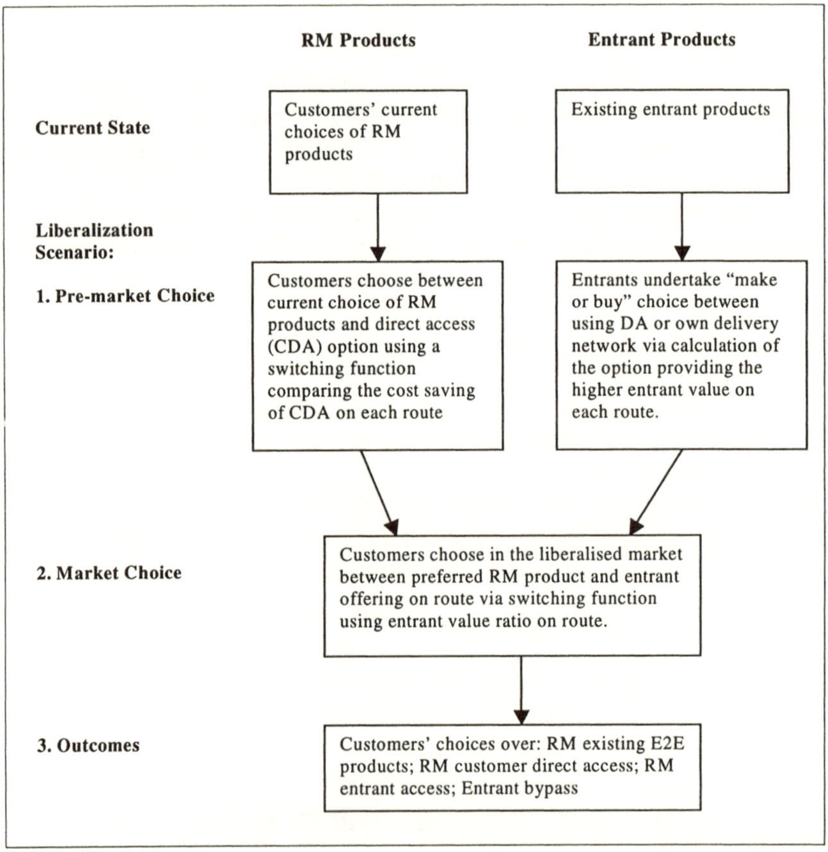

Given the existence of a uniform and weight-based pricing structure, the average price for a segment of traffic is determined by product and weight but costs vary by each of the other characteristics in defining segments outlined above. Consequently, contribution (defined as average price minus LRMC) for individual segments of traffic varies significantly being high in easy to service segments of the market (e.g. delivery to businesses in urban areas) and low or negative where LRMCs are high (e.g. delivery to households in rural areas).

A "liberalization scenario" is required to specify the nature and timing of the extent of the opening of the market. An example of a liberalization scenario is the EU Directive's reduction in the reserved area to a weight limit of 50g in January 2006 which will open all traffic between 50g and 100g to competition (Official Journal, L176/21, 2002). As shown in figure 2, there is a two-stage procedure in evaluating a particular liberalization scenario. First, there is a "pre-market choice" stage. With regard to Royal Mail products, customers can choose between existing products and directly accessing Royal Mail's delivery network (customer direct access (CDA)). Entrants also undertake a pre-market choice which is the "make or buy" decision between the use of DA and setting up their own delivery networks. The outcomes of these pre-market choices determine which products and prices form the potential basis for the market and to determine how much traffic switches to entrants and how much is retained by Royal Mail[17].

At the second stage (the "market choice") entrants' products are now available to Royal Mail customers who, to a greater or lesser extent, may decide to move to competitors. The factors which affect this movement will be both price and non-price for it is the overall price/quality offering that matters to a mailer's decision as to whether or not to switch to an entrant's service. This market process is modeled through the use of a switching function approach which has been used in the telecoms sector and elsewhere. The impact of entry is modeled on the assumption that there is no response by Royal Mail (for example, in terms of the prices it sets) in the face of entrants coming into the market. This allows a clear line to be drawn between the effect of further liberalization, which is modeled by the EPM, and the effect of a response to entry (subject to competition and regulatory constraints) which needs to be considered separately. The analysis in the current paper makes use of the EPM for this purpose as well by taking the outputs from a base case run of the model and then evaluating the use of price to offset the loss of contribution arising from entry.

---

[17] In practice, the alternatives of CDA and using an entrant's service, either with or without DA, are available simultaneously subject to phasing. However, it is useful to make the distinction between pre-market and market choices in understanding the logic of the model.

A.2 Entrant's Value Ratio and Extent of Switching

The "value ratio" of entrants is fundamental to both the "make or buy" choice of entrants regarding delivery and the market choice. Consider initially a situation where only price impacts on a mailer's decision of which postal operator to choose[18]. Then switching to an entrant occurs if its price, p_i^E, is sufficiently below Royal Mail's, p_i^{RM}, or if:

$$\frac{p_i^E}{p_i^{RM}} < b_i^p \qquad (3)$$

where i is the segment of traffic or route ($i = 1, \ldots. N$ where N is the total number of segments of traffic) and b_i^p is the price ratio below which switching starts on that segment. No switching would occur if the entrant's price were above this ratio and the lower this ratio the more switching would be likely to occur.

However, because the mailer's choice will be affected also by non-price factors, two relativities between Royal Mail services and those of entrants matter – price as set out in expression (3) and "quality" or non-price factors widely defined. These ratios are weighted together by the relative importance mailers appear to place on these factors. Rather than switching being identified purely in terms of a price ratio, this extended case does so in terms of a weighted average of two ratios or a value ratio, V. Then switching from a particular segment of traffic occurs if:

$$V_i = \delta_i . \left(\frac{p_i^E}{p_i^{RM}} \right) + (1 - \delta_i) . \left(\frac{v_i^{RM}}{v_i^E} \right) < b_i^v \qquad (4)$$

where V_i is the value ratio of Royal Mail for a particular segment of traffic; δ_i is the weight (as a proportion of 1) that the mailer gives to price; $(1 - \delta_i)$ is the weight the mailer gives to quality or non-price factors; $\left(\frac{v_i^{RM}}{v_i^E} \right)$ is the ratio of Royal Mail's quality level to that of entrants (=1 where the two quality levels are equal) and b_i^v is the value ratio below which switching starts If the entrant's price and/or Royal Mail's quality is sufficiently low, mailers will switch and clearly the lower this overall ratio (the lower the

[18] This treatment follows that set out in Robinson and Rodriguez (2000)

value offered by Royal Mail) the greater the extent of switching. Here, b_i^p, a price ratio, is replaced by b_i^v, a value ratio.

Expression (3) can be rewritten as:

$$\frac{p_i^{RM} - p_i^E}{p_i^{RM}} > 1 - b_i^p \tag{5}$$

or that where the price of entrants is lower (and so the price difference with Royal Mail larger) then the greater will be the switch of traffic to entrants from that segment of traffic. Extending this formulation to include non-price factors and applying the manipulation applied to (3) in the same way to (4) leads to switching occurring if:

$$I_i = \frac{p_i^{RM}\left(1-(1-\delta_i)\left(\frac{v_i^{RM}}{v_i^E}\right)\right) - \delta_i . p_i^E}{p_i^{RM}} > 1 - b_i^v \tag{6}$$

where $I_i = (1 - V_i)$ and can be thought of as the entrant's value ratio for that segment of traffic. If only price matters $(\delta_i = 1)$, then (6) reduces to (5). But more generally non-price factors are important to mailers (so that $0 < \delta_i < 1$) and I_i is used in the model. The poorer the value offered by Royal Mail (the lower the value of V_i), the higher the value of I_i, then the better the offering of the entrant because of price and/or non-price factors and, hence, the greater the expected switch of traffic[19].

As noted previously, entrants undertake a "make or buy" choice with regard to whether the product they offer involves delivery via their own network (bypass) or through DA. This choice is made by selecting that option which has the higher value ratio on a route or:

$$I_i = max\{I_{DA,i}, I_{bi}\} \tag{7}$$

where $I_{DA,i}$ is the entrant's value ratio associated with the service being offered through DA and I_{bi} is the entrant's value ratio for a service offered

---

[19] More formal models can allow the quality of an entrant's service to increase as the number of routes it serves increases although in an operational model such as the EPM it is complex to incorporate such an extension explicitly (Cremer et al, 2001).

through bypass. Non-price factors may also differ between these alternatives but it is likely to be price and cost differences which dominate an entrant's choice of whether service is offered through DA or bypass.

The market structure underpinning the pricing approach of entrants is one of monopolistic competition (De Donder et al, 2002b). Under this entrants have an explicit fixed cost to recover which they achieve by setting their price at marginal cost plus a mark-up. Entrants disregard the pricing of other operators in setting their own price (either because they are relatively small scale or behave myopically) and entry occurs up to the point where entrants break-even, after recovering their fixed cost.[20] The overall marginal cost of an entrant for a given segment of traffic can be separated into two components: all elements other than delivery, c_{ni}^{E}, and delivery, c_{di}^{E}. The entrant's offer price for service through bypass on a given route, p_{bi}^{E}, which is used to calculate I_{bi} in (7) then can be formulated as:

$$p_{bi}^{E}=c_{ni}^{E}\left(1+\pi_{i}^{E}\right)+c_{di}^{E}\left(1+\pi_{di}^{E}\right) \qquad (8)$$

where π_{i}^{E} is a set of uplift factors or mark-ups to cover fixed costs (including a return on capital) on cost components other than delivery and π_{di}^{E} is the overall uplift factor to recover fixed costs in delivery. For certain segments of traffic e.g. deep rural areas, π_{di}^{E} might be very, very large[21]. The corresponding price potentially charged by an entrant using DA, p_{ai}^{E}, which is used to calculate $I_{DA,i}$ in (7) can be formulated as:

$$p_{ai}^{E}=c_{ni}^{E}\left(1+\pi^{E}\right)+a_{i} \qquad (9)$$

---

[20] In a full theoretical formulation, the solution of such a model would be driven by the demand side and, in particular, by the price elasticity of demand. From this, the number of entrants that can be sustained by that part of the market can be calculated from the overall contribution raised and the fixed costs for each entrant such that, after entry, each entrant is just able to break-even and recover its fixed cost as well as a return at a normal rate of profit (De Donder et al, 2002b).

[21] Under monopolistic competition and free entry the overall sum recovered through the mark-ups or uplift factors π^{E} and π_{di}^{E} jointly is just sufficient to recover an entrant's fixed cost (including a return on capital) but no more than this for a higher mark-up would encourage further entry so driving down price to the sum of marginal and fixed cost. The overall amount of fixed cost to be recovered is identified by assuming a proportionality between marginal cost and fixed costs with a different factor or mark-up for different components of cost; in particular, that there is more fixed cost to an entrant in putting in place a delivery network than there is for other elements of cost such as the sorting of letters.

where a_i is the access price to Royal Mail's delivery network for that segment of traffic.

The relationship between the value ratio of entrants on a route, I_i, and the share of traffic that they gain, s_i, is defined by a switching function which is cumulative Normal in form[22]. An example is shown in figure 1. At higher values of I_i entrants gain a greater share of traffic but the rate at which they do so depends also on the value ratio itself. The curve is steeper in its central region but flatter to the extremes. Very few mailers may wish to switch unless the additional value offered by entrants is significantly higher than Royal Mail but once a certain differential in value opens up traffic may move to entrants in greater quantities. However, even at very high values of I_i some mailers would be reluctant to switch so that the curve again flattens[23]. Note that following entry there are two prices on a route, p_i^{RM} and p_i^E, and in general, $p_i^E < p_i^{RM}$. Consequently, the new average price for a segment after entry is lower than previously and so volumes higher. In particular:

$$p_i^L = s_i \cdot p_i^E + (1 - s_i) \cdot p_i^{RM} \tag{10}$$

where p_i^L is the overall average price on segment i after entry and hence:

$$q_i^L = q_i^M \cdot \left[1 + \left(\frac{p_i^L - p_i^{RM}}{p_i^{RM}} \right) \cdot \eta_i \right] \tag{11}$$

where q_i^M is the level of traffic (Royal Mail's) on route i prior to entry and η_i is price elasticity of demand for traffic on that segment so that q_i^{RM} is $(1 - s_i)$ of (11). Total traffic retained by Royal Mail is its original traffic level factored by the growth of traffic on the route due to the new average price and scaled down by the proportion it retains of this new market volume.[24]

---

[22] The context for switching functions of this form is outlined in Crew and Kleindorfer (1992)

[23] A switching function approach is also used for the pre-market choice of the extent of CDA chosen by customers. For this choice, the percentage of traffic switching to CDA depends on the extent of the cost saving from direct access compared with the service currently taken up by customers.

[24] The demand function at (11) is linear in form, the slope being determined by the opening (p, q) pair and η_i at that point, so that the price elasticity varies with price.

A.3 Impact on Royal Mail's Contribution of a Given Liberalization Scenario

The impact on Royal Mail's contribution of a given liberalization scenario can be calculated from the output of the evaluation of market choices and the extent to which Royal Mail volumes switch to entrants. Prior to the liberalization scenario, Royal Mail's overall contribution from its postal network, π^M, is given by:

$$\pi^M = \sum_i^N q_i^M . \left(p_i^{RM} - c_i\right) \tag{12}$$

where c_i is Royal Mail's LRMC on route i. With liberalization, segments of traffic divide into those where entry occurs by entrants offering their own E2E service ($i \in$ E2E) and those where entry occurs through entrants offering a service by making use of DA ($i \in$ DA). Furthermore, access through CDA can occur on either type of route ($i \in$ CDA).

For each segment of traffic, liberalization results in a new lower value of Royal Mail E2E traffic after entry, q_i^{RM}. The entry pricing calculation assumes no price response in the base case and that LRMCs per item are invariant with volume over the ranges considered in the model. Additionally, on CDA and DA routes Royal Mail is paid an access price and incurs a cost in providing access to customers or entrants respectively. Hence, Royal Mail's overall contribution following liberalization, π^{RM}, is given by:

$$\begin{aligned} \pi^{RM} = & \sum_i^N q_i^{RM} \left(p_i^{RM} - c_i\right) + \sum_{i \in DA} q_i^{DA} \left(a_i - \left(c_{di}^{RM} + c_{ai}^{RM}\right)\right) \\ & + \sum_{i \in CDA} q_i^{CDA} \left(a_i - \left(c_{di}^{RM} + c_{ai}^{RM}\right)\right) \end{aligned} \tag{13}$$

where q_i^{DA} is the level of DA traffic for segment i; q_i^{CDA} is the level of CDA traffic for segment i; and $\left(c_{di}^{RM} + c_{ai}^{RM}\right)$ is Royal Mail's LRMC of providing DA or CDA for segment i expressed as the sum of a delivery and an acceptance charge. The first term in expression (13) is the contribution Royal Mail achieves on its E2E traffic under the liberalization scenario; the second term is the contribution it achieves by selling access on segments where entrants provide service through DA; and the third is the contribution it achieves by selling access on segments where customers make use of CDA. Royal Mail's E2E volumes after competitive entry will be at or below their levels pre-liberalization $\left(q_i^{RM} \leq q_i^M\right)$ and consequently overall contribution from Royal Mail's E2E traffic will be lower. The first term in (13) is therefore less than π^M given by (12) but the introduction of DA leads to new sources of contribution as indicated by the second and third terms in (13).

A.4 Algorithm for Changing Prices to Eliminate Contribution Loss

It is the case, in general, that $\pi^{RM} < \pi^M$. As explained in the main paper an algorithm is applied within the EPM which seeks to recover this loss of contribution by either an across the board increase in prices or by one differentiated by product. Expression (1) is a simplified version of:

$$\pi_{\beta}^{RM} = \sum_{i}^{N} q_{i,\beta}^{RM}\left(p_i^{RM}(1+\beta_i)-c_i\right)$$
$$+\sum_{i\in DA,\beta} q_{i,\beta}^{DA}\left(a_i(1+\beta_i)-\left(c_{di}^{RM}+c_{ai}^{RM}\right)\right) \qquad (14)$$
$$+\sum_{i\in CDA,\beta} q_{i,\beta}^{CDA}\left(a_i(1+\beta_i)-\left(c_{di}^{RM}+c_{ai}^{RM}\right)\right)$$

which subsumes the J groups of products in (1) within the N segments of traffic, disaggregating these also by E2E, DA and CDA. In (14), β_i is a factor indicating the proportionate increase in price on the ith segment of traffic and the subscript β applied to q_i^{RM}, q_i^{DA} and q_i^{CDA} represents the values of these variables when all prices are factored up by the proportion β_i.

Note that as prices are increased there are significant effects on relative prices as well as the level of prices and hence on each of these variables relating to volumes in (14). In terms of figure 2, an increase in Royal Mail prices encourages customers to switch to CDA compared with Royal Mail's E2E products because this widens the absolute price difference between these alternatives for customers (for pre-market choice, $\frac{\partial q^{CDA}}{\partial p^{RM}} > 0$).[25] Secondly, an increase in Royal Mail access prices encourages entrants to favor offering service through bypass, whose offer price is unaffected, and lowers the demand for DA whose price has increased, $\left(\frac{\partial q^{DA}}{\partial a_i} < 0\right)$. Finally, in terms of the market choice, an increase in Royal Mail prices worsens its E2E prices relative to those of entrants and lowers its traffic relative to the base. This is a second, direct factor leading to a fall in Royal Mail E2E volumes in addition to the encouragement of CDA, $\left(\frac{\partial q^{RM}}{\partial p^{RM}} < 0\right)$.

All these effects and their consequential impact on contribution are modeled in the EPM as part of the algorithm to search for β_i to satisfy the condition $\pi_{\beta}^{RM} = \pi^{M}$. The pre-market choices of customers and entrants directly follow from the revised prices. However, the market choice is more complex to track. In terms of the switching functions illustrated by figure 1, higher Royal Mail prices improve the entrants' value ratio, I_i, defined in (6) leading to a greater share of that segment of traffic being attracted to entrants, s_i. As Royal Mail's prices rise the non-linearity of the switching function implies and contributes to variations in own price elasticities for Royal Mail's products which have their greatest absolute value close to the steepest part of the switching function. As shares, s_i, change so too does the average price for that segment of traffic, p_i^L, which may rise or fall, from (10); this determines the overall demand, q_i^L, through the size of the price change and the price elasticity for traffic on that segment from (11); and hence, finally, Royal Mail's lower traffic volume, q_i^{RM}, as $(1 - s_i)$ of (11).

A.5 Routes, Calibration and Sensitivities

Entry is modeled in EPM (2003) at the level of the "entrant route". These are defined as segments of traffic from combinations of products (29); size (2, letter, packet); distance (2, local, non-local); delivery area (3, city, suburban, rural); mail recipient (2, business, household); and weight steps (4) yielding a total of some 2,570 non-empty segments of traffic in the

---

[25] If access prices were set on a strict avoided cost basis then the retail price alone could be increased and this would maintain the absolute price difference between access and E2E products.

2001/02 base year of the model. The large number of segments reflect, in part, Postcomm's approach to the opening of the UK postal market (Postcomm, 2002) which requires modeling of phased liberalization. The model has been calibrated using information from various sources including the EU liberalization studies (MMD, 1999); internal market research and cost information; operational assessments; and demand studies (Nankervis et al, 2002). Some of the calibration values are as set out previously in Robinson and Rodriguez (2000) but others have been updated to take account of new information. The values used in the base case of the current paper are set out below.

Beginning with the entrants' value ratio, (6), δ_i is 0.4 for all First Class public tariff segments of mail, 0.5 for Second Class and 0.7 for all other (mainly presort) mail. The quality ratio $\left(\frac{v_i^{RM}}{v_i^E}\right)$ is set at 1 as the default and for the base case in the current paper.[26] The entrant offer price for a bypass service, p_{bi}^E, starts from the cost elements summing to Royal Mail's LRMC, c_i, and then applies mark-ups $\pi_{nd,i}^E$ and π_{di}^E to these cost elements reflecting fixed costs entrants could be expected to incur in offering service. For the base case these mark-ups are as follows: stamped mail: business mail –0.4, consumer 1; sorting and access cost: presort mail 0.4, other 0.15; distribution cost: local 0, non-local 0.5; local distribution 0.5; delivery: packet 4, flat 2; delivery to business: city –0.3, suburban 0, rural 3; delivery to household: city 0.4, suburban 0.8, rural 5; seven-day presort mail to households: city and suburban 0, rural 5. For delivery cost elements mark-ups are additive so that, for example, packets delivered to rural business would have a factor of (4+3) = 7 over and above delivery LRMC or equal to eight times RM's LRMC for delivery of such an item. These parameters imply that, while not impossible, entry will be very costly and hence extremely limited in rural areas and in mail originating from consumers and abroad; and quite restricted for other segments such as flats and packets relative to the margins gained by Royal Mail. For each segment of traffic, the model also calculates $p_{DA,i}^E$, entrants' offer price using downstream access, by replacing entrants' delivery cost as derived above by the access price for that segment of traffic, a_i. The access prices are those reported in Postcomm (2003) and equation (7) identifies which type of service entrants offer by segment of traffic.

---

26 The quality ratio is set to 1 for end-to-end competition and to 0.75, 1.1, 1.3 for downstream access to first, second and third class services respectively. The access ratios vary because a single access offering is assumed and this can be used for any service. This would typically provide a worse than first class service but a better than second (or third) class service.

Parameterization of the switching function defines the mean and variance of the cumulative Normal distribution. More intuitively, the two parameters are set by assumptions on the percentage of traffic switching to entrants at an equal price/quality offering and the value of I_i at which switching is at its most rapid rate. For the former, 15% of all direct mail segments are assumed to switch to entrants at an equal price quality offering (so that 85% would remain with Royal Mail), 10% of other bulk mail and 3% of all other (mainly public tariff) mail (so that 97% of such mail would remain with Royal Mail at an equal price/quality offering). The values of I_i at which switching is at its most rapid are assumed to be 0.15 (direct mail), 0.18 (all other bulk mail) and 0.26 (all other mainly public tariff mail). These assumptions jointly imply that customers are more likely to switch to service from entrants for presort, direct mail and least likely to do so for public tariff, single piece mail. Price elasticities to calibrate the demand functions for each segment of traffic in (11), η_i, are -0.5 for direct mail, -0.3 for other bulk mail and –0.2 for all other (mainly public tariff) mail.

The results of sensitivities on the switching function and entrants' costs are reported in the main paper. For the switching function the value of the means have been lowered in small steps from 0.15, 0.18 and 0.26 respectively while readjusting the value of the variance of the distribution to maintain (approximately) the values above for the extent of switching at an equal price/quality offering. Given the uncertain nature of some these values, and the prospect that some will change over time particularly with regard to those impacting on the propensity of customers to switch at different price/quality offerings and entrants' prices, it is essential that extensive sensitivity testing is undertaken once a liberalization scenario is defined for use in the model. It is also possible and important to use various simulation approaches (e.g. Monte Carlo techniques) to identify ranges around central estimates produced by the model.

REFERENCES

Cohen, Robert H., Matthew Robinson, Renee Sheehy, John Waller and Spyros Xenakis. 2004. "An Empirical Analysis of the Graveyard Spiral". In *Competitive Transformation of the Postal and Delivery Sector*, edited by M.A. Crew and P.R. Kleindorfer. Boston, MA: Kluwer Academic Publishers.

Cohen, Robert H, Matthew Robinson, Renee Sheehy, John Waller and Spyros Xenakis. 2005. "Would Entry into a Liberalized Delivery Market Attract Investors." In *Regulatory and Economic Challenges in the Postal and Delivery Sector*, edited by M.A. Crew and P.R. Kleindorfer. Boston, MA: Kluwer Academic Publishers.

Crew, Michael A. and Paul R. Kleindorfer. 1992. *The Economics of Postal Service*. Boston, MA: Kluwer Academic Publishers.

Crew, Michael A. and Paul R. Kleindorfer. 2000. "Liberalization and the Universal Service Obligation in Postal Services". In *The Current Directions in Postal Reform*, edited by M.A. Crew and P.R. Kleindorfer. Boston, MA: Kluwer Academic Publishers.

Crew, Michael A. and Paul R. Kleindorfer. 2004. "Access and the USO for Letters and Parcels". In *Competitive Transformation of the Postal and Delivery Sector*, edited by M.A. Crew and P.R. Kleindorfer. Boston, MA: Kluwer Academic Publishers.

Crew, Michael A. and Paul R. Kleindorfer. 2005. "Competition, Universal Service and the Graveyard Spiral." In *Regulatory and Economic Challenges in the Postal and Delivery Sector*, edited by M.A. Crew and P.R. Kleindorfer. Boston, MA: Kluwer Academic Publishers.

D'Alcantara, Gonzales and Bernard Amerlynck. 2004. "Financial Viability of the Universal Postal Service Provider". In *Competitive Transformation of the Postal and Delivery Sector*, edited by M.A. Crew and P.R. Kleindorfer. Boston, MA: Kluwer Academic Publishers.

De Donder, Philippe, Helmuth Cremer, Andre Grimaud, Jean-Pierre Florens and Frank Rodriguez. 2001. "Uniform Pricing and Postal Market Liberalization". In *Future Directions in Postal Reform*, edited by M.A. Crew and P.R. Kleindorfer. Boston, MA: Kluwer Academic Publishers.

De Donder, Philippe, Helmuth Cremer and Frank Rodriguez. 2002a. "Funding the Universal Service Obligation under Liberalization: An Analysis of the Postal Market". In *Postal and Delivery Services: Pricing, Productivity, Regulation and Strategy*, edited by M.A. Crew and P.R. Kleindorfer. Boston, MA: Kluwer Academic Publishers.

De Donder, Philippe, Helmuth Cremer and Frank Rodriguez. 2002b. "Access Pricing and Parcels Delivery". In *Postal and Delivery Services: Delivery and Competition*, edited by M.A. Crew and P.R. Kleindorfer. Boston, MA: Kluwer Academic Publishers.

De Donder, Philippe, Helmuth Cremer and Frank Rodriguez. 2005. "Access Pricing in the Postal Sector: Results from a Model with Bypass and Customer Direct Access." In *Regulatory and Economic Challenges in the Postal and Delivery Sector*, edited by M.A. Crew and P.R. Kleindorfer. Boston, MA: Kluwer Academic Publishers.

Official Journal of the European Communities, 10/06/02, No L176/ 21, "Directive No 2002/39/EC of the European Parliament and of the Council amending Directive 97/67/EC with regard to the further opening to competition of Community postal services".

Kolin, Marshall and Edward J. Smith. 1999. "Mail Goes Where the Money Is: A Study of Rural Mail Delivery in the United States". In *Emerging Competition in Postal and Delivery Services*, edited by M.A. Crew and P.R. Kleindorfer. Boston, MA: Kluwer Academic Publishers.

MMD. 1999. Studies on the Impact of the Liberalization of the Postal Sector, Lot 5: Modeling and Quantifying Scenarios for Liberalization.

Nankervis, John, Sophie Richard, Soterios Soteri and Frank Rodriguez. 2002. "Disaggregated Letter Traffic Demand in the UK". In *Postal and Delivery Services: Pricing, Productivity, Regulation and Strategy*, edited by M.A. Crew and P.R. Kleindorfer. Boston, MA: Kluwer Academic Publishers.

Postcomm. 2002. Promoting Effective Competition in UK Postal Services

Postcomm. 2003. Notice of a Proposed Direction to Royal Mail on Downstream Access by UK Mail to Royal Mail's Postal Facilities: Reasons.

Robinson, Richard and Frank Rodriguez. 2000. "Liberalization of the Postal Market and the Cost of the Universal Service Obligation: Some Estimates for the UK". In *Current Directions in Postal Reform*, edited by M.A. Crew and P.R. Kleindorfer. Boston, MA: Kluwer Academic Publishers.

Chapter 5

Barriers to Entry in Post and Regulatory Responses*

Richard Moriarty and Paul Smith
Postcomm

1. INTRODUCTION

Models that have previously been proposed to explain *ex-ante* the expected pattern of new entry in liberalized postal markets have tended to focus on how new entrants can take advantage of profit opportunities created by the margin between the incumbent's geographically uniform tariff and actual cost structure (Liddiard et al 1999). Royal Mail put forward such a model when Postcomm began its consideration of how to open the UK postal market to competition. Notably, Royal Mail predicted that by 2004, it would have lost about 8% of its market share. Actual entry in the UK postal market has been very limited. As of January 2004, Postcomm estimated that new entrants had captured about 1/4 of one per cent of the regulated market, defined as items weighing less than 350g or priced at less than £1 (Postcomm 2004a). Combined, these new operators handle[1] fewer letters in one year than Royal Mail would expect to carry in one day.

This paper examines an alternative approach for understanding the likely pattern of entry in a liberalized UK postal market and the implications for regulatory policy. Rather than start from the premise of the incumbent's cost

---

* The views expressed in this paper are the authors and do not necessarily reflect the views of Postcomm.

[1] Some of the items handled by new entrants are 'end to end' covering all of the postal processes from collection to delivery, while other items will only be handled for part of the process, with other activities carried out by the customer, e.g. sortation, or Royal Mail (final delivery).

functions and business models, we take the perspective of a new entrant trying to build a business case for entering the market. Section 2 states how Postcomm, to date, has opened the market to competition and what has happened. Section 3 examines some key strategic considerations for potential entrants when assessing whether to invest in the UK market. Section 4 discusses how the regulatory regime can address the barriers to entry that may impede the development of effective competition. Section 5 states our conclusions.

2. MARKET OPENING IN THE UK

The EC Directive currently permits competition for mail items weighing more than 100g and/ or priced at more than three times the basic postal tariff of the incumbent. In addition, Postcomm's market opening strategy enabled operators to compete directly with Royal Mail from 1 January 2003 ("phase one") in three ways. First, operators could undertake conveyance of bulk mail, from collection through to delivery. Bulk mail is defined as mailings of more than 4000 identical format mail items from one customer (about 30% of the regulated market by revenue). Second, operators could perform upstream consolidation of mail from more than one customer for injection into Royal Mail's network for final delivery ("access"). Third, operators could apply for a license for certain 'defined activities,' such as enhanced document exchange services for closed user groups. These 'defined' activities generally involve handling mail end to end.

Postcomm's market opening strategy envisaged that from 1 April 2005 ("phase two") a further 30% of the market by revenue would be exposed to competition. At the time, Postcomm considered that this might be achieved by lowering the bulk mail volume threshold from 4000 items to around 500 items. The most significant aspect of Postcomm's market opening strategy was that from 1 April 2007 ("phase three"), the market should be fully opened to competition (the "end date"). Postcomm is currently reviewing this strategy and will announce its proposals for further market opening in autumn 2004.

So what has happened in "phase one" of Postcomm's market opening strategy? Almost 18 months on, Postcomm has granted 13 licenses to operators to compete with Royal Mail. These operators provide a range of services including document exchange for closed user groups, tracked business-to-business mail, and most recently, upstream consolidation of mail for final delivery by Royal Mail.

Although the range of entry is quite "broad," it is not "deep" in the sense of significant volumes of mail being handled by new entrants. So far, new entrants combined have captured volumes amounting to 51 million items per year. This pales into insignificance compared to Royal Mail's annual volume of 20 billion items (1/4 of one per cent at the last calculation in January 2004). Although entry has involved a broad range of different services, no entrant has chosen to compete directly with Royal Mail for the delivery of bulk mail to residential customers.

Market shares and the number of competitors are not the only indicators of the effectiveness of competition. A lot also depends on how Royal Mail reacts to competition and the threat of competition, including how it changes its behavior and culture to become more customer-focused and innovative. There is some evidence that over the last 2 years, Royal Mail has begun to grapple with turning its business into a commercial organization. Its 3 year "Renewal Plan" (Consignia 2002), for example, is beginning to deliver changes to its internal processes to improve its efficiency, including through reviewing its transport strategy, further use of sorting technology and eliminating the second daily delivery.

Royal Mail has also begun to turn around its relatively poor financial position (Royal Mail 2004). This financial improvement has so far been driven by strong volume growth and price increases on regulated products rather than significant cost reductions. However, some of the efficiency improvements carried out as part of the renewal plan might feed through into lower costs in the coming year.

It is debatable at this stage whether these positive signs of change are mainly a response to the threat of competition, or a reaction to the dire financial state the company was in 2002. There is a lot of concern among the public and other interested parties that quality of service has declined at the same time as the financial performance has improved. For the year 2003/4 Royal Mail failed to meet all 15 of its regulated quality of service performance targets, including the target that 92.5% of first class letters arrive the next working day (Royal Mail's performance was 90.1% during this period). This decline in service quality has prompted significant public concern about Royal Mail's lack of customer focus. It has also prompted Postcomm to begin an investigation that could lead to fines on the company, if it finds that Royal Mail did not use all reasonable endeavors to meet its targets (Postcomm 2004c).

3. STRATEGIC CONSIDERATIONS FOR POTENTIAL ENTRANTS

Successful entry in post and in other newly liberalized markets can be expected to depend on a number of important conditions. Principally successful entry requires rival operators to discover profit opportunities that compensate for the opportunity cost of entry. In order for new entrants to make profits they need as a minimum to have some form of competitive advantage over the incumbent, which might be found through keener prices or better service quality, e.g. through an innovative product specification.

As noted above, the regulated postal market in the UK covers all postal items weighing up to 350g or costing less than £1. This amounts to about 20 billion items a year.[2] It has been a steadily growing market, with growth rates showing a reasonably clear relationship with the growth rate of the economy and averaging 2 to 3% per annum over the past 10 years. This growth in volumes has been driven largely by increasing second class (D+3) products reflecting a growth in business-to-consumer mail, principally direct marketing and advertising mail. The regulated market has a turnover of about £6 billion. Outside the regulated market is a thriving market for courier and time-sensitive items. It has been estimated that this market has being growing at a faster rate than the basic mails market, experiencing a volume average growth rate of 4% per annum over the past 10 years, with some 4000 operators in this market (Postcomm 2004a).

One of the key questions for the development of the market is the balance between the threats and opportunities posed by alternative media such as electronic communications (email) and the internet. There appears to be a common consensus among postal commentators that electronic media will start to replace certain postal volumes at some stage. In the UK, anecdotal evidence can be found in the business-to-consumer (B2C) market segment through moves from utilities and financial institutions to encourage their customers to receive bills and statements online rather than hard copy by post.[3]

Although incumbent postal operators tend to focus on the threats from e-substitution to their core mail volumes, electronic commerce also offers opportunities. Internet shopping facilities and online market places such as 'EBay' require physical distribution for getting the goods to the customer. This market has two interesting characteristics. First, to the extent that it relates to time sensitive deliveries or to postal packets containing goods, the value to the postal operator will tend to be greater per item than for a basic letter. Second, this market is largely outside of the regulated postal market.

---

2 A small proportion of these items are over 100g and/or 3 times the basic tariff. These products are regulated to ensure the universal service up to 2kg or because Royal Mail retains a strong position in these market segments.

3 For example, Centrica, the UK's largest gas and electricity supplier offers customers a £10 discount on their bill if they agree to receive all statements online rather than through the post.

In summary, although there is volume risk, expectations of a collapsing postal market do not appear to be driving the limited entry we have witnessed[4].

Customer perspectives are also critical. Postcomm recently commissioned the consultant Roland Berger to undertake a market research study of customers' needs from a competitive postal market, their awareness of competition and their switching behavior (Roland Berger 2004). Roland Berger interviewed about 550 business postal customers of varying sizes. This is the first time Postcomm has sought primary data from customers rather than relying on information provided by Royal Mail. In a market with a company that has a very strong monopoly position, this type of survey is perhaps the best available means of establishing the views of customers and monitoring how they might evolve over time, until competition starts to reveal customers' needs and preferences.

This research identified that whereas most large customers ("Top 500" by size of postal spend per annum) concentrate on mailings to households (B2C), the majority of smaller mailers concentrate on mailings to other businesses (B2B). Customers' views about how they might react to competition produced some interesting results.

Customer awareness is low. There is a relatively low awareness amongst all customers, but particularly smaller businesses, about competition, and when and how it is happening. There is a variable level of awareness about new entrants. Strongest awareness is of those companies that already operate in unregulated sectors, e.g. express and parcel operators. Only 11% of businesses had been contacted by another operator. New operators need to raise the awareness amongst customers about their presence in the market. Given the concentration of mailing activity amongst a relatively small number of large business customers (almost 50% of mail is sent by the top 500 businesses); this might not be very costly.

Rival operators need to 'beat' Royal Mail's benchmark in terms of price and quality. Although some large customers are frustrated by what they perceive as Royal Mail's relative inflexibility, there is generally a perception that Royal Mail does a reasonable job.[5] Therefore, in order to be persuaded to switch, customers need assurances on service quality and a reasonably significant price discount. Price is the main factor that they take account of when deciding which postal operator to use, closely followed by reliability and overall service quality. 13% of customers would start negotiating for a 5% lower price and the same service quality. 28% of customers said that

[4] Companies are less likely to want to enter a market characterized by declining volumes because any profit opportunities are likely to be transitory and limited in size.

[5] The survey was conducted before the recent public concern about Royal Mail failing to meet all 15 of its service quality targets for 2003/4.

they would start negotiating with a new entrant that offered the same service quality but 10% lower prices than Royal Mail. These discount expectations could be quite demanding for product lines like basic letter products that may experience low margins and are subject to strong economies of scale for delivery activities. A quarter of businesses expected there to be costs associated with switching operator.

Royal Mail's quality is fairly well perceived but opportunities exist for innovation. Two thirds of customers have a positive perception of the general quality level provided by Royal Mail. Although Royal Mail's actual performance against targets had declined over the period, customers still valued the fact that Royal Mail was striving for targets, which were generally higher than many of its European counterparts. Not surprisingly, given the decline in performance against its targets, reliability of service delivery was the aspect of Royal Mail's service identified as needing the greatest improvement. Specific delivery times were the main value added service that businesses wanted. 45% of items sent to domestic customers were considered 'time critical.' This does not mean that the items required next day delivery, but simply that delivery is required within a certain time period.

Switching intentions are mixed. Only 18% of businesses said that they might consider switching (more) mail to other operators in the near future, although this rose to 31% for the largest businesses ("Top 500"). Direct mail was the main type of mail that businesses expected to give to new entrants.

Network reach is critical. National (universal) delivery coverage was considered an important qualifying factor for rival operators. 43% of customers considered the geographic coverage of the delivery network as the most important attribute that a rival postal operator had to offer.[6] We discuss below some of the implications for competitors of this aspect of customers' requirements given the costs of providing a universal delivery network. Customers did not want to split their mail streams between different operators to undertake delivery in different geographic regions.[7] Customers did not generally appreciate that operators might collect all their mail, delivering where they could and injecting the rest into Royal Mail's network.

A common perception of the postal services industry is that barriers to entry (and exit) are low. Contrasts are often drawn between the economics

---

[6] Other customers might have also considered network coverage an important factor when considering rival operators even if it was not the most important factor.

[7] Customer perceptions on this issue may have been influenced at the time by the background of Royal Mail publicly criticizing Postcomm's approach to third-party access. We note that that in Sweden, competition centers on the ability of customers to split their mail streams into various segments, either by type of mail (e.g. computer generated) or location (e.g. city centers).

of entry in post, where a localized 'network' can rely on little more than a van and some flexible manpower, to the economics of network utilities, where large sunk cost investments are necessary in order to establish a fixed infrastructure of pipes, wires or rails (Panzar 1991 and 2002). Others have argued that profits are easily available to new entrants because of statutorily required cross subsidies in incumbents pricing structures. The most commonly cited example is the incumbent's geographically uniform pricing constraint (Liddiard et al 1999).

This may be oversimplified for the UK market. This is because barriers exist that may prove to be non-transitory and therefore distort the profit seeking opportunities available to new entrants. These barriers might include the incumbent's economies of scale, the application of value added tax (VAT) rules and the incumbent's response to entry. The effect of these barriers could be compounded if the regulator's intentions towards addressing them are insufficiently clear.

Economies of scale are defined as decreasing unit costs as volume rises. In itself, not necessarily a barrier to entry. However, scale is important in determining the unit costs of postal operators and therefore their competitive position. In most countries there is a general acceptance that competition between different providers of electricity wires, gas pipes or water pipes is not in customers' best interests because these activities have the properties of a 'natural monopoly,' i.e. significant economies of scale. However, there has been some debate about the cost structures of the postal sector, and in particular, whether the final mile (local delivery) is characterized by significant economies of scale, such that competition between competing delivery companies is not likely to be economic or in customers' best interests (De Bijl et al 2003, Cohen and Chu 1997).

A decomposition of the postal value chain would suggest that some of the activities could be undertaken profitably by other businesses (e.g. transportation).

This may not, however, be the case for local delivery, particularly to residential and small business customers. Unless the postal operator is handling the maximum amount of items for a delivery route, the marginal cost for each new item to be delivered will be relatively small, particularly if it is to an address that would otherwise have received a delivery. Average costs will decline as volumes increase, up to the point when volumes reach a level that requires an additional postmen or alternative delivery strategy, e.g. an interim point on route where additional mail is stored.[8]

---

[8] This analysis is premised on the basis that delivery costs are driven by four main elements – the volume of mail items to be delivered, the average number of drops per delivery point, the distance between delivery points and labor/ vehicle costs depending on the delivery method. The model uses the underlying cost information supplied by Royal Mail.

We have adapted a model developed by Royal Mail that looks at delivery costs in the UK by dividing the UK into five geographical zones based on delivery characteristics – mainly the density of delivery points. The model shows the market share that a new entrant would have to achieve to face the same unit costs as Royal Mail (indexed to 100 in Figures 1 and 2). The model allows the frequency of delivery by the new entrant to be anything between 1 and 6 days a week, with 6 days a week being equivalent to the universal service obligation in the UK that Royal Mail provides for letters.

Figure 1: The Costs for Postal Delivery in the UK Based on Delivering 1 and 6 Days a Week

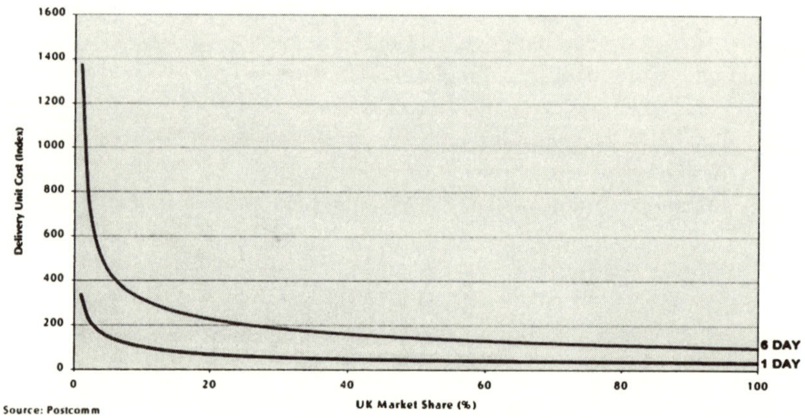

Figure 1 sets out the results from running the model for delivery on a nationwide basis 1 and 6 days a week based on representative labor and vehicle costs. It shows that for delivery both 1 and 6 days a week there are significant economies of scale, with average costs declining as volume increases. The figure also shows that for both 1 and 6 day a week delivery, a new entrant would require a significant market share before becoming competitive with Royal Mail's unit costs. For example, to match Royal Mail's present unit costs for delivery 6 days per week, and depending on the assumptions about new entrants costs compared to Royal Mail, a new entrant might need to capture more than 50% market share.[9] This limits the number of operators that could realistically compete with Royal Mail for a daily

---

[9] In reality, it is likely to be less because if new entrants take volume away from Royal Mail, its unit costs could rise as it starts to lose some of the advantages of economies of scale. However, the static representation in Figure 1 makes the point that significant volume is required to compete profitably head-to-head with Royal Mail.

delivery service across the country.[10]This model is a stylized representation of reality. New entrants might not seek to compete against Royal Mail for nationwide delivery 6 days per week. By reducing the frequency of delivery to 1 day per week, new entrants would probably need a lower market share (depending on the assumptions about new entrants costs compared to Royal Mail) to match Royal Mail's average unit costs of delivery (less than 20%). This supports the view expressed by some other authors that the real cost of the universal service delivery constraint is not the geographic coverage *per se* but the frequency of delivery (Bernard et al 2002). The simple premise underlying this point is that volume drives the average cost of delivery.

Figure 2 compares the costs of delivery 1 day a week based on representative labor and vehicle costs in 'rural' and 'urban' areas.[11]

Figure 2: The Costs for Postal Delivery in the UK Based on Delivering 1 Day a Week

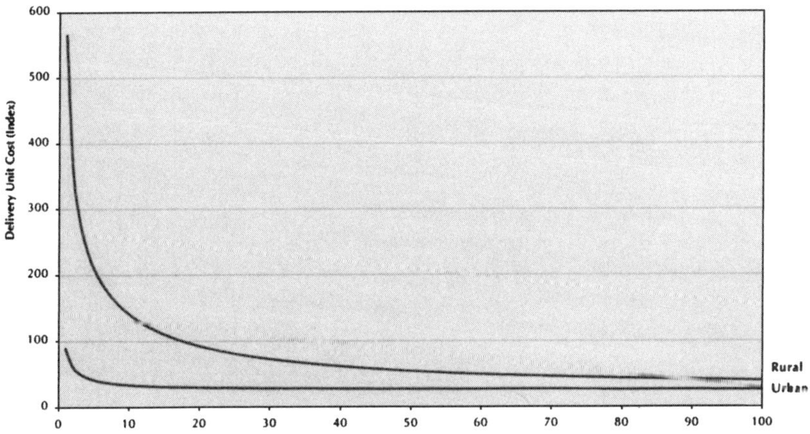

Source: Postcomm

Figure 2 shows that delivery in both rural and urban areas is characterized by economies of scale, but that the average cost curve for urban areas is significantly flatter and lower than the average cost curve for rural areas.[12] This is principally because of the lower volume per drop and

[10] Where an entrant pursues an alternative strategy of selective entry into high density routes only it is going to be much easier to achieve the requisite market shares.

[11] Rural areas are defined as areas of the UK with a delivery density of up to 23 delivery points per square kilometer, while urban areas are defined as areas of the UK with a delivery density of over 1715 delivery points per square kilometer.

[12] Postcomm had previously used information from Royal Mail to estimate the costs and benefits to it of providing the universal postal service ("An assessment of the costs and

the distance between drops. The unsurprising implication is that less market share is required in urban than rural areas to be cost competitive with Royal Mail.

To place these cost structures in some context, the only way for a new entrant to profitably compete against Royal Mail would be to reduce the frequency of delivery to say once per week and then concentrate on high volume drop areas such as financial or business districts.

This analysis suggests that even after full market opening, Royal Mail's incumbent economies of scale for delivery activities, particularly to residential and small business customers are likely to constitute a barrier to significant competitive entry for postal delivery activities in the UK market. The prospects for competitive entry for delivery activities in less densely populated areas appear particularly weak. When combined with business customers' desire for competitors to have universal coverage, it suggests that regulators will need to consider whether forms of access will be necessary for competition to develop in all geographic areas. This is discussed further below.

Under various legal statutes, Royal Mail has various legal rights ('privileges') that are not available to other postal operators. The most significant of these privileges is the exemption from having to charge VAT on its services, as a result of Royal Mail being the UK supplier of public postal services.[13] Postcomm has published an explanation of the nature of Royal Mail's other legal privileges (Postcomm 2004b)

As a result of this exemption, Royal Mail does not charge VAT on services that it provides, while other postal operators are required to charge VAT at 17.5%. When a postal customer sells goods and services that are subject to VAT it can reclaim its input VAT, i.e. the VAT that the suppliers to this postal customer levy on their goods and services. Where a postal customer cannot reclaim this 17.5% input VAT, the VAT charged by non-Royal Mail operators amounts to an additional cost. Postal customers that cannot reclaim all of their input VAT include some very large mailers such as financial institutions (banks and insurance companies) and educational establishments. Additionally, private individuals cannot reclaim VAT.

Postcomm has carried out some analysis to estimate the likely economic effect of Royal Mail's VAT exemption (Postcomm 2004b). As Royal Mail cannot reclaim the VAT it is charged, but other postal operators can, the

---

benefits of Consignia's current Universal Service Provision, A Discussion Document," Postcomm, June 2001"). This approach to assessing the costs and benefits of providing the universal service was based on an 'avoidable cost' approach rather than calculating overall unit costs.

[13] Royal Mail's VAT exemption is set out in the 6th VAT Directive (77/388/EEC) adopted in 1977 and transposed into UK law by the VAT Act 1994.

extent of the cost advantage for Royal Mail is not the full 17.5% VAT rate. Postcomm estimates that Royal Mail's postal prices could be around 3% lower (before VAT) if it was able to recover its input VAT. Another way of interpreting this is that Royal Mail has an approximate 13% to 14% cost advantage over competitors for 50% of the mail it handles due to the fact that it does not charge VAT on its services.

Postcomm estimates that the imposition of a VAT rate of somewhere between 4% and 5% on all postal operators could be absorbed by Royal Mail as it could then recover its input VAT. The net effect would be to leave Royal Mail's prices slightly lower for those customers able to recover input VAT and unchanged for those unable to recover input VAT.

A concern of new entrants in any market is how the incumbent will react to their presence. This is generally not a fear of competition, but a fear of anti-competitive behavior, such as predatory pricing, and to what extent particular behavior will be allowed by regulators and competition authorities. New entrants are particularly concerned that the incumbent will seek to unfairly undermine their entry into the market before they have time to become established and when they are financially at their weakest. Potential entrants therefore need to keep in mind whether they could still compete *after* Royal Mail has made its likely response.

In addition to calculating the incumbent's range of legitimate responses to market entry, potential entrants will also need to consider the assurances and processes provided by the rules prohibiting anti-competitive behavior. Disputes with the incumbent before competition authorities can be protracted and costly. It is too early to tell how Royal Mail is responding to the threat of entry in order to judge the weight of this risk. However, there is evidence from other countries (most notably Sweden) that protracted competition cases that have arisen in the early stages of postal competition.

4. REGULATORY RESPONSES TO THE BARRIERS TO ENTRY

Barriers to entry granting the incumbent monopoly power provide a rationale for economic regulatory intervention in postal markets.[14] Barriers might not be a problem *per se* if they can be expected to be transitory and eroded by the pace of innovation over a reasonable time period and if competition can be expected to deliver real benefits to postal users. The acid

[14] Of course, regulation may also be needed for social requirements and for good governance requirements, such as processes for 'integrity of the mail.'

test is the counter-factual: what would happen if the market were liberalized with no further regulatory action?

In the case of the UK, we would argue that entry is likely to be limited in the foreseeable future without further regulatory action, given the combination of Royal Mail's economies of scale in delivery activities, the VAT rules, and Royal Mail's actual and perceived responses to entry.

Liberalization and the removal of the statutory impediment to competition is a necessary requirement for competition, but it is unlikely to be sufficient to lead to truly effective and vigorous competition.[15] While the threat of competition might go some way toward providing Royal Mail with incentives to improve its processes and become more responsive to customers' needs, if the threat is not seen to be credible through the emergence of actual competition, then the incentives will gradually be reduced.

If fully opening the market is insufficient, what else can a regulatory authority do to facilitate effective competition that furthers postal users' interests?

Clarity on non-economic requirements. To the extent that it has not been done prior to opening the market, the regulatory authority should provide clarity over the nature of any social obligations on the incumbent (e.g. the products that constitute the universal service obligation).

Identification of contestable and non-contestable activities. This requires the regulatory authority to distinguish between those parts of the market that might be expected to be contestable and those parts of the market that might not. This enables regulatory policy to be tailored to the differing circumstances of the market segments to ensure that customers' interests are protected. The boundary between contestable and non-contestable activities might be expected to change over time.

Pro-competitive regulation. In those parts of the market where competition is possible and desirable, the regulator should adopt a 'pro-competitive' stance to identify and address all barriers to entry to 'level the playing field.'

Incentive based regulation. In those parts of the market where competition is unlikely, uneconomic or else not desirable, the regulator should adopt an 'incentive based' stance to counter the effect of the incumbent's market and monopoly power. The target incentives need not be solely to cut costs and reduce inefficiency: they could also include incentives to invest and innovate. These arrangements should also include preventing

[15] Experience in those countries that have fully liberalized (e.g. Sweden and New Zealand) suggests that without more pro-active regulatory action it may take a long time for entry to circumscribe the market power of the incumbent.

anti-competitive cross-subsidies between the *de facto* monopoly and competitive market.

Deregulation. This balance of measures needs to be reviewed over time as it may need to change as the scope of the non-contestable activities reduces. In this case, the regulatory authority can start to de-regulate, with more of the market being regulated by general competition law rather than sector specific regulation. Although clichéd, the success criterion of the economic regulatory authority under this strategy is the point at which deregulation happens to such an extent to remove the rationale for the regulator itself. There might also be a lot of focus on the pace at which the incumbent moves to align its prices with its costs, not just with regard to the geographic uniformity required by the USO, but also for other historical cross-subsidies that might have existed.

The sections below apply this strategy in the current context of the UK.

Strong economies of scale can result in barriers to competition, with the consequence that there is little pressure on the company to improve its efficiency. Strong economies of scale in the incumbent's operations allow it to maintain a cost advantage against potential rivals.

The regulatory response to economies of scale acting as a barrier to entry is not to remove the economies of scale. This might cause unit costs and prices to rise to the detriment to customers and the market. Rather than "throw the baby out with the bathwater," a more reasoned regulatory response to promote effective competition would be to "share" the incumbent's benefits with other operators. This can be achieved by allowing operators to have access to the incumbent's network and facilities.

In the UK, Postcomm and Royal Mail agreed to the inclusion within Royal Mail's regulatory license a condition requiring Royal Mail to negotiate in good faith with access seekers. If the two parties cannot reach a commercial agreement on the price or other terms and conditions for access, then the access seeker can ask Postcomm to determine the dispute. In doing so, Postcomm must ensure that access prices recover a reasonable allocation of costs. At any time Royal Mail can propose an access code setting out prices and other terms and conditions for Postcomm to approve to replace the individual negotiation process.

Access enables operators to compete 'upstream' of the access point for consolidation activities. It also enables those operators wishing to develop end-to-end operations to build up the necessary customer relationships and scale to make such investments worthwhile. Given the evidence discussed above about the market shares likely to be required by new entrants to compete in delivery activities, access arrangements are likely to be particularly important for promoting competition in less densely populated areas and for delivery frequencies similar to that provided for the universal service.

Strategically, in the early days of the market's development, the incumbent might react strongly against the imposition of third-party access arrangements. Incumbents tend to view access as a zero-sum game under such circumstances. However, over time, the incumbent may see at least two benefits from access. First, if the price is set such that it recovers an appropriate share of costs and a profit margin, then the incumbent may see access as a profit centre. Second, the incumbent may see access 'competition' as a defense against losing volumes to end-to-end rivals.

Access might lead to market distortions that will require quite delicate judgments by the regulator in order to mitigate their risks.

Distortions to dynamic efficiency. If the access price is set too high, then it will discourage operators from using the access arrangements. Conversely, an access price that is too low might encourage operators to use access when the alternative might be that these operators would set up delivery networks. In setting the access price the regulator will need to balance these factors and bear in mind that the access price might need to change over time as market conditions evolve.

Distortions to allocative and productive efficiency. Entrants might decide to develop end-to-end networks in areas where their delivery costs are less than the access price. If the access price is based on geographically averaged costs (including an appropriate return to capital providers) then new entrants will only set up delivery networks where they are more cost efficient than the incumbent. However, if the access price is set above cost, for example, from the imposition of a geographically uniform pricing constraint, then this could encourage 'inefficient' entry in the sense that rivals can attack profit opportunities whilst maintaining cost structures that are less cost efficient than the incumbent's cost structure. Conversely, in areas where the access price is set below cost due to the geographic uniform pricing constraint, entrants might be provide with incentive to hand over mail in those areas to the incumbent. One approach for overcoming these risks is for the incumbent to set access prices on a geographically non-uniform basis.[16]

One initial barrier regarding access provision that is now hopefully overcome in the UK is the uncertainty that surrounded the first downstream

---

[16] Under this condition the rise in the access price in high cost areas will be bounded by tariffs that remain in the uniform pricing constraint, for example the public tariffs. It should be noted that a geographical non-uniform access pricing regime might be in tension with the objective of promoting dynamic efficiency and competition because it is likely to result in lower access prices in urban and high volume per drop areas. At the margin, this could deter some entrants from establishing delivery networks in those areas.

access price and terms. This uncertainty worked in two ways – delaying the development of delivery networks to compete with Royal Mail and preventing the development of upstream only competition facilitated by downstream access. UK Mail (a licensed operator in the UK and a wholly owned subsidiary or Business Post plc) made a request to Postcomm in April 2002 to determine the price and terms for access to Royal Mail's downstream network. This request followed a failure to agree terms with Royal Mail. Postcomm began a process to make a determination, and was close to issuing its determination when Royal Mail and UK Mail reached agreement in February 2004 (UK Mail and Royal Mail 2004). Subsequently Royal Mail has reached agreement with TPG (Royal Mail and TPG 2004) and Deutsche Post (Royal Mail and Deutsche Post 2004) for downstream access.

The agreements have been important in setting an initial framework for future access arrangements. However, they relate to the specific circumstances of the bilateral negotiations. They do not cover every access 'product' that operators might want or Royal Mail could offer. In these cases there could still be significant uncertainty while Postcomm considered a determination request. Postcomm recently published guidance about how it would expect to treat future requests for downstream access agreements, which might remove some of this uncertainty (Postcomm 2004c).

As the access agreements have now been reached in the UK, we will be able to see how competition develops with an access price and terms and conditions in place. This can be compared to some of the recent predictions in the literature about the impact of access arrangements (Crew and Kleindorfer 2002, Cremer et al 2004). The arrangements in place at present can be described as a 'negotiated' access model. If this model fails to promote effective upstream competition, then other arrangements may need to be considered, including an access code or ring-fencing and greater separation between the monopoly and contestable businesses.

One of the benefits, however, of a 'negotiated' access model that should not be overlooked is that commercial parties are much better placed to find a commercially viable proposition than the regulator. This is perhaps more relevant to post than in other regulated industries, such as telecoms, gas and electricity, with long histories of access and separation arrangements. This is because post is not a fixed network with a homogenous product. The nature of these 'operational' terms and conditions are complex and there is a risk that the regulator can be dragged into 'micro-managing' the business.

Value Added Tax (VAT) is an area in which Postcomm has no power to make changes because changes to primary parliamentary legislation are required. Indeed, changes to European legislation are required first.

From a postal market perspective, a solution that 'levels the competitive playing field' without imposing significant price increases on customers would seem the optimum solution. A number of potential approaches might suit this objective. For example, a reduced rate of VAT of 5% might be competition 'neutral' to the extent that Royal Mail's present prices already implicitly include an allowance for VAT that it cannot presently reclaim. Another approach might be to exclude from VAT only those services used by the public. This might have certain drawbacks in the sense of distorting price signals between the VAT and non-VAT segments of the market. If VAT was applied on non-public products at its full rate of 17.5%, this could have negative volume effects. However, it is likely that this market segment is most likely to benefit from price competition that could result from a 'level playing field.'

In terms of incumbents' reactions to entry and the threat of entry. Member States have general competition law provisions based on the articles in the European Union Treaty that prohibit anti-competitive behavior within the Single Market. In the UK, the Competition Act 1998 prohibits abuses of a dominant position and anti-competitive agreements.

Ex post enforcement of such requirements can often be a lengthy process requiring the gathering of significant amounts of information and careful consideration of previous precedents, where they are relevant. The relative complexity of competition issues and the limited previous precedent in the UK postal sector will make it more difficult for new entrants to be confident in advance about whether a particular action by the incumbent will or will not breach statutory provisions.

Regulators cannot entirely remove these risks, but *ex ante* guidance about how anti-competitive provisions will be interpreted can give new entrants more confidence about what types of incumbent behavior will raise concerns with the regulator. Such guidance might also give the incumbent more confidence about which of its actions would raise concerns with the regulator. This approach of *ex ante* guidance must complement that already used by the UK competition authority for general competition law[17]. It is also important for a regulator in responding to concerns about anti-competitive behavior by the incumbent to demonstrate that it acts professionally and in a timely manner in response to any complaints from competitors. For Postcomm, this involves enforcing sector specific license conditions and working effectively with the UK competition authority to ensure enforcement of general competition law.[18]

---

17 See Office of Fair Trading website at www.oft.gov.uk.

18 Unlike any economic regulators in the UK, Postcomm does not have concurrent powers with the Office of Fair Trading for the enforcement of general competition law, in particular the Competition Act 1998.

Where competition does not circumscribe the market power of the incumbent, this may risk creating (or sustaining) a situation whereby the incumbent can impose costs on its customers. This could be in the form of higher prices and poorer quality of service than would otherwise be the case. These costs may also manifest in terms of a lack of innovation and inefficiency.

It is therefore important to decide which products should be subject to price caps. Where competition cannot be relied upon to protect customers interests, then price and service regulation are needed. In the UK, the most popular form of incentive based regulation is the 'RPI-X' framework, which links price rises to the general level of price inflation (the Retail Price Index) minus an efficiency factor. Companies have an incentive to 'beat' the X factor in terms of efficiency improvements because they keep the financial gains for the duration of the price control period. In other regulated UK utilities, the drive to outperform the regulator's price control has come from shareholders.

The regulator will need to balance short term and long term customer interests. A particular challenge is to strike a balance between pressures from customer representatives for prices to be reduced to reflect cost savings and pressure from new entrants not to do this in case it depresses the competitive 'headroom.' To inform this judgment, it is important that the regulator identifies the prospects for competition in various market segments to ensure that regulation is appropriately tailored to their specific characteristics.

Another challenge for the regulator will be how it manages the pace at which the incumbent better aligns its pricing structure with its cost structure. Any unwinding of historical cross-subsidies is likely to create winners and losers amongst customer groups and the regulator needs to take account of their interests.

5. CONCLUSIONS

Postcomm has implemented the gradual removal of Royal Mail's statutory monopoly in the UK postal market by licensing other operators to compete in the part of the market opened to competition. Postcomm's original intention was to have a three stage market opening with 30% of the market by revenue opened in April 2003 followed by a further 30% in April 2005, and the remainder opened in April 2007. The gradual market opening rather than opening the market all at once was intended to give Royal Mail more time to prepare for competition.

Given the relative lack of actual and prospective competition as a result of the first stage of market opening and the lack of any significant threat to the continued provision of the universal service, it seems appropriate to consider a broader range of options for phase two than just opening up a further 30% of the market by revenue. It might be preferable to fully open the market ahead of April 2007.

Although such a move might be necessary to ensure some competition, this paper suggests that it is very unlikely to be sufficient to lead to vigorous and ultimately effective competition. Other barriers to entry exist that make it harder than commonly perceived for potential entrants to build practical and profitable business models. These barriers include Royal Mail's strong economies of scale in delivery activities; its VAT treatment and a lack of customer awareness of competition.

The existence of these barriers and the continuing market power of the incumbent, Royal Mail, provide a rationale for sector specific regulation in addition to statutorily opening the market. It is important regulatory strategy identifies the non-economic obligations on the incumbent, distinguishes between the contestable and non-contestable activities and applies 'incentive based' and 'pro-competitive' regulation accordingly. It is also important the regulatory model changes over time, preferably in a way that sees sector specific regulation removed.

REFERENCES

Stephane Bernard, Robert Cohen, Matthew Robinson, Bernard Roy, Joelle Toledano, John Walker and Spyros Xenakis. 2002. "Delivery Cost Heterogeneity and Vulnerability to Entry." In *Postal and Delivery Services: Delivering on Competition*, edited by M.A. Crew and P.R. Kleindorder. Kluwer Academic Publishers.

Robert Cohen and Edward Chu. 1997. "A Measure of Scale Economies for Postal Systems." In *Managing Change in the Postal and Delivery Industries*, edited by M.A. Crew and P.R. Kleindorder. Kluwer Academic Publishers.

Consignia. March 2002. "Consignia announces first moves in three year renewal plan."

Helmuth Cremer, Phillippe De Donder and Frank Rodriguez. 2004. "Access Pricing and the Uniform Tariff in the Postal Sector." In *Competitive Transformation of the Postal and Delivery Sector*, edited by M.A. Crew and P.R. Kleindorder. Kluwer Academic Publishers.

Michael A. Crew and Paul R. Kleindorfer. 2002. "Balancing Access and Universal Service Obligation." In *Postal and Delivery Services: Delivering on Competition*, edited by M.A. Crew and P.R. Kleindorder. Kluwer Academic Publishers.

Paul De Bijl, Eric van Damme and Pierre Larouche. August 2003. "Towards a liberalized postal market." Tilburg Law and Economics Center.

Paul Liddiard, Richard Robinson and Frank Rodriguez. April 1999. "Estimates of the cost of the universal service obligation using the Entry Pricing approach."

John Panzar. 1991. "Is Postal Service a Natural Monopoly?" In *Competition and Innovation in Postal Services*, edited by M.A. Crew and P.R. Kleindorder. Kluwer Academic Publishers.

John Panzar. 2002. "Reconciling Competition, Downstream Access, and Universal Service in Postal Markets." In *Postal and Delivery Services: Delivering on Competition*, edited by M.A. Crew and P.R. Kleindorder. Kluwer Academic Publishers.

Postcomm. January 2004. "The UK Letters Market 2000-2003, A Market Report."

Postcomm. January 2004. "A Review of Royal Mail's Special Privileges, A Consultation Document."

Postcomm. March 2004. "Promoting Effective Competition in UK Postal Services Through Downstream Access, Observations on the Agreement Between Royal Mail and UK Mail Ltd on Access to Royal Mail's Delivery Network."

Postcomm. May 2004. "Postcomm to probe Royal Mail's serious service quality failings."

Roland Berger. April 2004. "Monitoring developments in the postal market – market survey."

Royal Mail. May 2004. "Royal Mail Back in Profit – Unofficial industrial action hits quality of service."

Royal Mail and Deutsche Post. April 2004. "Royal Mail and Deutsche Post access deal."

Royal Mail and TPG. April 2004. "Royal Mail and TPG Post agree access deal."

UK Mail and Royal Mail. February 2004. "UK MAIL/ ROYAL MAIL – Historic agreement signed for access to postal facilities."

Chapter 6

Competition and the Coverage of Price Controls in the Postal Sector*

Paul Dudley,[1] Helen Jenkins,[2] Leonardo Mautino,[2] and Sophie Richard[1]
Royal Mail Group[1] and Oxera[2]

1. INTRODUCTION

In general, the introduction of competition into a market is seen as a means to maximize economic efficiency and welfare. Competition and competition law act irrespective of whether a price control is in place and protect customers from, among other things, any behavior considered to be an abuse of a dominant position. The opening of a market to competition may provide an adequate level of pressure to incentivize the universal service providers (USPs) to become more efficient and may in itself be sufficient to protect the interests of the customer. Nevertheless, in most utility industries in the EU, regulators have been provided with powers to set price controls and further constrain prices, while competition is developing in the market.

In the postal sector, the EU Postal Directive[1] required Member States to partially open their postal markets in 2003. The Directive allows for the possibility of requiring full market opening in 2009. In such an environment, price controls have been applied to ensure the provision of statutory undertakings (e.g. universal service), encourage efficiency and

* The analysis contained in this paper reflects the views of the authors. These views are not necessarily those of Oxera and the Royal Mail Group.

1 European Commission, European Directive 97/67/EC and amending Directive 2002/39/EC.

economy, protect customer groups, as well as encourage competition through providing sufficient headroom for market entry.

In other utility sectors,[2] with the prospect of developing a competitive market, price controls have been applied as temporary measures while competition develops. There are three significant and closely related effects to be considered when setting the control. First, the form of the price control may be designed to encourage competition into segments of the market. Second, the scope of the price control may be adjusted over time to match the pace of developing competition. Finally, the universal service obligation for the USPs may call into question the compatibility of such an obligation and fully competitive markets; therefore, regardless of whether there is a price control, there are issues over the financial viability of the USP in the presence of competition.

Price controls may not only provide additional protection to customers while competition develops, but may also alter the market to encourage competition into segments of the market. Price controls can hinder the USP's development of its service in order to meet customer needs by restricting its changes in non-price characteristics. The price-control arrangements may limit its flexibility in adjusting the output and quality of any given service. For example, if the services offered by the USP go beyond the mandated requirements of the universal service in terms of collection and delivery, the USP may wish to rationalize its services to meet the universal service requirements. Price controls can also limit the ability of the USP to amend prices and pricing structures in order to make them more cost-reflective.

Regarding the services included in price controls, there are essentially three ways in which the coverage of the price controls can evolve over time and ultimately be removed. The USP's services that become competitive can be removed from the coverage of the controls. Such an approach requires detailed analysis of the developing markets and the allocation of costs between the competitive and non-competitive market segments. Alternatively, the USP's services that could prospectively become competitive during the price-control period can be removed from the main control and either temporarily placed in a separate control (e.g. safety caps) or have no control applied to them. Finally, the USP's services that are competitive can be included in the same control as those services that are non-competitive until such time as all of those services are either competitive or prospectively competitive.

For example, Laffont and Tirole (1996) have stated that, in the presence of universal access to part of a USP's network that cannot be readily replicated by a competitor (and thereby forms a bottleneck), a global price

---

[2] For example, telecommunications, and the electricity and gas retail business in the UK.

control covering end-to-end and access prices, with floors on end-to-end services and ECPR (efficient component pricing rule) ceilings on access services, has several beneficial economic properties. The global control provides the USP with the flexibility to set prices in order to maximize welfare and move prices to become more geared to cost,[3] while the overall level of allowed revenue is constrained within the control. It also avoids the need for the regulator to review the allocation of costs in detail between competitive and non-competitive markets or between the product prices.

Regarding the universal service obligation, an extensive literature has identified, and continues to investigate, significant welfare implications arising from competitive entry (Crew and Kleindorfer 2002). Much of this literature has focused on issues related to the financing of the universal service in the presence of competition (De Donder et al 2002). The USP's delivery network, particularly the outdoor element, has cost elasticities with respect to volume that are significantly below unity (Cazals et al 2001, Cazals et al 2005), which indicates a potential bottleneck. Nevertheless, competitors are not constrained by an obligation to provide a universal delivery service, and have the option to circumvent major parts of the bottleneck through selective entry into market segments where high margins are available (cream-skimming). Competitors may also select access to the USP's network if it is available. Similar selective entry may be expected in end-to-end services. The specific nature of entry may vary but may also be easily distorted by price controls that seek to control price changes in one particular segment relative to those of another.

In the presence of costs related to maintaining the provision of the universal service and volume loss to entrants' cream-skimming, the average unit costs increase. However, there are ways in which the structure of the price control may address such issues. For example, the price-control can allow the average revenue to be adjusted upward accordingly. In addition, it can allow the USP greater market segmentation, with distinct prices offered by the USP – subject to the universal service obligation – to reflect different costs, to reduce the extent to which the entrants can capitalize on cream-skimming opportunities. Whether these policies are sufficient to ensure the continued sustainability of the universal service, or, indeed, the opposite (i.e. a "graveyard spiral"), is explored elsewhere (Cohen et al 2004, Crew and Kleindorfer 2005).

This paper focuses on the second of the significant issues (identified above) for setting the price control, namely the coverage of the control in a developing competitive market. It develops tests for removing from the

---

[3] Cost reflective prices are required by the European Commission. See European Directive 97/67/EC and amending Directive 2002/39/EC

main control services that are prospectively competitive during the price control and illustrates their application to a service in the UK.

In the UK, the regulator, acting under the Postal Services Act 2000,[4] has proposed full market opening in 2007. Of the USP's inland addressed mail services, 99% of revenue is price-controlled. The first price control after the Act had individual price caps that prevented prices from becoming more geared to costs. The present control is a form of global price control that allows rebalancing between all prices. However, the price control effectively affects the ability of the USP to reflect underlying costs in its pricing through individual secondary caps and additional regulatory hurdles to be met before changes to non-price and pricing structures are allowed. Most of the remaining inland addressed mail service revenues correspond to products with multiple prices and relatively small revenues that, for simplicity, are outside of the main control but are under individual price caps. In addition, the USP's unaddressed and international mail (with the exception of public tariffs)[5] is deemed to be competitive and outside of any control.

The UK price control also allows the USP to apply for services that are in competitive markets to be removed from the control.[6] This envisages the main control shrinking over time, to avoid a situation in which the USP reduces prices in competitive markets only to recover additional revenue through price increases in non-competitive markets. This paper does not consider the relative merits of the present form of price control and its alternatives, which are attracting an increasing amount of attention from academics. Rather, it examines the tests that could be applied to remove prices from the control from the perspective of a practitioner.

The remainder of this paper is structured as follows. Section 2 outlines the economic principles that underlie the approaches used to assess the effectiveness of competition. Sections 3 and 4 identify practical tests that have been applied to assess the effectiveness of competition, which can be used to determine the coverage of the price control. In particular, Section 3 deals with calculations of market power in the postal sector, while Section 4 considers market analysis in postal services. Section 5 presents some critical

---

[4] The Postal Services Act 2000, subject to the primary objective of ensuring the provision of the universal service, has a second objective vested in the regulator, which is to "further the interests of users of postal services, wherever appropriate by promoting effective competition between postal operators".

[5] International public tariffs are within the main control.

[6] An application to remove a service can be made when "competition in the provision to customers, or to classes of customers, of the service in question, is sufficiently developed for the interest of customers to be protected without the application of the [price control] condition". Postcomm 2003b. 'Royal Mail Group Licence Condition 19(17) on 23 March 2001 and amended on 1 April 2003'.

values in proposed tests for Royal Mail's magazine mail. Section 6 concludes.

2. THEORY AND APPLICATION BEYOND THE POSTAL SECTOR

Competition law prohibits excessive, predatory and discriminatory pricing, amongst other types of behavior. It is an *ex post* instrument. Price controls, instead are *ex ante* instruments that are usually imposed on undertakings that are deemed to be dominant; that is in markets where competition is not sufficiently developed. For example, in the case of a developing competitive market, the regulator may intervene to set the price cap below the profit-maximizing price for the incumbent with residual market power, in order to ensure that the price charged reflects the price expected in a fully competitive market and to increase consumer welfare (Newbery 1997). As a market is liberalized, it will be essential to match increasing competition with deregulatory action. The price cap would be deemed still to be effective and necessary if its removal would be likely to result in a significant price increase. This leads into the economic concept of significant market power (SMP) that is widely used in competition law, and also in some regulatory frameworks.[7] SMP is usually defined in terms of a firm's ability to raise prices consistently and profitably above competitive levels.[8] This definition, which has its origins in micro-economic theory, is the basis for assessing market power.

The condition for profit maximization by a monopolist is that the marginal revenue equals marginal costs such that $p(1 - 1/\eta) = c$, where p denotes the price; η is the elasticity of demand; and c is the marginal cost. This condition is normally presented as:

$$\frac{p-c}{p} = -\frac{1}{\eta} \tag{1}$$

This expression indicates that the price–cost margin is inversely related to the elasticity of demand for the provider. When the elasticity of demand is very high, p is close to c. Conversely, the lower the value of η, the greater the difference between p and c.

---

[7] This is the case of the new European electronic communications regulatory framework. See, for example, Commission of the European Communities (2002).

[8] See, for example, the UK Office of Fair Trading's market power guidelines (OFT, 1999, para 1.2).

The left-hand side of the condition shows that observed mark-ups can be used to measure market power. In practice, this is less appropriate when there are significant issues concerning the allocation of costs (e.g. common costs), the definition of marginal costs, or the fact that prices have not been set to maximize profits, but set to other objectives or regulatory constraints. In such cases, the assessment of market power focuses on the factors that affect the right-hand side of the condition.

In theory, the *critical elasticity of demand* at which it is not profitable for the provider to increase prices can be calculated and compared with the *actual elasticity of demand.* If the actual elasticity of demand is higher than the critical elasticity of demand, it will not be profitable for the provider to increase prices. The critical sales loss can also be calculated from the *critical elasticity of demand* for a given price. This is defined as the proportionate decrease in quantity sold resulting from a price increase that is just large enough to ensure that the provider will not impose a price increase of at least the given amount once price regulation is removed. Assuming that, once regulation is lifted, the provider increases its price from p_1 to p_2, the critical elasticity, for the case of linear demand (Werden 1998), is equal to:

$$-\frac{1}{m+2t} \qquad (2)$$ [9]

where t is the price increase, $(p_2 - p_1)/p_1$, and m is the price–cost margin before price regulation is removed, $(p_1 - c)/p_1$.

There are different approaches to estimating the elasticity of demand. If historic data is available, an econometric approach could be used. This entails writing down a firm-specific demand equation for the product or service, and using price and quantity data at the firm level to estimate the own-price demand elasticity. A more sophisticated approach is to measure the firm-specific own-price elasticity by estimating a complete demand system in which the quantities demanded of each product depend on the price of the product itself and on all the prices of all the other products. This approach was used, for example, in a study of the US Federal Communications Commission to address directly the question of whether AT&T would be able to raise its prices in the long-distance market if the regulatory controls were removed (Ward 1995). However, if sufficient data

[9] The formula for the critical elasticity is $-(1 + t)/(m + t)$ if demand is assumed to be iso-elastic. A derivation of the formulae can be found in Werden (1998).

is not available, the simplest way would be to ask customers how they would respond to a 10% price change.[10]

In practice, the approach taken by some UK regulators outside of the postal sector[11] is not to assess or estimate the elasticities directly, but to make observations of the market to assess indirectly whether the market is competitive. The approach is summarized in Figure 1. Assuming that the starting point is the case where regulation of the USP's services is in place, first, the relevant market is defined by reference to the product's characteristics (including cost characteristics) and close substitutes. Second, observations of customer switching, market shares, provider entry (and exit), and provider offers are collated and reviewed. From this, an assessment of SMP is made. Finally, the regulator determines the appropriate response if any market power is identified.

For the UK postal sector at least, this paper shows that, in the second step of Figure 1, there is scope for the primary focus to be directly on the elasticities of forecast and observed customer switching, including own- and cross-price elasticities (Cazals et al 2003, Fève et al 2003), within the price-control review. This is subsequently referred to as Test A. Test A may be supplemented by observations and requirements of market shares, provider entry (and exit), provider offers, and whether any barriers to further entry exist. These are subsequently referred to as Test B.

Figure 1: Standard regulatory approach

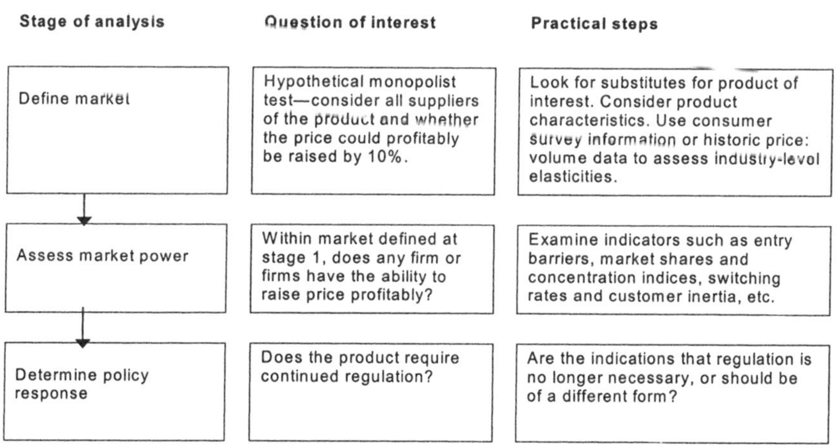

---

[10] This could be done for example using a stated preference survey. A more complex alternative would be the use of conjoint analysis.

[11] For example, Ofgem (2000) and Oftel (2000).

3. MARKET POWER CALCULATIONS IN THE POSTAL SECTOR (TEST A)

Price controls limit the upward movement in prices and can restrict a supplier's tendency to apply an increment to its prices to increase profit. If the USP cannot *expect to* increase its profit through increases in prices within a price-control period, the service is prospectively competitive. This is consistent with the view that if the USP cannot *actually* increase its profit through increases in prices within a price-control period, the service is competitive. Under prospective competition, the service could then be removed from the control with the potential for only limited upward pressure on prices. This approach has been used in UK telecommunications (Oftel 2000, 2002).

For a price-control/rates review, the USP provides business plans to the regulator. These plans include volume forecasts that necessitate an assessment of the development of the market and the impact of price changes. If a market is liberalizing and entry is expected within the timeframe of the control, the incumbent USP can expect to lose volume even if prices do not increase. Hence volume forecasts use estimates of own- and cross-price effects on the USP's substitute end-to-end services, USP's access services, or competitors' services.[12] If, in addition, the marginal cost and prices are known, the USP's planning assumptions can be used to assess whether it believes it has the incentive to increase prices profitably. Thus the first test for taking a service out of the control (Test A) is satisfied if the USP's plans imply that it is not expected to be able to increase profit by applying an increment to the price in question.

As set out in Figure 1, the definition of the relevant market is the first step in the analysis. A product may serve several sub-markets (customer sub-groups) or may be related to other products that could service the market (substitutes). The choice of the relevant market may be informed by the own- and cross-price elasticities. For the purpose of illustration in this paper, the relevant market is assumed to include the product under investigation, its closest substitute and their respective access services.

The USP's profit (π) in the relevant market(s) is then calculated as follows:

[12] In the UK, the regulator could seek to access this information through the license and review of the price control.

$$\pi = \sum_{i=1}^{4} (p_i - c_i)x_i(p_i) - F$$

(3)

$$\frac{\partial \pi}{\partial p_1} = x_1 + \sum_{i=1}^{4}(p_i - c_i)\frac{\partial x_i}{\partial p_1} = x_1 + \sum \frac{(p_i - c_i)}{p_1}\delta_i x_i$$

where: x_1 is volume of the product under investigation

x_2 is volume of the substitute product of the USP

x_3 is volume of the access product relating to product x_1

x_4 is volume of the access product relating to product x_2

p_i, c_i are price and marginal cost for product i

F is fixed cost

δ_i is $\frac{p_1}{x_i}\frac{\partial x_i}{\partial p_1}$

The volume change arising from the price increment in a market after additional entry (as a result of liberalization)[13] can be calculated from a comparison of (a) the volume before and after additional market entry at the existing price; (b) the volume at the existing and incremented prices for the market before additional market entry; and (c) the volume before and after additional market entry at the incremented price. Hence, if:

	Pre-price change at p_1^1	Post-price change at p_1^2
Volume before additional market entry	x_1^{11}	x_1^{12}
Volume after additional market entry	x_1^{21}	x_1^{22}

then:

[13] That is, ∂x_1 in δ_1. The own-price elasticity for x_1, after additional entry.

$$\partial x_1 = \left(x_1^{22} - x_1^{21}\right) = \left(x_1^{22} - x_1^{12}\right) + \left(x_1^{12} - x_1^{11}\right) - \left(x_1^{21} - x_1^{11}\right)$$
$$= \frac{\eta_1 x_1^{12}\left(p_1^2 - c_1\right)}{c_1} + \frac{\eta_4 x_1^{11}(p_1^2 - p_1^1)}{p_1^1} - \frac{\eta_5 x_1^{11}\left(p_1^1 - c_1\right)}{c_1} \tag{4}$$

and

$$\eta_4 = \frac{\left(\eta_2 x_1^{11} - \eta_3 x_2^{11}\right)}{x_1^{11}}$$

where η_1 is the elasticity of demand representing the change before and after additional market entry at the incremented price relative to marginal cost[14]

η_2 is the specific-price elasticity before additional market entry[15]

η_3 is the cross-price elasticity before additional market entry

η_4 in the own-price elasticity after additional market entry

η_5 is the elasticity of demand representing the change before and after additional market entry at the existing price relative to marginal cost

If $\frac{\partial \pi}{\partial p_1} \leq 0$ then Test A will be satisfied.

Equation (4) includes the own-price elasticity (specific- and cross-price effects) on the product that has undergone the price change plus switching effects arising from entry. In a developing competitive market, the volumes x_1^{11} and x_1^{12} are first estimated with and without the price increment in the absence of competition. Second, the volumes x_1^{21} and x_1^{22} are estimated with and without the price increment for the case of expected competition.

In the practical application of Test A, two additional assumptions need to be made: the increment in the price, and the period of time used.

The price increment applied for such a test in other sectors is usually 5% or 10% of the existing price. The greater the percentage increment applied,

---

[14] More specifically, the analysis used switching functions and the Entry Pricing Model developed and discussed in Hill et al (2004).

[15] This reflects the volume transferring out of the product that does not transfer elsewhere following the price change.

the greater the likelihood of Test A being satisfied, because it will generate more switching.

The period of time will typically correspond to the period of the price control. The price-control review may establish that Test A is not satisfied in the first year of the control but is satisfied in the final year.[16] In such circumstances, the service could be taken out of the global control and placed in a separate control for the period of the price control, or for the period until the start of the final year of the control when Test A is satisfied. This removal of the service from the main (global) control and into a separate control would mean that the USP would no longer be able to reduce the prices of that service and then recover the lost revenue through price increases in other services. Alternatively, the service could be removed from the control from the start of the period on the basis that any upward scope to increase prices is only temporary, with the underlying price pressure being downward.

4. MARKET ANALYSIS IN POST (TEST B)

Before removing the service from the control under Test A, the USP's assumptions relating to the development of the market over the period of the control will need to be assessed for reasonableness.

In the period of the price-control review, there would be an expectation firstly to observe a propensity by customers to switch in response to price differentials consistent with the USP's switching assumptions, and secondly to observe a loss of volume heading towards the threshold levels at which the USP's market power becomes limited. These would show the existence and level of competition, and test whether the switching assumptions are realistic and whether the threshold level is attainable during the price control, based on the historical and present market development. The greater the loss of market share at the time of the price-control review, the more credible the forecasts of significant volume loss over the future price-control period.

Nevertheless, historical and present trends may belie the actual developments in the market. In particular, when a few large customers hold significant volume, the USP's market share could change significantly quite quickly. This has two further implications. First, it implies that Test B needs to be reviewed at frequent intervals, with the controls being relatively short in duration (i.e. two or three years in length) during the development of the market. Second, it requires records to be kept of offers from alternative

[16] This is close to Oftel's definition of a prospectively competitive market (Oftel 2000).

supplier(s), as this indicates (a) the stability of offers and therefore the continued presence of alternative supplier(s) in the market, and (b) the proportion of credible offers not taken up, and therefore, potential growth of the competitors' volume.

The number of offers made by competitors and the proportion of those offers taken up, could also be investigated before making a decision. For example, an investigation could be made as to (a) whether the durability of competitive offers is any different for a single alternative supplier with a range of offers, or many individual suppliers with the same range of offers, or (b) whether the proportion of take-up is influenced by the USP's behavior or other factors. While such investigations may lead to a clearer understanding of the market, their inclusion would introduce significantly more subjectivity into the test. This could reduce transparency and understanding of regulatory decisions by customers, competitors and the USP. Test B could be limited to the relatively more objective criteria of checking (a) the reasonableness of the switching assumptions used in the business plan against observed switching; (b) the USP's loss of volume approaching the threshold; (c) the stability of offers; and (d) the proportion of credible offers not taken up.

Test B on the availability of offers also raises the possibility that one segment of the service faces competition while another segment of the same service does not. One approach would be to take out those segments that satisfy both Test A and B. However, for universal services, the requirement of uniform and affordable tariffs acts as a constraint on the USP's ability to apply different prices in different geographical areas, and on the geographical segmentation of the market in such an approach.

If there is erosion of the USP's volume in the competitive segment and the withdrawal or removal of the universal service from that segment, market segmentation will lead to the competitive segment being removed from the control and possibly the withdrawal of the USP's offering in the competitive market.[17] Conversely, if there is erosion of the USP's volume in the competitive segment and no scope for segmentation, while the service remains within the price control, the loss of volume and network costs of the universal service will place upward pressure on costs and prices, as discussed in Section 1. In such a case, the worsening of the financial position for the USP (and ultimately a graveyard spiral) may be delayed initially using prices that segment the market while retaining the geographic extent of universal service, but may reappear once all of the available pricing levers have been used and competition enters a geographical segment within the universal service.

[17] This is illustrated by the case of standard parcels weighing over 20kg in the UK. Standard parcels above 20kg are not a universal service (Postcomm 2003c).

In conclusion, the regulatory decision could be based on Test A, and the more objective and observable switching, actual volume loss and offers of Test B. In practice, this involves detailed monitoring of the switching, volume loss and offers, which requires both the USP and competitors to provide market information in a transparent form for review by the regulator. While such an approach is consistent with that adopted by some regulators,[18] the different measurements of volume, different license obligations with respect to the provision of information by USPs and competitors, and the universal service make its application to the postal sector more challenging.

5. ILLUSTRATIVE CALCULATION FOR THE CRITICAL ELASTICITIES FOR MAGAZINE MAIL

For illustration, the critical elasticities of Test A were estimated for Royal Mail's services for businesses publishing newsletters, magazines and in-house journals on a regular basis (Presstream). The Presstream services of Royal Mail include a next-day (PS1) or three-day (PS2) service. The service has a minimum mailing of 4,000 letters or 1,000 packets, at least 90% must be fully postcoded, postings must be made on fixed dates, and its availability is limited to magazines and publications. The service is used by four customer types: (a) businesses sending consumer magazines of general interest that are available in the news-stands; (b) businesses sending business (industrial and professional) magazines that are not generally available from the news-stand; (c) businesses sending customer magazines as a form of marketing their services; and (d) businesses sending membership magazines. The Presstream services are deemed to be outside of the universal service.[19]

For the calculation of critical elasticities for PS1, p_1^1 to p_1^2 price increments of 10% were applied to PS1 prices.[20] The analysis used access prices,[21] entrant prices[22] and expected levels of switching out of the USP's service in response to price increases. The parameters of expected demand elasticities represent a non-linear demand curve in a competitive market such that the critical own-price elasticity was no longer represented by equation

---

[18] In the UK gas, electricity and telecommunications sectors.

[19] Postcomm (2004)

[20] The results for a 5% price increment are similar, with marginally higher critical elasticities.

[21] These were based on the approach set out in Postcomm (2003d).

[22] This assumed that the entrant prices were below those of Royal Mail for about 40% of Presstream 1 market.

(2) but by δ_1 (η_1, η_4, η_5,) in equation (3). The analysis calculated the specific- and cross-price elasticities {η_2, η_3}, and own-price elasticity before additional entry, η_4, to identify the values at which $\frac{\partial \pi}{\partial p_1} \le 0$ is met and yield the critical own-price elasticity after additional entry.

Table 1 shows examples of demand elasticities from the analysis, assuming a level of switching whereby the USP's volume is reduced by 17% relative to the level of volume before additional market entry. It shows that, for a specific-price elasticity equal to zero and a cross-price elasticity equal to zero, $\frac{\partial \pi}{\partial p_1} \rangle 0$. It also shows values of the specific- and cross-price elasticities{η_2, η_3} at which $\frac{\partial \pi}{\partial p_1} = 0$. For example, the critical own-price elasticity δ_1 is –1.5 when the specific-price elasticity is –1.1 and cross-price elasticity is zero. Table 1 shows that the price increase is not profit enhancing, if the specific-price elasticity exceeds 1.1 (in absolute terms) or the cross-price elasticity exceeds 1.9.[23]

Table 1: Test A elasticities for PS1

Specific-price elasticity (before entry) η_2	Cross-price elasticity with PS2 (before entry) η_3	Own-price elasticity (after entry) δ_1	Change in profit to change in price
0.0	0.0	–0.4	>0
0.0	1.9	–5.9	0.0
–0.5	1.0	–3.8	0.0
–1.1	0.0	–1.5	0.0

Table 2 shows a similar analysis and examples for PS2 in which the USP's volume is reduced by 30% relative to the level of volume before additional market entry. For example, the critical own-price elasticity is -1.6 when the specific-price elasticity is –0.6 and cross-price elasticity is zero. Table 2 shows that the price increase is not profit-enhancing, if the specific-price elasticity exceeds 0.6 (in absolute terms), or the cross-price elasticity exceeds 8.9.

[23] If it is assumed that $\eta_2 \le 0$ *and* $\eta_3 \ge 0$.

Table 2: Test A elasticities for PS2

Specific-price elasticity (before entry) η_2	Cross-price elasticity with PS1 (before entry) η_3	Own-price elasticity (after entry) δ_1	Change in profit to change in price
0.0	0.0	–1.1	>0
0.0	8.9	–3.8	0.0
–0.5	1.8	–2.1	0.0
–0.6	0.0	–1.6	0.0

There are several special cases that are also worthy of note arising form this type of analysis. Firstly, if the PS1 price was less than 10% above the PS2 price, a unilateral increase in the PS2 price of 10% would be expected to lead to a high cross-price elasticity as volume transferred to PS1 and $\frac{\partial \pi}{\partial p_2} \langle 0$. Secondly, in such a case, the USP may have an incentive to increase the price for PS1. Clearly this would arise if $\frac{\partial \pi}{\partial p_1} \rangle 0$; however it also may arise in a special case even when $\frac{\partial \pi}{\partial p_1} \leq 0$. If $\frac{\partial \pi}{\partial p_1} \leq 0$, the USP may still have an incentive to increase PS1 prices beyond the price at which $\frac{\partial \pi}{\partial p_1} = 0$ to enable the PS2 price to increase if $\frac{\partial \pi}{\partial p_1} + \frac{\partial \pi}{\partial p_2} \rangle 0$. Finally, if the USP cannot increase PS1 prices beyond the point at which $\frac{\partial \pi}{\partial p_1} = 0$, and a unilateral increase in the PS1 price results in $\frac{\partial \pi}{\partial p_1} \leq 0$, a 10% price increase in the PS2 price USP will result in $\frac{\partial \pi}{\partial p_2} \langle 0$. In such a scenario, if PS1 satisfies Test A, PS2 would also satisfy Test A.[24]

In addition, the approach lends itself to sensitivity analysis of some of the assumptions. For example, the degree of switching may be analyzed to establish the impact on the specific- and cross-price elasticities $\{\eta_2, \eta_3\}$ at which $\frac{\partial \pi}{\partial p_1} = 0$. A higher level of switching in equation (5) reduces the

24 In the same way, other services to PS2 (e.g. presorted, next-day service of Mailsort 1) may be close substitutes to PS1. If the USP cannot apply the increment to this close substitute service to increase profit, it may suffice to protect customers from a 10% price increase of PS1.

absolute values of the specific- and cross-price elasticities $\{\eta_2, \eta_3\}$ and own-price elasticity η_4 at which $\frac{\partial \pi}{\partial p_1} = 0$.

The results indicate that the critical elasticities with specific- and cross-price, and there own-price elasticities, are lower for PS2 relative to PS1. If there is a 10% increase in the PS2 price, PS1 satisfies Test A, and the original difference in price between PS1 and PS2 is less than 10%, then PS2 should satisfy Test A as well. In addition, critical elasticities for specific- and cross-price elasticities, and thereby own-price elasticities, are lower in the case of a high level of switching relative to a low level of switching. Finally, as discussed in preceding sections, if the parameter values used in the forecasting for the price-control period are consistent with $\frac{\partial \pi}{\partial p_1} \leq 0$ (Test A), and are consistent with observed developments in the competitive market (Test B), the service may be removed from the control with the expectation that there would be no significant price increase by the USP.

6. CONCLUSION

This paper has reviewed the conditions necessary for services to be removed from price controls for the postal sector, consistent with the present regulatory environment in the UK. In particular, it has developed the approach used by UK regulators outside of the postal sector into one that places more emphasis on testing whether a market is likely to be prospectively competitive within the price-control period. First, the assumptions used by the USP in its forecasts for the price-control period can be assessed to see if they are consistent with there being no significant market power for any service within that period (Test A). In particular, the paper illustrates with an example of magazine mail how the critical demand elasticity values could be derived from the USP business plan for comparison with actual values in assessing whether Test A is satisfied. Second, the observations of the market can be used to confirm whether the USP's forecasts contained in the business plan are indeed reasonable and compatible with the developments of the market (Test B). The removal of services then requires costs to be allocated between competitive and non-competitive markets to enable the coverage of the main control to shrink over time as the competitive market develops.

REFERENCES

Cazals, Catherine, Jean-Pierre Florens, Bernard Roy. 2001. "An Analysis of Some Specific Cost Drivers in the Delivery Activity." In *Future Directions in Postal Reform*, edited by M.A. Crew and P.R. Kleindorfer, Boston, MA: Kluwer Academic Publishers.

Cazals, Catherine, Frederique Fève, Patrick Fève, Jean-Pierre Florens. 2003. "Simple Structural Econometrics of Price Elasticity." *Economics Letters*.

Cazals, Catherine, Jean-Pierre Florens, Soteri Soterios. 2005. "Delivery Costs for Postal Services in UK: Some Results on Scale Economies with Panel Data." In *Regulatory and Economics Changes in the Postal and Delivery Sector*, edited by M.A. Crew and P.R. Kleindorfer, Boston, MA: Kluwer Academic Publishers.

Cohen, Robert, Matthew Robinson, Renee Sheehy, John Waller and Spyros Xenakis. 2004. "An Empirical Analysis of the Graveyard Spiral." In *Competitive Transformation of the Postal Delivery Sector*, edited by M.A. Crew and P.R. Kleindorfer, Boston, MA: Kluwer Academic Publishers.

Commission of the European Communities. 2002. "Commission Guidelines on Market Analysis and the Assessment of Significant Market Power under the Community Regulatory Framework for Electronic Communications Networks and Services", July 9th.

Crew, Michael A. and Paul R. Kleindorfer. 2002. "Balancing Access and the Universal Service Obligation." In *Postal and Delivery Services: Delivering on Competition*, edited by M.A. Crew and P.R. Kleindorfer, Boston, MA: Kluwer Academic Publishers.

Crew, Michael A. and Paul R. Kleindorfer. 2005. "Competition, Universal Service and the Graveyard Spiral." In *Regulatory and Economics Changes in the Postal and Delivery Sector*, edited by M.A. Crew and P.R. Kleindorfer, Boston, MA: Kluwer Academic Publishers.

De Donder, Philippe, Helmuth Cremer, and Frank Rodriguez. 2002. "Funding the Universal Service Obligation under Liberalisation." In *Postal and Delivery Services: Delivering on Competition*, edited by M.A. Crew and P.R. Kleindorfer, Boston, MA: Kluwer Academic Publishers.

Fève, Frédérique, Patrick Fève, Jean-Pierre Florens. 2003. "Attribute Choices and Structural Econometrics of Price Elasticity of Demand." IDEI working paper.

Hill, Roger, Richard Robinson and Frank Rodriguez. 2005. "The Financial Equilibrium of Universal Service Providers in a Liberalized Postal Market." In *Regulatory and Economics Changes in the Postal and Delivery Sector*, edited by M.A. Crew and P.R. Kleindorfer, Boston, MA: Kluwer Academic Publishers.

HM Government. 2000. "The Postal Services Act".

Laffont, Jean-Jacques and Jean Tirole. 1996. "Creating Competition through Interconnection: Theory and Practice." *Journal of Regulatory Economics* 10(3): 227–256.

Ofgem. 2000. "Review of British Gas Trading's Price Regulation: Initial Proposals", December.

OFT. 1999. "Assessment of Market Power", OFT 415, Office of Fair Trading, September.

Oftel. 2000. "Implementing Oftel's Strategy: Effective Competition Review Guidelines," August.

Oftel. 2002. "Protecting Consumers by Promoting Competition: Oftel's Conclusions."

Newbery, David. 1997. "Privatisation and Liberalisation of Network Utilities", *European Economic Review* 41: 357–383.

Postcomm. 2003a. "Assessing Competitiveness in Postal Services: Postcomm's Proposed Criteria." Consultation Document, November.

Postcomm. 2003b. "Royal Mail Group Licence Condition 19(17) on 23 March 2001 and amended on 1 April 2003."

Postcomm. 2003c. "Proposed Changes to Royal Mail's Standard Parcels and Special Delivery Products – Decision Document." October.

Postcomm. 2003d. "Access by UK Mail: Nature of Proposed Determination, Reasons." Consultation Document, May.

Postcomm. 2004. "Decision Document: The UK's Universal Postal Service." June.

Ward, Michael. 1995. "Measurement of Market Power in Long Distance Telecommunications." Bureau of Economics Staff Report, Federal Trade Commission, Washington, April.

Werden, Gregory. 1998. "Demand Elasticities in Antitrust Analysis." *Antitrust Law Journal* 66(2): 364–414.

Chapter 7

Worksharing, Pricing and Competition in the Postal Sector*

Etienne Billette de Villemeur,[1] Helmuth Cremer,[1] Bernard Roy[2] and Joëlle Toledano[2]
University of Toulouse (IDEI and GREMAQ)[1] *and La Poste*[2]

1. INTRODUCTION

In the postal sector, the practice of worksharing has been introducing a measure of competition even when the industry was otherwise monopolistic. When the customers have the possibility to "bypass" part of the postal network, there is effectively competition in the relevant segments between the operator's activities and those of the customers. From that perspective, one can think of the processing of workshared mail as a form of "downstream access" which is provided to the customers. The relevant question is then to know how the workshared product ought to be priced and more generally, how the possibility of worksharing ought to affect the operators pricing structure. This subject has been extensively studied in the literature (Billette de Villemeur et al. 2002, 2003,. Crew and Kleindorfer 1995, Mitchell (999, Sherman 2001 and Panzar 2002).[1]

When the market is liberalized and when entry occurs, a new kind of demand for workshared mail may emerge if the other operators do not have

---

* We would like to thank Michael Crew, Philippe De Donder and Paul Kleindorfer for their comments. The views expressed in this paper are those of authors and do not necessarily reflect the views of La Poste.

1 See also Crew and Kleindorfer (1995), Mitchel (1999), Sherman (2001) and Panzar (2002).

their own delivery network, at least in some areas. The pricing of the services provided to competing operator raises the problem of "access pricing". The phenomenon of "downstream access" has been heavily debated in many network industries like telecommunication, electricity and gas, as part of the ongoing liberalization process; see for instance Laffont and Tirole (1996, 2000) and Armstrong (2002). A few recent papers have also looked at this problem for the postal sector, see Crew and Kleindorfer (2002) and Billette de Villemeur et al. (2003b, 2004). However, these contributions neglect the more traditional form of worksharing by customers. A fully fledged model of postal sector pricing would have to account for both the customers and the competitors demand for workshared mail. Panzar (2003) represents a first step in that direction. He uses the worksharing model of Billette de Villemeur et al. (2003a) in which he introduced upstream and downstream competition. However, he uses a rather specific setting and he does not characterize the optimal pricing structure. The current paper tries to bring together competitive access and monopoly worksharing models in a more systematic way.

Before proceeding it may be interesting to take a look at the fundamental issues underlying our problem. The regulatory design of postal prices including those for workshared mail is essentially a Ramsey-Boiteux pricing problem. The incumbent operator offers different products to different types of customers and we can think of workshared mail as one of these products. While some of these products are final goods, some like workshared mail may be intermediate goods which are used as inputs by other firms. The pricing of this intermediate good then indirectly determines the prices paid by the final consumers of these products. In a "perfect" (first-best) world the prices of all these products are equal to (long-run) marginal cost for all products. This provides consumers with the correct signals and ensures that the decentralized outcome is efficient.

In an industry like the postal sector, where technology involves "fixed" costs (like the cost of maintaining the delivery network) it is however, typically the case that marginal cost (even long-run marginal costs) are well below average costs.[2] Strict marginal cost pricing is then problematic because it implies that the operator cannot break even, which is usually considered as not acceptable for a number of reasons (including political economy considerations).[3] Consequently, one would have to impose positive markups on at least some products in order to meet the break-even constraint. The determination of these markups is precisely what the

---

[2] Like most of the regulation literature we use the term fixed cost for the part of cost which is independent of output, *even in the long run.*

[3] In a first-best setting this problem can be overcome by a lump-sum transfer to the operator covering its fixed cost.

Ramsey-Boiteux problem is all about. The question is simply how to distort the different prices away from marginal cost in order to break-even while keeping the efficiency cost of these distortions as small as possible. The exact specification of this problem and hence the specific results depend on the characteristics of the industry (costs, technology and demand) the general regulatory environment (e.g., the presence of a uniform pricing constraint) and on the type of competition there is between the incumbent and the entrant(s) (competitive fringe, monopolistic competition, some form of oligopoly, etc.). The literature so far has concentrated on the competitive fringe case for which a number of interesting results have been obtained.[4] Pricing rules for final goods and for workshared mail are typically inverse-elasticity rules, properly amended to account for cross-price effects (if any). Consequently, optimal prices depend on demand consideration and not just on cost considerations. This is different from the first best setting where prices simply reflect marginal costs. In a recent contribution, Billette de Villemeur et al. (2003b) show that these rules can be generalized to account for imperfect competition

Summing up, it appears that the economists' toolbox regarding pricing in the postal sector, though still in need to be expanded, does already have the potential to offer valuable guidance in the regulatory debate. In many instances, however, all these studies are ignored by the various parties involved, regulators and postal representatives alike. Instead, the debate concentrates on the relative merits of two essentially ad hoc rules (or classes of rules). The first of these ad hoc approaches is the so called Efficient Component Pricing Rule (ECPR) which (roughly speaking) consists in applying the same (per unit) markup on workshared that is applied on the corresponding final product offered by the incumbent operator. Consequently, worksharing per se does not appear to affect the incumbent's profits and more generally its ability to cover its fixed costs. This rule has the theoretical merit that it leads (under some conditions) to efficient entry decisions: entry occurs if and only if the entrant is more efficient. However, these apparent properties often do not stand under closer scrutiny because ECPR does not account for the demand side of the problem. Further, the rule is incomplete and does not explain how the markup on the incumbent's relevant final product ought to be determined. In addition and most significantly, it does not in general yield an efficient Ramsey-Boiteux pricing, even when one ignores the determination of all the other prices.

Another *ad hoc* rule which is sometimes advocated by regulators (for instance in the UK) is a "cost-plus" rule, where the access price is obtained from the long run marginal cost by applying some *ad hoc* markup. This may

---

4 See e.g., Cremer et al. (1995, 1997), Crew and Kleindorfer (2002), De Donder et al. (2002, 2003), Billette de Villemeur et al. (2004).

at first sound similar to a Ramsey-Boiteux approach and there exists of course a specific level of the markup for which we obtain the Ramsey price (or alternatively the ECPR level). The crucial difference, however, is that no effort in made to optimize the markup by accounting for instance for demand considerations. Instead the markup is set in a ad hoc way. For instance a small markup is added in order to cover the cost of universal service which in turn is calculated in a questionable way (and thus often significantly underestimated; see Cremer et al. (2000)). There is no reason to expect that such a procedure can yield anything which comes close to the optimal prices.

The main features of our setting are as follows. We consider a stylized representation of the postal sector, with two activities (e.g. distribution and a composite activity) and two types of operators: the incumbent universal service operator on the one hand and the potential entrants on the other hand. There are two types of customers and at least three different products. Households consume single piece mail which uses the entire network. Business customers may or may not engage in worksharing depending on the price structure. Business customers can also consume the entrant's product. The incumbent operator processes workshared mail which emanated both from its customers and from the competitors. The incumbent's and the entrants' product may or may not be perfect substitutes.

We start by characterizing the first-best allocation which essentially involves marginal cost pricing. Consequently, differences in prices reflect solely differences in marginal costs. Then we proceed to a more realistic setting where a fixed network cost has to be covered through the pricing scheme.

Our model can be used to study a number of settings depending on the specific assumptions which are made on demand, costs and on the regulatory environment. The current paper is meant to be a first step and we concentrate on a very stylized setting. Specifically, we assume throughout that the entrant does not deliver (there is no bypass). We also concentrate on the case where the access price for competitors is restricted to equal the rate charged for workshared mail to customers. We make no specific assumption at first on the degree of product differentiation between the incumbents' and entrant's product. However, we also look at the special case of perfect substitutes for which crisper results emerge.

2. MODEL

2.1 Operators, customers and preferences

There are two operators: the incumbent universal service operator *I* and an entrant *E*. The stylized postal network we consider consists of two segments. Segment 1 corresponds to a composite activity including collecting, sorting and transportation. This activity implies a constant marginal cost of c_1 for operator *I* and of k_E for operator *E*. Segment 2 is delivery. Operator *I*'s marginal delivery cost is c_2; Operator *E* does not have its own delivery network. In addition, there is a fixed cost of $F^I > 0$ for operator *I* and $F^E \geq 0$ for operator *E*.

There are two types of senders and two goods. The n_h senders of type *h* (households) consume good x which is supplied by *I* and uses both segments. The marginal cost of x is thus given by $c_1 + c_2$. The n_f customers of type *f* may or may not use segment 1 of operator *I*'s network. If they do not use segment 1 they consume good *z* which implies a marginal cost of $k + c_2$, where *k* is distributed over $\left[\underline{k}, \overline{k}\right]$ according to the cumulative distribution $G(k)$ with density $g(k)$. Observe that c_2 is the operator's cost, while *k* is directly born by the customer. Alternatively, they can consume good x for which they pay the same price as households,[5] or good *y* supplied by operator *E*. Prices are given by p_x and p_z for operator *I* and by p_y for operator *E*.

Let $S_h(x_h)$ denote the (gross) surplus of a households, while $S_f(x_f + z, y, k)$ represents the (gross) surplus of a sender of type *f* with characteristic *k*.[6] Observe that *k* represents not only the preparation cost, but also determines surplus and hence demand. Net surplus is obtained by subtracting total cost: payment to the operator plus cost of activity 1, if applicable. The demand function for a household is given by:

---

5 Except for the cost difference x and z are considered as perfect substitutes.

6 For simplicity we use surplus as a welfare measure for firms. From a strict welfare economics point of view, this can be understood as representing the surplus of the consumers who buy the goods produced by firms *f* which use postal services as inputs. One can easily show that our shortcut does not involve any loss of generality in the case where all downstream markets are competitive.

$$x_h(p) = \arg\max_x \{S_h(x) - px\}. \tag{1}$$

The demand functions of the representative sender f are obtained by maximizing

$$S_f\left(x_f + z, y, k\right) - p_x x_f - (p_z + k)z - p_y y$$
$$\text{s.t} \quad x_f, z \geq 0.$$

To characterize the solution to this problem define $\tilde{k} = p_x - p_z$. This yields the demand functions:

$$\begin{cases} x_f(p_x, p_y, k) \text{ and } y(p_x, p_y, k) & \text{when } k > \tilde{k} \text{ (so that } p_z + k > p_x) \\ z(p_z + k, p_y, k) \text{ and } y(p_z + k, p_y, k) & \text{when } k \leq \tilde{k} \text{ (so that } p_z + k \leq p_x). \end{cases}$$

To understand the determination of the demand functions, note that all users of type f for which $p_z + k \leq p_x$ (i.e., when $k \leq p_x - p_z = \tilde{k}$) find it profitable to buy good z (rather than x) at a level $z(p_z + k, p_y, k)$. Overall per-unit cost of z is equal to $p_z + k$; it is this overall cost rather than just p_z which determines demand. On the other hand, when $p_z + k > p_x$, it is cheaper to consume x (which is otherwise a perfect substitute of z) and demand is $x_f(p_x, p_y, k)$. Observe that when $p_z + k = p_x$ we have $x_f(p_x, p_y, k) = z(p_z + k, p_y, k)$; this property arises because, except of cost considerations, x and z are perfect substitutes. Either way, the firms may also consume the (differentiated) product offered by E, at levels specified by $y(\cdot)$.

Substituting demand functions into net surplus yields the following indirect utility functions:

$$V_h(p_x) = S_h\left[x_h(p_x)\right] - p_x x_h(p_x), \tag{2a}$$

$$V_f(p_x, p_z, p_y, k) = \begin{cases} S_f\left[z(p_z + k, p_y, k), y(p_z + k, p_y, k), k\right] \\ -(p_z + k)z(p_z + k, p_y, k) - p_y y(p_z + k, p_y, k) \\ \text{if } p_z + k \leq p_x, \\ S_f\left[x_f(p_x, p_y, k), y(p_x, p_y, k), k\right] \\ -p_x x_f(p_x, p_y, k) - p_y y(p_x, p_y k) \\ \text{if } p_z + k > p_x. \end{cases} \tag{2b}$$

2.2 Market demand, cost and profits

We are now in a position to determine market demand functions for the various (final) goods. The aggregate demand functions for the incumbent products are:

$$X(p_x, p_z, p_y) = n_h x_h(p_x) + n_f \int_{p_x - p_z}^{\bar{k}} x_f(p_x, p_y, k) g(k) dk \tag{3}$$

$$Z(p_x, p_z, p_y) = n_f \int_{\underline{k}}^{p_x - p_z} z(p_z + k, p_y, k) g(k) dk \tag{4}$$

The demand function for the operator E is:

$$\begin{aligned} Y(p_x, p_z, p_y) = n_f \int_{\underline{k}}^{p_x - p_z} y(p_y, p_z + k, k) g(k) dk \\ + n_f \int_{p_x - p_z}^{\bar{k}} y(p_y, p_x, k) g(k) dk \end{aligned} \tag{5}$$

Expression (3) provides the *total* demand for the incumbent's single piece mail. The first term on the RHS of this expression is the total demand by households, while the second term represents the total demand by the firms who do not workshare their mail (those with high levels of k). Expression (4) gives the firms' total demand for commercial (workshared) mail. It is the sum of individual demand levels for the firm with a low level of k. Finally, equation (5) represents the demand level for the entrants product. This demand *potentially* emanates from all firms; however, we do not rule out the case where $y = 0$ for some firms and especially those with a low level of *k*. This will of course be particularly relevant when the products are close substitutes; see the case of perfect substitutes below.

For the remainder of the paper, it is important to keep in mind that these demand levels are for *final* products (as opposed to intermediate goods). Since operator *E* does not deliver, *Y* will also be delivered through the incumbent's network. Consequently, the total (final and intermediate) demand for the incumbent's workshared mail will effectively be equal to $Z + Y$.

Per the assumptions introduced in subsection 1 we can write the costs functions as follows.

$$C^I = (c_1 + c_2)X + c_2(Z + Y) + F^I \tag{6}$$

$$C^E = (k^E + p_z)Y + F^E \tag{7}$$

To understand these expressions, recall that marginal costs are constant, that X used both segments of the network, while the $(Z+Y)$ units workshared mail only use the delivery network. Then entrant pays p_z *in lieu* of the delivery cost and it has a preparation cost of k^E (rather than c_1 for the incumbent).

Finally, profits can be expressed as follows.

$$\begin{aligned} \pi^I &= p_x X + p_z(Z + Y) - C^I, \\ &= [p_x - (c_1 + c_2)]X + [p_z - c_2](Z + Y) - F^I, \end{aligned} \tag{8}$$

$$\begin{aligned} \pi^E &= p_y Y - C^E, \\ &= \left[p_y - (k^E + p_z)\right]Y - F^E. \end{aligned} \tag{9}$$

Observe that both costs and profits can be expressed as functions of prices (and of the exogenous cost parameters). To obtain these functions is sufficient to substitute aggregate demand functions (3)–(5) in the expressions for costs and profits (6)–(9).

Our formal analysis concentrates on the competitive fringe case, where E price at marginal cost so that $p_y = k^E + p_z$. This assumption is of course only meaningful if we assume $F^E = 0$.

3. FIRST-BEST SOLUTION

The first-best solution constitutes an interesting benchmark. To obtain it, we maximize total surplus which is given by

$$W = V_h(p_x) + \int_{\underline{k}}^{\bar{k}} V_f(p_x, p_z, p_y, k) + \pi^I(p_x, p_z, p_y) + \pi^E(p_x, p_z, p_y), \tag{10}$$

with respect to prices (p_x, p_z, p_y). The result is well known and we skip the derivation here.[7] Differentiating (10) with respect to (p_x, p_z, p_y) and rearranging yields the following solution:

$$p_x = c_1 + c_2, \tag{11}$$

$$p_z = c_2, \tag{12}$$

$$p_y = k^E + c_2. \tag{13}$$

In words, all prices are set at marginal cost. Event though these expressions are standard, it has to be pointed out that they have an number of interesting implications in our setting.

First, we can think about $p_x - p_z$ as the "worksharing discount". From (11) and (12) it follows immediately that this discount is simply equal to c_1, that is the avoided cost. This in turn implies that we have "production efficiency" in the sense that a firm will workshare its mail if and only if its preparation cost is less than that of the operator. To see this recall that all firms with $k < \tilde{k} = p_x - p_z$ consume workshared mail and under marginal cost pricing this reduces to $k < c_2$.

---

[7] It can be obtained from expressions (27)–(28) in the appendix by setting $\lambda = 0$.

Second, we have assumed from the outset that p_z represents both the discounted price charged to customers and the access price charged to the competitor. Put differently, price discrimination between competitors and customers has been ruled out. It is interesting to note that in a first-best setting this does not effectively impose a restriction. Since the (marginal) delivery cost is the same whatever the "origin" of the mail product, its price ought to be the same for everyone anyway.

Third, we have solved this problem as if the regulator would control directly the entrant's price p_y. This is a technical simplification which is of no relevance in the competitive fringe case where $p_y = k^E + p_z$ so that when p_z is set according to (12), (13) is automatically satisfied. Finally, one can easily verify that with first-best prices, operator *I* realizes a deficit equal to F^I. Put differently, revenues do not cover fixed costs and the first-best solution is not feasible when the operator is required to break even. We now turn to the second best problem which arises when budget balancing is imposed.

4. SECOND-BEST SOLUTION

Set $p_y = k^E + p_z$ (competitive fringe) and maximize the welfare function subject to the constraint that the incumbent realizes nonnegative profits. The Lagrangian is given by:

$$L = V_h(p_x) + \int_{\underline{k}}^{\bar{k}} V_f(p_x, p_z, p_y, k) + (1+\lambda)\pi^I(p_x, p_z, p_y) + \pi^E$$

where $\lambda > 0$ is the Lagrange multiplier of the firms break-even constraint. Observe that $\pi^E \equiv 0$ by assumption (competitive fringe and $F^E = 0$). The FOCs are as follows:

$$\frac{\partial L}{\partial p_x} = -x_h(p_x) - \int_{p_x - p_z}^{\bar{k}} x_f(p_x, p_y, k) g(k) dk$$
$$+ (1+\lambda)\left[X + [p_x - (c_1 + c_2)]\frac{\partial X}{\partial p_x} + [p_z - c_2]\left(\frac{\partial Z}{\partial p_x} + \frac{\partial Y}{\partial p_x}\right)\right], \quad (14)$$

$$\frac{\partial L}{\partial p_z} = -\int_{\underline{k}}^{p_x - p_z} z(p_z + k, p_y, k) g(k) dk$$
$$-\left(\frac{dp_y}{dp_z}\right)\left[\int_{\underline{k}}^{p_x - p_z} y(p_z + k, p_y, k) g(k) dk + \int_{p_x - p_z}^{\bar{k}} y(p_x, p_y, k) g(k) dk\right]$$
$$+(1+\lambda)\left[Z + Y + \left[p_x - (c_1 + c_2)\right]\left(\frac{\partial X}{\partial p_z} + \frac{\partial X}{\partial p_y}\frac{dp_y}{dp_z}\right)\right]$$
$$+(1+\lambda)\left[\left[p_z - c_2\right]\left(\frac{\partial Z}{\partial p_z} + \frac{\partial Y}{\partial p_z} + \frac{\partial Z}{\partial p_y}\frac{dp_y}{dp_z} + \frac{\partial Y}{\partial p_y}\frac{dp_y}{dp_z}\right)\right], \tag{15}$$

where $dp_y / dp_z = 1$. For the sake of interpretation it is interesting to redefine the demand functions to account for the induced price variation of the entrant:

$$\tilde{X}(p_x, p_z) = X(p_x, p_z, p_y(p_z)), \tag{16}$$

$$\tilde{Y}(p_x, p_z) = Y(p_x, p_z, p_y(p_z)), \tag{17}$$

$$\tilde{Z}(p_x, p_z) = Z(p_x, p_z, p_y(p_z)), \tag{18}$$

where $p_y(p_z) = k^E + p_z$. Observe that these demand functions $\tilde{X}, \tilde{Y}$ and $\tilde{Z}$ only depend on operator I's prices which is convenient because these prices are the relevant decision variables in our problem.

We show in the appendix that the FOC can be rearranged to yield the following pricing rules:

$$\frac{p_x - (c_1 + c_2)}{p_x} = \frac{\lambda}{1+\lambda}\frac{1}{\hat{\sigma}_X} \tag{19}$$

$$\frac{p_z - c_2}{p_z} = \frac{\lambda}{1+\lambda}\frac{1}{\hat{\sigma}_{Y+Z}} \tag{20}$$

where $\hat{\sigma}_X$ and $\hat{\sigma}_{Y+Z}$ are the superelasticities of $\widetilde{X}$ and $\widetilde{Y}+\widetilde{Z}$ respectively. These expressions are the counterparts to equations (15) and (16) obtained by Billette de Villemeur et al. (2003a) for the monopoly case. To interpret them, one has to recall first that superelasticities are generalized demand elasticities which account for cross-price effects. When demand functions are independent, superelasticities are equal to ordinary price elasticities. In that case (19) and (20) reduce to "inverse elasticity rules". However, in our setting demand functions are not independent. A variation in one of the prices affects demand levels of the other goods and this brings about distortions which are accounted for in the superelasticities. Observe that when the goods are substitutes (as is the case here) one can show that superelasticities are smaller than ordinary price elasticities.

In spite of this complication it remains that the pricing rules have the familiar flavor and interpretation of Ramsey type rules. This point was made by Billette de Villemeur et al. (2003a) for a monopoly setting. Here we obtain similar expressions under competition. The main difference is that we have $Y+Z$ rather than just Z in the second expression. In either case this has to be interpreted as the total demand for workshared mail which here also emanates from the competing operators. The interesting feature is that while the incumbent's and the entrant's products are not perfect substitutes (for the customers) they are here treated as if they were perfect substitutes: only the sum of demands matters. This is because from operator I's perspective the two types of mail are indistinguishable; they have the same marginal cost (delivery only) and they are priced alike.

Combining these pricing expressions, we can determined the second best worksharing discount which is given by:

$$p_x - p_z = c_1 + \frac{\lambda}{1+\lambda}\left(\frac{p_x}{\hat{\sigma}_X} - \frac{p_z}{\hat{\sigma}_{Y+Z}}\right). \tag{21}$$

Under the plausible assumption that $\hat{\sigma}_{Y+Z} > \hat{\sigma}_X$ expression (21) implies that $p_x - p_z > c_1$. Observe that the application of the ECPR rule would require the discount to equal avoided costs, namely c_1. This would amount to apply the tradeoff which warrants first-best production efficiency. Not surprisingly this rule has to be amended in a second-best setting and under plausible assumption on the demand elasticities one can expect the discount to exceed avoided cost. Comparing this expression to its counterpart in Billette de Villemeur et al. (2003a), namely equation (17) it appears that the presence of competition does not appear to fundamentally affect the structure of the pricing rule. In either case, we obtain a *rule* which can be qualified as

"ECPR, adjusted for demand (super)elasticities". This does of course not imply that the actual *levels* prices are the same or are similar. The demand functions underlying the superelasticities are affected by the presence of competition. We shall have a closer look at this issue for the special case of perfect substitutes to which we now turn.

5. THE CASE OF PERFECT SUBSTITUTES

We now turn to the special case where the incumbent and the entrant's products are perfect substitutes. Observe that this is the case on which Panzar (2003) concentrates. Though extreme, this does not appear to be a totally meaningless setting to consider here. One can argue that any degree of differentiation there may be between the two operators is likely to be mitigated by the fact that operator *E* uses operator *I*'s delivery network. In other words, once they get to the delivery segment the three products *X, Y* and *Z* become indistinguishable.

With $p_y = k^E + p_z$ (competitive fringe), the demand of type *f* customers has the following properties:

$$\begin{cases} x_f = 0; \quad y = 0; \quad z_k > 0 \quad \text{if } k < \inf\left\{k^E, p_x - p_z\right\} \\ x_f = 0; \quad y > 0; \quad z_k = 0 \quad \text{if } k^E < \inf\left\{k, p_x - p_z\right\} \\ x_f > 0; \quad y = 0; \quad z_k = 0 \quad \text{if } p_x - p_z < k^E < k. \end{cases}$$

Observe that demand function are now discontinues when $k^E < p_x - p_z = \tilde{k}$. To determine the solution, two regimes have to be considered separately. We have either $k^E \leq \tilde{k}$ (Regime *I*) or $k^E > \tilde{k}$ (Regime *II*).

5.1 Regime $I : k^E \leq \tilde{k}$

In this case, no customers of type *f* consume product x. The demand functions for the incumbent products are:

$$X(p_x) = x_h(p_x),$$

$$Z(p_z) = \int_{\underline{k}}^{k^E} z_k(p_z + k)g(k)dk.$$

The demand function for the operator E is:

$$Y(p_z) = \int_{k^E}^{\bar{k}} y_k(p_z + k^E) g(k) dk.$$

Remark that, since y and x (hence z) are perfect substitutes, $y_k(p) = z_k(p)$. As a result, this is "as if" the entry of firm E were allowing firms with $k \geq k^E$ to sort their mail at a cost of only k^E. Firm I is now facing a set of firms with a distribution of k which is cut from above at the level k^E and all these firms consume the workshared mail.

Appendix B shows that the optimal pricing rules are now given by

$$\frac{p_x - (c_1 + c_2)}{p_x} = \frac{\lambda}{1+\lambda} \frac{1}{\varepsilon_{X_h}} \tag{22}$$

$$\frac{p_z - c_2}{p_z} = \frac{\lambda}{1+\lambda} \frac{1}{\varepsilon_{Y+Z}} \tag{23}$$

Where ε_{X_h} and ε_{Y+Z} are ordinary price elasticities (absolute values). Observe that we have returned to ordinary price elasticities rather than superelasticities which where obtained in the general case. This is because, with perfect substitutes, cross-price elasticities (between X on the one hand and $Z + Y$ on the other hand) are zero *within a given regime.*

5.2 Regime $II : k^E > \tilde{k}$

In the case where $k^E > p_x - p_z$, the demand for the operator E is zero and the demand functions for the incumbent products are:

$$X(p_x, p_z) = x_h(p_x) + \int_{p_x - p_z}^{\bar{k}} x_f(p_x, k) g(k) dk$$

$$Z(p_x, p_z) = \int_{\underline{k}}^{p_x - p_z} z(p_z + k, k) g(k) dk$$

and we are back to the model of worksharing. Optimal pricing rules are then given by expressions (15) and (17) in Billette de Villemeur and *al.* (2003a).

5.3 Which Regime is relevant?

The condition defining the applicable regime depends on $\tilde{k}$ and thus on the prices. Formally, one would have to evaluate welfare at the solutions achieved in either regime and compare welfare levels to determine the global optimum. This is a complicated task and the problem cannot be done based on the first order conditions alone. However, it is quite clear that the solution will depend on the relative efficiency of the two operator's on segment 1, i.e. on the comparison between k^E and c_1.

The first interesting property one can show is that when $k^E \leq c_1$, Regime *II* cannot occur. In other words, it is never optimal to (totally) exclude an efficient competitor from the market. To see that, recall from Billette de Villemeur et *al.* (2003a) that Regime *II* yields $\tilde{k} = p_x - p_z > c_1$, hence $k^E \leq c_1$ is incompatible with the condition for *this regime to arise,* namely $k^E > \tilde{k}$.

By continuity, this property implies that when $k^E > c_1$ but not "too large", Regime *I* will continue to prevail. In other words, at the second best optimum, it may be interesting to "tolerate" a competitor who is slightly less efficient than the incumbent (even though its product is a perfect substitute to that of operator *I*). This is because the presence of *E* allows for a solution which differentiates between firms with high *k* (who will consume *Y*) and households (who consume *X*). If the competitor is not in the market, both of these groups consume *X* at a uniform price.

Finally, when k^E become sufficiently large the solution will imply Regime *II* there is no room at a second best optimum for a very inefficient entrant.

5.4 Discounts under monopoly and under competition

Having characterized the solution under competition we can now attempt to compare it to the monopoly case. In particular it is interesting to study how the worksharing discount $p_x - p_z$ is affected by the presence of the competitor. To do this we shall remain within the setting of perfect substitutes.

Not surprisingly, the answer depends (among other things) on the cost of the entrant k^E. To see this let us start from the monopoly solution denoted p_x^m and p_z^m, with $\tilde{k}^m = p_x^m - p_z^m$. We know from Billette de Villemeur et al. (2003a) that $\tilde{k}^m > c_1$ (under plausible assumptions on demand elasticities). Depending on the entrant's cost we can then have three configurations. First, there is the rather trivial case where the entrant has large preparation costs, $k^E \geq \tilde{k}^m$. In that case, we have Regime *II* and monopoly prices (and discounts) will continue to prevail. Second and at the other extreme, we can have $k^E < c_1$, which of course implies $k^E < \tilde{k}^m$. As shown in the previous subsection Regime *I* prevails and the solution is given by (22) and (23). To compare these to their monopoly counterparts, expressions (15) and (16) of Billette de Villemeur et al. (2003a), we have to assess the impact of the presence of the competitor on the demand elasticities. Roughly speaking, the firms with the larger *k* (which are also the ones with the relatively less elastic demand) consume x under monopoly and *y* (and thus indirectly also *z*) under competition. It is quite clear that this tends to make the demand for *X* less elastic *(*as the consumers*)* with the more elastic demand switch to *Y*.[8] Consequently, we can expect p_x to increase.[9] Furthermore, the switching consumers have smaller elasticities than the low *k.* firms. Consequently, they will cause the elasticity for *Z* to be lower than in the monopoly case. But then p_z would also tend to increase and the overall impact on $\tilde{k}$ appears to be ambiguous.[10]

Finally, there is the case where $c_1 \leq k^E \leq \tilde{k}^m$. In words, the entrant's preparation cost is between that of the incumbent and the monopoly level of the worksharing discount. In particular, consider the case where $k^E = \tilde{k}^m - \varepsilon$ where $\varepsilon > 0$ is small. Now, if operator *I* maintains its monopoly prices, all consumers to the right of $\tilde{k}^m$ will switch from x to *y* (while essentially nothing else changes). With $k^E > c_1$ this switch can only

[8] The demand of firms with high preparation cost is expected to be nevertheless more elastic than that of houselholds.

[9] This is a very rough argument of course because the monopoly expression involve superelasticities. Our arguement assumes thus implicitely that cross-price effects are not too significiant.

[10] All these arguments are for a given level of λ. In reality λ would of course change. Practically speaking this means that when both prices increase (starting from the Ramsey solution) we can expect profits to increase. But then prices can again be lowered without violating the break-even constraint. This introduces yet another effect which of course does not make the result any less ambiguous.

decrease welfare (because total preparation costs increase). This welfare loss can easily be avoided when operator *I* changes its prices to reduce $\tilde{k}$ to a level below k^E. Since ε is small and since we start from a optimal solution, this variation will have no first order impact on welfare. It does, however, avoid the increase in preparation cost. Consequently, it will clearly dominate the status quo (maintaining monopoly prices upon entry) with higher preparation costs. To sum up, in this case we can conclude unambiguously that competition decreases the level of the discount. Now, as ε increases, so that k^E will become closer and closer to c_1 we can continue to make this argument. However, the price adjustment need to match k^E become larger and larger and this will also imply a welfare loss. This has to be balanced against the reduction in preparation cost (which becomes of course smaller and smaller as k^E approaches c_1). Thus at some point we will switch to Regime *I* and return to case where the impact on $\tilde{k}$ is ambiguous.

6. CONCLUDING REMARKS

The current regulatory debate in the postal sector calls for an in depth study of the appropriate pricing rules in a competitive environment. Such an investigation has to encompass both worksharing discounts granted to customers and the pricing of the mail which is prepared by competitors but delivered by the incumbent postal operator. Building on our earlier paper which had studied the pricing of worksharing under monopoly, we have provided a framework which is suitable to study jointly access and worksharing in a liberalized industry. However, in the current paper we have not fully explored the potential of our framework. We have looked only at one scenarios and probably one of the simplest. The natural next steps would be for instance to introduce bypass (in delivery), to consider delivery areas with different costs, etc. This is left for future research.

In the meantime we can already learn from our partial results that the optimal prices are not going to be determined according to simple ad hoc rules which moreover would be valid in all circumstances. The pricing rules are complex in the sense that many factors, including demand, cost and regulatory rules will matter. We have already discussed the role of the entrant sorting cost k^E in the previous section. More interestingly, one can easily see that the arguments used to asses the impact of entry on the worksharing discount (in Subsection 5.4) crucially depend on the requirement the same p_z applies to both to operator *E* and to customers. The impact of bypass can be expected to be even more significant. As long as there is no bypass operator *I* set positive markups on *all* products, including the one sold by competitors to finance its fixed cost. The other operators' products are of course only "taxed" indirectly, through the access charge. However, as long the operator *E* has no delivery network this is of no relevance. With the possibility of bypass, on the other hand, it is more difficult or may even be impossible to realize markups on the competitor's products. Summing up, the main conclusion to be drawn is thus that the impact of liberalization is very difficult to assess and will very much depend on the exact (competitive) environment which is considered.

A. APPENDIX

A.1. Derivation of expressions (19) and (20)

The derivatives of the redefined demand functions are given by

$$\frac{\partial \tilde{X}}{\partial p_x} = \frac{\partial X}{\partial p_x} \quad \text{and} \quad \frac{\partial \tilde{X}}{\partial p_z} = \frac{\partial X}{\partial p_z} + \frac{\partial X}{\partial p_y}\frac{dp_y}{dp_z} \tag{24}$$

$$\frac{\partial \tilde{Y}}{\partial p_x} = \frac{\partial Y}{\partial p_x} \quad \text{and} \quad \frac{\partial \tilde{Y}}{\partial p_z} = \frac{\partial Y}{\partial p_z} + \frac{\partial Y}{\partial p_y}\frac{dp_y}{dp_z} \tag{25}$$

$$\frac{\partial \tilde{Z}}{\partial p_x} = \frac{\partial Z}{\partial p_x} \quad \text{and} \quad \frac{\partial \tilde{Z}}{\partial p_z} = \frac{\partial Z}{\partial p_z} + \frac{\partial Z}{\partial p_y}\frac{dp_y}{dp_z} \tag{26}$$

Using (16)–(18) and (24)–(26), the FOCs can be rewritten as:

$$\frac{\partial L}{\partial p_x} = \lambda X + (1+\lambda)\left[p_x - (c_1 + c_2)\right]\frac{\partial X}{\partial p_x} + (1+\lambda)\left[p_z - c_2\right]\left(\frac{\partial Z}{\partial p_x} + \frac{\partial Y}{\partial p_x}\right), \tag{27}$$

$$\frac{\partial L}{\partial p_z} = \lambda(Z+Y) + (1+\lambda)\left[p_x - (c_1 + c_2\right]\frac{\partial \tilde{X}}{\partial p_z} + (1+\lambda)\left[p_z - c_2\right]\left(\frac{\partial \tilde{Z}}{\partial p_z} + \frac{\partial \tilde{Y}}{\partial p_z}\right), \tag{28}$$

which gives the "standard" Ramsey-like system:

$$\frac{p_x-(c_1+c_2)}{p_x}=\frac{\lambda}{1+\lambda}\frac{1}{\varepsilon_X}+\left[p_z-c_2\right]\left(\frac{(\partial Z/\partial p_x)}{(-\partial X/\partial p_x)}+\frac{(\partial Y/\partial p_x)}{(-\partial X/\partial p_x)}\right)$$

$$\frac{p_z-c_2}{p_z}=\frac{\lambda}{(1+\lambda)}\frac{1}{\sigma_{Y+Z}}(Z+Y)+\left[p_x-(c_1+c_2)\right]\frac{\partial\tilde{X}/\partial p_z}{\left(-\partial\tilde{Z}/\partial p_z\right)+\left(-\partial\tilde{Y}/\partial p_z\right)},$$

where

$$\varepsilon_X=\frac{p_x}{X}\left(\frac{-\partial X}{\partial p_x}\right),$$

$$\sigma_{Y+Z}=\frac{p_z}{Z+Y}\left(\frac{-\partial\tilde{Z}}{\partial p_z}+\frac{-\partial\tilde{Y}}{\partial p_z}\right)=\frac{Z}{Z+Y}\sigma_Z+\frac{Y}{Z+Y}\sigma_Y,$$

and

$$\sigma_Z=\frac{p_z}{Z}\left(\frac{-\partial\tilde{Z}}{\partial p_z}\right)\text{ and }\sigma_Y=\frac{p_Z}{Y}\left(\frac{-\partial\tilde{Y}}{\partial p_z}\right).$$

In matrix notation the FOC write:

$$\begin{pmatrix}\left(\dfrac{\partial X}{\partial p_x}\right) & \left(\dfrac{\partial Z}{\partial p_x}+\dfrac{\partial Y}{\partial p_x}\right)\\ \left(\dfrac{\partial\tilde{X}}{\partial p_z}\right) & \left(\dfrac{\partial\tilde{Z}}{\partial p_z}+\dfrac{\partial\tilde{Y}}{\partial p_z}\right)\end{pmatrix}\begin{pmatrix}p_x-(c_1+c_2)\\ p_z-c_2\end{pmatrix}=-\frac{\lambda}{1+\lambda}\begin{pmatrix}X\\ Z+Y\end{pmatrix},$$

which is easily be solved to yield

$$p_x-\left(c_1+c_2\right)=-\frac{\lambda}{1+\lambda}\frac{X\left(\dfrac{\partial\tilde{Z}}{\partial p_z}+\dfrac{\partial\tilde{Y}}{\partial p_z}\right)-(Z+Y)\left(\dfrac{\partial Z}{\partial p_x}+\dfrac{\partial Y}{\partial p_x}\right)}{\left(\dfrac{\partial X}{\partial p_x}\right)\left(\dfrac{\partial\tilde{Z}}{\partial p_z}+\dfrac{\partial\tilde{Y}}{\partial p_z}\right)-\left(\dfrac{\partial\tilde{X}}{\partial p_z}\right)\left(\dfrac{\partial Z}{\partial p_x}+\dfrac{\partial Y}{\partial p_x}\right)},$$

$$p_z-c_2=-\frac{\lambda}{1+\lambda}\frac{\left(\dfrac{\partial X}{\partial p_x}\right)(Z+Y)-\left(\dfrac{\partial\tilde{X}}{\partial p_z}\right)X}{\left(\dfrac{\partial X}{\partial p_x}\right)\left(\dfrac{\partial\tilde{Z}}{\partial p_z}+\dfrac{\partial\tilde{Y}}{\partial p_z}\right)-\left(\dfrac{\partial\tilde{X}}{\partial p_z}\right)\left(\dfrac{\partial Z}{\partial p_x}+\dfrac{\partial Y}{\partial p_x}\right)},$$

that can be rewritten as

$$\frac{p_x-\left(c_1+c_2\right)}{p_x}=\frac{\lambda}{1+\lambda}\frac{\dfrac{p_z}{Z+Y}\left(\dfrac{-\partial\tilde{Z}}{\partial p_z}+\dfrac{-\partial\tilde{Y}}{\partial p_z}\right)+\dfrac{p_z(Z+Y)}{p_xX}\left(\dfrac{p_x}{Z+Y}\right)\left(\dfrac{\partial Z}{\partial p_x}+\dfrac{\partial Y}{\partial p_x}\right)}{\left(\dfrac{p_x}{X}\right)\left(\dfrac{-\partial X}{\partial p_x}\right)\dfrac{p_z}{Z+Y}\left(\dfrac{-\partial\tilde{Z}}{\partial p_z}+\dfrac{-\partial\tilde{Y}}{\partial p_z}\right)-\left(\dfrac{p_z}{X}\right)\left(\dfrac{\partial\tilde{X}}{\partial p_z}\right)\left(\dfrac{p_x}{Z+Y}\right)\left(\dfrac{\partial Z}{\partial p_x}+\dfrac{\partial Y}{\partial p_x}\right)}$$

$$=\frac{\lambda}{1+\lambda}\frac{\sigma_{Y+Z}+\dfrac{p_z(Z+Y)}{p_xX}\sigma_{(Z+Y)X}}{\varepsilon_X\sigma_{Y+Z}-\sigma_{XZ}\sigma_{(Z+Y)X}},$$

$$\frac{p_z-c_2}{p_z}=-\frac{\lambda}{1+\lambda}\frac{\dfrac{p_x}{X}\left(\dfrac{-\partial X}{\partial p_x}\right)+\dfrac{p_xX}{p_z(Z+Y)}\left(\dfrac{p_z}{X}\right)\left(\dfrac{\partial\tilde{X}}{\partial p_z}\right)}{\left(\dfrac{p_x}{X}\right)\left(\dfrac{\partial X}{\partial p_x}\right)\left(\dfrac{p_z}{Z+Y}\right)\left(\dfrac{\partial\tilde{Z}}{\partial p_z}+\dfrac{\partial\tilde{Y}}{\partial p_z}\right)-\left(\dfrac{p_z}{X}\right)\left(\dfrac{\partial\tilde{X}}{\partial p_z}\right)\left(\dfrac{p_x}{Z+Y}\right)\left(\dfrac{\partial Z}{\partial p_x}+\dfrac{\partial Y}{\partial p_x}\right)}$$

$$=\frac{\lambda}{1+\lambda}\frac{\varepsilon_X+\dfrac{p_xX}{p_z(Z+Y)}\sigma_{XZ}}{\varepsilon_X\sigma_{Y+Z}-\sigma_{XZ}\sigma_{(Z+Y)X}}$$

where

$$\sigma_{XZ} = \left(\frac{p_z}{X}\right)\left(\frac{\partial \tilde{X}}{\partial p_z}\right),$$

$$\begin{aligned}\sigma_{(Z+Y)X} &= \left(\frac{p_x}{Z+Y}\right)\left(\frac{\partial Z}{\partial p_x}+\frac{\partial Y}{\partial p_x}\right)\\ &= \left(\frac{Z}{Z+Y}\right)\left(\frac{p_x}{Z}\frac{\partial Z}{\partial p_x}\right)+\left(\frac{Y}{Z+Y}\right)\left(\frac{p_x}{Y}\frac{\partial Y}{\partial p_x}\right)\\ &= \left(\frac{Z}{Z+Y}\right)\sigma_{ZX}+\left(\frac{Y}{Z+Y}\right)\sigma_{YX}.\end{aligned}$$

Rearranging these expressions and defining superelasticities in the usual way:

$$\hat{\sigma}_X = \frac{\varepsilon_X \sigma_{Y+Z} - \sigma_{XZ}\sigma_{(Z+Y)X}}{\sigma_{Y+Z}+\sigma_{XZ}},$$

$$\hat{\sigma}_{Y+Z} = \frac{\sigma_{Y+Z}\varepsilon_X - \sigma_{XZ}\sigma_{(Z+Y)X}}{\varepsilon_X+\sigma_{(Z+Y)X}},$$

yields expression (19) and (20). To simplify the expression we have used the property that demand functions for $\tilde{X}$ and for $\left(\tilde{Z}+\tilde{Y}\right)$ have symmetric cross derivatives:

$$\begin{aligned}\frac{\partial \tilde{X}}{\partial p_z} &= \frac{\partial X}{\partial p_z}+\frac{\partial X}{\partial p_y}\\ &= x_f\left(p_x,p_y,\tilde{k}\right)g\left(\tilde{k}\right)+\int_{p_x-p_z}^{\bar{k}}\frac{\partial x_f(p_x,p_y,k)}{\partial p_y}g(k)dk\\ &= z\left(p_z+\tilde{k},p_y,\tilde{k}\right)g\left(\tilde{k}\right)+\int_{p_x-p_z}^{\bar{k}}\frac{\partial y(p_x,p_y,k)}{\partial p_x}g(k)dk\\ &= \frac{\partial Z}{\partial p_x}+\frac{\partial Y}{\partial p_x}=\frac{\partial \tilde{Z}}{\partial p_x}+\frac{\partial \tilde{Y}}{\partial p_x},\end{aligned}$$

which in turn arises because

$$\frac{\partial x_f\left(p_x, p_y, k\right)}{\partial p_y} = \frac{\partial y\left(p_x, p_y, k\right)}{\partial p_x},$$

and which implies $p_z(Z+Y)\sigma_{(Z+Y)X} = p_x X \sigma_{XZ}$.

A.2. Derivation of expressions (22) and (23)

First observe that in this case we have:

$$\frac{\partial \tilde{X}}{\partial p_x} = \frac{\partial x_h}{\partial p_x} \text{ and } \frac{\partial \tilde{X}}{\partial p_z} = 0$$

$$\frac{\partial \tilde{Y}}{\partial p_x} = 0 \quad \text{and } \frac{\partial \tilde{Y}}{\partial p_z} = \frac{\partial Y}{\partial p_y}$$

$$\frac{\partial \tilde{Z}}{\partial p_z} = 0 \quad \text{and } \frac{\partial \tilde{Z}}{\partial p_z} = \frac{\partial Z}{\partial p_z}.$$

Using these properties to simplify the FOCs (27) and (28) one obtains

$$\frac{\partial L}{\partial p_x} = \lambda x_h + (1+\lambda)\left[p_x - (c_1 + c_2)\right]\frac{\partial x_h}{\partial p_x}$$

$$\frac{\partial L}{\partial p_z} = \lambda(Z+Y) + (1+\lambda)\left[p_z - c_2\right]\left(\frac{\partial Z}{\partial p_z} + \frac{\partial Y}{\partial p_y}\right),$$

which can easily be rearranged to yield (22) and (23).

REFERENCES

Armstrong, M. 2002. "The Theory of Access Pricing and Interconnection." In *Handbook of Telecommunication,* vol 1., edited by M. Cave et al., 295–386.

Billette de Villemeur, E, H. Cremer, B. Roy. and J. Toledano. 2002. "Pricing and Worksharing Discounts in the Postal Sector." In *Postal and Delivery Services: Delivering on Competition*, edited by M. A. Crew and P. R. Kleindorfer. Boston, MA: Kluwer Academic Publishers.

Billette de Villemeur, E, H. Cremer, B. Roy, and J. Toledano. 2003a. "Optimal Pricing and Global Price-Cap in the Postal Sector." *Journal of Regulatory Economics* 24: 49-62.

Billette de Villemeur, E, H. Cremer, B. Roy, and J. Toledano. 2003b. "Pricing and Imperfect Competition in the Postal Sector", mimeo, IDEI, University of Toulouse.

Billette de Villemeur, E, H. Cremer, B. Roy, and J. Toledano. 2004. "Access and (Non-) Uniform Pricing in the Postal Sector." In *Competitive Transformation of the Postal and Delivery Sector*, edited by M. A. Crew and P. R. Kleindorfer. Boston MA: Kluwer Academic Publishers, 43–68.

Cremer, H., M. De Rycke and A. Grimaud. 1995. "Alternative Scenarios for the Reform of Postal Services: Optimal Pricing and Welfare." In *Commercialization of Postal and Delivery Services*, edited by M. A. Crew and P. R. Kleindorfer. Boston, MA: Kluwer Academic Publishers, 247–267.

Cremer, H., M. De Rycke and A. Grimaud. 1997. "Costs and Benefits of Universal Service Obligations in the Postal Sector." In *Managing Change in the Postal and Delivery Industries*, edited by M. A. Crew and P. R. Kleindorfer. Boston, MA: Kluwer Academic Publishers, 22–41.

Cremer, H., A. Grimaud and J.-J. Laffont. 2000. "The Cost of Universal Service in the Postal Sector." In *Current Directions in Postal Reform*, edited by M. A. Crew and P. R. Kleindorfer. Boston MA: Kluwer Academic Publishers, 47–68.

Cremer, H., J.P. Florens, A. Grimaud, S. Marcy, B. Roy. and J. Toledano. 2001. "Entry and Competition in the Postal Market : Foundations for the Construction of Entry Scenarios", *Journal of Regulatory Economics* 19: 107-121.

Crew M. and P. Kleindorfer. 1995. "Pricing in Postal Service under Competitive Entry", in *Commercialization of Postal and Delivery Services*, edited by M. A. Crew and P. R. Kleindorfer, Boston, MA: Kluwer Academic Publishers, 117–136.

Crew M. and P. Kleindorfer. 2002. "Balancing Access and the Universal Service Obligation." In *Postal and Delivery Services: Delivering on Competition*, edited by M. A. Crew and P. R. Kleindorfer. Boston, MA : Kluwer Academic Publishers, 3–32.

Laffont, J.J. and J. Tirole. 1996. "Creating Competition through Interconnection: Theory and Practice." *Journal of Regulatory Economics* 10: 227–256.

Laffont, J.J. and J. Tirole. 2000. *Competition in Telecommunications.* Cambridge MA: MIT Press.

Law, P. 1997. "Welfare effects of pricing in anticipation of Laspeyres." *Bulletin of Economic Research* 49: 17–27.

Panzar, J. 2003. "The Economic Effects of Combining Liberalization and Unbundling in Postal Markets," mimeo.

Sherman, R. 2001. "Optimal Worksharing Discounts." *Journal of Regulatory Economics* 19: 81–92.

Chapter 8

Access Pricing in the Postal Sector

Results from a Model with Bypass and Customer Direct Access

Philippe De Donder[1], Helmuth Cremer[1], and Frank Rodriguez[2]
University of Toulouse, IDEI & GREMAQ[1] and Royal Mail Group[2]

1.

The economics of access pricing to the postal network has attracted a significant amount of research interest, much of it arising from the EU Postal Directive of 2002 (Official Journal, L176/21).[1] The Directive requires that access prices should be on an avoided cost basis and that, in addition to being available to entrants, "any such tariffs shall also be available to private customers who post under similar conditions."[2] In a liberalized environment, some private customers, at least, then effectively have three alternatives with regard to their choice over postal services. Customers, first, can use current end-to-end services of the universal service provider (USP); secondly, customers can make use of alternative services offered by entrants which, in

[1] Recent contributions to this literature include papers by Billette de Villemeur et al (2004), Crew and Kleindorfer (2002, 2004), De Donder et al (2002a, 2004) and Panzar (2002).

[2] Official Journal, L176/21, 2002. Article 12. The full text reads:
"whenever universal service providers apply special tariffs, for example for services for business, bulk mailers or consolidators of mail from different customers, they shall apply the principles of transparency and non-discrimination with regard both to the tariffs and to the associated conditions. The tariffs shall take account of the avoided costs, as compared to the standard service covering the complete range of features offered for the clearance, transport, sorting and delivery of individual postal items and, together with the associated conditions, shall apply equally both as between different third parties and as between third parties and universal service providers supplying equivalent services. Any such tariffs shall also be available to private customers who post under similar conditions".

turn, may be provided either through the networks of entrants (bypass) or by the use, in part, of the USP's network (access); or, thirdly, customers can access the USP's network directly themselves. The latter already occurs in some countries through presortation of mail which attracts workshare discounts off public tariffs. However, the Directive opens explicitly the possibility of access to the delivery network of USPs, or downstream access, where previously access, in those countries where this has been possible, has applied only to upstream activities. The possibility of customer direct access to the delivery network of the USP (CDA) is an important development and extends the possibility of worksharing up to the final stage of delivery.

In an earlier paper (De Donder et al, 2004) we developed a model for deriving optimal rules for access pricing to the delivery network of a USP under conditions where only entrants were allowed access to the USP's network and where entrants could choose whether to use the USP's network or provide a full end-to-end (E2E) service themselves. In addition to access, the USP continued to offer a single retail, E2E service at a uniform tariff which applied across both an urban and a rural area. The paper concluded that optimal access charges follow the efficient component pricing rule (ECPR)[3], modified to take account of two additional factors. The first of these is the extent to which access displaces traffic previously using the USP's E2E service and the second is the extent of the financial loss arising from entry through bypass. The possibility that such entry results in a financial loss for the USP also raises the issue of whether the combined effect of bypass with access to the USP's network raises or lowers economic welfare.

In the current paper we extend that initial work in two significant ways. First, in the earlier model we assumed that an initial break-even price of the USP's retail service was constant and derived optimal rules on that basis. However, it is more satisfactory to derive also an optimal uniform tariff for the USP's retail service so that optimal prices for access and the uniform retail tariff are derived jointly. Secondly, the earlier model did not allow for the possibility of customer direct access to the USP's delivery network (CDA). As noted above, this option is now available to private customers which means that they can bypass both the USP's upstream network and entrants' services by undertaking upstream activity themselves.[4] The current paper considers the impact of CDA on optimal rules for the pricing of both access and the uniform retail tariff of the USP and the accompanying impacts on volumes, the USP's profit and economic welfare.

---

[3] The term ECPR is used in the narrow sense of the "margin rule" (Armstrong, 2002) equivalent to "avoided cost" as contained in the EU 2002 Postal Directive.

[4] Customers may use third parties for at least part of this work, for example, trucking of presorted mail to inward mail centers for final delivery by the USP.

The paper is structured as follows. Section 2 briefly sets out the model. Key formulae with regard to optimal pricing rules for access and uniform retail prices are reported in an appendix and the formal development and derivation of these results is set out in a separate paper. The main focus of the current paper is on results and implications for access rather than formal proofs. For this we make use of the calibration in De Donder et al (2004) extended to allow modeling of CDA. The calibration values used are also summarized in section 2. The results under optimal access and uniform retail prices are reported in three stages in order to gain insights into the impacts of the various components of the general case. These stages are entrant access only without bypass; entrant access only but allowing bypass; and thirdly, the most general case, which the EU Postal Directive mandates, of entrant access with bypass and with customer direct access. The results are reported in sections 3 to 5. A final section summarizes and concludes drawing out the main implications from our analysis.

2. MODEL AND CALIBRATION

2.1 Model

In this section, we describe the model in its most general formulation that is incorporating both entrant's bypass and CDA. The model includes two postal operators: the USP and an entrant which acts as a competitive fringe. Both the USP and the entrant offer a single E2E product (average mail) which can be sent to the rural or to the urban area. The USP has to serve both markets at a uniform price. The entrant is not subject to a universal service obligation and chooses which market (urban and/or rural) to serve and at which price. The entrant can choose to deliver mail itself or to access the USP delivery network. Consumers can also access the USP delivery network directly and the USP is required to post the same access price for the entrant and for CDA customers.

We model this situation as a 3-good (USP and entrant's E2E letters, CDA) and 2-market (urban, rural) economy, with a representative sender. We assume that the two markets are independent (the prices on one area do not affect the number of letters sent to the other area) and that the three goods offered are (imperfect) substitutes on any given market, so that a price increase in one market increases the quantity of the other products sold on the same market.

The price of CDA is the sum of the preparation cost (i.e. presorting and bringing the mail to the interconnecting point on the USP network) and the access charge. In reality, preparation costs differ significantly across mail senders. In order to incorporate this heterogeneity, we assume when introducing CDA that there are two representative senders of mail to the urban area: large scale senders and small scale senders (defined in such a way that they each represent one half of the market). Although, in principle, both large scale and small scale senders are able to take up the option of CDA, in practice effectively only large senders are in a position to choose CDA, since taking mail to the USP interconnection point is only likely to be economic when volumes are high. Similarly, we assume that no CDA happens to the rural area because volumes are low and this also simplifies the model.

Although the focus of this paper is not on the theoretical derivation of optimal prices, it is useful to set out the key elements of the model formally. We denote by an upper script I variables pertaining to the USP E2E product, by E to the entrant and by D to CDA. We use the lower script U for the urban market and R for the rural market. We denote by q_j^i the demand for E2E mail addressed to operator $i \in \{I, E\}$ for delivery in area $j \in \{U, R\}$ and by q^D the demand for CDA. The universal service obligation translates into a global fixed cost for the USP (denoted by F) while the entrant does not face any fixed cost. The USP uniform price for its E2E retail service is denoted by p.

We separate the postal activity into two segments: one for collection-sorting-transportation and a second for delivery. Both operators and large scale senders are active on the first segment. Their (constant) marginal cost is $c^i, i \in \{I, E, D\}$ respectively. Operator i*'s* constant marginal cost of delivery to area j is denoted by $d_j^{\,i}, i \in \{I, E\}, j \in \{U, R\}$. The USP charges a constant unit access price of a_j for each letter that the entrant or large scale senders ask the USP to deliver to area $j \in \{U, R\}$[5]. z_j^E measures the number of letters effectively delivered by the entrant in area $j \in \{U, R\}$, so that $q_j^E - z_j^E$ gives the amount of access to area $j \in \{U, R\}$ sold by the USP to the entrant.

The USP's profit is given by

[5] It would be straightforward to include also an explicit acceptance or metering charge incurred by the USP in providing access, as in Crew and Kleindorfer(2002). Such a charge enters the results below in the expected way and has been excluded from the discussion here to simplify the model.

$$\Pi^I = \left(p - c^I\right)\left(q_U^I + q_R^I\right) - d_U^I q_U^I - d_R^I q_R^I - F$$
$$+ \left(a_U - d_U^I\right)\left(q_U^E + q^D - z_U^E\right) + \left(a_R - d_R^I\right)\left(q_R^E - z_R^E\right),$$

where the first line gives the profit made on the E2E letters and the second line is the profit made on selling access. The USP sells access to its urban delivery network (at the same unit price) both to the entrant and to customers, while only the entrant accesses the USP rural delivery network. Entrant's profit is given by

$$\Pi^E = \left(p_U^E - c^E\right)q_U^E + \left(p_R^E - c^E\right)q_R^E - d_U^E z_U^E - d_R^E z_R^E$$
$$- a_U\left(q_U^E - z_U^E\right) - a_R\left(q_R^E - z_R^E\right),$$

with $0 \leq z_j^E \leq q_j^E, j \in \{U, R\}$. Maximization of entrant's profit gives that

$$z_j^E = \begin{cases} 0 \; if \, d_j^E \geq a_j \\ q_j^E \; if \, d_j^E < a_j \end{cases},$$

that is, that the entrant delivers itself only if it is strictly cheaper to do so rather than to ask access. We assume that the entrant acts as a competitive fringe i.e. that any positive profit made by the entrant would attract new competitors until prices are driven down to average (and marginal) costs. In other words, the entrant uses marginal cost pricing and we have $p_j^E = c^E + \min\left(d_j^E, a_j\right)$.

We look for the optimal access charges and USP retail price, i.e. access charges a_U, a_R and price p that simultaneously maximize total welfare (the sum of postal operators' profits and consumer surpluses) under the constraint that the USP profit is non-negative ($\Pi^I \geq 0$). This can be viewed as the regulator's maximization problem and optimal access and uniform retail price formulae derived from this model (with and without CDA and break-even constraint) are reported in the appendix.

We note here, however, that in this more general model we find that the optimal access charges take the same form as that in our earlier model. More precisely, the optimal access pricing formula in area j is

$$a_j = d_j^I + \left(p - c^I - d_j^I\right)\sigma'_j + \frac{\lambda}{1+\lambda}\frac{a_j}{\varepsilon_j^A}.$$

The access price is the sum of three terms. The first one is the delivery cost. The second one is the product of the margin made on the USP's E2E good (price minus upstream and downstream costs) and the displacement ratio

$$\sigma'_j = -\frac{\partial q_j^I / \partial a_j}{\partial\left(q_j^E + q_j^D\right) / \partial a_j}.$$

This displacement ratio measures the substitution between variations in the USP's E2E quantity (numerator) and in total quantity using access (denominator) when the access charge is increased. The third component is a markup relating to the break-even constraint, with λ being the Lagrange multiplier associated to this constraint. This markup increases with the strength of the break-even constraint (the value of λ) and decreases with the demand elasticity of total access (CDA and entrant's) to the access charge

$$\varepsilon_j^A = -\frac{\partial\left(q_j^E + q_j^D\right)}{\partial a_j}\frac{a_j}{q_j^E + q_j^D}.$$

The access charge formula reduces to the usual ECPR (or margin rule) under the conditions of the absence of the break-even constraint ($\lambda=0$) and when the displacement ratio equals one, i.e. when any letter sent using access simply displaces one USP's E2E letter. In other words, optimal charges are ECPR but modified to take account of the extent of displacement of USP's E2E traffic (which reduces access charges) and the impact of the break-even constraint (which increases access charges through a Ramsey term).

2.2 Calibration[6]

Calibration data for the demand side are obtained from De Donder et al (2002b). More precisely, we take linear demands that we calibrate to obtain that the total quantity sold by the USP under monopoly at an assumed current price p of 0.35€ is 8 900 millions items for urban delivery and 1 100 millions items for rural delivery. Both demand functions exhibit a direct price elasticity of –0.376 (obtained by averaging the elasticities on the households' and firms' markets in De Donder et al (2002b)) on both markets at the 0.35€ price.

---

[6] Parameter values are unchanged from those set out in De Donder et al (2004) for the corresponding elements of the model presented in the current paper.

Regarding the USP costs, the universal service obligation translates into a global fixed cost F of 1 701 millions €. The collection plus transportation and sorting unit cost is c^I=0.1€ for the USP and the unit delivery cost is d_U^I=0.07€ on the urban market and d_R^I=0.16€ on the rural market. The reader can easily check that the USP just covers its costs (including the fixed cost) at the 0.35€ price before opening of the market to competition.[7] The entrant's collection cost is c^E=0.13€. The entrant does not face a fixed cost but has a higher marginal delivery cost than the USP on both markets[8]: d_U^E=0.12€ on the urban area and d_R^E=0.35€ on the rural one.

In sections 3 and 4, we report results prior to including CDA and so study optimal USP E2E price and access charges when there are only 2 goods sent to each area: the USP's and the entrant's. Moreover, we report results from the model which highlight sensitivities relating to the extent and nature of entry and reflect the higher level of uncertainty relating to the value of two parameters. The first parameter is the share of each market (urban and rural) that the entrant would take if it were to post a price of 0.35€, the same as the uniform pre-liberalization tariff set by the USP. We analyze two values: 10% and 23.8%.[9] The second dimension highlighted in the results is the two-good displacement ratio, denoted by σ, which is a simplified version of the 3-good ratio, σ' in section 2.1. It measures the substitutability between USP's and entrant's products on a given market, i.e. by how much the USP's demand decreases when the entrant supplies one more unit of retail service in this market (see appendix for a formal definition of σ). This ratio is set at two values: σ=0.5 which implies that for every two items carried by the entrant, one is displaced from the USP and one is newly generated by the entrant's service and σ=0.75 where for every four items carried by the entrant, three are displaced from the USP and only one is new.[10]

In section 5, we report results including CDA. We do this by splitting the aggregate demand for mail sent to urban areas in two components, the first one representing demand by small scale senders who do not access directly to the USP delivery network while the second represents demand by large

7 Note that for ease of presentation the "fixed cost" includes a normal rate of return on capital or accounting profit so that the USP breaks even after allowing for this return (see De Donder et al, 2002b).

8 This can be due to the fact that the entrant has a different technology than the incumbent. Moreover, the marginal costs used here are long run marginal costs, which include many things which one may consider as 'fixed costs' from an accounting perspective.

9 The value of 23.8% is taken from De Donder et al (2002b) and is the value obtained there where the market share for business senders is 25% and that of residential senders is 15%. The alternative value assumes that the combined figure is only 10%.

10 We assume the same displacement ratio and market sharea price of 0.35 in both the urban and rural areas.

scale senders. Small scale senders may consume only two goods (the entrant's and the USP E2E's) while large senders may consume a third one (CDA). The three goods are imperfect substitutes, with the price of the CDA good being the sum of a preparation cost (0.08€) and the urban access charge paid to the USP for delivery.

We calibrate demands for the USP E2E and the entrant's products in such a way that the small scale senders represent exactly one half of the market when all goods are priced at 0.35€. We keep the same calibration assumptions as in sections 3 and 4 regarding demand by small senders for urban mail. As for demand by large scale senders, we make the following assumptions: the entrant's share of the total market (entrant + USP + CDA) is 10% when all 3 goods cost 0.35€ to the seller; and the CDA share of total USP volumes (i.e. E2E + CDA) is 40% when CDA represents a 20% cost saving for senders compared with the 0.35€ price of the E2E product.[11] The displacement ratio in the case where CDA is included needs to be modified from σ to σ' because the ratio reflects the substitutability between the USP E2E good on the one hand and both the entrant's product and CDA on the other hand rather than the entrant's product alone. The high substitutability likely, in the eyes of large scale senders, between CDA and the USP retail product implies that equivalent values for the modified displacement ratio are likely to be higher than where CDA is not included ($\sigma' > \sigma$). We consider two values: $\sigma' = 0.65$ and $\sigma' = 0.8$.

3. RESULTS: ENTRANT ACCESS WITHOUT BYPASS

We first analyze the optimal differentiated access charges when the entrant does not have the availability to bypass the USP's delivery network. The USP delivers its letters on both markets but we assume, as a first stage, that the entrant does not have its own delivery network and thus has to ask access to the USP delivery network in both areas. The urban (respectively rural) access charge represents the unitary price paid by the entrant for each letter that the USP delivers on its behalf to the urban (respectively rural) area. The USP optimally chooses its retail price and (urban and rural) access charges in order to maximize total welfare in the economy subject to the constraint that it breaks even, that is, the regulator's maximization problem as set out in section 2.1 and developed in the appendix. We solve this

[11] These values imply that the USP's retail E2E service retains a very high share of volumes at an equal price compared with the two alternative products. Clearly, if that share were lower then the extent of entry and switching would be higher than in the results reported in sections 3 to 5.

optimization problem by associating a Lagrange multiplier to the USP profit constraint. Moreover, we also study the case where the USP is obliged to post the same access charge for both urban and rural delivery.

We have looked first at the situation where the USP E2E price and access charges are set to maximize total welfare, without imposing the constraint that the USP break-even. Comparing the optimal pricing strategy under no bypass in this case with the pre-liberalization one, we obtain that both types of consumers (urban and rural) have a much higher consumer surplus after entry. The entrant breaks even, by definition of a competitive fringe. On the other hand, the USP makes a huge loss after entry. The reason for this loss is that the optimal pricing formula for the retail price p calls for marginal cost pricing (except for the fact it cannot differ in the urban and rural markets, so it is an average of marginal costs as given by equation (2) in the appendix). Moreover, the optimal pricing formula for access charges (as set out in equation (1) in the appendix) perfectly compensates the incumbent for any end-to-end profit foregone due to access being provided, the effect of this being to deter inefficient entry and the misallocation of resources that would result from entry of this type. The USP then covers exactly its variable costs and its loss equals its fixed costs.[12]

The unconstrained solution (when $\lambda=0$) results in a loss for the USP, indicating that the USP profit constraint is binding at the optimum. Table 1 provides results for the break-even constrained case. The column headed "monopoly" in the table shows results before the opening of the market to competition. Its main interest is in the value of the consumer surplus in the urban and rural areas[13], which will be used as benchmark values. We report next the results arising from access obtained when the USP just breaks even and the value of λ (the Lagrange multiplier of this constraint) is obtained endogenously when solving the regulator's maximization program.

We first comment on the case where the market share of the entrant at a price of 0.35€ (the pre-liberalization price of the USP) equals 10% and where σ equals 0.5, before looking at the impact of modifying σ and the market share assumption. The endogenous value of λ is quite low at 0.217, suggesting that it is not very costly in terms of aggregate welfare to require the USP to break-even in this case. This low value of λ feeds (through equations (3) for the optimal access charges by area and (4) for the optimal uniform price in the appendix) into relatively low values for p (0.346€) as

---

12 This contrasts with De Donder et al (2004) where $\lambda=0$ allows the USP to break-even. In that paper, the USP retail price p is held exogenously at the monopoly break-even price (0.35€) even after entry. Since the optimal access charge formula compensates the USP for the profit lost due to providing access, the USP still breaks even after liberalization.

13 More precisely, it is the welfare that the representative consumer gets from sending letters to, respectively, urban and rural addressees.

well as the urban (0.178€) and the rural (0.217€) access charges. As noted previously the access charge is ECPR in form, reduced to take account of the displacement ratio and raised to ensure break-even for the USP. Observe that the value of the retail price is even lower than its monopoly level! This is due to the fact that the USP makes some profit on selling access to its competitors and so can decrease its final price while still breaking-even. It is worth noting also that even though the USP's volume from its retail service declines the total volume of mail it delivers (of this type and delivery of the entrant's product) rises compared with the monopoly base case from 10bn to 10.821bn items.

Table 1 : Optimal Access Charges and Retail Price – No Bypass Allowed

		Monopoly	Entrant's Market Share if it Set Prices at 0.35€			
			10%		23.8%[1]	
			$\sigma = 0.5$	$\sigma = 0.75$	$\sigma = 0.5$	$\sigma = 0.75$
Access Charges, € :	Urban	-	0.178	0.213	0.189	0.219
	Rural	-	0.217	0.232	0.228	0.238
Entrant's Prices, € :	Urban	-	0.308	0.343	0.319	0.349
	Rural	-	0.347	0.362	0.359	0.368
USP Retail Price, €		0.35	0.346	0.349	0.337	0.345
Entrant's Quantities, bn:	Urban	-	1.145	1.050	2.716	2.193
	Rural	-	0.118	0.078	0.275	0.219
USP Quantities, bn:	Urban	8.9	8.213	8.123	7.662	7.304
	Rural	1.1	1.045	1.043	0.977	0.941
	Delivered[2]	10.0	10.821	10.294	11.630	10.657
USP Profit, bn €		0	0	0	0	0
Consumer Surplus, bn €:	Urban	4.142	4.257	4.178	4.544	4.298
	Rural	0.512	0.521	0.541	0.550	0.527
Value of λ			0.217	0.221	0.200	0.214
Total Welfare, bn €[3]		4.654	4.778	4.692	5.094	4.842
Compared with monopoly, bn €		-	0.124	0.038	0.440	0.170

1. Weighted average of business and residential sender mail as calculated in De Donder et al (2002a).
2. The USP delivers all of the entrant's mail so that the USP's delivered volumes equal the sum of its own quantities plus those of the entrant.
3. Sum of consumer surplus and operators' profit.

With a lower USP retail price and access to the goods sold by the entrant, both categories of consumers benefit from the opening of the market to competition. Such a move then constitutes a Pareto improvement (with respect to the monopoly situation) since some actors are strictly better off (consumers) while no one is worse off (postal operators break-even).

We now compare the results shown in the columns of table 1 to assess the impact of a higher displacement ratio σ and/or a higher entrant's market share. First note that, in all cases, the value of λ is low, the USP retail price is lower than its monopoly level and the USP's delivered volumes rise compared with the monopoly level. In this case of entrant access without bypass where access prices and the uniform retail price are set optimally, all consumers benefit from the opening of the market to competition which introduces a wider range of choice and leads to a more intensive use of the USP's delivery network. All these results are thus robust to the modifications of parameter values shown in table 1. As for the impact of the entrant's market share, we see that a higher share leads to a small decrease in λ, and to small decreases in the USP retail price and access charges which in turn increase consumer welfare. These results may seem surprising at first sight and deserve an explanation. Increasing the entrant's market share means increasing the desirability of the entrant's product and increasing the total size of the postal market. The small decrease in the optimal USP uniform retail price is not enough to prevent the USP retail quantities from falling. However, the USP compensates this loss in end-to-end revenues by increasing its revenues from selling access to the entrant, since the entrant's quantities roughly double with a higher market share, and so increases the total volume of mail delivered by the USP jointly from its own end-to-end service and delivery of the entrant's product. The increase in the consumers' surplus at these optimal prices thus has two sources: the higher desirability of the entrant's product associated with its higher market share and the (slightly) lower prices for both the USP and the entrant's goods. A lower displacement ratio has the same (qualitative) effects as an increase in the entrant's market share: a lower value of σ means that a higher proportion of the entrant's volumes corresponds to a generation of postal volume and not simply replacement of USP's by entrant's volume. The same mechanisms as above then explain why higher volumes tend to lower prices and increase consumers' welfare.

To summarize, when bypass is not a possibility, setting the USP retail price and access charges at their optimal levels leads to increases in consumers' welfare while allowing the USP to break-even. A higher entrant's market share and lower displacement ratio raise the total volume of mail delivered by the USP, decrease prices and increase welfare.

This appealing result incorporates within it the possibility for the USP to post access charges differentiated according to the delivery area. Such a differentiation may be technically cumbersome, legally prohibited or more simply may entail significant transaction costs for the USP. We now look at the consequences of imposing uniformity for the access charges as well as for the USP retail price in the case where bypass is not available to entrants[14]. Table 2 focuses on the no bypass case with σ=0.5 and the entrant's market share at 23.8% and an endogenous value of λ. It compares the welfare maximizing results obtained when the access charges may be differentiated according to the area (second column of figures) and where a

[14] This case is similar to that in the US under "dropshipment" discounts (Cohen et al, 2002).

uniform access charge must be posted (third column). The optimum value of the uniform access charge is set out in equation (6) in the appendix and is a weighted average of the optimal differentiated urban and rural access charges. For the case shown it is very close to the optimum urban access charge. We know from theory that imposing another constraint (uniformity of access charge) will decrease the value of the objective function at the optimum. However, we see in table 2 that the value of total welfare (as well as the value of λ) is barely affected by the uniformity constraint, and such is the case also for the USP retail price. The reason is that the rural market is sufficiently small not to matter much in these results. Imposing the access charge to be uniform also increases the entrant's urban price and decreases the entrant's rural price.

Table 2 : Optimal Uniform Access Charges and Retail Price - No Bypass[1]

		Monopoly	Access Charges	
			Differentiated[2]	Uniform
Access Charges, € :	Urban	-	0.189	0.194
	Rural	-	0.228	0.194
Entrant's Prices, € :	Urban	-	0.319	0.324
	Rural	-	0.359	0.324
USP Retail Price, €		0.35	0.337	0.337
Entrant's Quantities, bn:	Urban	-	2.176	2.662
	Rural	-	0.275	0.329
USP Quantities, bn:	Urban	8.9	7.662	7.689
	Rural	1.1	0.977	0.950
	Delivered[3]	10.0	11.630	11.630
USP Profit, bn €		0	0	0
Consumer Surplus, bn €:	Urban	4.142	4.544	4.532
	Rural	0.512	0.550	0.560
Value of λ			0.200	0.201
Total Welfare, bn €[4]		4.654	5.094	5.093
Compared with monopoly, bn €		-	0.440	0.439

1. Case where σ=0.5 and entrant's market share of 23.8% if it sets its prices at 0.35€.
2. As reported in fourth column of table 1.
3. The USP delivers all of the entrant's mail so that the USP's delivered volumes equal to the sum of its own quantities plus those of the entrant
4. Sum of consumer surplus and operators' profit.

Since the USP optimal price barely moves, this translates into a lower urban consumers' surplus and a higher rural consumers' surplus. Note that even with a uniform access charge (and USP retail price), at optimal prices all consumers have a higher welfare than under monopoly. Moreover, the net effect on total welfare compared with the case of differentiated access charges is only very slightly negative and this result is prior to the cost of a differentiation of access prices geographically.

To summarize, the results obtained with differentiated access charges are robust to the introduction of a uniform access pricing constraint when the uniform access price is derived and applied on an optimal basis. In particular, the welfare gain from geographical de-averaging of the access price in this case is small for the parameters chosen where recall that d_U^I = 0.07€, d_R^I = 0.16€ and about 10% of traffic is for delivery to the high cost rural area. We obtain a similar conclusion for the other cases of σ and market shares reported in table 1.

4. RESULTS: ENTRANT ACCESS WITH BYPASS

In this section we present the second stage of our results which cover the possibility for the entrant to deliver itself on any area but before including CDA. More precisely, the entrant will deliver through its own network in a given area if its delivery cost in this area is (strictly) lower than the corresponding access charge. We study in this section the optimal USP retail price and access charges when the entrant can bypass the USP delivery network and maintain the constraint that the USP must break even. We consider, with our calibration, the likeliest and hence most relevant case, namely that the entrant asks for access to the rural area but delivers itself in the urban area. If its delivery cost were above the access charge in the urban area the results and conclusions from section 3 would stand while if its delivery cost in the rural area were below that of the rural access charge, qualitatively the results would be similar to those reported below.

Unfortunately, even where optimal access and USP retail prices are set, the welfare-enhancing results for the case where bypass is not allowed do not carry through to the situation where bypass is available to the entrant. In all four cases reported in table 1 as well as in table 2, the urban access charge is higher than the entrant's delivery cost in the urban area (which is set at 0.12 €). Faced with this access charge, the entrant will deliver itself on the urban area. However, the entrant still asks for access to the rural area given that the rural access charge is in all cases lower than its rural delivery cost (set at 0.35€). The rural access charge is also lower than the USP retail price, so that the entrant is not tempted to reinject its rural mail through the USP's end-to-end network. In table 3, we provide results for this case where the entrant bypasses the USP delivery network in the urban area and uses it in the rural area.[15] As for table 1, we first discuss the results for the low

[15] We assume that the USP is prevented by legal or regulatory constraints from "undercutting" the entrant's urban delivery cost and so that urban bypass cannot be

entrant's market share, low displacement ratio case before analyzing the comparative static results with respect to these parameters.

Table 3 : Optimal Access Charges and Retail Price – Bypass Allowed
Case where Entrant Chooses Bypass in Urban Area and Access in Rural Area

		Monopoly	Entrant's Market Share If It Set Prices at 0.35€			
			10%		23.8%[1]	
			$\sigma = 0.5$	$\sigma = 0.75$	$\sigma = 0.5$	$\sigma = 0.75$
Access Charges, € :	Urban[2]	-	0.178	0.213	0.189	0.219
	Rural[3]	-	0.244	0.304	0.302	0.318
Entrant's Prices, € :	Urban	-	0.250	0.250	0.250	0.250
	Rural	-	0.374	0.434	0.432	0.448
USP Retail Price, €		0.35	0.383	0.429	0.415	0.407
Entrant's Quantities, bn:	Urban	-	2.419	4.392	4.096	5.374
	Rural	-	0.104	0.046	0.220	0.129
USP Quantities, bn	Urban	8.9	7.379	4.851	6.227	4.323
	Rural	1.1	1.009	0.972	0.913	0.936
	Delivered[4]	10.0	8.492	5.869	7.360	5.388
USP Profit, bn €[5]		0	0	-0.274	0	-0.518
Consumer Surplus, bn €:	Urban	4.142	4.087	3.911	4.239	4.310
	Rural	0.512	0.480	0.429	0.458	0.454
Value of λ			0.511	Infinite	0.841	Infinite
Total Welfare, bn €[6]		4.654	4.567	3.984[7]	4.697	4.091[7]
Compared with monopoly, bn €[9]		-	-0.087	-0.670	0.042	-0.563

1. Weighted average of business and residential sender mail as calculated in De Donder et al (2002a).
2. Optimal charge is greater than entrant's delivery cost per item of 0.12€ so entrant uses own delivery capability.
3. The rural access charge is the optimal uniform access charge given entrants deliver by their own network in the urban area.
4. The USP's delivered volumes for this case equal its own quantities plus the entrant's rural quantity.
5. Note that if the USP had set an access charge between the entrant's delivery cost per item of 0.12€ and its own delivery cost of 0.07€ it would have been able to reduce its financial loss.
6. Sum of consumer surplus and operators' profit (if profits are non-negative).
7. Sum of consumer surplus and $(1+\alpha)$ USP profits, where we have used $\alpha=0.3$ as measure of the welfare cost associated with funding the USP loss with distortionary means.

Fixing simultaneously the optimal rural access charge and the optimal USP retail price makes it possible in this case for the USP to break-even.[16] On the other hand, the welfare cost for society of requiring the USP to break-even is quite high, as shown by the high value of λ (0.511) at equilibrium. The reason why λ is so high, especially compared with the corresponding no bypass situation, is simply that the USP no longer earns revenue by providing access to the entrant in the urban area so resulting in a decline in the volumes it handles through its delivery network. These drop by over 20% from 10.821bn (table 1, column 2) to 8.492bn items. This leads to the USP needing to raise its prices for both its retail good and rural access. From equation (3) in the appendix, the optimal rural access charge is higher than without bypass (0.244€ compared with 0.217€) as a result of the effect of entry on the optimal retail price (equation (4) in the appendix). It turns out

prevented. We then maintain the urban access charge at its level in table 1, without any loss of generality.

16 This contrasts to the result for a similar case in De Donder et al (2004) where the retail price was fixed at 0.35€, lower than the 0.383€ price obtained here.

that the USP retail price (0.383€) and the entrant's rural price (0.374€) are both higher than not only the situation under access without bypass but also the USP pre-liberalization price (0.35€). Both types of consumers suffer from these higher prices and end up with less surplus than under monopoly! Such a scenario constitutes a Pareto worsening move away from monopoly, since some groups are worse off (consumers) while no group is better off (the postal operators just break even). Such results illustrate the very significant impact potentially of allowing entrant bypass since, even where optimal access and uniform retail prices are set, adding this possibility turns a Pareto improvement into a Pareto worsening move![17]

The impact of bypass is even more visible when the value of the displacement ratio is higher at $\sigma = 0.75$. In such a case there are no values of the rural access charge and the USP retail price that enable the USP to break-even, even though both of these prices are significantly higher than the corresponding case without bypass (table 1, column 3) or when $\sigma = 0.5$. The reason is straightforward: when the entrant mostly displaces retail volume from the USP, it reduces the revenue earned by the USP on these volumes, except by selling access to the rural area, which is a small market compared to the urban one. There is a very significant fall in the total number of items the USP delivers through its delivery network which declines to 5.869bn items compared with 10bn items pre-liberalization. For a high enough value of the displacement ratio, breaking even is then not possible for the USP.

In the case where $\sigma = 0.75$, table 3 reports the USP loss minimizing solution, which formally corresponds to the case where λ is set at plus infinity in the regulator's optimization program. In such a case, all prices are higher than when $\sigma = 0.5$, and surpluses are lower for both urban and rural consumers. It is difficult to give a value for total society's welfare, since the value of λ is infinite. Observe nevertheless that the sum of USP loss and consumers' surpluses is lower than under monopoly, since all three actors are worse off. But taking a simple sum overestimates total welfare, since it implies that there is no welfare cost in transferring money to cover the USP loss. A more reasonable assumption is that this loss would have to be funded by some form of distortionary means such as taxation. Using a value of 0.3 for the welfare cost associated with this transfer, we report results on this basis in table 3 and obtain that total welfare is lower than the monopoly level by 670 millions € in the ($\sigma = 0.75$, 10% entrant's market share) case and by 563 millions € in the ($\sigma = 0.75$, 23.8% entrant's market share) case.

As for the impact of a higher entrant's market share, we obtain that although it increases all prices, it increases consumers' surpluses in both the

---

[17] It is important to note that bypass is in itself socially inefficient in our setting since the entrant's delivery cost is higher than the USP's. A socially efficient bypass is a necessary but not sufficient condition for bypass to be welfare improving.

urban and rural (except when σ=0.5) areas. The reason for this result is that increasing the entrant's market share means that consumers derive more utility from the good provided by the entrant. This effect is stronger than the negative effect of higher prices (except for rural consumers when σ=0.5). As a consequence, the only case where, even with optimal access and uniform retail prices, total welfare is (very slightly) higher than under monopoly is when the displacement rate is low and the entrant's market share high. Even in this case, there is no Pareto improvement, since rural consumers are worse off. For the three other cases, both types of consumers are worse off. Although not reported here, optimal uniform access charges for this case would yield very similar results to those from optimal case of differentiated charges shown in table 3.

5. RESULTS: ENTRANT ACCESS WITH BYPASS AND CUSTOMER DIRECT ACCESS

In this section, we report results for the general case which incorporates also the impact of CDA. As in the preceding sections, the USP optimally chooses its uniform retail price and its access charges in order to maximize total welfare subject to its break-even constraint. The rural access charge only impacts on the entrant's situation on the rural area while the urban access charge affects both the entrant's urban market and, now, CDA by large scale senders to the urban area. We keep the possibility for the entrant to bypass the USP delivery network. Finally, we also study the case where the USP has to offer the same access charge to both the rural and urban (including CDA) areas.

Although the main components of the access charges incorporating the impact of CDA are the same as in the previous cases, both the displacement ratio and the elasticity in the Ramsey term are more complex in order to take account of the fact that access can be through CDA as well as by entrants.[18] The formulae for optimal differentiated access prices when direct access to the USP's delivery network is available to customers are reported in the appendix (equations (7) and (9)). The possibility of CDA also impacts on the formula for the optimal retail price (equation (8)). The fact that the formulae for the CDA case involve σ' rather than σ means it is difficult to use the calibration model to make strict comparisons between the general case including CDA and that without it. However, as noted in section 2.2, it is likely that the modified value for the displacement ratio is higher under CDA ($\sigma' > \sigma$) and we use two values $\sigma' = 0.65$ and $\sigma' = 0.80$.

[18] Hence in the 3-good case, σ' replaces σ and ε_j^A replaces ε_j^E (see the appendix).

Table 4: Optimal Access Charges and Retail Price – Bypass and Customer Direct Access Allowed

Case where Entrant Chooses Bypass in Urban Area and Access in Rural Area

		Monopoly	Entrant's Market Share if it Set Prices at 0.35€			
			10%			23.8%[1]
			$\sigma' = 0.65$	$\sigma' = 0.8$	$\sigma' = 0.8$ (Uniform access charges)	$\sigma' = 0.8$
Access Charges, € :	Urban[2]	-	0.178	0.214	0.234	0.214
	Rural[3]	-	0.333	0.271	0.234	0.290
Entrant's Prices, € :	Urban	-	0.250	0.250	0.250	0.250
	Rural	-	0.463	0.401	0.364	0.420
USP Retail Price, €		0.35	0.468	0.385	0.387	0.370
CDA Urban Cost, €[4]		-	0.267	0.294	0.314	0.294
Entrant's Quantities, bn:	Urban large[5]		1.167	1.967	2.132	2.532
	Urban small		1.872	1.980	2.005	2.459
	Rural		0.046	0.046	0.149	0.129
CDA Urban Quantity, bn:		-	1.954	1.232	0.916	0.952
USP Quantities, bn:	Urban large	4.45	1.563	1.726	1.836	1.568
	Urban small	4.45	2.667	2.701	2.671	2.388
	Rural	1.1	0.925	1.025	0.945	0.978
	Delivered[6]	10.0	7.155	6.730	6.516	6.017
USP Profit, bn €		0	-0.009	-0.441	-0.443	-0.649
Consumer Surplus, bn €:	Urban large	2.071	2.116	2.204	2.179	2.340
	Urban small	2.071	1.789	2.068	2.062	2.211
	Rural	0.512	0.390	0.475	0.476	0.493
Value of λ		-	Infinite	Infinite	Infinite	Infinite
Total Welfare, bn €[7]		4.654	4.284	4.175	4.141	4.201
Compared with Monopoly, bn €		-	-0.370	-0.479	-0.513	-0.453

1. Weighted average of business and residential sender mail as calculated in De Donder et al (2002a).
2. Optimal charge is greater than entrant's delivery cost per item of 0.12€ so entrant uses own delivery capability.
3. The rural access charge is the optimal uniform access charge given entrants deliver by their own network in the urban area.
4. Represents the effective price of customer direct access to large scale customers in urban areas as sum of urban access charge and customer preparation cost of 0.08€.
5. "Large" and "small" refer to large scale and small scale mailers.
6. The USP's delivered volumes for this case equal its own quantities plus the entrant's rural quantity plus CDA urban quantity.
7. Sum of consumer surplus and (1+α) USP profits, where we have used α=0.3 as measure of the welfare cost associated with funding the USP loss with distortionary means.

Results for the general case incorporating CDA are reported in table 4. New elements are the CDA urban cost (the sum of the urban access charge and a preparation cost of 0.08€) and the amount of CDA access. Table 4 also reports separate results for large scale and small scale senders to the urban area, given that within the model only the first category finds it economic to use CDA. In all cases reported here, the optimal urban access charge given by (9) is greater than the entrant's delivery cost, resulting in urban bypass. The first case shown is for $\sigma' = 0.65$ for a market share of 10% if the entrant set its price at 0.35€. There are nearly 2bn items of CDA traffic in this case. Compared with the case with bypass alone of $\sigma = 0.5$, significant increases in the USP retail price (0.468€ compared with 0.383€ under bypass alone) and in the rural access charge (0.333€ compared with 0.244€) nearly allow the USP to break even. In other words, most of the loss in profit from CDA and entrant volume can be recovered by raising prices for rural and small scale urban consumers who then face higher prices. Their welfare falls significantly compared with the pre-liberalization position. Although it is difficult to make direct comparisons with the results without CDA, in the case where $\sigma' = 0.65$, there is a considerable amount of CDA, a higher retail price and a pronounced distributional effect.

At a higher displacement ratio of $\sigma' = 0.8$, so that more of the volumes for entrants and CDA originate from the USP's retail traffic, the USP is no longer able to break-even. This result is consistent with those from table 3. The urban access charge is very similar to the bypass only case of $\sigma = 0.75$ in table 3 and so the results for CDA and bypass change in a similar direction at a higher displacement ratio[19]. CDA is substantially lower due to the higher urban access charge and the lower USP E2E price. Although CDA is lower, large scale customers still gain compared with the pre-liberalization position while small scale and rural customers lose.

The two remaining sets of results in table 4 are directly in line with results from the earlier stages. The results in the uniform access charge case broadly reinforce those reported earlier. For the mix of traffic between areas and parameter values in the calibration, differentiation of access charges has relatively little impact on the USP's optimal retail price and profit or on economic welfare although there are some changes to volumes between the urban and rural areas. The final column considers the case where the entrant has a higher market share if it were to set its price at 0.35€ reflecting a greater attractiveness and hence utility gained by customers from that service. CDA volumes are rather less than in the case where the entrant's share is 10% if it set its price at 0.35€. In other ways the results show a strong similarity to those for $\sigma = 0.75$ in table 3. The financial deficit of the USP is much higher than the case where market share is 10% but urban senders benefit compared to the pre-liberalization case.

Overall, comparisons of results from applying optimal access and USP uniform retail prices with and without CDA are difficult and dependent on the setting of the parameter values. However, there is little to suggest that CDA improves either the financial viability of the USP or economic welfare and may worsen the outcome arising from the situation where only entrants may ask for access. Although large mailers sending to the urban area always benefit (compared with the pre-liberalization situation) from the availability of the entrant's product and of CDA, rural consumers and to a lesser extent small scale senders to the urban area always lose (because of high E2E prices from both operators). All these results also point towards a trade-off

[19] Except for the variations in the USP's retail price.

between the ability of the USP to break-even and (urban) consumer surplus: the situation where the USP loss is the lowest (low displacement ratio and low entrant's market share) is also the situation where consumer welfare is the lowest.

6. SUMMARY AND CONCLUSIONS

We summarize our findings and conclusions under two main headings: first, the form of optimal prices for access to the delivery network of a USP and, secondly, the implications for volumes, break-even for the USP and economic welfare of access when the pricing of retail and access products is on an optimal basis. With regard to the form of optimal access prices we find that these are given by a second best efficient component pricing rule (ECPR), the effect of which is to deter inefficient entry and the accompanying misallocation of resources that would result from inefficient entry. The more general model developed here has therefore confirmed the conclusion from our earlier work (De Donder et al, 2004). Under this pricing rule, the optimal access charge equals, first, the cost to the USP of delivery plus, secondly, the profitability cost of an item lost from the retail service multiplied by the displacement ratio plus, thirdly, a mark-up to maintain the break-even position of the USP under entry.[20] The detail of this rule varies a little across the cases we consider but its general form is the same throughout. The optimal access charge in turn incorporates within it the optimal price for the USP's uniformly priced retail product as part of the component to calculate the profit foregone by an item lost from the USP's retail service. If access charges are also uniform and not differentiated by area then the optimal uniform access charge is a weighted average of the optimal charges by area. Detailed formulae for all of these prices are reported in the appendix.

We have presented our results in three stages leading up to a general case relevant for modeling access. The general case, which is mandated by Article 12 of the 2002 EU Directive, includes the possibility of bypass as well as access by entrants and also of direct access by (at least some) customers (CDA). First, access without bypass and CDA when access and retail prices are set optimally leads in each of the cases we examine to an increase in welfare for each group of customers as a rise in delivered volumes allows the retail price to fall (see table 1). This result is little

[20] The displacement ratio measures how the USP's demand decreases when the entrant supplies one more unit of traffic and the third term is a Ramsey term appearing when the profit constraint is binding which it is in all cases of interest. Break-even is assumed to include a normal rate of return on capital.

affected if the access price is uniform rather than differentiated but this may be due partly to our model having a relatively small proportion of traffic which is rural (see table 2). The improvement in welfare is greater when the displacement ratio is lower and more access traffic is new rather than displaced retail traffic of the USP.

The welfare outcome when incorporating bypass as well as access by entrants, the second stage, is much different from that for entrant access alone if entrants' delivery costs are less than the access charge so that bypass does indeed occur. Such bypass is much likelier in urban areas. Compared to the first stage of introducing access without bypass, even with access prices and uniform retail prices set optimally in all cases the USP's delivered volume is lower and its retail price is higher, while in some cases it is not able to break-even (see table 3). Economic welfare is always lower, even assuming that it is possible to find a means of funding deficits. Indeed only if the proportion of access traffic which is new is very high and the entrant's service is highly valued by customers does access with bypass lead to a better outcome on economic welfare than under monopoly.

The availability of CDA to customers, the third stage which represents the general case, leaves this conclusion little changed although the complexity of the analytical results for optimal access and uniform retail prices from the model makes calculation of the incremental effect of CDA over that of bypass difficult (see table 4). The impact of CDA is sensitive to the degree of switching created by this alternative for it both reduces the potential volume of entrants (adding to USP contribution) but also reduces the USP's retail volumes (so reducing USP contribution). Although the total impact of CDA on welfare is uncertain it has a clear distributional effect. Large scale customers switch some volume to CDA which increases optimal retail and access charges so that large scale customers gain and small scale customers lose. Overall, the impact of CDA and bypass compared with economic welfare pre-liberalization is dependent on the specific setting of parameter values but it clearly leads to a level of economic welfare which, at optimally set prices, is below that from access alone.

The optimal rules for access we have derived are complex but also intuitive. They confirm that the appropriate starting point for the pricing of access to the postal network of a USP is ECPR, interpreted here in the sense of the "margin rule." That is the position set out in the EU Postal Directive. If the purpose of liberalization is to increase economic welfare while ensuring that the USP continues to meet the universal service obligation then these rules indicate the factors, starting from ECPR that would need to be taken into account in setting optimal prices. In particular, these factors include the impact of entry on the USP's volumes, the extent to which access volumes are new or displaced from the USP's retail product and the extent of

CDA. Except by chance, simpler rules will not capture these factors fully but the optimal rules can act as a benchmark against which to develop and assess access prices in practice.

APPENDIX: OPTIMAL PRICING

The objective of the USP/regulator is to maximize total welfare (the sum of consumer surplus and of the USP profit) under the constraint that the USP break-even. The instruments used by the USP are the USP retail (or E2E) price p and the access charges, a_U and a_R. Formally,

$$\underset{p,a^U,a^R}{Max}\ W = V_U\left(q_U^I, q_U^E, q^D\right) + V_R\left(q_R^I, q_R^E\right) + \Pi^I$$

$$s.t.\ \Pi^I \geq 0,$$

where V_U is the utility from sending letters to the urban area, V_R to the rural area[21] and Π^I the USP profit, as defined in section 2.1. We associate the Lagrange multiplier λ to the break-even constraint.

We list hereunder the optimality formulae and refer the reader to the companion paper for derivations and comments. We start with the simpler, two-good model where CDA is not an option and introduce it later in the analysis.

The model with 2 goods (no CDA)

The results will depend on whether the break-even constraint is binding at the optimum. We first give the optimal pricing formulae when the constraint is not binding ($\lambda = 0$) and then when it binds ($\lambda > 0$).

A. $\lambda = 0$

The access price formula is given by

$$a_j = d_j^I + \left(p - c^I - d_j^I\right)\sigma_j \tag{1}$$

[21] To simplify notation, we abstract here from the distinction between large scale and small scale senders and assume that CDA may be used to send letters to the urban, but not the rural, area.

where $\sigma_j = -\frac{\partial q_j^I / \partial p_j^E}{\partial q_j^E / \partial p_j^E}$ is the displacement ratio which measures the substitutability between USP's and entrant's products on market *j*, i.e. by how much the USP's demand decreases when the entrant supplies one more unit of retail service in this market. Multiplying this displacement ratio by the difference between the letter price and its marginal cost, one obtains the USP's lost profit on the retail market caused by providing access. This is thus an ECPR formula, which compensates the USP for the opportunity cost in terms of foregone profit (and hence contribution towards the network cost of providing universal service) of any traffic lost to the entrant (see Armstrong, 2002).

If we denote by

$$\frac{dq_j^I}{dp} = \frac{\partial q_j^I}{\partial p} + \frac{\partial q_J^E}{\partial p}\sigma_j$$

the **total** derivative of q_j^I with respect to *p*, we obtain the following formula for the optimal value of *p*

$$p = \left(c^I + d_U^I\right)\frac{dq_U^I / dp}{d(q_U^I + q_R^I)/dp} + \left(c^I + d_R^I\right)\frac{dq_R^I / dp}{d(q_U^I + q_R^I)/dp}. \tag{2}$$

B. $\lambda > 0$

The access pricing formula is

$$a_j = d_j^I + \left(p - c^I - d_j^I\right)\sigma_j + \frac{\lambda}{1+\lambda}\frac{p_j^E}{\varepsilon_j^E} \tag{3}$$

where ε_j^E is the (absolute value) of the direct price elasticity of the demand for entrant's letters addressed to area *j*. Formula (3) builds on (1) and adds the usual Ramsey term as a mark-up, which is inversely proportional to the demand direct price elasticity. The intuition for this last term is that it is less costly in terms of welfare to raise prices on markets where the demand is less sensitive to price, i.e. where demand direct price elasticity is lower.

The formula for the optimum USP retail price is more complicated and given by the following first-order condition

$$\left(p-c^{I}-d_{U}^{I}+\frac{\lambda}{1+\lambda}\frac{p}{\hat{\varepsilon}_{U}^{I}}\right)\frac{dq_{U}^{I}}{dp}+\left(p-c^{I}-d_{R}^{I}+\frac{\lambda}{1+\lambda}\frac{p}{\hat{\varepsilon}_{R}^{I}}\right)\frac{dq_{R}^{I}}{dp}$$
$$+\frac{\lambda}{1+\lambda}\left(\frac{p_{R}^{E}}{\varepsilon_{R}^{E}}\frac{\partial q_{R}^{E}}{\partial p}+\frac{p_{U}^{E}}{\varepsilon_{U}^{E}}\frac{\partial q_{U}^{E}}{\partial p}\right)=0. \tag{4}$$

C. Uniform access charge

Introducing the new notation

$$\alpha=\frac{\partial q_{U}^{E}/\partial p_{U}^{E}}{\left(\partial q_{U}^{E}/\partial p_{U}^{E}\right)+\left(\partial q_{R}^{E}/\partial p_{R}^{E}\right)},$$

we obtain that the optimum uniform access charge is given by

$$a=\alpha\left(d_{U}^{I}+\left(p-c^{I}-d_{U}^{I}\right)\sigma_{U}\right)+(1-\alpha)\left(d_{R}^{I}+\left(p-c^{I}-d_{R}^{I}\right)\sigma_{R}\right) \tag{5}$$

in the case where $\lambda=0$, and by

$$a=\alpha\left(d_{U}^{I}+\left(p-c^{I}-d_{U}^{I}\right)\sigma_{U}+\frac{\lambda}{1+\lambda}\frac{p_{U}^{E}}{\varepsilon_{U}^{E}}\right)$$
$$+(1-\alpha)\left(d_{R}^{I}+\left(p-c^{I}-d_{R}^{I}\right)\sigma_{R}+\frac{\lambda}{1+\lambda}\frac{p_{R}^{E}}{\varepsilon_{R}^{E}}\right) \tag{6}$$

if $\lambda>0$.

The model with 3 goods (including CDA)

D. λ =0

The access price formula is given by

$$a_{j}=d_{j}^{I}+\left(p-c^{I}-d_{j}^{I}\right)\sigma'_{j} \tag{7}$$

where

$$\sigma'_j = -\frac{\partial q_j^I / \partial a_j}{\partial\left(q_j^E + q_j^D\right) / \partial a}, \qquad \partial q_j^I / \partial a = \frac{\partial q_j^I}{\partial p_j^E} + \frac{\partial q_j^I}{\partial p_j^D},$$

$$\partial q_j^I / \partial a = \frac{\partial q_j^I}{\partial p_j^E} + \frac{\partial q_j^I}{\partial p_j^D} \text{ and } \partial q_j^D / \partial a_j = \frac{\partial q_j^D}{\partial p_j^E} + \frac{\partial q_j^D}{\partial p_j^D}.$$

If we denote by

$$\frac{dq_j^I}{dp} = \frac{\partial q_j^I}{\partial p} + \sigma'_j \left(\frac{\partial q_j^E}{\partial p} + \frac{\partial q_j^E}{\partial p} \right)$$

the total derivative of q_j^I with respect to p, we obtain the following formula for the optimal value of p

$$p = c^I + d_U^I \frac{dq_U^I / dp}{d(q_U^I + q_R^I)/dp} + d_R^I \frac{dq_R^I / dp}{d(q_U^I + q_R^I)/dp}. \tag{8}$$

E. $\lambda > 0$

The access pricing formula is

$$a_j = d_j^I + \left(p - c^I - d_j^I\right)\sigma'_j + \frac{\lambda}{1+\lambda} \frac{a}{\varepsilon_j^A} \tag{9}$$

with $\varepsilon_j^A = -\dfrac{\partial\left(q_j^E + q_j^D\right)}{\partial a} \dfrac{a}{q_j^E + q_j^D}$,

the elasticity of total access (CDA and entrant's) to the access charge. The formula for the optimum USP retail price is more complicated and we refer the reader to the separate paper containing the derivation of the technical results.

REFERENCES

Armstrong, Mark. 2002. "The Theory of Access Pricing and Interconnection." In *Handbook of Telecommunications Economics*, edited by M. Cave, S. Majumdar and I. Vogelsang. North Holland.

Billette de Villemeur, Etienne, Helmuth Cremer, Bernard Roy and Joelle Toledano. 2004. "Access Pricing and (Non-) Uniform Pricing in the Postal Sector." In *Competitive Transformation of the Postal and Delivery Sector*, edited by M.A. Crew and P.R. Kleindorfer. Boston, MA: Kluwer Academic Publishers.

Cohen, Robert H., William W. Ferguson, John D. Waller and Spyros S. Xenakis. 2002. "Impacts of Using Worksharing to Liberalise a Postal Market." In *Liberalization of Postal Markets*, edited by G. Kulenkampff and H. Smit. Bad Honnef: WIK.

Crew, Michael A. and Paul R. Kleindorfer. 2002. "Balancing Access and the Universal Service Obligation." In *Postal and Delivery Services: Delivering on Competition*, edited by M.A. Crew and P.R. Kleindorfer. Boston, MA: Kluwer Academic Publishers.

Crew, Michael A. and Paul R. Kliendorfer. 2004. "Access and the USO for Letters and Parcels." In *Competitive Transformation of the Postal and Delivery Sector*, edited by M.A. Crew and P.R. Kleindorfer. Boston, MA: Kluwer Academic Publishers.

De Donder, Philippe, Helmuth Cremer and Frank Rodriguez. 2002a. "Access Pricing and Parcels Delivery." In *Postal and Delivery Services: Delivering on Competition*, edited by M.A. Crew and P.R. Kleindorfer. Boston, MA: Kluwer Academic Publishers.

De Donder, Philippe, Helmuth Cremer and Frank Rodriguez. 2002b. "Funding the Universal Service Obligation under Liberalization: An Analysis of the Postal Market." In *Postal and Delivery Services: Pricing, Productivity, Regulation and Strategy*, edited by M.A. Crew and P.R. Kleindorfer. Boston, MA: Kluwer Academic Publishers.

De Donder, Philippe, Helmuth Cremer and Frank Rodriguez. 2004. "Access Pricing and the Uniform Tariff in the Postal Sector." In *Competitive Transformation of the Postal and Delivery Sector*, edited by M.A. Crew and P.R. Kleindorfer. Boston, MA: Kluwer Academic Publishers.

Official Journal of the European Communities, 10/06/02, No L 176/21, "Directive No 2002/39/EC of the European Parliament and of the Council amending Directive 97/67/EC with regard to the further opening to competition of Community postal services."

Panzar, John. 2002. "Reconciling Competition, Downstream Access and Universal Service in Postal Markets." In *Postal and Delivery Services: Delivering on Competition*, edited by M.A. Crew and P.R. Kleindorfer. Boston, MA: Kluwer Academic Publishers.

Chapter 9

Delivery Costs II

Back to Parametric Models

Catherine Cazals[1], Frédérique Fève[1], Jean-Pierre Florens[1], and Bernard Roy[2]
University of Toulouse (IDEI & GREMAQ)[1], and La Poste[2]

1. INTRODUCTION

It is commonly accepted that the outdoor mail delivery process exhibits strong scale economies, even if models differ on the precise measurement of this phenomena. Engineering models based on analytical analyses of the delivery process estimate scale factors in excess of 4 or, equivalently, to a scale elasticity smaller than 0.25, so that an increase of 1% of the quantity of mail would imply a cost variation of only 0.25% (see Roy 1999 and Bernard et al 2002). Econometric models have also provided estimates of significant scale factors (around 2 or 3) (see Cazals et al 1997 and 2001). The econometric models are based on the estimation of a relation between the cost and the quantity of mail. Such a relation is usually estimated using micro data measured at the level of delivery offices. Then the cost function should incorporate variables describing the heterogeneity between offices. This diversity is introduced through observable explanatory variables and, if the sampling scheme permits, using unobservable heterogeneity components. One of the strongest conclusions of ten years of estimation of delivery cost models is that the more precise the treatment of heterogeneity between delivery offices, the lower the estimated scale elasticity. In particular the use of panel data and of individual unobservable effects leads to estimations of scale elasticity around 3 if the model also incorporates some observable heterogeneity components; the same argument applies when using a nonparametric specification, which allows very different cost structures between "small" and "large" offices.

Using a new data set describing the cost of outdoor delivery for French offices in 2001 we estimate a very simple constant elasticity model where the cost is modeled as a function of the total traffic and of two heterogeneity components, the surface[1] and the population (measured by the 1999 census; hereafter referred to as population99). As we note below, this model is also equivalent to representing delivery cost as a function of the traffic, the population density and the traffic per capita. Section 2 presents the main result of such an elementary econometric model: The elasticity of the cost with respect to the traffic is estimated to be 0.28. Furthermore, if the sample is sub-divided according to the traffic it appears that the elasticity is almost zero for the very small offices (costs are essentially fixed) and jumps to 0.7 for very large offices.

The models presented in section 2 are more "descriptive" than "structural" because they do not incorporate technology choices or design of delivery offices, which introduce selection bias or endogeneity bias in the estimation. In this paper we carry out two steps in the direction of the specification of a more structural model. Actually, we consider two (partial) phenomena.

Section 3 presents the first one. We show that two technologies may be used for the delivery of packets: The packets may be delivered jointly with the rest of the mail or by specific motorized rounds. We consider a model which incorporates this choice as an endogenous selection mechanism.

Secondly, the model of section 4 shows that the surface of the office is an important explanatory variable. However the strategy of the design of the offices is conducted in order to reduce the cost. The decomposition of the territory into delivery offices defines units of observation with a surface depending on unknown heterogeneity components of the costs. Then the surface should be treated as endogenous: This is the goal of the last section of this paper. The model we present is not fully satisfactory because the process of construction or regrouping offices is not explicitly modeled and in particular the number of offices[2] is kept exogenous.

---

[1] Surface: size of the geographical postal area covered by a delivery office (denoted for simplicity the surface in the paper).

[2] The sample size is also kept exogenous.

2. AN ELEMENTARY COST MODEL OF OUTDOOR DELIVERY OFFICES

Econometric costs models are specified by a relation between the total cost of the production unit as a function of the level of the output, input prices and some other explanatory variables. We estimate the model using a single cross section. The input prices are then constant and their effect is not identified.

This model is based on the empirical analysis of elementary Cobb Douglas models estimated in this section by ordinary least squares method. These models have the form:

$$\ln C = \alpha \ln T + \sum_{j=1}^{K} \beta_j \ln Z_j + \gamma + \mu$$

where C is the total cost of outdoor delivery, T the total traffic and $Z_1,\ldots,Z_K$ several cofactors describing the demographical/geographical structure of the offices. The parameter γ is a constant and u is a random unobservable component.

This type of model is, inevitably, a simplification and is certainly an imperfect summary of the reality. However it provides the best approximation of the real complex cost function by a constant elasticity function. The value of α (or its inverse $1/\alpha$ defining the scale economy factor) represents the relations between traffic and cost.

Our data set comprises 4739 observations, each one corresponding to a delivery office in France; for each office we observe the total outdoor cost[3], the total number of delivered items, and several heterogeneity variables. A selection of most relevant explanatory variables based on usual t-statistics and on economic interpretation of the results suggests two leading observable heterogeneity components, namely the population and the surface. Let us recall that each office is attached to a well defined geographical area and its population was measured by the 1999 census. The surface is defined by the number of square meters of this area. In comparison with previous studies, we have less observations[4] and this new data set concerns a unique year only. The introduction of an unobservable heterogeneity component is then impossible.

---

[3] Total outdoor cost : mixed rounds (on foot +bicycle) charges + motorized mixed rounds charges +dedicated rounds charges

[4] Some of the delivery offices consist of a main office and satellite offices ("echelon de distribution"). In previous studies these satellite offices were considered separated production units but they are now regrouped with the main office to which they are attached. This procedure is more relevant for the measurement of cost and of traffic.

The model may be written in two equivalent ways

$$\ln C = \underset{(26.1)}{0.28}\ln T + \underset{(40.8)}{0.48}\ln P + \underset{(50.3)}{0.19}\ln S + \underset{(5.9)}{0.64} \qquad R^2 = 0.88 \qquad (1)$$

Where *C, T, S* and *P* represent, respectively, cost, traffic, surface and population; the numbers in parentheses are the student-t values.

An equivalent form of the previous equation is:

$$\ln\frac{C}{T} = \underset{(-7.8)}{-0.05}\ln T - \underset{(-56.5)}{0.67}\ln\frac{T}{P} - \underset{(-50.3)}{0.19}\ln\frac{P}{S} + \underset{(5.9)}{0.64} \quad R^2 = 0.88 \qquad (2)$$

In this relation the explanatory variable is the unitary cost (C/T) defined by the ratio of the total cost divided by the quantity of mail.

The relations between the coefficients of the two models are obvious consequences of elementary computations. For example, the elasticity of the total cost to the traffic equal to 0.28 is decomposed in 1-0.05-0.67 in the second model: The elasticity of unitary cost to the traffic (with a traffic per capita constant) is -0.05; the elasticity to the traffic per capita (with a traffic constant) is 0.67. The difference between the cost elasticity and the unitary cost elasticity is one, by definition of the elasticity. The estimate of the elasticity of the total cost to the traffic of 0.28 corresponds to a scale factor greater than 3.5.

Model (2) shows that the main unitary cost drivers are the traffic per capita and the density (a smaller effect of the traffic). A change in the traffic has more of an impact on the cost than does the direct influence of the traffic per capita.[5]

In order to capture a more complex relation between cost and cost drivers, we have divided the sample into sub groups.

We have first stratified the sample into three groups of equal size function of the traffic per capita

$$\text{Low}\frac{T}{P} \quad \ln\frac{C}{T} = \underset{(-8.1)}{-0.08}\ln T - \underset{(-44.3)}{0.88}\ln\frac{T}{P} - \underset{(-29.2)}{0.22}\ln\frac{P}{S} + \underset{(11.4)}{1.90} \quad R^2 = 0.74 \qquad (3)$$

$$\text{Intermediate}\frac{T}{P} \quad \ln\frac{C}{T} = \underset{(-6.5)}{-0.06}\ln T - \underset{(-6.5)}{0.6}\,T\ln\frac{T}{P} - \underset{(-39.4)}{0.23}\ln\frac{P}{S} + \underset{(0.2)}{0.024} \quad R^2 = 0.67 \quad (4)$$

[5] Traffic per capita: traffic divided by population99.

$$\text{High}\frac{T}{P} \qquad \ln\frac{C}{T} = \underset{(-1.2)}{-0.001}\ln T - \underset{(-14.3)}{0.4}\ln\frac{T}{P} - \underset{(-32.2)}{0.19}\ln\frac{P}{S} - \underset{(-6.0)}{1.38} \quad R^2 = 0.69 \qquad (5)$$

The elasticity of the cost to the total traffic of the three groups is respectively 0.04, 0.36 and 0.58; elasticity increases with the traffic per capita.

A second stratification of the sample is based on the level of the density.

$$\text{Low } \frac{P}{S} \quad \left(\frac{P}{S} < 42 \ \text{ hab/km}^2\right):$$

$$\ln\frac{C}{T} = \underset{(-9.4)}{-0.12}\ln T - \underset{(-31.3)}{0.69}\ln\frac{T}{P} - \underset{(-31.5)}{0.29}\ln\frac{P}{S} + \underset{(5.4)}{1.38} \quad R^2 = 0.55 \qquad (6)$$

$$\text{Intermediate } \frac{P}{S} \quad \left(42 \le \frac{P}{S} \le 118 \ \text{ hab/Km}^2\right):$$

$$\ln\frac{C}{T} = \underset{(-1.2)}{0.008}\ln T - \underset{(-53.2)}{0.89}\ln\frac{T}{P} - \underset{(-16.3)}{0.26}\ln\frac{P}{S} + \underset{(2.0)}{0.48} \quad R^2 = 0.7 \qquad (7)$$

$$\text{High } \frac{P}{S} \quad \left(\frac{P}{S} > 118 \ \text{ hab/Km}^2\right):$$

$$\ln\frac{C}{T} = \underset{(-36.4)}{0.001}\ln T - \underset{(-31.1)}{0.69}\ln\frac{T}{P} - \underset{(-4.3)}{0.098}\ln\frac{P}{S} + \underset{(-5.2)}{0.7} \quad R^2 = 0.63 \qquad (8)$$

The elasticity of the cost to the total traffic of the three groups is 0.19, 0.03 and 0.3. This U shape of the elasticity function of the density is one of the main results of this empirical study. In intermediate density, the cost is almost completely independent from a small variation in the traffic. In low or high density regions the cost reacts to a variation of traffic and this variation is more important in the high density areas.

Finally the joint effect of stratification by traffic per capita and by density is analyzed by the estimation of nine models. The empirical evidence is summarized by graph (figure 1) representing total cost elasticity to traffic or to unit cost to traffic per capita.

The U shape of the relation between elasticity and density is preserved and this curve is shifted up when the traffic per capita increases.

The graph also gives the relative mean unit cost by group of delivery offices. The higher elasticities correspond to the lower mean unit cost but the mean unit cost increases when the density or the traffic per capita increases (numbers in brackets are mean unit cost)

The mean unit cost (where, by convention, the mean unit cost of high traffic and high density offices is 1) is computed from the data and not from the estimated model.

Table 1: Mean unit costs

Density / Traffic per Capita	Low	Intermediate	High	
Low	4.25 (7.25)	3.125 (10.6)	3 (13)	3.5 (10.3)
Intermediate	3 (1)	1.75 (0.37)	1.25 (0.37)	2.125 (9.75)
High	2.5 (1)	1.375 (0.37)	1 (0.25)	1.5 (9.5)
	3.25 (4.25)	2.25 (7.125)	1.5 (6.37)	2.375 (6.125)

(Numbers in brackets are the standard deviation)

Figure 1: Total cost Elasticity to Traffic (Surface and population given)

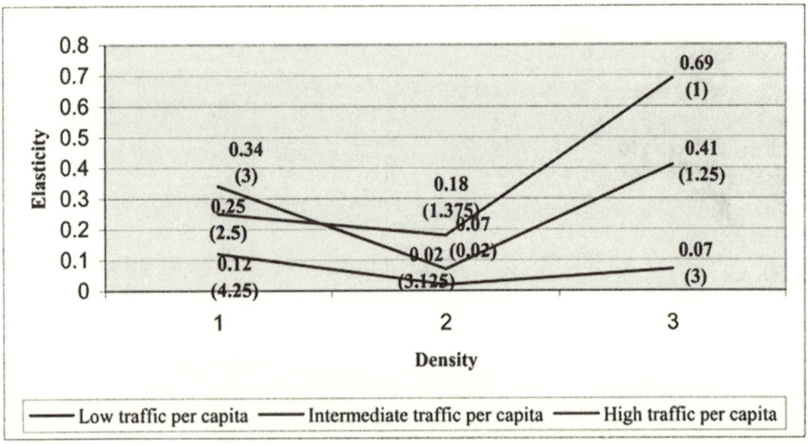

These different values of cost elasticities and the particular shape of the function need an explanation, drawn from the economics of delivery, as described in Cohen and Chu (1997), Roy (1999), and Bernard et al (2002).

To make things clearer, we can briefly recall that in the delivery process, the fixed costs are accounted for by the need for the carrier to move from one stop to another, whereas the variable costs consist in loading the mailboxes. The stop time needs particular attention. Indeed, the delivery model is made more complex by the fact that the proportion between fixed and marginal costs is not constant. According to the level of traffic, the stop time can be either considered as fixed or variable. For very low levels of traffic, a single letter requires its own stop. But for very high levels of traffic, a letter just adds to an existing stop as described in Jasinski and Steggles (1977) through a Poisson process. Therefore, the marginal cost (i.e., the derivative of the cost function) is not constant and depends on the level of traffic.

These effects exist in the econometrics presented here, while we examine the range of elasticities obtained over the different values of traffic. As the level of traffic increases, the scale economies are exhausted, because the relative weight of loading time increases whereas the route time and stop time remain fixed. The average cost goes down as the marginal cost has become constant. Therefore, the value of cost elasticity with respect to traffic increases, although the value of average cost decreases. This explains why costs elasticity obtained with higher levels of traffic are above the ones obtained with lower levels.

The singular result is the U shape, which leads to an analysis of the cost elasticities with respect to traffic over the different values of density. For a very high value of density, it is easy to understand that the relative amount of fixed costs is lower than in medium density: The distance between two stops is lower, and the stops are shared with more addresses.

The quite interesting case occurs for very low levels of density. In these areas, we should expect the value of cost elasticity to be even lower than in medium density, since the distance between two stops is even greater. But if we look at it closer, one stop may correspond to one addressee only.

For an equal level of traffic, the probability that an extra letter generates an extra stop is higher in low density areas than in medium density areas, in which one stop can serve several addresses. So, as described above, the stop-part of the costs can be considered more as a variable cost in very rural areas.

It also can be mentioned that in very low density areas, an extra letter can lead to a detour (increasing the route costs), or conversely a decrease of volumes may allow short cuts in the delivery process, because some parts of the route can be avoided. This is very accurate when the levels of traffic are quite low. Again, this explains why we can find higher cost elasticities in areas with very low density.

3. AN ENDOGENOUS SELECTION MODEL FOR OPTIMAL DELIVERY OF PACKETS

As described in Roy (1999) and Bernard et al (2002), in France, the optimal mode for delivering letter mail is often by foot or bicycle. But the existence of parcels renders quite complex the choice of the mode of delivery in these areas. If we assume that it is impossible to deliver parcels in something other than a van (ignoring the special cases of very small or very few parcels), then it is quite difficult to determine whether routes must be dedicated for parcels or integrated with letter mail.

In the case where the optimal mode for delivery for letter mail is the van, the question is straightforward. In the case where the optimal mode for delivery is foot or bicycle, the trade-off is the following: Is the loss made by a van constraint (sub-optimal) lower than the gains made by sharing the fixed costs of the route?

In very high-density areas, using a van for delivering letter mail can be significantly more expensive. As the distance between two stops becomes smaller, the speed of traveling becomes very slow, perhaps even slower than a pedestrian. This is amplified by the necessity of parking the van at each stop (or so), which creates prohibitive extra costs. For a dedicated parcel delivery, however, the stop coverage is quite low, so the van does not have to stop at every point. It is quite natural therefore to organize dedicated routes in very dense areas.

So the key question is that of the "grey zone": The zones with medium density, where the problem of organizing dedicated routes or not becomes relevant. In La Poste, an engineering model (taking its roots in Roy 1999), has assisted the decision making process. It is interesting to study now *ex post* how econometrics can treat the results.

Two categories of delivery offices appear in the sample:

- in most of the offices (3937 of 4739[6]) packets are delivered jointly with the other mail ($D = 0$)
- - in 802 offices (17%) packets are delivered by specific motorized rounds ($D = 1$)

This decision is considered endogenous and the model incorporates this mechanism by an endogenous switching model (see Gourieroux 2000), which has the following structure:

- the counterfactual model: Each delivery office has two cost functions depending on the choice between D equal to either 0 or 1

---

[6] Due to a few missing data, the sample size has been modified a little depending on the variables.

- the assignment equation which explains how the decision between 0 and 1 is taken.

The model assumes that for any office only one of the two regimes is observed and that the decision rule is not independent of the potential outcome, even conditionally on the explanatory variables.

The estimation is conducted using Heckman's two-step method and gives the following results:

Cost function without dedicated rounds:

$$\ln C = \underset{(9.1)}{0.18} \ln T + \underset{(21.4)}{0.43} \ln P + \underset{(39.0)}{0.23} \ln S + \underset{(8.2)}{1.66} \tag{9}$$

or equivalently

$$\ln \frac{C}{T} = -0.16 \ln T - 0.66 \ln \frac{T}{P} - 0.23 \ln \frac{P}{S} + 1.66 \tag{10}$$

Cost function with dedicated rounds

$$\ln C = \underset{(7.0)}{0.39} \ln T + \underset{(10.2)}{0.91} \ln P + \underset{(11.4)}{0.11} \ln S - \underset{(-2.9)}{4.46} \tag{11}$$

or equivalently

$$\ln \frac{C}{T} = 0.41 \ln T - 1.02 \ln \frac{T}{P} - 0.11 \ln \frac{P}{S} - 4.46 \tag{12}$$

Decision equation (Probit model):

$$\text{Prob}(D=1) = \Phi\left(+\underset{(5.4)}{0.36} \ln T + \underset{(3.9)}{0.51} \ln P + \underset{(1.9)}{0.18} \ln \text{Re}\, vp - \underset{(-25.2)}{13.4} \right) \tag{13}$$

where Φ is the cumulative function of the normal distribution and Revp is the average household revenue.

The two lambda coefficients of the Mills Ratio are significant and confirm that the selection between the two regimes is not merely random.

As the decision whether or not to use dedicated rounds is highly correlated to the size of the office, it is not surprising to verify that the size of the elasticity is smaller for offices without dedicated rounds.

In the linear case under consideration, identification of the model with an endogenous selection rule does not require specific instrumental variables in the selection equation. However we have selected the number of firms as an instrument in order to increase the robustness of the procedure.

An interesting validity test of this model is to compare actual decisions and optimal ones. Indeed for each office the models (9) and (11) permit a computation of the (latent) costs in the two regimes given T, P and S. We can then compute the difference[7] Δ and the office is classified as either one, which should use dedicated rounds or one which should deliver all mail jointly. The results are in the following table:

Table 2: Actual decisions and optimal ones

	Number of offices which should		
Number of Offices that actually	use dedicated rounds	not use dedicated rounds	
Used dedicated rounds	488	314	802
Did not use dedicated rounds	168	3 769	3937
	656	4 083	4739

The number of mismatches between prediction and reality is 482 (10% of the offices).

4. ENDOGENEITY OF DELIVERY OFFICES' DESIGN

Let us consider a territory with a particular density of inhabitants and mail distribution per capita. The postal operator will divide this territory into n units with a particular spatial shape. This division minimizes the total delivery cost. In such a model the number and the shape (in particular the surface area) of the delivery offices become endogenous. Indeed the cost structure depends on local heterogeneity factors known by the operator and then incorporated into the optimal partition of the territory.

Even if in reality, the division of France into delivery offices is largely the consequence of historical considerations, it is certainly also partially based on cost minimization considerations. It would be difficult to write a theoretical model of optimal division and to estimate such a fully structural specification.[8] However we want to consider the surface of each delivery

7 Δ is the exact average treatment effect of the use of dedicated rounds.

8 This problem is strongly related to the problem of observing the integral of a continuous time process between random times. This question has been considered recently in finance. In the case of delivery offices, time processes become spatial processes and the

office as an endogenous variable in the model and to estimate the cost function using an instrumental variables method. This approach is an approximation of the implicit structural model and, in particular, the number of observations is treated as exogenous.

Then we just consider the same equation as equation (1) (in section 2) but in the case in which the surface is endogenous and the estimation is done by instrumental variables[9] (or $2SLS$ in that case). The obtained estimation is:

$$\ln C = \underset{(27.9)}{0.33}\ln T + \underset{(36.3)}{0.44}\ln P + \underset{(44.4)}{0.26}\ln S - \underset{(-6.3)}{0.97} \tag{14}$$

or equivalently

$$\ln\frac{C}{T} = \underset{(4.2)}{0.03}\ln T - \underset{(-55.9)}{0.7}\ln\frac{T}{P} - \underset{(43.9)}{0.26}\ln\frac{P}{S} - \underset{(-6.2)}{0.97} \tag{15}$$

A test of endogeneity has been performed. This test estimates the previous equation by OLS but introduces the estimated residuals of the instrumental equation. Endogeneity is then equivalent to the significance of the coefficient of the residuals and is not rejected in our case.

Despite this evidence in favor of endogeneity the model does not provide dramatically different results from our previous ones[10]: In particular, the scale factor for the whole sample is around 3. The increment of the elasticity of traffic between model (1) and model (6) depends upon the surface where the traffic changes. The model estimated in this section shows that if the traffic increases, the surface will decrease.

If we allow a variation of the surface to a modification of traffic, the elasticity becomes:

$$\begin{aligned}\frac{\partial \ln C}{\partial \ln T} &= 0.33 + 0.26\frac{\partial \ln S}{\partial \ln T} \\ &= 0.33 + 0.26(-0.40) = 0.226\end{aligned}$$

Finally, it should be noted that it is valid to consider the surface of the density as endogenous, given the hypothesis of the exogeneity of the population.

---

question becomes extremely complex. To our knowledge no econometric model is based on this kind of computation.

9 Instruments selected are the household revenue index, the number of firms and the average mailboxes by block of flats.

10 See section 2.

5. CONCLUDING REMARKS

This paper presents several parametric log linear models for the outdoor delivery cost functions based on a survey of all the French delivery offices in 2001. The main empirical results derived from this set of estimations are the following:

The best approximation of the model by a constant elasticity model gives an elasticity of the cost to the traffic equal to 0.28, confirming the existence of a strong scale economy in the delivery process. A relevant selection of cost drivers for the unit cost of a delivery office uses the traffic per capita, the density and, at a lower level, the total traffic. The total cost elasticity is actually not constant: It increases with the traffic per capita and is a U shape function of the density.

This U shape, highlighted econometrically for the first time, is one of the main contributions of this paper: It is very well explained by the Economics of delivery and it reconciles different anterior results upon costs elasticities.

The design of the delivery process should be treated endogenously. In most of the previous models of the cost of delivery, the design of the process, i.e. the division of the territory into delivery area and the organization of rounds, is considered as given. We have shown that it is useful to treat it as an endogenous component and to explain this by the model. In this paper the design was catch by the use of rounds not dedicated and by the surface of area of each office. In future research we plan to consider jointly endogeneity of the design of the delivery offices and non constant elasticity models.

APPENDIX: THE DATA

Definition of the variables

Sample Size 4 764 Metropolitan French Post Delivery Offices (2001) 25 Delivery Offices with missing data	
Lcost (Cost)	Mixed rounds (on foot+bicycle) charges+motorized mixed rounds)charges + motorized dedicated rounds charges
LTrafic (Traffic)	Mixed rounds (on foot+bicycle) traffic+motorized mixed rounds) traffic + motorized dedicated rounds traffic
Lpop99 (Population 99)	INSEE[11] definition
Lsurface (Surface)	Surface covered by each Delivery Office
Lnb_etab (Number of firms)	INSEE definition
Ltraf_tete (Unit cost)	Traffic per capita
Ldensity (population density)	Population99 divided by surface
LIRE (average mailboxes index)	Number of mailboxes divided by block of flats
Lrev_moy_men (average Households revenue)	= Number of Households x Households Delivery Offices revenue index[12]

REFERENCES

Bernard, Stéphane, Robert H. Cohen., Matthew H. Robinson, Bernard Roy, Joëlle Toledano, John D. Waller, and Spyros S. Xenakis. 2002. "Delivery Cost Heterogeneity and Vulnerability to Entry, in Postal and Delivery Services." In *Delivering on Competition*, edited by M.A.. Crew, and P.R. Kleindorfer, Boston, MA: Kluwer Academic Publishers.

Bradley, Michael D., Jeff Colvin, and John Panzar.1997. "Issues in Measuring Incremental Cost in a Multi-Function Enterprise." In *Managing Change in the Postal and Delivery Industries*, edited by M.A. Crew, and P.R. Kleindorfer, Boston, MA: Kluwer Academic Publishers.

Cohen, Robert H. and Edward H. Chu. 1997. "A Measure of Scale Economies for Postal Systems." In *Managing Changes in the Postal Delivery Industries*, edited by M.A. Crew, and P.R. Kleindorfer, Boston, MA: Kluwer Academic Publishers.

Cazals, Catherine, Robert M. De Rycke, Jean-Pierre Florens, and Séverine Rouzaud., 1997. "Scale Economies and Natural Monopoly in the Postal Delivery: Comparison between Parametric and Non Parametric." In *Managing Change in the Postal and Delivery Industries*, edited by M.A. Crew, and P.R. Kleindorfer, Boston, MA: Kluwer Academic Publishers.

---

[11] INSEE : Institut National de la Statistique et des Etudes Economiques (French census bureau).

[12] DGI : Direction Générale des Impôts, France (French Taxes Administration).

Cazals, Catherine, Jean-Pierre Florens, and Bernard Roy. 2001. "An Analysis of Some Specific Cost Drivers in the Delivery Activity." In *Future Directions in Postal Reform*, edited by M.A. Crew, and P.R. Kleindorfer, Boston, MA: Kluwer Academic Publishers.

Cohen, Robert H. and Edward H. Chu. "A Measure of Scale Economies for Postal Systems." In *Managing Change in the Postal and Delivery Industries,* edited by M.A. Crew, and P.R. Kleindorfer, Boston, MA: Kluwer Academic Publishers.

Cremer Helmuth, André Grimaud,, Jean-Pierre Florens, Sarah Marcy, Bernard Roy, and Joëlle Toledano. 2001. "Entry and Competition in the Postal Market: Foundations of the Construction of Entry Scenarios." *Journal of Regulatory Economics* 19(2): 107-121.

Davidson, Russel and James G. Mac Kinnon. 1993. *Estimation and Inference in Econometrics*. New York, NY: Oxford University Press.

Gourieroux, Christian. 2000. *Econometrics of Qualitative Dependant Variables.* Cambridge, U.K.: Cambridge University Press.

Jasinski, K. M. and T.J. Steggles. 1977. "Modelling Letter Delivery in Town Areas." *Computers and Operations research* 4(4): 287-294

Roy, B. 1999. "Technico-Economic Analysis of the Costs of Outside Work in Postal Delivery." In *Emerging Competition in Postal and Delivery Services*, edited by M.A. Crew, and P.R. Kleindorfer, Boston, MA: Kluwer Academic Publishers.

Chapter 10

Delivery Costs for Postal Services in the UK

Some Results on Scale Economies with Panel Data

Catherine Cazals[1], Jean-Pierre Florens[1], and Soterios Soteri[2]
University of Toulouse (IDEI & GREMAQ)[1], and Royal Mail Group[2]

1. INTRODUCTION

A key assumption underpinning some of the most important issues in postal economics is that high fixed costs in delivery give rise to substantial economies of scale in the delivery network. For example, as Cohen and Chu (1997) make clear, fixed costs and the notion of economies of scale in delivery underpin two of the modern justifications for maintaining a letter monopoly. First, that the delivery network is a natural monopoly. Second, a letter monopoly is necessary to assure universal service at a uniform price. During the past decade a number of cost (or production) models have been estimated for the mail delivery activity of postal services in France and the US and the main conclusion drawn from this work is that this activity is indeed characterized by economies of scale (see for example, Rogerson and Takis (1993), Cazals, DeRycke, Florens and Rouzaud (1997), Cohen and Chu (1997), Roy (1999), Cazals, Florens and Roy (2001)). A further result derived from this literature is the importance of taking the heterogeneity of delivery offices into account when estimating returns to scale. For example, Cazals et al (2001) show that such estimates can be considerably higher when heterogeneity between delivery offices is taken into account.

This paper extends the literature on the estimation of economies of scale for outdoor delivery activity to mail services in the United Kingdom (Royal Mail). To this end we use a data set for a large representative sample of delivery offices in the UK observed for two years to estimate cost functions.

The panel dimension of these data allows us to take into account unobservable heterogeneity by specifying individual-specific effects. The cost function we consider is a relationship between outdoor costs of delivery (financial costs) and the output, defined as the quantity of delivered mail (number of items), and environmental characteristics. The environmental variables we include are the surface of the delivery area and the number of delivery points in this area. A log-linear functional form is then specified for the cost function.

In order to increase our control of heterogeneity factors between delivery offices we take into account an additional potential cost driver for delivery which is the proportion of total traffic delivered by town ('non rural') routes in each delivery office. This variable enters in a non-linear way in our cost model as we estimate cost functions for some stratifications of the sample with respect to different values for this proportion. We obtain results about the behaviour of economies of scale with these stratifications, showing that this variable is a useful way to capture heterogeneity in delivery offices. In order to emphasise the importance of the treatment of heterogeneity and the usefulness of panel data in dealing with this issue we test whether outdoor delivery cost models estimated with panel data encompass models estimated with cross-section data.

By reparameterising our estimated models we also give an alternative representation of this simple log-linear model, which provides useful insights in terms of postal policy and planning. In this model outdoor delivery costs can be expressed as a function of the number of delivery points, area and traffic per delivery point. This specification allows us to examine the relative importance of traffic and delivery point growth and their different impacts on economies of scale in outdoor delivery.

2. SPECIFICATION OF THE COST MODEL

We are interested in the estimation of an outdoor cost function for the mail delivery activity. Generally, a cost function is defined as a relation between the production cost, denoted by C, and the level of production, denoted by Q, (here the delivered mail volume), the prices of inputs, denoted by the vector P, and possibly some environmental (exogenous) variables, denoted by the vector X.

When data are available on these variables for n decision units, we can undertake an empirical analysis of this cost function, which can be written as follows:

$$C_i=f(Q_i, P_i, X_i, u_i), \qquad i=1,\dots, n \tag{1}$$

where u represents the usual random error term, assumed to be well behaved (zero mean and constant variance), which captures statistical noise and unobserved heterogeneity.

We must then decide on whether to specify a functional form for f(.) or not. In the case where no specification is assumed for f(.) we could apply a non-parametric estimation methodology (kernel method, local polynomial regression, ... see Cazals, DeRycke, Florens and Rouzaud (1997)).

In this paper we adopt a traditional parametric analysis approach and assume a log-linear specification for f(.). As we have no information on input prices in our data, the cost function we consider can be interpreted as a mean cost function with respect to the distribution of these prices. The cost function can then be written as follows:

$$LnC_i = a + bLnQ_i + cLnX_i + u_i \tag{2}$$

The estimation of this model can be performed by standard least squares . In this study, we use panel data, that is data for *n* decision units which are observed over a number of time periods. The main advantage of estimation with panel data over cross-sectional data, is that we can control better for individual heterogeneity, with an appropriate decomposition of the error term. More precisely, the previous cost model with panel data becomes, for *i*=1,...N, and *t*=1,..., T:

$$LnC_{it} = \alpha + \beta LnQ_{it} + \gamma LnX_{it} + u_{it} \tag{3}$$

where u_{it} is decomposed by the sum of a standard random error term e_{it} and an unobservable individual specific effect a_i such that $u_{it} = a_i + e_{it}$.

Typically two approaches can be used for the estimation: fixed effects or random effects. With the fixed effect approach, the estimation is performed conditionally on the distribution of the individual effect a_i. With the random effect approach, we assume a specific marginal distribution for a_i (for technical details, see Hsiao (1986), Baltagi (1995)). The main drawback of the fixed effect model is that time invariant explanatory variables are not allowed. We then use in this study the random effect model, because we introduce time invariant environmental variables.

3. RESULTS

The decision unit in this study is a delivery office. We use data for a sample of 509 delivery offices from Royal Mail (UK), which are observed over 2 years: 2001/02 and 2002/03.

More precisely, for each delivery office i (i=1, ..., 509) at time t (t=1, 2), we consider the following variables to estimate the cost model: C_{it} outdoor delivery costs (in £); Q_{it}, number of delivered items; NDP_i, number of delivery points in the delivery office zone; and $AREA_i$, area of the delivery office zone in square km. The variables *NDP* and *AREA* are environmental variables (then, corresponding to the previous section, we have *X= (NDP, AREA))* which are time invariant.

Model (3) can be finally expressed as:

$$LnC_{it} = \alpha + \beta LnQ_{it} + \gamma_1 LnAREA_i + \gamma_2 LnNDP_i + a_i + e_{it} \tag{4}$$

where $e_{it} \sim IDD\left(0, \sigma_e^2\right)$, and $a_{it} \sim IDD\left(0, \sigma_a^2\right)$, and we assume the e_{it} are independent of the a_i.

We consider an additional characteristic of delivery offices in the estimation of this cost function, the proportion of traffic delivered by non rural routes (that is mail delivered by town routes, to firms and very large users). This variable is introduced in a non-linear way, by a stratification of the sample into different ranges for this proportion.

Table 1: Estimated coefficients of outdoor cost functions

Proportion of Q delivered by non rural routes	n	Ln Q (β)	Coefficient of Ln AREA (γ_1)	Ln NDP (γ_2)	Constant (α)	R^2	ρ
<0.65	110	0.228 (0.055)	0.145 (0.019)	0.583 (0.061)	3.412 (0.434)	0.928	0.909
[0.65; 0.85]	110	0.359 (0.052)	0.125 (0.014)	0.570 (0.057)	1.470 (0.369)	*0.967*	*0.864*
[0.85; 1]	149	0.416 (0.048)	0.050 (0.014)	0.555 (0.049)	0.99 (0.394)	*0.953*	*0.861*
=1	140	0.543 (0.047)	0.047 (0.015)	0.427 (0.051)	0.156* (0.434)	*0.915*	*0.686*
Full sample	509	0.418 (0.027)	0.087 (0.004)	0.476 (0.028)	1.624 (0.218)	*0.939*	*0.845*

Note: Standard errors are reported in parentheses. All coefficients are statistically significant at the 5% level except where indicated by an asterisk.

Our main objective is the estimation of the outdoor cost elasticity with respect to traffic. With the log linear specification for the cost function, this elasticity corresponds to β, the coefficient of the logarithm of traffic. Table 1 gives the results of estimated coefficients of cost functions for each sub-sample corresponding to different values of the proportion of traffic delivered by non rural routes. This table gives also the value of R^2, and the value of $\rho = \frac{\sigma_a^2}{\sigma_a^2 + \sigma_e^2}$, which represents the proportion of the variance of residuals due to the variance of the individual-specific effect. The estimation methodology used is generalized least squares (GLS). We also performed maximum likelihood estimates which yielded very similar results.

A first general comment of these results is that the goodness of fit of these models is high (i.e. all R^2 are greater than 0.9). We can also notice that most of the variance in the residuals, for each sub-sample, is due to the variance in the delivery office-specific effect (ρ varies from 68% to 91%), while the remainder is due to purely statistical noise.

The estimated coefficients for traffic reported in table 1 suggest that outdoor delivery activity in the UK exhibits a high degree of economies of scale. For example, the model estimated over the full sample yields a total returns to scale estimate for mail volumes of 2.4, as given by the reciprocal of the coefficient on traffic variable, *Q*, for the total sample ($\beta = 0.418$). This overall result is consistent with studies on outdoor delivery costs in the USA and France (see for example Cazals et al (2001) and Postal Rate Commission (2003)). It should be noted, however, that the returns to scale estimate lies in the range 1.8 to 4.4 when the sample is estimated for different values of the proportion of traffic delivered by non-rural routes. This range of estimates highlights the non-linear nature of the estimated outdoor delivery cost function and the importance of taking heterogeneity into account when estimating economies of scale. In general, the results indicate higher returns to scale in delivery offices with a lower proportion of traffic delivered by non- rural routes and suggest that more rural areas, which tend to have lower levels of traffic per delivery point than more urban areas, have greater scope for economies of scale.

4. ENCOMPASSING TEST

This section is devoted to the analysis of the ability of the previous panel cost model to encompass rivals models. More precisely we want to test if this model can explain results of models estimated with cross-section data (that is using observations for only one period). For a theoretic version of the encompassing principle and test, see for example Mizon and Richard (1986).

To this end, we use the models estimated with panel data in the previous section for each stratum to generate samples for cost variable for one period and we regress this simulated cost on exogenous variables (*Q, AREA* and *NDP*), in logarithms. Then, we compare the values of the estimated coefficients with observed data with the distribution of the estimated coefficients obtained with the simulated samples.

More precisely, we compute the adjusted values of the dependant variable (logarithm of cost) in each model (each stratum), as follows (for notational convenience we now denote the logarithm of variables by small letters, then c = *Ln C, q=Ln Q, area=Ln AREA* and *ndp=Ln NDP*):

$$\hat{c}_{it} = \hat{\alpha} + \hat{\beta} q_{it} + \hat{\gamma}_1 area_i + \hat{\gamma}_2 ndp_i + \hat{a}_i$$

where t=1,2 and i=1, ...,n_k and n_k is the number of observations in the kth stratum, k=1,...,4.

For each stratum we draw then 1000 samples of the residual e_{it}, denoted e_{it}^S, from a normal distribution with a mean 0 and a standard deviation equal to the estimated value of the standard deviation of residual in each model. The sizes of these samples are compatible with the number of observation in each stratum (that is for example, we draw 1000 samples of size n=110 for the 1st stratum). We obtain then for each stratum, 1000 simulated samples for the logarithm of cost, defined as:

$$c_{it}^S = \hat{c}_{it} + u_{it}^S$$

Finally we estimate the coefficient of $\hat{c}_{it}^S$ on $(q_{it}, ndp_i, area_i)$, for t=1 (that is 2001/02).

If the panel model encompasses the cross-section model, then data generated by the panel model and used to estimate models with cross-section data must give results such that the value of estimated parameters from observed data can be viewed as a random drawing on the distribution of parameters obtained with simulated data.

Table 2 gives the results of these estimations. In the first column we give the values of estimated coefficients using only a cross section with real (observed) data for one period (t=1). In the following columns we give the mean, the standard deviation and a confidence interval for estimated parameters from simulated data. In the last column we give for comparison the value of coefficient obtained with panel data for two periods.

The first comment is about the values of estimated cost elasticities with respect to the traffic (coefficient of *Ln Q*) when we use observed cross-section data compared to the values obtained with panel data. We obtain greater values in all classes when the estimation is performed with cross-section data, implying smaller returns to scale than with panel data. This indicates that the use of cross-section data alone will tend to bias up the size of the estimated coefficients and hence understate the extent of returns to scale in outdoor delivery. At the same time the results for the estimated cost elasticities with respect to delivery points (coefficient of *Ln NDP*) show the opposite effect. Here, cross-section data in general (except for the most urban areas) tend to bias downwards the size of the cost elasticity with respect to the number of delivery points and so overstate returns to scale from delivery point growth.

Secondly, we notice that the values of estimated coefficients in models with observed cross-section all belong to the confidence intervals calculated from estimation with simulated samples. This indicates that panel models encompass "cross-section models" and implies that no additional information can be obtained from estimates using cross-section data. This result shows that the use of panel structure of data, when available, is important. Such a panel dimension of data allows us to take into account a greater degree of heterogeneity amongst delivery offices in the estimation procedure and yields better estimators.

Table 2: Regression results from observed and simulated cross-section data

	From observed data (t=1)	From simulated samples				From observed panel data
Prop. Of Q del. By non rural routes		Mean (m)	Std. Dev. (s)	Confidence interval ($m \pm 2s$)		
Coefficient of *Ln Q*						
0.65	0.378	0.374	0.023	0.326	0.420	0.228
[0.65; 0.8]	0.519	0.510	0.024	0.463	0.558	0.359
[0.8; 1]	0.595	0.581	0.019	0.543	0.621	0.416
=1	0.583	0.590	0.029	0.532	0.649	0.613
Coefficient of *Ln AREA*						
0.65	0.149	0.151	0.008	0.117	0.167	0.145
[0.65; 0.8]	0.118	0.124	0.005	0.113	0.135	0.125
[0.8; 1]	0.049	0.051	0.005	0.041	0.061	0.050
=1	0.054	0.048	0.009	0.030	0.066	0.047
Coefficient of *Ln NDP*						
0.65	0.431	0.434	0.024	0.386	0.482	0.583
[0.65; 0.8]	0.419	0.414	0.026	0.362	0.465	0.570
[0.8; 1]	0.390	0.399	0.020	0.360	0.439	0.555
=1	0.413	0.385	0.031	0.322	0.448	0.427

5. MAIL VOLUMES, DELIVERY POINTS AND DELIVERY COSTS

Over the medium to long-term mail volumes tend to change in response to changes in the number of households and firms which impact directly on the number of delivery points. However, in addition, a number of other factors, for example economic growth and competition from non-mail media and entrants into the mail market, are likely to impact on mail volumes. The impact on delivery costs of these alternative sources of volume growth is quite different and it is important to understand this from a postal policy and planning perspective. For this purpose it is useful to reparameterise equation (4) and specify the outdoor delivery cost function in terms of the number of delivery points (*NDP*) and traffic per delivery point (Q_{it}/NDP_i), as follows:

$$LnC_{it} = \alpha + \delta LnNDP_{it} + \gamma_1 Ln\, AREA_i + \beta\, Ln(Q_{it}/ NDP_i) + a_i + e_{it} \qquad (5)$$

where: $\delta = \beta + \gamma_2$

Table 3: Estimate coefficients of model (5)

Proportion of Q delivered by non rural routes	Coefficient of		
	Ln NDP $(\delta = \beta + \gamma_2)$	Ln (AREA) γ_1	Ln (Q/NDP) β
<0.65	0.811 (0.024)	0.145 (0.019)	0.228 (0.060)
[0.65; 0.85]	0.929 (0.018)	0.125 (0.014)	0.359 (0.052)
[0.85; 1]	0.971 (0.027)	0.050 (0.014)	0.416 (0.048)
=1	0.970 (0.020)	0.047 (0.015)	0.543 (0.047)
Full sample	0.894 (0.009)	0.087 (0.004)	0.418 (0.027)

Note: The coefficients reported above are based on a reparameterised version of model (4). The constant, R^2 and ρ parameters are therefore identical to these reported in table 1. Standard errors are reported in parentheses. All coefficients are statistically significant at the 5% level.

We report the values of δ, γ_1 and β in table 3. These estimated values suggest that, in general, δ is close to unity and β is well below unity. Given that Royal Mail is a universal service provider of mail services in the UK and there is empirical evidence to suggest that the elasticity of mail volumes with respect to the number of delivery points is close to unity (see Nankervis and Rodriguez, 1995), expression (5) suggests that economies of scale in outdoor delivery are mainly due to economies of scale from traffic per delivery point rather than traffic *per se*.[1] Therefore if in the near future Royal Mail delivered traffic increases faster than the number of delivery points this will exert downward pressure on average delivery costs. In contrast, however, if Royal Mail traffic volumes per delivery point decline in the near future, due for example to competition from non mail media or losses to entrants into the UK mail market, this will exert upward pressure on Royal Mail average costs. These are powerful conclusions to draw from the estimated cost model and ones that UK postal policy makers and business planners should take into consideration when developing evidence-based policies and business decisions.

6. CONCLUSION

This paper stresses the importance of the treatment of heterogeneity between delivery offices when estimating economies of scale in outdoor mail delivery activity. We show that models estimated with cross-section data can give biased results and that panel data models encompass cross-section models. In practice this means that empirical estimates of economies of scale in delivery will be underestimated when using cross-section data and researchers should, where possible, adopt panel estimation techniques. In line with these findings we have estimated cost functions for UK outdoor mail activities using panel data that take into account observed heterogeneity by using variables describing the environmental characteristics of delivery offices. Among these variables, the proportion of traffic delivered by non rural routes is introduced in a non linear way (with a stratification of the sample) into the cost models and we find strong evidence of UK outdoor mail delivery activities exhibiting returns to scale with respect to volumes per delivery point that lie in the range of less than 2 to over 4 according to the value of this proportion. These results are consistent with other studies on outdoor delivery costs in France and the USA and add to the growing international literature that substantial fixed costs are incurred in outdoor mail delivery activities.

Reparameterising the estimated model allows further insights into the key factors underpinning the existence of economies of scale in UK outdoor mail delivery activities. Namely, that economies of scale are primarily due to the concentration of traffic per delivery point and that the extent to which Royal Mail benefits from economies of scale depends on the relative growth rate of mail volumes versus the number of delivery points. In general the estimated cost model suggests that the greater the rate of traffic growth relative to the

---

1 This is similar to the conclusion reached in previous work by Christensen et al (1993) on US data.

number of delivery points the greater the degree to which Royal Mail benefits from economies of scale and vice versa. These are powerful conclusions to draw from the estimated cost function and suggest that postal policy makers take such factors into account when forming evidence-based policies on the future of the postal market.

REFERENCES

Baltagi, B. 1995. *Econometric analysis of panel data.* John Wiley & Sons

Cazals, Catherine, Marc DeRycke, Jean-Pierre Florens, and Séverine Rouzaud. 1997. "Scale Economies and Natural Monopoly in the Postal Delivery: Comparison between Parametric and Nonparametric Specification." In *Managing Change in the Postal and Delivery Industries*, edited by M.A. Crew and P.R. Kleindorfer. Boston, MA: Kluwer Academic Publishers.

Cazals, Catherine, Jean-Pierre Florens and Bernard Roy. 2001. "An Analysis of Some Specific Cost Drivers in the Delivery Activity". In *Future Directions in Postal Reform*, edited by M.A. Crew and P.R. Kleindorfer, Boston, MA: Kluwer Academic Publishers.

Christensen, Dianne C., Laurits R. Christensen, Charles E. Guy and Donald J. O'Hara. "U.S Postal Service Productivity: Measurement and Performance". In *Regulation and the Nature of Postal and Delivery Services,* edited by M.A. Crew and P.R. Kleindorfer, Boston, MA: Kluwer Academic Publishers.

Cohen, R.H. and Edward H. Chu. 1997. "A Measure of Scale Economies for Postal Services". In *Managing Change in the Postal and Delivery Industries*, edited by M.A. Crew and P.R. Kleindorfer, Boston, MA: Kluwer Academic Publishers.

Hsiao, C. 1986. *Analysis of panel data.* Cambridge University Press.

Mizon, G.E. and J.F. Richard. 1986. "The encompassing principle and its application to testing non-nested hypotheses". In *Econometrica*, vol.54.

Nankervis, John and Frank Rodriguez. 1995. "Aggregate Letter Traffic Demand in the United Kingdom and the Economy". In *Commercialization of Postal and Delivery Services: National and International Perspectives*, edited by M.A. Crew and P.R. Kleindorfer, Boston, MA: Kluwer Academic Publishers.

Postal Rate Commission. 2003. "The City Carrier Street Time Study: A Presentation to the Postal Rate Commission".

Rogerson, Cathy and William Takis. 1993. "Economies of Scale and Scope and Competition in Postal Services". In *Regulation and the Nature of Postal and Delivery Services*, edited by M.A. Crew and P.R. Kleindorfer, Boston, MA: Kluwer Academic Publishers.

Roy, Bernard. 1999 . "Technico-economic analysis of the costs of outside work in postal delivery". In *Emerging Competition in Postal and Delivery Services*, edited by M.A. Crew and P.R. Kleindorfer, Boston, MA: Kluwer Academic Publishers.

Chapter 11

The Effects of Worksharing and Other Product Innovations on U. S. Postal Volumes and Revenues*

Edward S. Pearsall
U. S. Postal Rate Commission

1. INTRODUCTION

Since 1975 the U. S. Postal Service (USPS) has made many product innovations creating new categories of services, either directly, as with Express mail and the Priority mail envelope, or indirectly, by unbundling existing services as was done for large mailers with discounts for presorting, prebarcoding and drop shipping. In all of these instances economic theory tells us that postal volumes should have increased *ceteris paribus* after the changes. This occurs because mailers are able to use the new mix of services more efficiently than the old, especially after they have had the time to develop necessary worksharing technologies, and because delivery has always remained a bundled component of all of the offerings. In effect USPS has liberalized potential competitors' access to postal markets but has strictly limited the liberalization to upstream service components involving collection, mail processing and transportation while retaining its monopoly on delivery.

---

* The views expressed in this paper are my own and do not necessarily represent the opinions of the U. S. Postal Rate Commission. I am particularly indebted to Kevin Harle, a member of the Commission's technical staff, for his invaluable assistance in assembling the data that I used to fit the econometric model for this paper. I am also thankful for the many helpful comments and suggestions made by readers of earlier drafts.

Although mail volumes should have increased, it is not necessarily true that postal revenues would have increased proportionately. Postal revenues may have increased less than proportionately, or even decreased, because some existing mail would typically shift categories to obtain a lower discounted rate. This effect usually lowers the revenues per piece received by the Service when mailers are given the opportunity to workshare.

This paper presents an econometric model of the demand for U. S. mail services by subclasses and major discount categories[1] and applies the model[2] to estimate the impact that worksharing and other product innovations have had on mail volumes and revenues. Adaptive processes are used to model the impact of innovations and other events on volume per household and revenue per piece. Innovations are assumed to initiate the processes by creating new, usually higher, equilibrium levels for volumes and new, usually lower, levels for revenues per piece. Actual volumes and revenues per piece then adapt over time at rates that are proportionate to the remaining displacement from the new equilibria.[3] The effects of the 9/11-Anthrax attack are also modeled as adaptive processes in which volumes and revenues per piece grow back to their equilibrium levels after an initial, usually downward, displacement.

The adaptive processes are represented in the equations by variables that follow an exponential time-path from the old equilibrium to the new. Both the size of the displacements caused by innovations and the rates of adaptation that determine the exponential paths are estimated econometrically. The econometrics is outlined in Appendix A.

The entire econometric model consists of two mostly-matching sets of equations describing quarterly postal volumes per household and revenues per piece in constant dollars. Altogether there are 36 equations for volumes (or volume ratios for discount categories) and 31 equations for revenues per piece at a level of detail generally corresponding to that found in the Service's annual Revenue, Pieces and Weight (RPW) reports (USPS, 1971 to 2004).[4]

---

[1] An early version of the econometric model used in this paper is described in Cohen *et al* (2001). Other recent econometric studies of U. S. postal demand include those by Musgrave (2001) and Thress (2001) on behalf of USPS for the R2001-1 postal rate proceeding. Nikali (1997) has studied postal volumes in Finland, and Cazals and Florens (2002) have made a recent econometric study of postal demand in France.

[2] For an earlier empirical discussion of worksharing innovations and the pricing of workshared products using USPS estimates, see Mitchell (1999).

[3] Strictly speaking, this proportionality applies to the dependent variables of the econometric model which are natural logarithms and logits.

[4] The entire set of fitted equations is too large to be attached as an appendix. Readers wishing to examine the estimated equations of the model can find them assembled in 16 tables and posted on the PRC web site at www.prc.gov. The site also holds a copy of the

The basic methodology for deriving the historical impact of product innovations is back-casting with the fitted model. Projections of volumes per household and revenues per piece were generated over the sample period beginning at the date of the first innovations for each subclass. The (quarterly) projections were made both with and without the exponential path variables representing the demand effects of the innovations. Direct comparisons of the generated time series disclose how the product innovations have altered volumes per household and revenues per piece over the time periods spanned by the projections.

The fitted model shows that the product innovations made by the U. S. Postal Service (USPS) beginning in 1975 were responsible for generating about 37 percent of the total volume of mail and special service transactions by the end of 2003. The volume increases, in turn, have caused an increase in total revenue of about 26 percent despite the lowering of average rates for most subclasses due to discounts. These percentages will eventually grow to 46 and 27 percent, respectively, when the adaptive processes have run their course. Therefore, upstream liberalizations of access to U. S. postal markets and other product innovations have greatly stimulated the aggregate growth of both U. S. postal volumes and revenues since 1975.

2. WORKSHARING AND OTHER PRODUCT INNOVATIONS

The modern USPS inherited from the federal department it replaced in 1971 a system of postal product offerings consisting entirely of composite services. A composite service combines two or more basic services in given proportions in a single bundle at a single price. Prior to 1971 all mail was collected, transported, processed and delivered exclusively by the Service at undiscounted rates.

This cradle-to-grave marketing doctrine changed in 1976 when USPS began to offer discounts to First-Class mailers for presorting cards and letters. This was soon followed by discounts for other subclasses of mail and for other kinds of worksharing. By 1990 the Service was offering discounts for several levels of presorting, prebarcoding and drop shipping on many categories of First-Class, Priority mail, Periodicals (Second-Class), Standard (Third-Class) mail and Parcel Services. For large mailers, the discounts first offered during this period effectively expanded the Service's original short list of composite services into a much larger menu of simpler

Lotus 1-2-3 worksheet used to compile the data, derive the estimates, and construct the various tables and figures.

composites consisting of bundles of different basic services with delivery always included as part of the mix.

In 1975 USPS also introduced two new services, Express mail and Mailgrams. Later, the Service added more new products such as the two-pound envelope for Priority mail, and made innovations in its pricing formulas such as un-zoned rates up to five pounds for Priority mail.

Offering a larger less bundled selection of services has the same effect on postal demand as offering an a la carte menu to customers in a restaurant. Since delivery is always included in the mix, a more diverse menu of postal services increases the overall volume of mail delivered. This occurs because the expanded list of services usually makes it possible for mailers to choose for themselves a more efficient mix of the basic collection, processing, transportation and delivery services that are included in different proportions in the composites. Overall volume will increase when postal customers are offered a discount for worksharing because the difference between the discount and the lower cost of presorting or drop shipping to mailers who take the discount has the same effect on their demand as a reduction in the price of the original composite. When mailers are offered a new product some of the demand for the new service constitutes new pieces that would not have been mailed in other forms under the old offerings.

The immediate impact of unbundling is limited to mailers with a worksharing cost advantage conferred by the available technology. Similarly, new services and other product innovations have an immediate impact largely on the demands of mailers who have anticipated their introduction. But the immediate effects are not the only, and may not be the most important, stimulus to postal demand resulting from the Service's innovations in its product offerings. The unbundling of basic mail services and the introduction of new services also have the delayed effect of promoting the development of better commercial technologies for generating and processing mail. Mailing is actually a sequence of connected processes beginning with the generation of the mail, which is always performed by the mailer, and ending with delivery, which has always been performed by USPS. Between generation and delivery, the intermediate collection, transportation, and processing activities were performed by USPS until about 1981 using a limited range of simple manual technologies. With the introduction of worksharing, mailers had the opportunity to perform some of these activities for themselves. However, the gain to undertaking a worksharing activity depends upon the mailer having a cost advantage over the offered discount, or being able perform the activity with superior results. Thus worksharing discounts gave mailers an incentive to develop specialized technologies that were cheaper or more effective than those used by USPS for the workshared activities.

As specialized technologies were developed, mail volumes grew as more mailers discovered a cost advantage to performing the activities themselves and taking the discount. USPS has also encouraged the development of more efficient technologies by adapting its own technology and regulations to smooth its interface with large mailers. The discounts for most kinds of worksharing also tended to increase in relation to the rate for undiscounted mail during the period prior to the general reclassification proceeding of 1995. So the economic incentive to develop better technologies for most kinds of worksharing was maintained or increased by the rate structure for many years following the introduction of the discounts.

3. A MODEL OF ADAPTIVE PROCESSES

Adaptive processes occur whenever postal customers must adapt over time to new market conditions. In the case of worksharing, for example, customers must learn how to exploit the opportunities offered by new partially unbundled composite services. In the case of the 9/11-Anthrax attack, mailers had to relearn the U. S. mail's characteristics of speed, reliability and safety after an event that temporarily degraded all three. Put simply, adaptive processes are often just learning curves, or, in the case of the 9/11-Anthrax attack, a relearning curve.

The demand for new service offerings takes time to develop for a reason that is fundamental to the study of marketing. The demand develops as postal customers learn of the new product and then adapt their personal habits and business practices to use it. It is this process that marketing tries to speed up, since, unassisted, it would proceed only slowly as customers learned mostly from the example of others. However, heavy marketing campaigns for new products have never been a hallmark of USPS. Consequently, the adaptive response of postal customers to new services and to other product innovations may be fairly slow.

Adaptive processes also may take time to develop because adaptation can be costly. In order to do worksharing, it is usually necessary for postal customers to make investments in capital equipment, training and/or computer software. The speed of adoption of new practices is then constrained by customer investment rates.

Even a casual examination of the time series for most major subclasses of mail is sufficient to show that adaptive processes have been important determinants of postal volume since 1975. For example, the volume per household of First-Class letters was declining from 1971 to 1976, leveled off between 1976 and 1982, grew rapidly but at a declining rate from 1982 to 1996, was level again until 2000, and has since declined. This growth pattern corresponds to the growth path one would expect from the introduction of successively less effective innovations beginning with the discounts for basic 3/5-digit presorting in 1976 and ending with the automation discounts accompanying the mail reclassification of 1996. It also tracks closely a simultaneous migration of First-Class letters away from single-piece and into the discounted rate categories.

First-Class letters, cards and Standard mail all exhibit growth paths with periods of rapidly changing demand per household that are much too large to be explained as the response to the usual economic suspects such as long term trends, population growth, relative rate changes and changes in the gross domestic product (GDP). As with First-Class letters, the episodes of rapid growth typically follow in the wake of major innovations in service offerings. Furthermore, the changes usually are accompanied by redistributions toward new discounted rate categories. Parcel Service volume per household after 1985 also exhibits a pattern that is almost impossible to explain except as a slowly developing response by large mailers to new worksharing discounts.

Adaptive processes are represented in the equations of the econometric model by variables whose values follow exponential paths. The assumption that underlies this treatment is that the effect of an adaptive process is proportional to a function $D(t;\ t_0)$ that is zero for $t \leq t_0$ and ranges from zero to one along a time path that obeys a linear differential equation for $t \geq t_0$. The time t_0 corresponds to the date that the adaptive process begins. The linear differential equation that sets the time path of $D(t;t_0)$ after t_0 is $\frac{dD(t;t_0)}{dt} = r[1 - D(t;t_0)]$. The equation makes the rate of change in the level of $D(t;t_0)$ proportional to the difference remaining between $D(t;t_0)$ and it's limiting value of one. The coefficient r is the rate of adaptation for the process. If time is measured in years then r is roughly equal to the fraction of the difference, $1 - D(t;t_0)$, that the adaptive process attempts to make up each year. The solution to the linear differential equation is $D(t;t_0) = 1 - e^{-r(t-t_0)}$ for $t \geq t_0$. Therefore, the effect of the adaptive process is represented as a path beginning at the time t_0 and growing exponentially over time at the rate r from an initial value of zero towards a limiting value of one.

$D(t;t_0)$ is a continuous function of time, however, the econometric model is necessarily specified for variables measured over finite intervals. Therefore, the variables that are used as regressors in the equations of the econometric model are averages of $D(t;t_0)$ over calendar quarters. For a quarter beginning at time t_1 and ending at t_2 the average value of the variable, $\overline{D}$, is found by evaluating the integral $\overline{D} = \int_{t_1}^{t_2} \frac{D(t;t_0)}{(t_2 - t_1)} dt$. The form of the integral depends upon whether the start of the adaptive process occurs after the end of the quarter, during the quarter, or before the quarter begins. The three cases are:

$$\overline{D} = 0 \text{, if } t_1 < t_2 \le t_0,$$

$$\overline{D} = \frac{(t_2 - t_0)}{(t_2 - t_1)} + \frac{\left(e^{-r(t_2 - t_0)} - 1\right)}{r(t_2 - t_1)} \text{, if } t_1 < t_0 < t_2 \text{, and}$$

$$\overline{D} = 1 + \frac{\left(e^{-r(t_2 - t_0)} - e^{-r(t_1 - t_0)}\right)}{r(t_2 - t_1)} \text{, if } t_0 \le t_1 < t_2 .$$

For product innovations, an exponential path variable, $\overline{D}$, is inserted directly in a linear equation $Y = \alpha + .. + \beta\overline{D} + ...$ The equation may then be fit by standard econometric methods for a given rate of adaptation r. The coefficient β becomes the asymptotic limit to the change in the dependent variable Y for the adaptive process. It is the change in the equilibrium level of Y that triggers the process at the time t_0. It is also the addition to Y that occurs as $\overline{D}$ approaches its limiting value of one.

For the 9/11-Anthrax attack $\overline{D}$ is subtracted from an ordinary dummy variable to obtain a variable $\overline{R}$ that is inserted in the linear equation. $\overline{R}$ is called a reverse exponential path variable because the adaptive process returns the dependent variable Y to its original level after an initial disequilibrating change at time t_0.

An econometric model incorporating the exponential path variables $\overline{D}$ and $\overline{R}$ to describe the impact of product innovations, the effects of the 9/11-Anthrax attack and other events changing postal market conditions comprises a technical advance beyond the common econometric practice of representing the impact of such events with ordinary dummy variables. In fact, when an ordinary dummy is used to approximate an adaptive process, the resulting coefficient tends to underestimate the impact of the event. This occurs because the coefficient for the ordinary dummy measures an average effect on Y that is present when the dummy variable is set to one and is absent otherwise. The average effect of an innovation will include smaller effects during many early quarters when postal customers have only partially adapted to the new or improved service. With an event such as the 9/11-Anthrax attack, the coefficient for the ordinary dummy will include in the average the impact for later quarters after the initial impact has somewhat attenuated. In both cases the result is an underestimate.

Each exponential path variable used in the econometric model is completely defined by just two parameters – the initial time t_0 and the rate of adaptation r. The initial dates for postal product innovations and events such as the entry of postal competitors were taken from postal sources.[5] The date for the 9/11-Anthrax attack was chosen as September 11, 2001 even though the anthrax mailings were unknown until several weeks later. All of the initial times for the exponential paths were treated as fixed and given in the econometrics. The same rate of adaptation is used for all the exponential path variables found in the equations pertaining to a single class or, in some cases, a large subclass.

There are both theoretical and practical reasons for adopting a one-size-fits-all assumption for the rate of adaptation for equations grouped together by a class or large subclass. First, an exponential path variable for the same innovation or event often appears in several of the equations for a class or subclass. The representations for each innovation or event ought to mirror each other in these equations. Second, the rates of adaptation for different innovations and events should roughly be the same if they describe similar behavior by a single group of mailers. When an adaptive process is a learning curve, the rate of adaptation is the underlying rate at which mailers acquire and act on new information and should not differ too much with respect to what is being learned. When adaptive processes are constrained by capital formation, the rates of adaptation should also be similar.

The practical reason for using a single rate of adaptation for a single class/subclass everywhere in the model is that the maximum likelihood method of estimating these rates is not particularly robust. Formally, the model can be generalized fairly easily by introducing unique rates of adaptation for each of the adaptive processes affecting demand. However, relaxing the single-rate assumption in this way, while complicating the

---

[5] The most important of these sources is the Domestic Mail Rate History filed by USPS with the PRC for every general rate proceeding. Most of the initial dates used to define exponential path variables for the introduction of worksharing discounts, new postal services and other product innovations were taken from the Service's R2001-1 filing (USPS 2001). In several instances dates have been obtained from the testimony of Service witnesses Thress (2001) and Musgrave (2001), or from USPS Library References (USPS, 2001).

econometrics, would be unlikely to lead to a better understanding of mailer behavior.

4. AN OUTLINE OF THE COMPLETE MODEL

The model comprises a complete system of fitted equations describing U.S. postal volumes and revenues for domestic mail and special services at a level of detail that is approximately the same as that found in the Service's annual RPW reports (USPS, 1971 to 2004). International mail volumes and revenues are treated as aggregates.

There are two sets of equations with mostly matching explanatory variables. The first set describes volumes per household by subclass and major discount category. The second set describes revenue per piece for the same subclasses and categories. The first set of equations, but not the second, have a rough counterpart in the demand model that the Service must submit to the PRC at the start of an omnibus rate proceeding.[6]

Projections of postal volumes alone may be made with the first set, but projections of postal revenues require both sets of equations. The second set of equations is needed because postal revenues per piece may be expected to respond to all of the same influences as postal volumes per household. The volumes and revenues given in the RPW reports are actually vast aggregates of somewhat heterogeneous pieces of mail and transactions. Since 1971 postal tariffs for mail and special services have undergone many structural changes and have become quite complex, especially for large mailers. As a result mailers now respond to changing rates and other market conditions not only by changing the volume of mail sent but also by changing the characteristics of the pieces or by choosing different combinations of worksharing. When mailers do this it affects the average revenue per piece.

USPS, in its filings, and the PRC, in its recommended decisions, employ behavioral equations to forecast volumes but not to project revenues per piece. Instead, both make calculations based on the simple assumption that the relative proportions of mail with different characteristics found in an annual survey of mail and services will not change.[7] Revenues are estimated

---

[6] The PRC's current rules (PRC 2004, 52) require the submission of "an econometric demand study relating postal volumes to their economic and non-economic determinants..." The most recent filed version of this model, submitted for the R2001-1 general rate proceeding, is described at considerable length in the testimony, workpapers, responses to interrogatories and library references of Service witnesses Thress (2001) and Musgrave (2001).

[7] The results of these surveys are called "billing determinants". They are estimates of the weights, numbers of pieces by shape, or whatever, to which each element of the postal

by applying new rates to forecasts of volumes with an unchanged distribution of characteristics. In effect, revenues per piece are assumed to be unit-elastic with respect to a fixed-weight average of the rates.

There is little about this assumption that seems attractive as a description of economic behavior. Faced with a complex tariff based not only on pieces but frequently also on their weights, dimensions, content, size of mailing, entry point, destination, workshared characteristics, etc., mailers will re-optimize their selection of services and discounts whenever rates and other market conditions change. These re-optimizations can be expected to alter the characteristics of the mail in ways that predictably relate revenues per piece to postal rates and to the other determinants of postal demand. Therefore, a complete model of the demand for postal services should include behavioral equations for revenues per piece rather than depend upon the simplistic assumption that the relative proportions of the mail with different characteristics remain fixed.

The overall design of the volume equations in the model partly reflects a need to preserve degrees of freedom for the econometrics. A problem arises because the Service has occasionally revised its RPW reports to disaggregate mail streams into sub-streams in order to report workshared mail in greater detail. This has occurred several times with all four subclasses of First-Class and Standard mail, most recently in 1996. A model that simply adopted the categories currently in use in the definitions of its dependent variables would limit the econometrics to using time series that began in 1996 even though there are quarterly RPW reports of volumes and revenues using more aggregated category definitions that reach continuously back to 1971.

A solution to the problem is to fit an equation for aggregate subclass volume using the entire sample, and then to fit equations for subsequent subdivisions of the aggregate using the shorter time series that start later after USPS had begun reporting the components. The equations for First-Class letters illustrate how this is done. First, an equation for volume per household is fit to the entire sample for total First-Class letters. The next equation explains the division of First-Class letters into single-piece and worksharing segments. This equation is a logit that is fit to the sample beginning in 1976 after the Service began reporting single-piece and workshared mail separately.[8] Another logit explains the division of workshared letters into its carrier-route presorted and non-carrier-route

---

tariff applies. The billing determinants for a recent base year are filed by the Service for every general rate proceeding , for example, see USPS (2001).

[8] Suppose that a variable has two components, e.g., $Y = Y_1 + Y_2$. The logit is defined as the natural logarithm of the ratio of the components $\lambda = \ln(Y_1 / Y_2)$. The logit divides Y into its components as follows: $Y_1 = Ye^{\lambda}/(1+e^{\lambda})$ and $Y_2 = Y/(1+e^{\lambda})$.

presorted components. The time series for the fit of this equation begins in 1981. The subdivision of non-carrier-route presorted mail into automation and non-automation components is explained by a final logit. This last equation is the only one in the set whose fit must be made using a short time series beginning in 1996.

5. DETERMINANTS OF THE DEMAND FOR MAIL AND POSTAL SERVICES

Except for the exponential path variables, the model relies on standard economic determinants of demand and on conventional forms for the variables representing their effects. The dependent variable for each equation is the natural logarithm of either volume per household, the volume ratio for two rate categories (a logit), or, revenue per piece in constant dollars. All of the explanatory variables, except for dummies, trends and exponential path variables, appear in the equations as natural logarithms. This includes the variables relating the dependent variables to levels of economic activity, indexes of U.S postal rates, prices of competitive services, and other measures of market conditions. The equations are linear in the transformed variables with additive disturbances.

The determinants of postal demand and the ways they are represented in the equations are as follows.

Demographics – Mail is the sum of messages and packages exchanged over the postal network by individuals, households, businesses, nonprofit organizations and government agencies. Volumes should be roughly proportional to the number of participants. However, the number of postal customers is not known and must be represented indirectly by a demographic measure. The overwhelming bulk of postal transactions involve a household at either the sending or the receiving end. Therefore, the equations use RPW volumes converted to calendar quarters and divided by the number of domestic households from the Census (2003). Income and other activity variables found in the equations as regressors are expressed as flows per quarter per household. The equation for Classroom mail also includes the school age (5 to 21 years of age) population per household as an explanatory variable.

Long Term Trends – Gradually encroaching indirect competition forms the background economic environment for most non-competitive subclasses. "Gradually encroaching indirect competition" is a term that describes the effect of the telegraph, telephone, newspapers, radio, television, messenger services, time-shared computers, faxes, e-mails, the Internet and cell phones. In fact the term applies to any alternative method for communicating messages between the same points served by the postal network. In the case of competitive services, the effects that predominate in the long run are the entry and growth of successful direct competitors such as United Parcel Service and Federal Express. All but four of the equations include a linear trend beginning with the quarter corresponding to the first observation in the time series to which they are fit. The four exceptions are four logit equations that must be fit to time series beginning only in 1996.

Seasonality – The volumes per household and revenues per piece for most categories of mail exhibit seasonal patterns that are clearly evident when volumes are plotted against time. The reason for the seasonality is that some of the mail is closely linked to social customs and business practices that are also seasonal (e.g., Christmas mail). All of the equations therefore include an intercept and dummy variables for the second, third and fourth quarters of the calendar year. These would suffice if social customs and business practices did not change over time. To account for changes in the seasonal patterns, the equations also include seasonal trends obtained by interacting the seasonal dummies with the linear trend.

Reclassifications, Redefinitions and Eligibility Changes – One time shifts in the volumes and revenues in the Service's RPW reports are occasionally caused simply by revisions in the ways that these variables are defined, measured and reported. On other occasions changes in the Service's eligibility rules have caused sudden migrations of mail from one category to another that are largely involuntary. Changes of these kinds can be represented by simple dummy variables because the changes are instantaneously and do not occur as the result of an adaptive process. Suitably defined simple dummy variables have been included in selected equations for the redistribution of government mail that occurred in 1988, for the MC95-1 reclassification that took effect in 1996, for the separate accounting of return receipts in 1996, and for a heterogeneous collection of subclass-specific changes in eligibility, sampling methods and RPW reporting.

Market Conditions – Postal markets have been transformed from time to time by the entry and exit of competitors such as Federal Express, by the business decisions of major customers such as Sears' discontinuation of catalog mailings, by the misfortunes of competitors such as strikes by United Parcel Service's delivery men, and by pricing anomalies such as the ones that have sometimes made First-Class cards cheaper than comparable Standard cards. When a change in market conditions can be related to a specific dateable cause, the effect is represented in the equations by an exponential path variable or by a simple dummy variable, depending upon whether the circumstances require adaptive behavior by mailers or not. In some other cases, for example, to represent the effect of the maximum weight for a First-Class letter on Priority mail, a tracking variable has been inserted in the equations.

Economic Activity – USPS surveys of the composition of the mail stream have always shown that the mail is primarily business-driven. The volumes in most categories are derived demands that arise from the broad range of other production, distribution and marketing activities taking place in the economy. This argues that the demand for postal services is related to economic activity in a way that is best represented by broad aggregate measures of income and product. The measure of general economic activity that is used in all-but-one of the equations is the constant dollar Gross Domestic Product (GDP) per household. The series that is used is the chained GDP in year 2000 dollars (U. S. Dep't. of Commerce 2004).

Special Services – Special service transactions are complementary services to First-Class letters, Priority mail or Parcels. These complementary relationships are represented in the model by the inclusion of First-Class letters, Priority mail and Parcel Post pieces per household in the equations for their complementary special services.[9]

Worksharing and Other Product Innovations –The effects of these innovations are represented in the equations by exponential path variables as described earlier. Typically, several such variables appear in an equation, one for each major product innovation that has occurred since the start of the time series used to fit the equation. Variables are not included for innovations that predate the time series.

9/11-Anthrax Attack – A reverse exponential path variable for the effect of the 9/11-Anthrax attack is included in every equation. All of these paths are assumed to begin on 9/11/2001 and to converge over time to zero, i.e., it is assumed that the effects of the 9/11-Anthrax attack are disappearing without leaving any permanent changes in volumes per household or revenues per piece. It is also assumed that the rates of adaptation for the reverse exponential path variables of the attack are the same as the rates for the exponential paths representing the effects of product innovations.

Postal Rates and the Rates of Substitutes – The demand functions for monopoly services like First-Class letters can be expected to be fairly price-inelastic because of the absence of direct competition and because postage is rarely large in proportion to a person or business's total outlay. Services with direct competition like Priority mail should tend to have more price-elastic demands since mailers have the option of switching to a similar service offered by a postal competitor when USPS raises its rates. The rates

---

9 The equations for Special Services were fit last using the predicted values for First-Class volume per household etc. This procedure avoids an errors-in-variables bias that would arise from using the series for First-Class letters etc. as regressors without the errors removed.

enter the demand equations in the deflated form of fixed-weight indexes divided by the implicit deflator for the GDP. The fixed weights for the indexes are derived from postal billing determinants for either GFY 1997 or GFY 2000[10]. Billing determinants were not available for International mail, Mailgrams or Special Delivery. For these subclasses rates were represented by revenue per piece divided by the GDP deflator. No rates appear in the equations for Penalty mail or Free-for-the-Blind mail. All of the rates found in the equations are unlagged. If the expectations of postal customers are rational, there should be no lags in the responses of demand to changes in any of the rates.

Auto Regressive Disturbances – The sources of errors in quarterly observations of volumes per household and revenues per piece are diverse and may include causes that persist for more than a quarter or tend to recur seasonally for several years. The model copes with these possibilities by treating the disturbances as auto regressive. Specifically, the current disturbance for each equation is assumed to be a linear function of the disturbances for each of the preceding four quarters plus a serially uncorrelated error. This is known as an AR-4 process.

Estimation procedures for the AR-4 process and for the rates of adaptation used to derive the exponential path variables are described in Appendix A.

6. OVERALL RESULTS

The selected equations for First-Class letters shown in Appendix B are generally characteristic of the equations that have been fit for all subclasses and rate categories. This similarity exists because the individual equations were derived by adapting a single prototype with as few alterations as necessary. All of the equations for First-Class letters are fit to the same basic set of regressors, so the equations are structurally similar except for the dependent variable. The regressors for the revenue-per-piece equations exactly match the regressors found in the corresponding volume-per-household equations. The reason for this mirroring is that the matched equations are just different manifestations of the same economic behavior.

The estimates in Appendix B, and the corresponding estimates for the other 63 fitted equations, tell us generally that the econometric model

[10] Most of the fixed-weight indexes used to fit the model were derived by modifying and consolidating USPS worksheets submitted to the PRC for the R2001-1 rate proceeding. In several instances the worksheets provided a choice of 1997 or 2000 billing determinants for computing the indexes. The 1997 billing determinants were usually selected. The fixed-weight indexes were calculated as averages for the calendar quarters.

successfully explains the data to which it has been fit. This is apparent from the high adjusted R-squares, the high proportion of statistically significant estimates among the coefficients, and the fact that the coefficients almost always have estimated values that conform to expectations. So the estimates demonstrate that a fairly conventional model of the demand behavior of postal customers can be made to succeed statistically.

Next in importance, the estimates reveal that revenues per piece respond to the same behavioral determinants as volumes per household. Many of the variables in the revenue equations have estimated coefficients that differ from zero at high levels of confidence. It turns out that revenues per piece have all of the same general behavioral characteristics as volumes. They have seasonal patterns and trends; they are affected by reclassifications, market conditions and the level of economic activity; they have adapted over time to worksharing and other innovations; they were changed by the 9/11-Anthrax attack and are recovering; and, finally, they are almost always less than unit-elastic with respect to postal rates.

The non-zero coefficients for the AR-4 processes show why it is difficult to accurately forecast postal volumes and revenues using an econometric model. The autoregressive process is usually an important part of the mechanism that explains the time series in each equation. But this part of the mechanism must be partially omitted when making forecasts more than one quarter beyond the end of the sample period; and must be completely omitted when making forecasts more than four quarters out. These omissions leave forecasts with errors that are typically larger in magnitude than the high adjusted R-squares of the fitted equations would indicate.

Table 1. Long Run Trends and Income Growth

		Volume per Household		Revenue per Piece		Revenue per Household	
	d.f.	Rate of Chg.	t-value	Rate of Chg.	t-value	Rate of Chg.	t-value
First-Class Letters	106	-1.58%	-3.84	0.57%	2.41	-1.01%	-2.12
First-Class Cards	105	-1.88%	-2.95	0.98%	4.90	-0.91%	-1.35
Periodicals	106	-1.87%	-3.87	-0.61%	-0.81	-2.48%	-2.77
Standard Regular	106	0.55%	2.12	0.60%	1.72	1.15%	2.65
Standard Nonprofit	106	3.42%	7.02	2.14%	8.00	5.57%	10.01
Parcel Post	105	-14.00%	-15.75	2.04%	3.06	-11.96%	-10.77
Bound Printed Matter	109	-2.56%	-1.94	0.07%	0.13	-2.50%	-1.77
Priority Mail	108	2.05%	5.27	-0.14%	-1.52	1.92%	4.80
Certified Mail	111	2.58%	3.68	2.20%	3.20	4.78%	4.87
International Mail	115	0.25%	1.21			0.25%	1.21

Table 1 was derived from the estimates to show how volumes and revenues tend to change over the long run when they are affected only by the linear trends and the long run growth in GDP per household of about 1.51

percent per year.[11] The t-values in Table 1 indicate that the estimates of the long term rates of change in volume per household, revenue per piece and revenue per household are mostly significant, many at very high levels.

The long run rates of change in volume per household for all First-Class letters and cards, Periodicals, Parcel Post and Bound Printed Matter are negative. Most of these negative long-term trends can be explained as the effect of gradually encroaching indirect competition. In the case of Parcel Post the competition from United Parcel Service is direct and its effect has not been particularly gradual. Altogether, the subclasses with negative long term rates of growth account for slightly more than half the mail and a considerably larger proportion of USPS' revenue.

The long-term trends for revenues per piece are mostly upward as mailers gradually change the characteristics of the mail to increase the weight and size of the average piece, send the average parcel over a greater distance, perform less worksharing on the average bulk piece, and opt in other ways to select a more expensive average mix of basic services. The long-term trends in volume per household and revenue per piece combine to produce the long-term rates of change in revenue per household shown in the right-hand columns of Table 1.

The long-term trends in Table 1 are mostly gradual and are not apparent in time plots of the data for most subclasses of mail and services. They are obscured by the effects of the large-scale introduction of worksharing discounts and other innovations beginning in 1976. Table 2 shows that the cumulative effects of the innovations on volume per household and revenue per piece for the affected subclasses were enormous. The columns labeled "Sum of Effects" in Table 2 are the sums of the estimated coefficients expressed as percentages for the exponential path variables for the innovations affecting the subclass. Most of the sums are significantly different from zero as seen from their high t-values. These sums constitute the total displacements of equilibrium volumes per household and revenues per piece driving adaptive processes in the equations of the demand model. Even with slow rates of adaptation, these displacements are so large that the changes in volumes and revenues they caused dwarfed the long-term trends for many years after the innovations occurred.

---

[11] The rates of change for volume per household and revenue per piece in Table 1 are equal to the equation coefficient for linear trend plus the coefficient for GDP per household times its annual growth rate (see Appendix A). The percentage for revenue per household is the sum of the percentages for volume per household and revenue per piece. The two coefficient estimates are assumed to be uncorrelated.

Table 2. Worksharing and Other Innovations

		Volume per Household		Revenue per Piece		Revenue per Househol	
	d.f.	Sum of Effects	t-value	Sum of Effects	t-value	Sum of Effects	t-value
First-Class Letters	106	70.80%	5.80	-16.73%	-2.35	54.06%	3.83
First-Class Cards	105	52.32%	2.17	-43.24%	-5.79	9.07%	0.36
Periodicals	106	13.60%	1.21	35.87%	1.93	49.48%	2.28
Standard Regular	106	94.11%	11.78	-20.21%	-1.97	73.89%	5.68
Standard Nonprofit	106	-50.50%	-3.26	-35.31%	-3.63	-85.81%	-4.70
Parcel Post	105	469.62%	13.54	-96.06%	-3.80	373.56%	8.70
Bound Printed Matter	109	304.12%	4.14	-52.65%	-1.75	251.48%	3.16
Priority Mail	108	45.27%	5.13	-3.70%	-1.92	41.57%	4.61
Certified Mail	111	-35.27%	-2.21	-16.50%	-1.14	-51.76%	-2.40
Return Receipts	17	187.25%	4.55	-145.39%	-5.30	41.86%	0.85

The estimates of the long-term trend and the effects of innovations may explain a puzzle concerning the recent slowdown of growth in the volume of First-Class letters. For many years in the late 1970s and 1980s the volumes per household of First-Class letters grew robustly year after year. But during the 1990's this growth slowed down. By the year 2000 it had stopped altogether and has since been replaced by a decline. The *ad hoc* explanation most often advanced for this reversal is that e-mail and electronic bill payment over the Internet are displacing letters as the preferred method for written communications and payment by many households. There is nothing actually wrong with this hypothesis; however, the estimates place these effects within a broader context. The model does not distinguish between the effects of the growth of the Internet and the effects of any of the other developing communication technologies that have encroached on the market for First-Class letters since 1971. All of these effects are merged by the model into a single linear trend. The estimates indicate that the annual rate of change in First-Class letters per household is simply reverting to its long-term trend as the adaptive processes caused by product innovations run their course.

An examination of the coefficients in Appendix B for the various innovations that have affected First-Class letters reveals a pattern that is also characteristic of other subclasses. The Service's innovations have tended to be successively less effective. The original introduction of 3/5-digit presort discounts in 1976 initiated an adaptive process that grew toward a 17.1 percent increase in volume per household. Discounts for carrier-route presorting in 1981 caused an increase of 19.9 percent and discounts for Zip+4 addressing added 17.1 percent in 1983. More recently, discounts for 5-digit prebarcoding raised equilibrium volumes per household by 3.4 percent in 1988; discounts for 3-digit prebarcoding raised volumes 9.4 percent in 1991; automation discounts raised volumes 3.9 percent in 1996.

The estimate of the rate of adaptation for First-Class letters is 19.86 percent per year so the Service's innovations stimulated growth in letter volumes for many years. However, the percentage increases caused by the innovations decreased over time while the long-term trend did not. Sometime during the year 2000 the tortoise finally caught the hare.

Although the Service's innovations have usually increased volumes per household, they have simultaneously depressed revenues per piece. This is hardly surprising since most of the innovations involve discounts for various forms of worksharing. Most large mailers can be expected to eventually use the opportunity provided by the discounts to do all of the worksharing for which they have a cost advantage. As they take more of the offered discounts, revenues per piece decline. However, this is not the only way that worksharing can affect revenues per piece. Worksharing discounts can also encourage mailers to increase the weight and the size of their pieces thus driving up revenue per piece. This is apparently what happened with publishers of Periodicals who cannot readily change the numbers of their subscribers but can easily change the size and weight of their publications.

To economists the most important behavioral characteristic of postal demand functions is the elasticity of volumes per household with respect to postal rates. The sums of the elasticities for all postal rates appearing in the demand equations are shown in Table 3. These values are the elasticities for simultaneous proportional changes in all postal rates. This is the way that real rates change between rate proceedings as the result of movements in the general level of prices. It also approximates the changes in the nominal rates recommended by the PRC at the conclusion of general rate proceedings. Typically, the PRC alters relative rates only gradually over several consecutive proceedings.

Table 3. Postal Rate Elasticities

		Volume per Household		Revenue per Piece		Revenue per Household	
	d.f.	Elasticity	t-value	Elasticity	t-value	Elasticity	t-value
First-Class Letters	106	-12.87%	-4.40	98.12%	-0.91	85.25%	23.77
First-Class Cards	105	-48.23%	-4.33	97.47%	-0.81	49.24%	4.26
Periodicals	106	-9.63%	-1.95	74.76%	-3.94	65.12%	8.05
Standard Regular	106	-29.95%	-5.97	76.24%	-5.39	46.29%	6.93
Standard Nonprofit	106	-13.23%	-2.55	74.85%	-7.01	61.61%	9.77
Parcel Post	105	-67.00%	-5.62	78.23%	-2.72	11.23%	0.78
Bound Printed Matter	109	-2.01%	-0.09	76.14%	-2.65	74.14%	3.21
Priority Mail	108	-63.51%	-5.33	95.22%	-1.57	31.71%	2.58
Certified Mail	111	-9.58%	-1.39	85.68%	-2.69	76.10%	8.76
Money Orders	113	-43.60%	-9.88	90.44%	-1.91	46.84%	7.02

The demand elasticities with respect to postal rates of the non-competitive subclasses of mail are all quite small. The non-competitive subclasses of mail and special services in Table 3 are First-Class letters and cards, Periodicals, Standard Regular, Standard Nonprofit, Bound Printed Matter and Certified mail. All of the other subclasses have fairly direct competitors and tend to be more rate-elastic. However, none of the rate elasticities are less than minus 100 percent. Therefore, even the demand functions for the competitive services are somewhat rate-inelastic.

The t-values for revenue per piece are calculated for tests of the null hypothesis that the elasticity with respect to rates is 100 percent. These t-values allow us to test the assumption that revenues per piece are unit-elastic with respect to changes in postal rates as measured by changes in fixed-weight rate indexes computed from billing determinants. Table 3 shows that this assumption is simply wrong.

Revenues per piece are less than unit-elastic with respect to rates in every category. The t-values show that many of the elasticities are less than 100 percent at very high levels of significance. This result is exactly what would be predicted for mailers who re-optimize in response to changes in a complex tariff. These less-than-unit elasticities may be partly responsible for the Commission's tendency to over-estimate postal revenues when recommending higher rates.

The elasticities in the last column of Table 3 are the percentage increases in revenue per piece by subclass that would result from a 100 percent increase in postal rates under current conditions. All of these elasticities, with the exception of the elasticity for Parcel Post, are greater than zero by margins that are statistically quite large. This means that USPS presently has the power to raise revenues by raising rates in every postal market with the possible exception of the market served by Parcel Post.

The last columns of Table 3 also help to inform the current debate on whether the USPS could fall into a death spiral because of decreasing business demand and electronic substitutes. A death spiral for a subclass can happen only when the elasticity of revenue with respect to postal rates is below zero; a death spiral for USPS as an enterprise can occur only when all of these elasticities are negative. Even then, the drop in postal revenues has to exceed the cost saving from lower volumes in order to create a situation in which higher rates produce a self-defeating drop in revenue net of costs. The estimated rate elasticities of postal revenues per household, with the possible exception of Parcel Post, come nowhere near meeting this condition. Of course, these elasticities are local measures and they could increase significantly as volumes fall out of the ranges circumscribed by the sample, so the information provided here, while assuring, does not entirely preclude a death spiral from emerging in the future.

The coefficient estimates for the reverse exponential path variables are direct estimates of the instantaneous effects of the 9/11-Anthrax attack. These estimates are collected and shown as percentages in Table 4 along with their t-values. Both volume per household and revenue per piece for most categories of mail were adversely affected by the attack. Reports of postal volumes during the weeks following the 9/11-Anthrax attack showed that postal customers had reacted measurably to the sudden realization that mail delivery was not as prompt, reliable or safe as had been previously believed.[12] In effect, mailers responded as might be expected to a degradation in service quality by reducing the levels of demand for most postal services. The estimates in Table 4 confirm these initial observations.

Table 4. Instantaneous Effects of the 9/11- Anthrax Attack

		Volume per Household		Revenue per Piece		Revenue per Household	
	d.f.	Pct. Change	t-value	Pct. Change	t-value	Pct. Change	t-value
First-Class Letters	106	-2.05%	-1.92	-1.62%	-2.23	-3.67%	-2.85
First-Class Cards	105	4.08%	1.41	0.95%	1.09	5.03%	1.67
Periodicals	106	-2.20%	-0.77	-1.69%	-0.53	-3.89%	-0.91
Standard Regular	106	-5.49%	-2.92	-0.57%	-0.29	-6.07%	-2.21
Standard Nonprofit	106	-7.61%	-2.26	-3.22%	-1.14	-10.83%	-2.46
Parcel Post	105	-7.88%	-1.32	2.45%	0.61	-5.44%	-0.76
Bound Printed Matter	109	-11.48%	-0.62	-4.15%	-0.48	-15.62%	-0.76
Priority Mail	108	-20.69%	-4.22	1.55%	1.27	-19.14%	-3.79
Express Mail	91	-12.29%	-2.85	-4.42%	-2.01	-16.71%	-3.45
Certified Mail	111	11.86%	1.54			11.86%	1.54
International Mail	115	-12.17%	-2.61			-12.17%	-2.61

Table 5 displays the maximum likelihood estimates of the rates of adaptation and confidence intervals for them obtained by reversing the arithmetic of a Wald test (see Appendix A). Most of the estimated rates of adaptation are low; the weighted average for all mail and services is only 21.81 percent per year. Most mailers, it seems, are slow learners. However, the confidence intervals bracketing the rates of adaptation are fairly wide. So this finding should be regarded with some caution.

Table 5. Rates of Adaptation

		99% Confidence Limits		95% Confidence Limits		90% Confidence Limit:	
	ML Rate	Upper	Lower	Upper	Lower	Upper	Lower
First-Class Letters	19.86%	31.56%	8.16%	29.20%	10.52%	28.03%	11.69%
First-Class Cards	11.15%	22.90%	-0.60%	20.53%	1.77%	19.36%	2.95%
Periodicals	60.94%	86.20%	35.69%	81.10%	40.78%	78.57%	43.31%
Standard Regular	21.08%	34.91%	7.26%	32.12%	10.05%	30.74%	11.43%
Standard Nonprofit	17.33%	34.37%	0.28%	30.93%	3.72%	29.23%	5.43%
Parcel Services	13.91%	18.51%	9.32%	17.58%	10.25%	17.12%	10.71%
Priority, Express,..	48.78%	62.54%	35.02%	59.77%	37.80%	58.39%	39.18%
Weighted Average	21.81%						

[12] Postal data systems continuously sample mail volumes. These reports are used to estimate volumes for postal accounting periods that are four weeks long. The reports for the accounting periods immediately before and after the 9/11-Anthrax attack showed a distinct drop in the volumes of most categories of mail and special services.

7. THE EFFECTS OF POSTAL PRODUCT INNOVATIONS

The historical effects of postal product innovations were gauged by comparing two sets of back-casts made with the fitted equations. The method is illustrated for First-Class letters volume per household in Figure 1. The first of the two back-casts is made with the same historical data used to fit the equations. This back-cast is just a reconstruction of the data but without the AR-4 process. In Figure 1 we can see that this back-cast tracks the actual First-Class letters volume per household fairly closely.

Figure 1. First-Class Letters Volume per Household
Projected Volumes with and without Service Inovations by Calendar Quarter

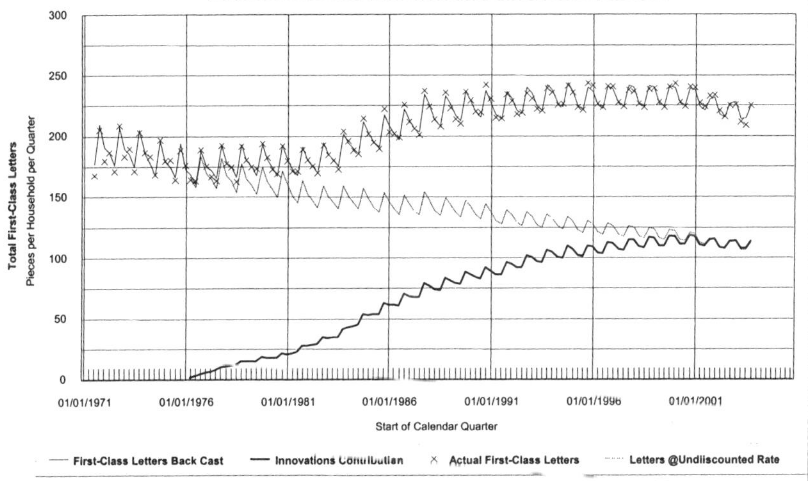

The second back-cast is also made with the historical data but with the exponential path variables for postal product innovations omitted and with undiscounted postal rates. If USPS had not undertaken an upstream liberalization of its service offerings beginning in the mid-1970s, postal rates would have been higher because most of the innovations created discounts for worksharing. The single-piece First-Class letters rate was used to approximate the average rate without the worksharing.

The contribution to volume per household by the product innovations is the difference between the first and second back-casts. This contribution begins in 1976 with the introduction of 3/5-digit presorting, accelerates with the introduction of carrier-route presorting and zip+4 addressing in the early 1980s, decelerates when later innovations prove less effective, and shares the long-run downward trend beginning around 2000 as the adaptive processes flatten out.

Revenues per piece were back-cast in the same way as volumes per household. Since 1976 this series has shown no overall tendency to increase or decrease. The sudden increases precipitated by rate decisions every 3 to 4 years have just about matched the intervening erosion caused by the rising general level of prices. However, this picture of rate stability is somewhat misleading. When revenue per piece is back-cast without the effects due to product innovations the result is a path that has slowly but unmistakably increased since 1976. Therefore, actual First-Class letter revenues per piece have not increased since 1976 largely because postal customers have lowered their average rates by taking the discounts offered by USPS for worksharing.

Although First-Class letter volumes per household have increased since 1976, postal revenues per piece have been reduced by innovations over the same period of time. The product of the back-casts of volume per household and revenue per piece is a back-cast of revenue per household. It is the volume effects that mostly dominate this combination. USPS product innovations acted to increase postal revenues per household from 1976 up until about 1996. Since then the innovations contribution has remained essentially flat.

The effects of product innovations on all classes and subclasses of mail are summarized in Table 6. The back-casts of volumes per household and revenues per piece used to construct Table 6 were made as they were for First-Class letters. The undiscounted rates used for First-Class letters and cards are the Single-Piece rates; the rates for Periodicals exclude discounts for drop shipping and presortation, the rates for Standard Regular and Standard Nonprofit bulk mail are the rates for the minimum required level of presorting; and, the rates for Parcels are the non-discounted rates for ordinary Parcel Service.

Table 6. Volume and Revenue Effects of Innovations with Undiscounted Rates

		Effect from Start Date		Percent Difference		Asymptotic Difference	
	Start Date	Volume	Revenue	Volume	Revenue	Volume	Revenue
First-Class Letters	07/01/1976	787,372	$181,435	36.27%	23.62%	51.63%	37.53%
First-Class Cards	07/01/1976	37,905	$3,568	34.20%	16.04%	42.47%	8.31%
Periodicals	04/01/1978	34,212	$8,692	13.20%	18.10%	13.29%	28.98%
Standard Regular	01/01/1979	701,993	$84,035	53.81%	36.21%	66.60%	45.58%
Standard Nonprofit	01/01/1979	(35,900)	($16,832)	-12.30%	-56.79%	-67.33%	-121.18%
Parcel Services	01/01/1981	10,770	$16,450	57.66%	48.10%	99.88%	66.25%
Priority, Express,..	07/01/1975	7,775	$42,325	40.54%	46.24%	39.28%	37.54%
Special Services	10/01/1996	3,186	$1,962	45.29%	22.27%	55.19%	14.12%
Total		1,547,314	$321,635	37.00%	26.05%	46.23%	27.07%

Volumes and revenues per household were multiplied by projections of the number of households (Census, 1996 and 2004) and aggregated from the date of the first important innovation shown as the "start date". Volumes are in millions of pieces; revenues are in millions of constant dollars. Current dollar values are converted to constant (2000) dollars using the implicit deflator for the chained GDP. The percent differences are the effects expressed as percentages of total volumes and revenues projected from the start date with the innovations at undiscounted rates. For example, the percent difference for First-Class letters volume (36.27%) is the ratio of the difference between accumulated volumes since 7/1/1976 back-cast with and without the innovations divided by the back-cast of accumulated volumes with the innovations.

The asymptotic differences are the percentage differences corresponding to the new equilibrium levels of volume per household and revenue per piece. These are the percentage differences that the innovations will cause when the adaptive processes have run their course. They are the limiting changes that the combined exponential paths approach over time. For example, 51.63 percent of First-Class letters volume and 37.53 percent of revenue will eventually be attributable to the product innovations affecting this subclass since 1976.

Most of the asymptotic percent differences are larger in magnitude than their corresponding historical percent differences. This occurs, first, because most of the innovations had a positive effect on volume, and second, because the effects grow along the time path described by the exponential path variables toward their asymptotic limits. Typically, the rates of adaptation are not very high so it takes several years for an innovation's effects to fully develop.

The percent differences and the asymptotic percent differences mostly conform to expected patterns. The innovations have produced increases in volumes in every subclass except Standard Nonprofit bulk mail.[13] They have also produced increases in revenues, which are proportionately smaller in most of the subclasses.

However, Periodicals mailers have responded somewhat differently. Periodicals volumes have increased very little as a result of the many discounts for presorting and drop shipping that have been offered to them. Instead, these mailers have taken advantage of the discounts to increase the average weight of their pieces. Therefore, the response to innovations in this class has been a large increase in revenue per piece accompanied by a much smaller percentage increase in volume.

---

[13] An explanation for this exception to the general pattern may be found in the timing of the innovations. All of the innovations for Standard Nonprofit bulk mail were made at times that corresponded to almost identical innovations in Standard Regular bulk mail and, in some cases, First-Class letters. Standard Nonprofit bulk mailings tend to be much smaller than mailings in these other subclasses so the combined effect of the innovations may have been to shift mail out of Standard Nonprofit bulk and into First-Class letters or Standard Regular bulk where it could be combined with other mail to qualify for discounts.

The last line of Table 6 provides the best estimates from the econometric model of the historic and long-run impacts of worksharing and other product innovations on aggregate postal volumes and revenues. From the start dates to the end of 2003, postal volumes increased by 37.00 percent as the result of worksharing and other product innovations. Revenues were enhanced by 26.05 percent despite the fact that the worksharing was necessarily accompanied by discounts and that revenues per piece tended to drop in response to the innovations. The asymptotic percent differences describing the long-run impact on volumes and revenues are 46.23 percent for volume and 27.07 percent for revenue.

8. CONCLUSIONS

The results presented in this paper bear on several questions that currently confront the international and the U. S. postal communities. For the international community, perhaps the most compelling of these questions is: what effect will liberalization have on the financial viability of the national postal services of the European Union? The results provide a partial answer. Upstream liberalizations of access to postal markets, of the kind increasingly allowed by USPS with worksharing discounts since 1975, are more likely to strengthen rather than weaken the financial position of a national postal service. The U. S. experience, repeated in all but one subclass, is that discounts for worksharing and other product innovations add substantially to both volumes and revenues. Revenues net of costs were also increased because the discounts were generally set equal to or below USPS' avoided costs per piece.

For the U. S. postal community the most compelling question may be: why have the rapid rates of growth in volume and revenue experienced in the 1980s and early 1990s slowed down? The short answer provided by the model is that USPS stopped innovating. The econometric results show that the historical growth pattern can be attributed almost entirely to the product innovations that USPS made starting about 1976. The early innovations were typically the most effective at stimulating postal demand. As their effects attenuated, the Service maintained the momentum for a while with more, but less effective, innovations. Eventually, during the 1990s, the adaptive processes for these additional innovations also largely ran their course. The last major product innovations by USPS were discounts introduced in 1996 for automation-related worksharing. These last innovations did little to stimulate additional demand in any of the larger subclasses, with the result that the long-run trends in postal demands are now reemerging as the predominant cause of the rates of growth of volumes and revenues. For many subclasses of mail and services the long-term trend of volume and revenue per household is downward.

For USPS the most compelling question may be whether to accept a long-run decline in the demand for many of its services, or try to restart the engine that once propelled volumes and revenues upward. Now that the econometrics has revealed how that engine worked, it is clear what USPS can do to restart it. USPS can continue to unbundle its remaining composite service offerings with respect to collection, processing and transportation - but not with respect to delivery. In addition, USPS can aggressively make other product innovations in the form of new or improved service offerings – again making delivery a part of every offering. USPS should also consider the possibilities for increasing the rather slow rates of adaptation that have been found to govern these processes. It may be advantageous for USPS to raise these rates by marketing new product offerings more intensively than has been its custom in the past.

APPENDIX A: NOTES ON THE ECONOMETRICS

There are two aspects of the model requiring special treatment in the econometrics. These are, first, the AR-4 processes for the disturbances, and, second, the rates of adaptation which enter the equations in a non-linear form. A non-iterative variant of the Cochrane-Orcutt procedure is used to deal with the auto-regressive disturbances while the rates of adaptation are held fixed.[14] This procedure is then performed iteratively to find the rates of adaptation that maximize the likelihood functions for the volumes equations taken in sets. The sets correspond to those equations with exponential path variables parameterized by the same rate of adaptation, for example, the four volume equations for First-Class letters.

The Cochrane-Orcutt procedure is more efficient than a direct least squares fit when the disturbances are generated by an auto-regressive process. First, an equation of the model is fit by least squares. The residuals from this preliminary fit are used to estimate the parameters of the AR-4 process by fitting a second linear equation, without an intercept, relating the residuals to their lagged values for the past four quarters. The coefficients from this second fit are used to perform an AR-4 transform on all of the variables (including a variable for the intercept) appearing in the equation. The equation is then refit by least squares to the transformed sample without the first four observations in the time series.

---

[14] The Cochrane-Orcutt procedure can be found described for an AR-1 process in almost any standard modern text, for instance, Maddala (1977, 277-84). The extension for an AR-4 process is straightforward.

A rate of adaptation is estimated by maximizing a likelihood function formed from the AR-4 transformed disturbances for the set of volume equations (including the logit equations) that use the rate to determine the values of exponential path variables in the equations. To construct the likelihood function it is assumed that the transformed disturbances are all independently and normally distributed errors. The errors from individual equations are serially independent if the AR-4 transform succeeds in removing all of the serial correlation caused by auto regressive processes in the disturbances. However, the form of the likelihood function also depends upon the transformed disturbances being uncorrelated across the equations. This condition is approximately met by the residuals from the equations for volumes per household but not by the residuals from the revenue per piece equations.

The likelihood function is maximized by minimizing the scaled sum of the squared residuals from the last step of the Cochrane-Orcutt procedure. The scaling is necessary if there is more than one equation in the set because the disturbances for the several equations can be expected to have different variances. The scaling is performed using prior approximate estimates of the variances of the equation errors so the scaled sum is a sum of squares of standardized residuals. In effect, the likelihood function is maximized over a parameter set that includes the rate of adaptation, all of the coefficients of the linear equations and (approximately) the coefficients of the AR-4 processes for the equation. However, the elements of the variance-covariance matrix of the disturbances are not part of the maximizing parameter set. Instead these elements are assigned predetermined values if they are on the diagonal and are assumed to be zero otherwise.

All of the parameters except the rate of adaptation are estimated within the Cochrane-Orcutt procedure. This allowed the procedure to be operated as a sub-optimization for each volume equation of a class or subclass. These sub-optimizations were embedded within a simple search process that converged iteratively on the value of the rate of adaptation that minimized the weighted sum of squares. The parameter estimates for the model are taken from the final least squares fits of the Cochrane-Orcutt procedure using the minimizing rate of adaptation. The coefficients for the autoregressive disturbances are also taken from the final iteration of the Cochrane-Orcutt procedure.

Confidence intervals for the estimates of the rates of adaptation were derived by reversing the arithmetic for a Wald test.[15] The second derivative of the logged likelihood function, which summarizes the information on the rate of adaptation contained in the sample, is used to construct a test statistic

[15] A clear and concise treatment of the subject of the Maximum Likelihood approach to nonlinearities in regression equations and the Wald test is Maddala (1977,176-81).

having asymptotically a χ^2 distribution with one degree of freedom. The test has the practical advantage that it only depends on the properties of the likelihood function at its maximum. To apply the Wald test a parabolic fit of the logged likelihood function was computed numerically in the vicinity of the final estimate of the rate of adaptation. The maximum likelihood estimate of the rate occurs at the peak of the parabola. The confidence intervals are found by inserting the second derivative of the parabola in the statistic for the Wald test and solving for the rates of adaptation corresponding to the critical values of χ^2. Confidence intervals computed in this way are symmetric about the maximum likelihood estimate.

Shown at the bottom of the table in Appendix B are the rate of adaptation for all of the First-Class letters equations, confidence intervals for 90, 95 and 99 percent Wald tests, and the coefficients of the AR-4 process for each equation.

The estimates also include t-values computed from the final variance-covariance matrices for three combinations of the coefficients. The first combination is the sum of the coefficient of the linear trend plus 0.0151 times the coefficient of GDP per household. GDP per household has increased at an average annual rate of 1.51 percent since 1971, so this sum describes the long-term trend of the dependent variable for each of the equations.

The second sum is the sum of the coefficients for the exponential path variables associated with postal innovations. This sum is an estimate of the asymptotic limit of the combined effect of the adaptive processes represented by the exponential path variables included in each equation. The t-value for the sum may be used to test the statistical significance of the combined effects of the innovations on volume per household, worksharing volume ratios and revenue per piece.

The third sum is the sum of the coefficients for all of the postal rates in the equation. In the volumes equations this sum shows the combined effect on volume-per-household of changing postal rates in the same proportion. The t-values for the volumes equations are computed in the usual way for tests of the null hypothesis that the sum of the rate elasticities is equal to zero (Ho: $\beta = 0$). The t-statistics for the revenue per piece equations are computed for tests of the null hypothesis that the sum of the elasticities is equal to one (Ho: $\beta = 1$).

APPENDIX B: SELECTED FIRST-CLASS LETTER VOLUME AND REVENUE EQUATIONS

Selected First-Class Letters Volume and Revenue Equations

Regressor	Effective Date	Ln 1st Cls Ltrs/ Household Estimate	t-value	Logit Single-Piece/ Work Shared Estimate	t-value	Ln 1st Cls Ltrs Real Rev/Pc Estimate	t-value	Ln Single-Piece Real Rev/Pc Estimate	t-value
Intercept		4.170	12.214	3.325	3.064	-0.500	-2.135	0.281	0.922
2nd Quarter Seasonal Dummy Variable		-0.017	-1.754	0.047	2.769	0.007	1.958	0.004	0.972
3rd Quarter Seasonal Dummy Variable		-0.075	-9.538	0.017	0.954	0.009	2.701	0.002	0.460
4th Quarter Seasonal Dummy Variable		0.096	10.010	0.174	10.711	-0.013	-3.733	-0.016	-4.407
Linear Trend		-0.019	-5.305	-0.014	-0.656	0.004	2.020	-0.003	-0.474
2nd Quarter Dummy Times Trend		-0.001	-2.857	-0.004	-3.644	0.000	1.053	0.001	3.485
3rd Quarter Dummy Times Trend		0.000	1.004	-0.002	-1.856	-0.000	-1.314	0.000	1.753
4th Quarter Dummy Times Trend		-0.003	-6.645	-0.008	-8.237	0.001	3.688	0.001	4.206
Government Mail Undistributed Dummy	09/24/1988	-0.033	-3.349	0.055	1.990	0.004	0.572	-0.013	-1.879
MC95-1 Mail Reclassification Dummy	07/01/1996	-0.002	-0.209	0.062	2.183	0.007	1.032	0.008	1.089
Ln of Gross Domestic Product per Household		0.242	2.869	0.091	0.331	0.100	1.729	-0.121	-1.591
3/5-digit Presort Introduction	07/06/1976	0.171	4.447	-3.419	-12.032	0.031	1.338	-0.009	-0.132
Carrier-Route Presort Introduction	03/21/1981	0.199	7.272	0.273	3.021	-0.060	-3.505	0.073	2.885
Zip+4 Discount	10/09/1983	0.171	4.236	0.176	1.478	-0.023	-0.870	0.000	0.016
5-digit Prebarcode Discount	04/03/1988	0.034	1.215	0.016	0.205	-0.017	-0.951	0.018	0.791
3-digit Prebarcode Discount	02/03/1991	0.094	2.827	-0.313	-2.906	-0.041	-1.942	0.075	2.651
MC95-1 Automation Discounts	07/01/1996	0.039	1.130	-0.220	-1.813	-0.058	-2.787	0.068	2.068
911 Attack/Anthrax Letters	09/11/2001	-0.021	-1.921	-0.035	-1.017	-0.016	-2.232	-0.007	-0.848
First Class Letters Rate		-0.165	-2.679			1.035	24.764		
First Class Cards Rate		0.037	0.642			-0.054	-1.407		
Single-Piece First Class Letters Rate				-0.667	-1.063			1.190	9.370
Workshared First Class Letters Rate				0.467	0.717			-0.280	-2.105
Carrier-Route First Class letters Rate									
Automated Non Car-Rte First Class Letters Rate									
Sum of Coefficients for the Long Term Trend		-0.016	-3.843	-0.013	-0.607	0.006	2.410	-0.004	-0.840
Sum of Coefficients for all Innovations		0.708	5.805	-3.487	-5.645	-0.167	-2.347	0.225	1.450
Sum of Coefficients for all Postal Rates		-0.129	-4.397	-0.200	-1.581	0.981	-0.908	0.910	-3.043
Regression Diagnostics		Adj. R^2	0.988	Adj. R^2	0.998	Adj. R^2	0.984	Adj. R^2	0.990
		Std. Error	0.013	Std. Error	0.037	Std. Error	0.008	Std. Error	0.008
		d.f.	106	d.f.	86	d.f.	106	d.f.	86
Estimated Annual Rate of Adaptation	19.86%	AR-1	0.003	AR-1	0.081	AR-1	0.144	AR-1	0.180
99 Percent Confidence Interval	+/- 11.70%	AR-2	0.104	AR-2	-0.043	AR-2	0.156	AR-2	0.118
95 Percent Confidence Interval	+/- 9.34%	AR-3	-0.036	AR-3	0.023	AR-3	0.042	AR-3	0.032
90 Percent Confidence Interval	+/- 8.17%	AR-4	0.215	AR-4	-0.277	AR-4	-0.094	AR-4	-0.147

REFERENCES

Cazals, C. and J. Florens. 2002. "Econometrics of Mail Demand: A Comparison between Cross-section and Dynamic Data." In *Postal and Delivery Services: Delivering on Competition*, edited by M. A. Crew and P. R. Kleindorfer. Boston, MA: Kluwer Academic Publishers.

Cohen, R. H., W.W. Ferguson, J.D. Waller, and S.S. Xenakis. 2001. "The Impact of Using Worksharing to Liberalize a Postal Market." In *Proceedings of the Wissenschaftliches Institut für the Kommunikationsdienste, 6th Köenigswinter Seminar on Postal Economics*, February 19-21.

Maddala, G. S. 1977. *Econometrics*, New York: McGraw-Hill.

Mitchell, R. W. 1999. "Postal Worksharing: Welfare, Technical Efficiency, and Pareto Optimality." In *Emerging Competition in Postal and Delivery Services*, edited by M. A. Crew and P. R. Kleindorfer. Boston, MA: Kluwer Academic Publishers.

Musgrave, G. L. 2001. Testimony and Workpapers on Behalf of the U. S. Postal Service, PRC Docket No. R2001-1.

Nikali, H. 1997. "Demand Models for Letter Mail and Its Substitutes: Results from Finland." In *Managing Change in the Postal and Delivery Industries*, edited by M. A. Crew and P. R. Kleindorfer. Boston, MA: Kluwer Academic Publishers.

Thress, T. 2001. Testimony and Workpapers on Behalf of the U. S. Postal Service, PRC Docket No. R2001-1.

U. S. Bureau of the Census. 2004. Households by Type and Projections of Households by Type, Series 14, May 1996 and January 2004.

U. S. Department of Commerce, Bureau of Economic Analysis. 2004. *National Economic Accounts*, Gross Domestic Product, January 2004.

U. S. Postal Rate Commission. 2004. *Rules of Practice and Procedure*. Washington, D.C.

U. S. Postal Service. 2001. Before- and After-Rates Fixed-Weight Indices (Tolley, G.), Library References J-122 and J-123, PRC Docket No. R2001-1. Washington, D.C.

U. S. Postal Service. 2001. Data, Programs and Results for Witness Thress's Econometric Work (Thress, T.), Library Reference J-129, PRC Docket No. R2001-1. Washington, D.C.

U. S. Postal Service. 2001. Derivation of Fixed-Weight Price Indices: Express and Priority (Musgrave, G. L.), Library Reference J-26, PRC Docket No. R2001-1. Washington, D.C.

U. S. Postal Service. 2001. Domestic Mail History, Library Reference J-90, PRC Docket No. R2001-1. Washington, D.C.

U. S. Postal Service. 2001. Special Services Fee History, Library Reference J-93, PRC Docket No. R2001-1. Washington, D.C.

U. S. Postal Service. 2004. *Revenue, Pieces, and Weight by Classes of Mail and Special Services for Government Fiscal Year*, Annual and Quarterly Reports to the PRC, Washington, D.C., 1971 to 2004.

Chapter 12

ETOEs—Arbitrageurs or Vehicles of Change in Postal Liberalization?*

Joy M. Leong, Daniel Bahar, and Dimosthenis Papakrivopoulos
Sidley Austin Brown & Wood LLP

1. INTRODUCTION

Extraterritorial Offices of Exchange (ETOEs) have proliferated recently, partly in response to arbitrage opportunities arising from the terminal dues system of the Universal Postal Union (UPU), which discriminates between mail sent by ICs and mail sent by DCs. At its 2004 Congress in Bucharest, the UPU will determine whether to place restrictions on ETOEs. This paper argues that the UPU should not seek to inhibit ETOEs. ETOEs are merely a symptom of an economically inefficient and outdated terminal dues structure. Rather than seeking to restrain ETOEs, the UPU should focus on reform of the underlying non cost-based, discriminatory terminal dues system that has given rise to arbitrage. Efforts to restrict ETOEs may also contravene trade rules and may in fact be counterproductive in the long run.

Indeed, the growth of ETOEs reflects the building pressure toward global postal competition. ETOEs can serve as helpful vehicles for change in a liberalized postal environment. The liberalized postal market in Europe provides a model of a more cost-based terminal dues system, where ETOEs are flourishing. Building on the postal liberalization policies of the European Union (EU), which allow competition in the cross-border mail market, the Agreement for the Remuneration of Mandatory Deliveries of

---

* The views expressed in this paper are those of the authors and not of Sidley Austin Brown & Wood LLP.

Cross-Border Mails ("REIMS II Agreement") establishes terminal dues based on a percentage of domestic rates. In such a regime, a postal administration in need of mail volumes may seek to compete outside its traditional territory for the cross-border mail (and eventually the domestic mail) of other countries. Through an ETOE, a postal administration can compete in newly-opened markets, leveraging its superior postal expertise and efficiencies to build a customer base. Thus, in a competitive environment, ETOEs offer benefits aside from their ability to arbitrage inefficiencies in the terminal dues structure.

This paper first examines the rise of ETOEs and describes two types of ETOEs: ETOEs established by DCs—which can exploit the difference between IC and DC terminal dues rates—and ETOEs established by ICs, which do not have universal service obligations in the territories in which they operate. Second, this paper describes the recent reactions to ETOEs at the UPU, where due to differing economic and social welfare incentives, Member States have hotly debated ETOEs. Third, this paper argues that, at the Bucharest Congress, the UPU should not restrict ETOEs because such an effort, at least with respect to IC ETOEs, may violate the General Agreement on Trade in Services (GATS) and may in fact be unworkable. Finally, this paper argues that UPU Member States should focus their attention on inefficiencies in the terminal dues structure and should take steps toward developing more cost-based terminal dues. Postal liberalization in Europe and the REIMS II Agreement can serve as a model for a transition to a more competitive international postal environment. In a liberalized postal environment, ETOEs have a role as vehicles for the entry of postal administrations into competitive cross-border mail markets.

2. THE ORIGIN OF ETOES

Competitive pressures in the international postal market have led to a proliferation of entities seeking to win cross-border mail volumes formerly reserved to Universal Service Providers (USPs). Private operators have begun to compete with USPs for mail volumes. Enterprising national postal administrations have also begun to compete for foreign mail volumes by establishing offices of exchange in the territories of other countries.

An Extraterritorial Office of Exchange or ETOE is an exchange office established by a postal operator in the territory of another country (UPU 2001). An ETOE may compete with the USP of the host territory and with private operators in any aspect of mail transport and delivery that is not subject to a monopoly in the host territory. An ETOE typically competes for outbound mail volumes that originate in its host territory and are destined for a third country (known as "ABC remail") (Emerson and Alverno 2002, p. 287). An ETOE could also compete with the USP in the market for domestic mail by collecting mail from the sender's country and placing it into the sender's mail system as inbound cross-border mail (known as "ABA remail") (Emerson and Alverno 2002, p. 287). As of March 2004, fifteen postal administrations had publicly registered approximately 112 ETOEs in foreign territories (UPU 2004); it is believed that many more are quietly operating without registering.

2.1 DC ETOES

The literature to date has focused on ETOEs' ability to exploit discrimination in the current system of terminal dues (D. Campbell, Cotton, and Power 2002, 277-84; Emerson and Alverno 2002, p. 288-9). Terminal dues are the fees paid by one postal administration to another postal administration to cover the delivery costs of inbound international mail (UPU Convention, art. 47.1). Under the current system, terminal dues paid by UPU member postal administrations vary depending on whether the sending and receiving countries are ICs or DCs (UPU Convention, art. 47.2). For example, terminal dues paid on lightweight cross-border letter traffic destined for an IC are generally lower if the letters are posted from a DC rather than an IC (Emerson and Alverno 2002, p. 288). An incentive thus exists to route mail originating in an IC and destined for another IC through a DC ETOE since mail that appears to be coming from a DC will be subject to lower terminal dues (Emerson and Alverno 2002, p. 288-9; D. Campbell, Cotton, and Power 2002, p. 278). Critics argue that such exploitation of the terminal dues system undermines the Universal Service Obligation (USO), distorts international postal markets, and raises legal issues under international trade rules (*see, e.g.*, D. Campbell, Cotton, and Power 2002, p. 281-3).

2.2 IC ETOES

While discrimination in the terminal dues system suggests that DC ETOEs have the strongest incentive to engage in arbitrage, available data shows that the recent growth in reported ETOEs results mainly from the establishment of ETOEs by ICs. Indeed, of the 112 ETOEs registered with the UPU in March 2004, approximately 100 were operated by IC postal administrations (UPU 2004). Critics argue that IC ETOEs should not be allowed to access the UPU terminal dues system—and thereby compete favorably against both USPs and private operators.

While IC ETOEs cannot exploit discrimination within the terminal dues system, these ETOEs can still offer rates for cross-border mail that are significantly lower than the rates charged by USPs and private operators. An IC ETOE can charge less than a USP because the ETOE is not subject to the Universal Service Obligation (USO) in the sender's country and thus does not include USO costs in its cross-border mail rates.[1] All else being equal, as long as ETOE shipments are treated as mail under the UPU Acts, an IC ETOE may also be able to underprice private operators, since (i) for the outbound leg, the ETOE and the private operator will presumably have similar costs, and (ii) for the inbound leg, the ETOE will pay terminal dues, while the private operator will pay domestic rates. Terminal dues are generally lower than domestic tariffs for lighter weight mail items (Emerson and Alverno 2002, 289; D. Campbell, Cotton, and Power 2002, p. 281-3).

3. CONTROVERSY OVER ETOES IN THE UPU

Differing economic incentives have caused some actors in the cross-border mail market to support ETOEs, while others strongly oppose them. IC USPs have divergent views. Some IC USPs oppose ETOEs, except where a USP gains more revenue as the result of its own ETOE operations than it loses to foreign ETOEs that take away its mail volumes. Private operators may also oppose ETOEs since, as discussed above, ETOEs can charge less than private operators for mail sent to any destinating country that treats items sent by ETOEs as mail under the UPU Acts. Notwithstanding these economic incentives to use ETOEs rather than USPs, it should be recognized that practical realities often place the USP at an advantage. The mere threat of non-delivery or of delay may prevent many senders from using an ETOE, even where the price differential would otherwise warrant using the ETOE (J. Campbell 2002, p. 13, n.12).

The UPU Convention is silent with respect to the legality of ETOEs and the treatment of ETOE mail as UPU mail falling under the UPU terminal dues system (UPU 2001, p. 2). Supporters of ETOEs have argued that Article 43 of the UPU Convention, which permits destinating administrations to charge higher rates for certain forms of remail, demonstrates the Convention's "recognition of the existence of competition" for outbound mail traffic, thus legitimizing ETOEs (Emerson and Alverno 2002, p. 293). Opponents of ETOEs have argued that Article 43 neither contemplates nor recognizes ETOEs, since Article 43 refers only to so-called "ABA" and "ABC" forms of remail, in which letters are "posted in a country

[1] It is also possible that the ETOE may be more efficient than the USP or may charge a smaller profit margin than the USP (in countries where the USP recovers a profit).

other than the country where the senders reside" (Emerson and Alverno 2002, p. 293). The quoted language, it is argued, would exclude ETOEs, which generally compete for outbound mail traffic posted by senders within the territory of the host country (UPU 2001, p. 3).

UPU Member States have previously acknowledged that the UPU Convention provides no guidance on ETOEs. In 2001, the UPU Council of Administration issued Resolution CA 17/2001, which noted that the UPU Acts "do not at present contain provisions for settling all the questions raised by the establishment of extraterritorial offices of exchange" (UPU 2002). The Council "recognize[d] provisionally . . . until the entry into force of the decisions of the next Congress . . . that administrations accepting dispatches from extraterritorial offices of exchange may apply the provisions of the Universal Postal Convention to such dispatches" (UPU 2002). The Council declared, however, "that nothing in this resolution can be construed as requiring an administration to accept items from extraterritorial offices of exchange as mail under the UPU Acts" (UPU 2002). The Resolution thus failed to resolve the central questions regarding the legality of (i) establishing an ETOE or (ii) treating ETOE mail as international mail under the UPU Acts (Emerson and Alverno 2002, p. 292).

At the UPU Congress in Bucharest, UPU Members are scheduled to consider—and, in theory, to reach agreement on—the legal status of ETOEs under the UPU Acts. As a temporary solution, the Council of Administration adopted a resolution proposed by Japan in October 2003, requiring ETOEs to obtain the approval of a host government before establishing operations in the host's territory (U.S. Dept. of State 2003). It is unclear whether this resolution applies retroactively to ETOEs already in existence, whether it is enforceable, and what penalties would be imposed for its violation. In February 2004, the Council of Administration postponed until the Bucharest Congress debate on a proposal that would prevent items sent by ETOEs from being treated as UPU mail to which UPU terminal dues apply, except where the government of the receiving administration specifically authorizes such treatment (U.S. Dept. of State 2004). In Bucharest, UPU Member States will also consider alternative proposals that would explicitly legitimize ETOEs under the UPU Convention (U.S. Dept. of State 2004).

4. THE BUCHAREST CONGRESS SHOULD NOT PLACE RESTRAINTS ON ETOES

As a symptom of an economically inefficient and unsustainable rate structure, ETOEs should not be treated as an anathema to postal administrations to be stamped out in order to preserve the monopoly status quo. Prohibiting ETOEs will not stem the pressure toward competition in the international postal arena caused by electronic diversion, multinational business operations, and the liberalization of many posts. UPU Members should address the underlying economic inefficiencies head on and encourage—not seek to stifle—new entrants and competition in the international postal delivery market. The UPU should adopt a long-term strategy—albeit with an acceptable transition period—to move toward an economically efficient terminal dues structure while making social subsidies explicit.

Basic economic policies for adopting a cost-based approach have been examined in detail in the literature on terminal dues and are beyond the scope of this paper. This paper identifies legal and practical reasons why the UPU should address ETOEs in the broader context of adopting a nondiscriminatory, cost-based rates approach rather than treating ETOEs as an isolated problem. The following discussion will address the possible legal challenges to restraints on ETOEs under the GATS and the practical problems in application and enforcement that may arise from such restraints.

4.1 Possible Challenges under GATS

A national measure that restricts ETOEs from paying UPU terminal dues—including a measure based on Article 43, which would allow UPU Members not to deliver certain forms of remail—might be successfully challenged under the Most-Favored Nation (MFN) obligation under GATS Article II:1. The possibility that a country would bring a World Trade Organization (WTO) case challenging restraints on ETOEs cannot be ignored. The existence of a large number of IC ETOEs means that several countries with the experience and resources necessary to aggressively pursue a WTO claim may also possess a strong economic incentive to do so. Strong legal arguments appear to support such a case, as outlined below.

Article II:1 of GATS provides, in relevant part:

> [E]ach Member shall accord immediately and unconditionally to services and service suppliers of any other Member treatment no less favorable than that it accords to like services and service suppliers of any other country.

Two elements would be required for a WTO member to establish that a measure restricting ETOEs constitutes a violation of GATS Article II:1. First, the challenged restriction on ETOEs must be "a measure covered by GATS"; second, it must "accord to services or service suppliers of the

Complainant's origin treatment less favorable than that it accords to the like services or services suppliers of any other country" (WTO 1997b, para. 7.344).

GATS obligations apply to all measures by WTO Members "affecting" trade in services such as postal services in the liberalized markets in which ETOEs operate. Under Article I:2, "trade in services" is defined, *inter alia*, as the "supply of a service . . . by a service supplier of one Member, through commercial presence in the territory of any other Member." ETOEs are service suppliers of one Member that trade in services by establishing a commercial presence in the territory of another Member. While GATS does not apply to "services supplied in the exercise of governmental authority," this category includes only services that are supplied "neither on a commercial basis, nor in competition with one or more service suppliers" (GATS, art. I:3). It would be difficult to argue that postal services offered in a liberalized market for outbound mail are not offered "on a commercial basis" (Perrazzelli and Vergano 2000, p. 741; WTO 1998c, p. 2). The ETOE issue in the UPU exists *because* USPs and ETOEs are commercial competitors for mail streams.

If a WTO Member were to implement measures preventing an ETOE (or all ETOEs) from accessing inbound delivery services of the USP under the terminal dues system, the ETOE would be charged domestic rates for inbound mail delivery while third country USPs would be charged the lower terminal dues rates. In this situation, any WTO Member whose ETOE was subject to such a measure could argue that the measure accords the ETOE less favorable treatment than that accorded to like service suppliers (*e.g.*, USPs) of third countries.

The key question is whether ETOEs and USPs are "like suppliers" for the purposes of GATS Article II:1. While some commentators have argued that these entities are not "like suppliers" due to the fact that USPs—unlike ETOEs—have an obligation to provide universal service (Emerson and Alverno 2002, p. 297), WTO jurisprudence indicates that a determination that entities are "like service suppliers" does not require a finding that such suppliers are alike in all or even most respects. Rather, service suppliers may be found to be "like" each other "at least to the extent that [the] entities provide . . . like services" (WTO 1997b, para. 7.346; WTO 1997a, paras. 242-244; WTO 2000, para. 10.248). Thus, where service suppliers provide the same service, they may be deemed to be "like" suppliers with respect to a challenge to a measure aimed at suppliers of the particular service. Under this reasoning, a WTO Panel would find that USPs and ETOEs are "like service suppliers" to the extent that they provide the same service—namely, the outbound transport of cross-border mail.

The fact that one service supplier has a universal service obligation or has a reciprocal obligation to deliver inbound cross-border mail should not destroy "likeness." As discussed above, a finding that service suppliers are "like" under the GATS MFN obligation depends on whether they provide *one or more* "like" services such as the outbound transport of cross-border mail. Suppliers thus need not be alike in *all* respects, nor provide all of the same services, nor be subject to all of the same legal obligations—including the obligation to provide reciprocal delivery of cross-border mail. Otherwise, a service supplier could take on additional obligations by contract, render itself "unlike" and benefit from special government treatment that would otherwise constitute impermissible discrimination. This result would likely be unacceptable to a WTO Panel.

While some commentators have argued that UPU rules should "trump" GATS rules due to the principle of *lex specialis*—in other words, the principle that specific rules prevail over general ones—it is unlikely that such an argument would succeed before a WTO Panel or the Appellate Body. The function of Panels and the Appellate Body is to apply the law embodied in the WTO Agreements, not the law embodied in other treaties such as the UPU Acts. The WTO's Dispute Settlement Understanding ("DSU"), which provides the legal framework for WTO dispute settlement, "appl[ies] to disputes brought pursuant to . . . the agreements listed in Appendix 1 to this Understanding"—a closed list that includes only WTO Agreements (DSU, art. 1.1). Panels convened for the purpose of settling a dispute between WTO Members are specifically charged with the task of interpreting and applying the relevant provisions *within* the WTO Agreements that are subject to dispute settlement (DSU, arts. 7, 11). The Appellate Body is similarly charged with applying and interpreting these WTO Agreements, since appellate review is limited to review of legal issues addressed in the underlying Panel Report (DSU, art. 17.6). The limited scope of WTO dispute settlement makes it very unlikely that a Panel or the Appellate Body would consider or apply UPU provisions. The prospect of UPU rules "trumping" WTO rules in a proceeding before a WTO Panel thus appears dim.[2] To date, neither a Panel nor the Appellate Body has applied *lex specialis* to "trump" an established rule of WTO law with a non-WTO treaty provision.

Even if a Panel were competent to analyze whether UPU provisions should prevail over the GATS obligation, it would apply *lex specialis* only where an unavoidable conflict exists between UPU and GATS provisions. According to WTO jurisprudence, a conflict will be found only where: (1)

---

[2] Under similar reasoning, it is doubtful that a WTO Panel or the Appellate Body would hold that UPU rules "trump" the GATS MFN obligation based on the principle of *lex posterior* (*i.e.*, the principle that a later law prevails over an earlier one).

the relevant agreements have the same signatories; (2) the relevant agreements operate in the same substantive area; and (3) the provisions in question (within the agreements) generate mutually exclusive obligations (WTO 1998b, para. 14.28, n.649). All three conditions present difficulties for a party arguing that *lex specialis* would privilege UPU rules over GATS. Perhaps the most significant obstacle arises in connection with the mutual exclusivity requirement. For the GATS MFN obligation and a UPU provision to be mutually exclusive, the UPU provision must *mandate* that UPU Members treat ETOEs in a WTO-inconsistent manner. A provision granting UPU Members *discretion* with respect to treatment of ETOEs would not conflict with GATS since a UPU Member could exercise discretion to act in a manner consistent with both UPU and WTO obligations (WTO 1998a, para. 65). It is not clear that sufficient consensus exists among UPU Members to enact provisions *mandating* WTO-inconsistent treatment of ETOEs.

Other aspects of the underlying terminal dues regime—which may impact an ETOE's profitability—may also be vulnerable to a GATS challenge. For example, a WTO member that is an IC might raise an MFN challenge asserting that a destinating country accords treatment less favorable to the service suppliers of the IC (*i.e.*, a USP or IC ETOE) than it accords to the like service suppliers of a DC (*i.e.*, a DC ETOE). The point here is not that national measures implementing the discriminatory terminal dues system would survive a challenge under GATS. Rather, an attempt to correct the problem of discrimination in terminal dues by restricting ETOEs would itself engender a GATS challenge. The policy proposal set forth in this paper would prevent both types of GATS challenges by replacing the underlying non-cost-based terminal dues system with a system that treats all countries' service suppliers equally.

As Emerson and Alverno have suggested, a country with a substantial interest in private operators might challenge a destinating country on the ground that treating ETOE mail as UPU mail (*i.e.*, charging an ETOE terminal dues rates rather than higher domestic rates) constitutes discrimination against private operators, since ETOEs and private operators are arguably "like suppliers" (2002, p. 297-8). In the competitive system proposed in this paper, open access and the same cost-based terminal dues would be applied to both ETOEs and private operators, thus avoiding such a GATS challenge.

4.2 Practical Problems with Restraints on ETOEs

Attempting to stamp out ETOEs to protect USP postal administrations may be counterproductive for practical reasons. The UPU's terminal dues system based on country borders is becoming outdated in light of technological innovations such as electronic mail and modern practices of multinational corporations in centralizing mailing operations. The fiction of postal administrations with strict boundaries may soon become untenable in places such as the EU, where integration across borders is encouraged.

Application of remail-type restrictions to ETOE mail would ignore the realities of the global business mailer. A large multinational mailer seeking to employ the most technologically efficient means of processing its mail—by consolidating mail in one country for sorting before sending the mail to several countries—would benefit from a wide variety of delivery alternatives, whether provided by the USP, an ETOE or a private operator. By squelching these competitive choices, the UPU may provide larger mailers with incentives toward electronic diversion, not only of international mail but also of domestic mail, and thus accelerate the decline of mail volumes.

In addition, enforcing ETOE prohibitions may be difficult in practice because the receiving postal administration must be able to track the volumes of mail over time. An ETOE that dumps into one country large volumes of mail from a single mailer in a short time period may be relatively easy to detect, but an ETOE intent on avoiding detection has several alternatives. For example, it can stagger mailing dates, vary volumes, enter the mail at different locations, and use various return addresses. ETOEs' ability to avoid detection is demonstrated by the fact that there is still no definitive data on the number or location of ETOEs (other than those that have registered) or of the amount of mail handled by ETOEs.

Finally, under Article 47.8 of the UPU Convention, UPU Members may choose to opt out of the UPU system of terminal dues in favor of payment provisions set forth in separate bilateral or multilateral agreements. Article 47.8 provides that "[t]he administrations concerned may, by bilateral or multilateral agreement, apply other payment systems for the settlement of terminal dues accounts." Many European countries have opted out of the UPU system in favor of the REIMS II Agreement, at least with respect to intra-REIMS II countries' terminal dues, the largest portion of their cross-border mail. Other countries could similarly circumvent UPU-imposed restrictions on ETOEs.

Restricting ETOEs may thus run afoul of both legal and practical considerations. Before placing restraints on ETOEs, the UPU should also consider the role ETOEs may play in a more competitive international postal system, such as the liberalized European postal market.

5. ETOES AS VEHICLES OF CHANGE IN A COMPETITIVE ENVIRONMENT

As explained earlier, ETOEs are a symptom of a larger problem caused by a noneconomic terminal dues structure. Moving toward competition and cost-based terminal dues would not only solve the ETOE issue but also position the UPU to play a significant role in the coming competitive international postal market. At the Bucharest Congress, the UPU should act with the goal of competition firmly in mind. This does not mean that social welfare considerations should fall by the wayside. Rather, the UPU should consider making more explicit any subsidies based on social welfare reasons such as universal service.

Although moving from a regulated monopoly regime to a competition-based market may seem a daunting task, such a feat has already been done in the European postal market. In the EU, the process of liberalizing cross-border mail has begun with dramatic results, including growing competition. EU postal liberalization and the REIMS II Agreement, described below, can serve as models for the process of introducing competition into the global postal market.

5.1 Liberalization of Postal Services in the EU

The European Court of Justice ("Court" or ECJ) in its landmark *Corbeau* decision established the legal framework for the liberalization of regulated industries in the EU, including postal services (ECJ 1993). In examining the legality of the Belgian postal monopoly under the EU Treaty, the Court stipulated that, while Member States may grant monopoly rights to postal operators when necessary to meet public service obligations (ECJ 1993, para. 17), such monopoly rights are not unlimited. Specifically, the USP's monopoly rights may not extend to separate services not traditionally provided by the postal service unless the USP's ability to meet its universal service obligation would be compromised (ECJ 1993, para. 19).

Similar principles formed the basis of Directive No. 97/67/EC, the "Framework Postal Directive," which provides the legislative framework for EU postal liberalization. The Framework Postal Directive has two main elements. First, it guarantees universal service, defining a minimum group of services that USPs must provide to all users at affordable rates (European Communities 1998, arts. 3.3 and 3.4, and recital 11). Second, it limits the postal services that Member States may reserve for their USPs. Article 7.1 of the Framework Postal Directive, as amended by Directive No. 2002/39/EC, provides that USPs may retain a monopoly regarding "clearance, sorting, transport and delivery of items of domestic and incoming cross-border correspondence"—within specified weight and price limits—but only "to the extent necessary to ensure . . . universal service" (European Communities 2002, art. 1). The market for outgoing cross-border mail is liberalized subject to a similar qualification (European Communities 2002, art. 1). Thus, a Member State seeking to reserve a service must demonstrate that the reservation is necessary for universal service. This exception mirrors Article 86(2) of the EU Treaty, under which EU competition rules apply to service providers such as USPs except where such application would impede universal service obligations (European Commission 1998).

While there has not yet been occasion for a ruling on the relationship between the UPU Convention and EU Law, a conflict in theory could arise if, for example, a revised UPU Convention restricted ETOEs in a manner incompatible with EU law. It is unlikely that such a conflict would arise, since EU Member States are under a legal obligation not to participate in international agreements that are incompatible with EU law. If a conflict were to arise, however, EU Member States might argue that the UPU Acts are subordinate to EU law under Declaration No. VIII made by the EU Member States on signature of the Acts of the 1999 Beijing Congress. Declaration VIII provides that EU Member States "will apply the [UPU] Acts . . . in accordance with their obligations pursuant to the Treaty establishing the EU and the General Agreement on Trade in Services (GATS) of the [WTO]."

5.2 The REIMS II Agreement on Terminal Dues

In October 2003, the European Commission adopted a Decision ("the Exemption Decision") extending through 2006 the exemption of the REIMS II Agreement from the application of EC competition rules concerning price fixing (European Commission 2004). The REIMS II Agreement is the instrument whereby seventeen European USPs collectively determined intra-party terminal dues. The Commission had previously exempted the Agreement for the period between 1999 and 2001 (European Commission 1999).

The REIMS II Agreement seeks, *inter alia*, "to provide the Parties with fair compensation for the delivery of cross-border mail which reflects more closely the real costs of delivery" (European Commission 2004, para. 35). Under REIMS II, terminal dues must bear a specified relation to the destinating country's domestic tariffs and are to progressively increase to a level of 78.5% of domestic tariffs in 2005-6 (European Commission 2004, paras. 37, 62).

The REIMS II Agreement provides that "each Party shall apply the same rates of terminal dues to all other parties provided that the transactions are equivalent" (European Commission 2004, para. 43). Thus, as described in the Exemption Decision, "two REIMS II PPOs competing for outgoing cross-border mail in a given REIMS II country to another REIMS II country would bear the same costs for . . . delivery . . . in the country of destination" (European Commission 2004, para. 43). Under the original, notified version of the Agreement, however, access to REIMS II terminal dues was not granted to non-REIMS II operators (*i.e.*, third-party postal operators), placing these third-party operators at a competitive disadvantage vis-à-vis the REIMS II parties. The Commission addressed this exclusion of third-party operators by exempting REIMS II from EC Competition rules subject to the condition, *inter alia*, that third-party operators competing in the intra-REIMS II market be granted access to REIMS II terminal dues under nondiscriminatory conditions (European Commission 2004, art. 3). The combination of postal liberalization in the EU and the REIMS II terminal dues system, as exempted by the Commission, has spurred a proliferation of ETOEs.

5.3 ETOES in the EU

The liberalization of postal services in Europe has led to the establishment of IC ETOEs that allow national postal administrations with shrinking mail volumes to build a customer base throughout the EU. To compensate for decreasing domestic mail volumes, postal administrations may look beyond their borders to creamskim mail from large customers of other postal administrations. In an earlier monopolistic era, this might have been perceived as an unacceptable threat to the universal service obligation of the postal administration located in the sender's country; however, economic principles dictate that such competition will encourage greater efficiencies and cost savings and ultimately benefit the consumer—the mailer.

The latest UPU listing of ETOEs, compiled from official registrations, shows that European postal administrations are rapidly deploying ETOEs. For example, the Belgian operator La Poste is currently operating twelve ETOEs (UPU 2004). Germany's Deutsche Post AG is currently operating twenty ETOEs (UPU 2004). Switzerland's Swiss Post is currently operating sixteen ETOEs (UPU 2004). The Netherlands' TPG Post is currently operating eighteen ETOEs (UPU 2004). The United Kingdom's Royal Mail is currently operating eleven ETOEs (UPU 2004). In the last year, the number of ETOEs in Europe has increased sharply.

As noted earlier, an ETOE operating in the sender's country may creamskim the most profitable mail of the postal administration of the sender's country. Most likely, the postal administration's charges for that mail would have included some recovery for the universal service obligation in addition to the attributable costs of carrying that mail. As discussed above, under the Framework Postal Directive, as amended, EU Member States may opt to maintain a monopoly with respect to outgoing cross-border mail only "to the extent necessary to ensure . . . universal service." To date, Member States do not appear to have invoked the universal service exception in order to block competition from ETOEs. It is possible that no challenges have been brought because many of the postal administrations that might otherwise raise such challenges have begun profitably operating their own ETOEs. It is also possible that cross-border mail revenues do not constitute a large enough portion of revenue such that their loss would threaten universal service.

5.4 ETOEs in a Competitive Environment

After witnessing the proliferation of ETOEs by European posts, one does not need much imagination to contemplate the future of ETOEs in a competitive global postal market. As postal administrations or even private operators collect and deliver cross-border mail with greater efficiency and innovation, competition in end-to-end international postal services will follow. The most efficient competitors will survive, with possible consolidation in, for example, the European market to a handful of posts (and/or private operators). These established global postal operators might then turn to competing with national postal administrations for domestic mail by creamskimming large mailers' domestic mail in countries where the national post is overpriced or of unsatisfactory quality. As the national post's monopoly is challenged, its universal service obligation may need to be met by an explicit subsidy or protected by regulation.

Depending on whether one has the perspective of a monopoly provider or of a consumer/mailer, ETOEs can be seen as a threat or a boon. The ultimate result of allowing ETOEs to grow can be improved cross-border mail service and competitive alternatives to inefficient national post services—offset by the loss of the hidden subsidy for universal service. One thing is clear, however: perpetuating an outdated monopoly system of non-cost-based, discriminatory terminal dues, attempting to police ETOEs and remail, and imposing noneconomic social welfare charges will only exacerbate the tension between those countries moving toward competition and those countries reluctant to recognize change.

6. CONCLUSION

The UPU should move away from a monopoly orientation, which perceives the proliferation of ETOEs only as a temporary aberration and a threat to universal service. Instead, the UPU should embrace a more economically efficient terminal dues structure that will correct non-cost-based discrimination, place the UPU in a position to lead the way to a competitive global postal market, and allow ETOEs to play a significant role in the growth of liberalized postal administrations.

REFERENCES

Campbell, Donald, Jeremy Cotton, and Gerard Power. 2002. "Extra-Territorial Offices of Exchange, the USO and International Trade: A Problem and a Solution." In *Postal and Delivery Services: Delivering on Competition*, edited by M.A. Crew and P.R. Kleindorfer. Boston, MA: Kluwer Academic Publishers.

Campbell Jr., James, I. 2002. "Evolution of Terminal Dues and Remail Provision in European and International Postal Law." In *The Liberalization of Postal Services in the European Union*, edited by D. Geradin. The Hague: Kluwer Law International.

Emerson, Lea, and Anthony Alverno. 2002. "Extra-Territorial Offices of Exchange: Examining New Forms of Competition under the UPU Umbrella." In *Postal and Delivery Services: Delivering on Competition*, edited by M.A. Crew and P.R. Kleindorfer. Boston, MA: Kluwer Academic Publishers.

European Commission. 1999. Decision of 15 September 1999 relating to a proceeding pursuant to Article 81 of the EC Treaty and Article 53 of the EEA, Case No. IV/36.748 – REIMS II. Official Journal of the European Communities, No. L 275/17 (26 October 1999).

European Commission. 2004. Decision of 23 October 2003 relating to a proceeding pursuant to Article 81 of the EC Treaty and Article 53 of the EEA, Case COMP/C/38.170 – REIMS II renotification. Official Journal of the European Communities, No. L 56/76 (24 February 2004).

European Commission. 1998. Notice from the Commission on the application of the competition rules to the postal sector and on the assessment of certain State measures relating to postal services. Official Journal of the European Communities, No. C 39/2 (6 February 1998).

European Communities. 1998. Directive 97/67/EC of the European Parliament and of the Council of 15 December 1997 on common rules for the development of the internal market of Community postal services and the improvement of quality of service. Official Journal of the European Communities, No. L 15/14 (21 January 1998).

European Communities. 2002. Directive 2002/39/EC of the European Parliament and of the Council of 10 June 2002 amending Directive 97/67/EC with regard to the further opening to competition of Community postal services. Official Journal of the European Communities, No. L 176/21 (5 July 2002).

European Court of Justice. 1993. *Criminal proceedings against Paul Corbeau*, Case C-320/91, ECR I-2533.

Perrazzelli, Alessandra, and Paolo R. Vergano. 2000. "Terminal Dues Under the UPU Convention and the GATS: An Overview of the Rules and of Their Compatibility." *Fordham International Law Journal* 23: 736-751.

Universal Postal Union. 2001. Extraterritorial Offices of Exchange. Annex 1 to circular letter No. 4415 (DER.PEP) 1535 of 16 August 2001.

Universal Postal Union. 2002. Extraterritorial Offices of Exchange. Resolution CA 17/2001, CA EP GTU 2002.1-Doc 4c, Annex 1.

Universal Postal Union. 2004. List of Registered Extraterritorial Offices of Exchange (ETOEs) as of 3 March 2004. http://www.upu.int/standards/etoes.txt.

U.S. Department of State. 2003. UPU: Council of Administration 2003 Annual Meeting, October 10-24, 2003. http://www.state.gov/p/io/rls/rpt/2003/26835.htm.

U.S. Department of State. 2004. UPU: Council of Administration and Postal Operations Council 2004 Annual Meetings, February 2-14, 2004. http://www.state.gov/p/io/rls/rpt/30742.htm.

World Trade Organization. 1997a. Appellate Body Report, *European Communities – Regime for the Importation, Sale and Distribution of Bananas*, WT/DS27/AB/R, adopted 25 September 1997, DSR 1997:II.

World Trade Organization. 1998a. Appellate Body Report, *Guatemala – Anti-Dumping Investigation Regarding Portland Cement from Mexico*, WT/DS60/AB/R, adopted 25 November 1998, DSR 1998:IX, 3767.

World Trade Organization. 2000. Panel Report, *Canada – Certain Measures Affecting the Automotive Industry*, WT/DS139/R, WT/DS142/R, adopted 19 June 2000, as modified by the Appellate Body Report, WT/DS139/AB/R, WT/DS142/AB/R, DSR 2000:VII.

World Trade Organization. 1997b. Panel Report, *European Communities – Regime for the Importation, Sale and Distribution of Bananas – Complaint by Ecuador*, WT/DS27/R/ECU, adopted 25 September 1997, as modified by the Appellate Body Report, WT/DS27/AB/R, DSR 1997:III.

World Trade Organization. 1998b. Panel Report, *Indonesia – Certain Measures Affecting the Automobile Industry*, WT/DS54/R, WT/DS55/R, WT/DS59/R, WT/DS64/R and Corr.1, 2, 3, and 4, adopted 23 July 1998, DSR 1998:VI, 2201.

World Trade Organization. 1998c. Postal and Courier Services, Background Note by the Secretariat 2, WTO S/C/W/39.

Chapter 13

Universal Service Providers

Defensive Moves on the Level Playing Field[*]

Mary Anne Gibbons
United States Postal Service

1. INTRODUCTION

For almost a decade major postal reform legislation has been considered in the U.S. Congress. In 2003, a nine-member, bipartisan commission appointed by President George W. Bush offered recommendations for structural reform of the U.S. postal market. Throughout the course of debates before the Congress and the President's Commission, postal competitors and watchdogs have alleged that competitive markets are tilted unfairly in favor of postal operators that receive government-granted protections and consequently more advantageous treatment than their private sector counterparts. Complaints about the U.S. Postal Service's (USPS's) immunity from "taxes, tags, and tickets" have become a familiar refrain in the halls of the U.S. Congress. Some observers allege that governments should "level the playing field" by subjecting postal operators to the same rules and laws as private operators, such as antitrust, customs, tort, traffic, and tax law.

These debates have transcended the halls of legislatures and academic circles and very recently were raised in arguments before the U.S. Supreme

---

[*] The views represented are solely those of the author and not necessarily those of the United States Postal Service. Special thanks to Gerald Robinson, Stephan Boardman, William Alvis, Lori Dym, Margaret Crenshaw, Fred Eggleston, Kent Smith, Kevin Rachel, Nancy Forden, Peter Henry, and Anthony Alverno for contributions towards this paper.

Court in *United States Postal Service v. Flamingo Industries,* an antitrust case in which the Court decided unanimously for the USPS and reaffirmed its governmental character, clearly distinguishing it from commercial operators. The impact of the *Flamingo* case should have profound implications for those on both sides of the level playing field argument.

While at first glance, arguments in favor of strict parity between public and private operators have superficial appeal, they oversimplify the differences between postal operators and their private sector competitors, minimize the financial impact of restrictions on postal operators, and ignore the costly public service functions and obligations of postal operators. This paper explores the "advantages" enjoyed by postal operators and surveys actions taken by regulators and independent commissions in several industrialized countries to address the "level playing field" arguments. This paper then reviews typical social and noncommercial policies that postal operators must fulfill, illustrated by the example of the USPS. This paper concludes that the market as currently structured imposes many costly, noncommercial objectives on universal service providers. The "level playing field" debate therefore cannot be fairly understood without recognizing the unique social policy responsibilities borne by postal operators.[1]

2. THE LEVEL PLAYING FIELD CHARGE

During the past decade, universal service providers around the world have been confronted with legal and political challenges. Debates in governments, independent legal bodies, and academic circles have challenged the longstanding treatment accorded to universal service operators by governments. These claims are closely linked to the growth of private sector companies in the communications field, the commercialization of postal operators, and liberalization in the scope of the letter monopolies. Historically, countries relied on government ministries to provide national postal services. In the past 20 years, that situation has been changing as more countries have created independent legal entities that provide their postal services. These entities have been granted discretion to act commercially, while governments have expanded opportunities to competing firms to participate in formerly protected markets. Following on the heels of this "corporatization" of postal authorities and the subsequent liberalization of the postal sector has been a move toward separating governmental

[1] Whether the social policy obligations imposed on the posts reflect sensible public policy goals for a business-oriented entity like the Postal Service, is a debate for another day. This paper is not intended to comment on the value to society of these obligations.

activities from commercial activities, even to the point in some cases of privatizing the postal operator and placing governmental oversight in specialized organizations within a ministry or in independent regulatory authorities.

As posts have commercialized and competition in postal markets has intensified, observers have debated whether private sector competitors are disadvantaged due to various governmental measures that grant postal operators different treatment under domestic law. This is illustrated by the experience of governments in Canada, Australia, the United Kingdom, and the United States.

2.1 Canada

In Canada, arguments about fairness in competition were heard before an independent panel known as the Canada Post Mandate Review. Commissioned in 1995, the Mandate Review analyzed Canada Post's business and provided an assessment of its ability to adjust to market conditions. In a report issued in 1996, the Mandate Review found that Canada Post was unfairly advantaged because it could leverage a network developed with public funds derived from a government-granted monopoly. This, according to the Mandate Review, gave Canada Post a pricing advantage over competitors. In addition, the Mandate Review found that Canada Post had a competitive advantage because it had exclusive access to mailboxes, could offer total market coverage for unaddressed advertising matter, and was immune from municipal laws allowing customers to refuse advertising material.

The Mandate Review concluded that Canada Post's structure and treatment under domestic law distorted competition by giving Canada Post an unfair advantage over private-sector competitors. In lieu of recommending the extension of Canada Post's preferential treatment to similarly situated competitors, the Mandate Review instead urged that Canada Post withdraw from all competitive activities that went beyond "core" responsibilities. Specifically, the Mandate Review recommended that Canada Post divest itself of its express delivery subsidiary, Purolator, exit the market for delivering unaddressed commercial advertising mail, and cease retailing of non-postal merchandise. While many of the Mandate Review's recommendations received a lukewarm reception, the Canadian government implemented certain reforms, including directing Canada Post's exit from the commercial unaddressed advertising mail business. More ambitious recommendations, such as divestiture of Purolator, were not adopted.

2.2 Australia

Similar to Canada, in 1997 the Australian government also directed an independent advisory body, the National Competition Council (NCC), to examine Australia Post. The issue of parity between postal and private providers was less of an issue in Australia, given that Australia Post was already corporatized and subject to private sector business procedures and taxes. Nevertheless, in a report issued in 1998, the NCC recommended that the Australian government implement a policy of "competitive neutrality" with respect to Australia Post's participation in competitive markets. The aim of this policy recommendation was to ensure that "significant government businesses" do not enjoy advantages over the private sector and that such businesses compete on an "equal footing" with their private sector counterparts.

The competitive neutrality policy envisaged by the NCC considered both advantages and disadvantages between the public postal operator and its private sector competitors. In furtherance of the competitive neutrality objective, the NCC recommended that equality of treatment be imposed on Australia Post in numerous contexts, including any remaining differences in tax, traffic, zoning, and customs administration, as well as immunity from liability. In the interest of promoting parity between public and private operators, however, the NCC recommended that privacy and mail security requirements be extended to all operators offering postal services. Although the expected outcome of the NCC review was a further agenda for reform of postal services, most of the key recommendations have not been implemented, with the exception of some changes in regulation of the Australian postal system.

2.3 United Kingdom

Debates about Royal Mail's treatment under domestic law are currently under scrutiny in the United Kingdom. The Postal Services Commission (Postcomm), the U.K.'s independent postal regulator, is in the process of soliciting public comment through a formal "consultation" process on whether ten of Royal Mail's "special privileges" present market distorting effects and should be remedied in some manner. Among the topics to be further explored include whether Royal Mail should: be exempt from value added taxes (VAT), continue to have the authority to set mail collection boxes on streets, retain immunity from parking restrictions, receive different customs treatment for postal articles, and have the ability to compel transportation providers to carry mail matter. In its initial consultation report, Postcomm suggests that certain immunities and treatment should be altered. For instance, Postcomm has preliminarily opined that Royal Mail's VAT exemption distorts competition. In other contexts, such as postal customs clearance, however, Postcomm observes that Royal Mail probably should continue to be treated differently. In Postcomm's view, postal customs clearance procedures may be justified on grounds that a great deal of postal traffic is anonymous and postal operators do not know, and cannot take responsibility for, the contents of packets.

The consultation is still ongoing. Although Postcomm has no power to make changes to any of the statutory privileges, the process should culminate in a series of recommendations for relevant action by Parliament or executive departments. Postcomm plans to publish its conclusions and recommendations for changes to Royal Mail's existing special privileges upon consideration of comments received.

2.4 United States

In the United States, debates about the USPS's treatment under domestic law are now subsumed in the postal reform debate. Major postal reform legislation has been considered in the U.S. Congress since 1996, and addressed with increasing intensity by several public policy think tanks. The arguments are fairly uniform and generally follow two themes. First, critics allege that the USPS unfairly leverages its monopoly network when it does business in competitive markets, and thereby "cross-subsidizes" competitive products. Interestingly, this argument is *not* supported by quantitative proof that postal competitive services fail to cover incremental costs. Rather, the competitors' argument appears to be premised on the notion that universal postal operators have an inherent cost advantage because they must create a delivery network to provide universal service. This, in turn, allows postal operators to offer competitive services at a relatively low unit cost, since a large portion of network costs are fixed or institutional and not attributed to competitive services. Apparently, the competitors believe that the remedy is to force the USPS to deal with its competitive services at arm's length, or to withdraw entirely from competitive markets, notwithstanding the economies and benefits to consumers associated with sharing postal network costs.

Second, and pertinent to the theme of this paper, critics allege that the USPS receives "indirect" subsidies and competitive advantages due to its status as a federal executive branch agency. For instance, critics allege unfair treatment in relation to the USPS's immunity from antitrust law, financial reporting requirements, and local zoning requirements, as well as its ability to exercise the power of eminent domain. Critics also complain that the USPS is exempt from federal, state, and local tax liability, borrows from the U.S. Treasury at preferential rates with the backing of the federal government, and is exempt from parking laws and state vehicular registration requirements.

By contrast, critics note that competitors are subject to tax liability, must pay parking tickets and registration fees, must retain their own defense in legal actions, lack regulatory power over competitors, and must comply with applicable commercial and antitrust law. According to the critics, the USPS's many governmental powers and privileges are tantamount to indirect subsidies that can hide inefficiency and distort competitive markets. Observers diverge on how the alleged perceived advantages should be remedied. On the one hand, some observers believe that privatization of the USPS would level the playing field and place it on the same footing as private competitors. Others fear that a privatized USPS would convert the postal industry's proverbial "sleeping giant" into competitors' worst nightmare.

Arguments addressing alleged unfair competition were aired in 2003 before the President's Commission on the USPS. Similar to the independent panels in Canada and Australia, the Commission was established to make recommendations on the USPS's future. The President's Commission issued its report to the President in July 2003. Interestingly, the President's Commission did not recommend privatization or strict parity between the USPS and private operators. Rather, it recommended retention of the USPS as a self-sustaining, independent executive branch establishment. The President's Commission also did not endeavor to recommend structural separation of postal competitive services, or complete withdrawal from competitive markets. Instead, it offered alternative solutions to address these arguments, such as, for example, recommending a "core mission" for the USPS, strengthened oversight by an independent regulator, and enhanced transparency and financial reporting under specially tailored guidelines.

The President's Commission recommendations have undergone further policy evaluation in the U.S. executive and legislative branches. In late 2003 and early 2004, both houses of the U.S. Congress held hearings to receive testimony from interested parties concerning a new postal reform legislative package. Once again, arguments about the "level playing field" have been injected into the congressional debate. Postal reform bills are currently pending in the U.S. House of Representatives and the Senate. The bills are designed in part to extend several commercial laws to the Postal Service. For example, the bills would require the Postal Service to pay an assumed federal income tax on competitive products, and subject the Postal Service to antitrust liability for its competitive, non-market dominant products, and Federal Trade Commission (FTC) jurisdiction. In addition, the bills would direct the FTC to prepare a report identifying the federal and state laws that apply differently to the USPS in its provision of competitive products as compared with private companies providing similar products. The report is to include the FTC's recommendations as to how such differences should be ended.

3. IMPACT OF FLAMINGO INDUSTRIES

One of the central arguments advanced by proponents of the "level playing field" has been the equal application of competition laws. Removing the USPS's longstanding immunity from federal antitrust law has been a key objective of some engaged in the "level playing field" debate. Momentum for extending the antitrust laws to the USPS through the judicial process gained some ground when the Ninth Circuit Court of Appeals ruled in 2002 in the *Flamingo* case that the USPS was a "person" subject to the antitrust laws. This ground-breaking precedent was short-lived, however, since the U.S. Supreme Court reversed the appellate court in a unanimous opinion issued in February 2004. The Supreme Court decision not only establishes an important holding about the governmental status of the USPS, but it also illustrates that questions of equal application to the USPS of private sector competition laws are matters reserved for the legislatures, not the courts.

The controversy in *Flamingo* began when Flamingo Industries, Ltd., a manufacturer of mail sacks, challenged the USPS's termination of a contract for mail sacks and Flamingo's subsequent nonselection for other contracts to provide mail bags. Among other claims, Flamingo alleged that the USPS sought to suppress competition and to create a monopoly in mail sack production by resorting to foreign manufacturers. The USPS prevailed in district court, which held that Congress did not intend for the antitrust laws to apply to the USPS. The Ninth Circuit Court of Appeals reversed. The appellate court ruled that federal law allowing the USPS to sue and be sued in its own name waived the USPS's sovereign immunity based on its "status." Since sovereign immunity was waived, the USPS should be treated as a "person" subject to the antitrust laws.

The USPS thereafter petitioned the Supreme Court to hear the case. Flamingo and its supporters asserted that when the USPS engages in activity outside the scope of its monopoly, it should be subject to antitrust liability. A contrary conclusion would pose a risk to competitors because the USPS could use its size and commercial freedom to harm competitors by expanding the scope of the letter monopoly. The USPS defended these claims by arguing that its commercial endeavors do not change the fact that it is performing a sovereign function required by statute. The Supreme Court held that the USPS is not a "person" subject to the antitrust laws. In reaching this decision, it applied a two-step analysis: whether there is a waiver of sovereign immunity against the USPS and, if so, whether the substantive provisions of the antitrust laws apply to the USPS as an independent establishment of the executive branch. The Court concluded that the first step is satisfied because the USPS's "sue-and-be-sued clause" is a broad waiver of sovereign immunity. However, the Supreme Court emphasized that this broad waiver of sovereign immunity does not change the USPS's status as a governmental entity.

The Supreme Court then determined that the second step is not satisfied because the USPS is not a "person" under the Sherman Act. The Sherman Act's definition of a "person" includes "corporations and associations existing under or authorized by the laws of ... the United States." The Court observed that it would be inconsistent with congressional intent to expose the United States to liability as an antitrust defendant. The Court noted that the USPS's goals, powers, and obligations are unlike those of private businesses. For instance, the USPS is not a profit-making enterprise, has responsibility for universal service and free mail delivery, and "increased public responsibilities related to national security." The Court also found instructive the fact that its powers are more limited than those of private businesses. For instance, the postal ratemaking process with the Postal Rate Commission deprives the USPS of the power unilaterally to set prices, and the USPS is subject to restrictions governing the closing of post offices. Thus, the Court concluded that the USPS's "public characteristics and responsibilities indicate it should be treated under the antitrust laws as part of the Government, not a market participant separate from it."

Flamingo confirmed that the USPS is legally governmental in nature. The *Flamingo* opinion also re-emphasizes the distinctions between the USPS and private sector competitors that do not shoulder public service functions and responsibilities. *Flamingo* further implies that reforms sought by proponents of the "level playing field" must be taken to legislatures, and not the federal courts, for resolution.

4. THE POSTS' ROLE IN FULFILLING SOCIAL AND ECONOMIC POLICIES

The "level playing field" reforms envisaged by critics focus on several discrete features of the USPS's treatment under domestic law. For example, critics emphasize tax and antitrust immunity, as well as differential treatment in customs, as evidence of unfair treatment favoring posts. Missing entirely from this debate is a comprehensive understanding of the financial and operational impact of the many noncommercial, public, and social missions that postal operators must fulfill. In the United States and many other countries, the postal system is not structured as an economic or commercial instrument alone. It is structured instead as an instrument of public policy which is required to balance economic efficiency objectives with other specified social policy goals. To be truly level, the playing field would look much different from the proposals advanced by proponents of the concept.

4.1 Universal Service

The universal service obligation, or USO, as provided in the Postal Reorganization Act of 1970, requires the USPS to "provide prompt, reliable, and efficient services to patrons in all areas" and to "render postal services to all communities" at "fair and equitable" rates. The extent of the USPS's universal service obligation is quite broad. It must serve as nearly as practicable the entire population of the United States. Further, the USPS is obligated to maintain a maximum degree of postal services to "rural areas, communities, and small towns where post offices are not self-sustaining."

The USPS also must adhere to frequency of delivery requirements. Six-day per week delivery service to virtually all addresses has been legislatively mandated on an annual basis. Additional requirements specify that the USPS must offer a uniform rate for sealed letters and books and other media. As a result, the USPS must accept high-cost shipments destined to the most remote locations and rely on internal cross-subsidies within subclasses of mail to cover unprofitable service.

The USPS must also maintain thousands of low activity, loss producing retail units throughout rural areas. To protect small communities from large-scale closings or consolidations of post offices, the Postal Reorganization Act stipulates that small post offices cannot be closed "solely for operating at a deficit." If the USPS seeks to close a rural office, it must provide advance notice to customers, and its decision to close the office is subject to appeal to the Postal Rate Commission, thereby staying the effective date of the decision until resolution of the appeal.

In light of the above requirements, the USPS clearly remains distinct from other providers. Universal service operators such as the USPS are charged with a statutory mandate to provide universal service to their country's population. In the United States and many other countries, universal postal services are subject to standards and requirements not common to private carriers. For instance, universal services are offered through a collection network that includes an extensive array of retail stores and collection boxes unlike that of any other provider. In the United States and elsewhere, this implies maintenance of unprofitable retail outlets, hardly a characteristic of the business practices of the private sector. Universal postal services are subject to regulation and statutorily-prescribed pricing standards, including principles of nondiscrimination, fairness, and equity that are not common to alternative providers. A clear example is the inability of the USPS to change domestic prices without a lengthy, external review process in which customers and competitors participate. Moreover, the regulatory process has not allowed the USPS to compete domestically through high-volume discounts.

In addition, unlike private sector providers, posts cannot unilaterally determine what markets to compete in and what markets to exit. Some posts offering universal postal service often may not offer new products or negotiate the prices of such products outside the purview of competitors or regulators. Universal postal services are also distinguished on grounds that they are delivered in a manner that requires passing all delivery points on a frequent, usually daily, schedule. This implies that universal postal services must be structured to provide services to all destinations. By contrast, private providers can tailor their networks to demand and profitability. They can decide what markets to serve, how often to serve them, and at what price. They also are not hampered by legislative requirements limiting their ability to close or consolidate retail outlets. Hence, private carriers have the luxury of being able to "cream skim" the most lucrative markets, leaving only the unprofitable and high-cost markets for the postal operator.

In the United States, private operators share no financial responsibility for executing universal service obligations. Moreover, a public service reimbursement from the government for maintenance of universal services was last provided in 1982. Since then, the total revenue of the USPS from the various classes of mail has had to cover the total cost of providing universal postal service. Postage for certain free services required by Congress, including mail for the blind and overseas voting materials, is subsidized with tax revenues; however, these amount to less than 0.1 percent of total revenue.

The universal service obligations represent a significant cost on the USPS. Based on a limited sample, Bradley and Colvin (2000) found that of 27,166 post offices, 4,525 had positive revenue, while 22,920 were operated at a loss or breakeven. The sum of these losses was estimated to be $1.27 billion, which represents an estimate of the cost of the retail aspect of the universal service obligation. Estimates of the delivery aspect of the USO cost from Cohen *et al.*, (2004) and Bradley and Colvin (2000) range from $2.5 billion to $9.8 billion, depending on the method of measurement.

4.2 Noncommercial Rate Policy

In addition to the USO, the USPS must adhere to numerous ratemaking requirements that incorporate social policy in pricing. These requirements have the effect of requiring the USPS to charge noncommercial prices, forgoing considerable revenue. For instance, the Postal Reorganization Act requires that all postage rates must be "fair and equitable." Further, the USPS must maintain at least one class of mail for letters for which the rate "shall be uniform" throughout the United States. For First-Class Mail the public policy aspects of the uniform rate policy imply that an internal cross-subsidy from low-cost users to high-cost users is the primary financing tool for universal service. This deprives the USPS of the ability to send the most efficient economic signals to mail users.

Another example of social policy reflected in U.S. ratemaking is the requirement that preferred rates be extended to certain categories of users. For instance, the USPS must offer highly discounted rates for advertising mail sent by nonprofit organizations. Under current law, nonprofit rates for advertising matter are roughly 40 percent below those for commercial users. The USPS lacks the power to control the volume of mail tendered at preferred rates, since Congress reserves to itself the right to decide to whom they are available.

In addition, as a matter of longstanding ratemaking practice, contribution margins on Periodicals and Media Mail have been kept at extremely low levels to further social policy. For instance, in FY 2003, the USPS reported a markup of 5.8 percent for Periodicals, while the Media Mail markup was a mere 6.3 percent. By contrast, the markup for "competitive" Express Mail was 111 percent, which ranked among the highest of all subclasses. These uneconomic outcomes result from rate policies in federal law that direct the Postal Rate Commission to consider the educational, cultural, scientific, and informational value ("ECSI value") of the mail in setting overhead cost assignments for purposes of rate recommendations. Mail matter having a high "ECSI value," such as Periodicals and Media Mail, traditionally receives relatively low overhead cost burdens. The Commission must also consider the impact of rate increases on competition, which creates upward pressure in relation to prices for competitive products like Express Mail.

By contrast, private industry serves only the most lucrative markets, engages in high degrees of price differentiation, and can elect to offer or cap any preferences extended to nonprofit users. For example, private operators can offer highly discounted negotiated rates to large volume customers. Hence, the noncommercial rate policies imposed on the USPS to promote certain social policies over economic and profitmaking principles in ratesetting distinguish the USPS from private providers.

4.3 Employment

The USPS provides employment opportunities for a large segment of the U.S. population. Currently, the USPS employs roughly 710,000 career employees, supports nearly 500,000 retired postal workers, and indirectly sustains thousands of other organizations that employ more than eight million individuals. As the second largest employer in the United States and the world's largest unionized employer, the USPS offers upward mobility for millions of U.S. families. It appears, moreover, that Congress has mandated rich benefits to aid in or expedite the upward mobility of postal employees.

Many federal statutes, such as the Postal Reorganization Act, the Civil Service Reform Act, and the Federal Employees' Compensation Act, to mention only a few, establish postal human-resources policies. These laws cover diverse employment matters ranging from the hiring of employees, to setting their wages and benefits, to governing employees' retention and retirement. In many instances, the USPS's discretion to establish or modify key components of its employment policies is quite narrow and highly circumscribed, especially compared to the broad latitude enjoyed by private businesses in the United States. Relevant to the issue of a "level playing field" between the USPS and private organizations providing delivery services, the annual cost to the USPS for its human resources significantly exceeds the employment costs of companies in the private sector. No assessment of the playing field can be accurate or complete if it fails to take full account of the costs of postal human-resources that are outside the USPS's control compared to the legally required costs of competing private enterprises.

The costs involved in postal employment far exceed those for employment in comparable positions in the private sector for a variety of reasons. Unlike private organizations, the wages and benefits of postal workers are determined by mechanisms established by the U.S. Congress. As a consequence, postal workers in collective-bargaining units (craft employees) earn an average salary of $42,500 and total annual compensation of nearly $60,000. Indeed, postal wage and benefit levels are so generous that there is a backlog in excess of 400,000 applicants for employment and an attrition rate that is virtually non-existent. Postal workers, once hired, typically stay with the USPS until retirement. Unlike employers in the private sector, the USPS lacks the ability or the discretion to set benefit levels based on market conditions. A review of how three important benefits – health insurance, retirement, and workers' compensation – are determined illustrates this point.

Postal workers enjoy a full range of comparatively generous health insurance plans offered by the federal government. The benefit levels in the federal health plans are set by the federal government without any significant input from the USPS. Federal law currently deprives postal management of considerable discretion in setting health benefits. The Postal Reorganization Act establishes the government benefits package in effect at the creation of the USPS in 1971 as a floor against which any alterations must be compared, ensuring that the benefits package, as a whole, remains favorable for employees. As a result, the USPS has little control over health benefits costs. The current cost of postal health insurance plans exceeds the cost for health insurance plans in the private sector by approximately 25 percent.

Retirement benefits for postal employees are also generous. Like other federal employees, certain postal employees with sufficient years of service can retire at age 55 and receive annuities that are indexed annually to inflation, a rare provision in private sector pension plans. Although the USPS absorbs the cost of these retirement programs, it has little influence on either the scope of the retirement plans or underlying policies. By contrast, private sector enterprises are free to establish and modify retirement plans based on market conditions. Indeed, private organizations are under no obligation to offer pension plans although, if they do, they must comply with various federal regulations.

Also, pursuant to a federal law passed in 2003 which sought to provide relief to the USPS in the retirement area, the USPS is now obligated to fund retirement benefits of its employees for periods earned while in the military service. Since the USPS, also by federal law, gives hiring preference to veterans, it has a large number of veterans in its workforce. This new requirement that the USPS cover these retirement costs, unique to federal agencies, will result in a cumulative pension obligation of $27 billion for a period beginning in 1971 and continuing prospectively through 2038.

Finally, the USPS falls under a federal workers' compensation plan, which, unlike the private sector, provides that benefits commence immediately upon the occurrence of a compensable injury. Under the federal plan, salaries are continued at full pay for the first 45 days and afterwards at a tax-free rate up to 75 percent of workers' pay, rather than the norm of 66-2/3 percent. There is no maximum cap on payments. The plan often results in take-home pay for an injured worker in excess of what the employee would have received if working. For those employees to whom this applies, most elect to remain on workers' compensation well beyond normal retirement.

As a rule, private organizations in the United States have wide freedoms to set benefit levels in accordance with their own circumstances, relevant market conditions, and profit targets. Although there are some few exceptions, such as various unemployment or worker injury benefits under state laws, private employers have much greater freedom to establish benefit policies appropriate to their circumstances in the marketplace. Many proponents of the "level playing field" principle take little, if any, account of respective employment costs, although the cost of employment is the single largest expense for organizations in most service industries. The human resources costs incurred by the USPS, while advancing public policies set by law, have a concomitant, significant impact on postal operations and costs which must be recognized in discussions of a "level playing field."

4.4 Social Policy in Procurement

The USPS fulfills numerous socio-economic policies that make it less able than a private sector company to acquire goods and services efficiently and at the lowest possible cost. For instance, Congress mandates wage levels for construction and service workers employed by contractors that do business with the USPS by requiring USPS suppliers to pay prevailing wage rates set by the Department of Labor (DOL). The Davis-Bacon Act requires all laborers on USPS construction contracts valued at more than $2,000 to be paid area prevailing wage rates established by DOL. Similar to the Davis-Bacon Act, the Service Contract Act also applies DOL-established wage rates and administrative requirements for service contracts. The effect of these laws is to deny the USPS the opportunity to contract at the lowest possible cost. The prevailing rates tend to be the union wage rates and require that even lower-cost (non-union) contractors must pay the higher wages on USPS projects. The impact of these laws is not trivial. The U.S. General Accounting Office concluded that the Davis-Bacon Act inflates federal construction costs considerably and repeal of the Act would reduce funds spent on federal construction.

While these policies promote the interests of their intended beneficiaries, they also add costs to USPS contracts, whether for supplies, services or facilities. In short, Congress, in an attempt to foster certain social goals, has imposed, either directly or by policy, numerous obligations and restrictions upon the USPS and its suppliers that prevent the USPS from obtaining products and services efficiently and at the lowest possible cost. Given the size of the USPS's purchasing program, which exceeds $11 billion annually, the combination of these requirements has a significant impact on the bottom line. Private sector companies do not share these obligations and restrictions, or the financial impacts that result.

5. COMPETITIVE CONDITIONS FOR UNIVERSAL SERVICE OPERATORS

The discussion above demonstrates that the level playing field argument cannot be boiled down to a simple set of discrete comparisons in narrowly-defined fields, as the critics have long suggested. Rather, there are a host of obligations that the USPS must fulfill in a variety of contexts. The economic effect of these policies may well dwarf whatever competitive advantages the USPS receives from its governmental status. Public objectives permeate and define the operations of the postal system to the extent that comparison to private economic entities is limited and questionable. At its core, the purpose of a private company is to maximize the value of its shareholders investments. The leadership of a private corporation is accountable for focusing on that effort. With its public service mission, the USPS is led and directed by Presidentially appointed Governors, expressly selected to "represent the public interest generally," not just the business interest of the institution.

Unlike the private sector, the USPS is subject to ongoing oversight by multiple executive and legislative branch bodies, and it is prohibited from lobbying or forming political action committees. The USPS is subject to rigorous independent review of domestic rates, product definitions, post office closings, and nationwide service changes. Pricing authority is limited, and even the most modest price and product changes are subject to lengthy advance scrutiny before the Postal Rate Commission. Not only are domestic postal rates set by a public process, but the Postal Rate Commission is bound by statute to consider the effect on postal competition before issuing recommended decisions on rates for any postal products. Private competitors and customers are also entitled to and do participate in these proceedings. The USPS is sometimes forced to disclose sensitive business and financial information to its competitors, and the effect of rate changes must consider the impact on competition. Because an explicit statutory provision limits its ability to price discriminate among mailers, the Postal Service also lacks considerable discretion in negotiating specially tailored price and product solutions. Private sector providers by contrast can engage in a higher degree of price discrimination.

The USPS also lacks independent control over its finances. Unlike the private sector, the USPS cannot borrow in public markets, or invest in securities, without first securing the consent of the Treasury Department. Like other federal agencies, the USPS is subject to certain administrative laws, such as open records and privacy restrictions, and it is explicitly denied commercial opportunities to sell or transfer lists of patrons or addresses.

Criticisms under the "level playing field" rubric would undoubtedly be more balanced if the principle required extension to private operators of the same restrictions and requirements imposed on public postal operators. Understandably, no private company could accept having its objectives and processes so heavily defined by public legislation and oversight, nor would that result merit consideration or be constitutionally permitted in the United States. Consideration of a "level playing field" analysis simply cannot ignore the tremendous impact these obligations and restrictions have on the competitive posture of postal operators like the USPS.

6. CONCLUSION

Posts around the world have been confronted with arguments that they receive competitive advantages and better treatment under domestic law than private sector operators. Independent bodies in several industrialized countries have issued recommendations urging governments to promote competitive equality principles under domestic law. While many critics urge that the playing field be leveled, they often do not take account of the many costly public responsibilities that postal operators must fulfill. The *Flamingo* opinion reaffirms that the USPS is a federal government entity and is not subject to competition laws applicable to private sector providers. As a governmental entity, the USPS must fulfill many social policies. Unlike private sector providers in the United States, it must execute universal service obligations. Postal rates must also reflect many noncommercial considerations, and product pricing is driven by social policy as opposed to economic principles. As an employer, the USPS must observe significant, costly restrictions on its ability to set wage and benefit policies. As a purchaser of billions of dollars of goods and services, the USPS must fulfill numerous socio-economic policies that make it less able to acquire goods and services efficiently and at the lowest possible cost. The "level playing field" debate cannot be fairly understood without recognizing the counterbalancing social policy responsibilities borne by postal operators.

REFERENCES

Australia National Competition Council. 1998. Report on the Competitive Restrictions in the Australian Postal Corporation Act 1989.

Bradley, M., and J. Colvin. 2000. "Measuring the Cost of Universal Service for Posts." In *Current Directions in Postal Reform,* edited by M.A. Crew and P.R. Kleindorfer. Boston, MA: Kluwer Academic Publishers.

Canada Post Mandate Review. 1996. The Future of Canada Post Corporation.

Canadian Union of Postal Workers. 2000. Submission to the Canadian Government on Public Postal Services and the World Trade Organization's General Agreement on Trade in Services.

Cannon, M.F. and D. Soifer. 2003. "With Flamingo Case, Supreme Court Can Help Level the Postal Playing Field." Lexington Institute.

Cohen, R., M. Robinson, R. Sheehy, J. Waller, and S. Xenakis. 2004. "An Empirical Analysis of the Graveyard Spiral." In *Competitive Transformation of the Postal and Delivery Sector,* edited by M.A. Crew and P.R. Kleindorfer. Boston, MA: Kluwer Academic Publishers.

Eskew, M. 2003. Written Statement of Mike Eskew, Chairman and CEO UPS before the President's Commission on the US Postal Service.

Eskew, M. 2004. Statement for the Record before the United States House of Representatives Committee on Government Reform, Special Panel on the US Postal Service.

Flamingo Industries, Inc. 2003. Brief for Respondent Flamingo Industries, Ltd. in *United States Postal Service v. Flamingo Industries,* No. 02-1290.

Flamingo Industries v. United States Postal Service, 302 F.3d 985 (9th Cir. 2002), *reversed,* 124 S. Ct. 1321 (2004).

Gattuso, J.L. 2004. "Regulation in Brief: US Postal Service Regulation." Heritage Foundation.

Geddes, R. 2003a. "Why We Need Serious Postal Reform." American Enterprise Institute.

Geddes, R. 2003b. *Saving the Mail: How to Solve the Problems of the U.S. Postal Service.* Washington, DC: The AEI Press.

Geddes, R. 2004a. "Bad Policy, Pure and Simple." Hoover Institution Weekly Essays.

Geddes, R. 2004b. "Competing With the U.S. Postal Service: Effects on Consumers, Competitors, and Virginia State and Local Government." Thomas Jefferson Institute for Public Policy.

General Accounting Office. 2001. *Supporting Congressional Oversight, Framework for Considering Budgetary Implications of Selected GAO Work* (GAO/ 01-447), App. I:78.

Oster, S. 1994. "The Postal Service as a Public Enterprise." In *Governing the Postal Service,* edited by G.M. Sidak. Washington, DC: AEI Press.

Postcomm, Postal Services Commission. 2004. A Review of Royal Mail's Special Privileges.

President's Commission on the US Postal Service. 2003. Embracing the Future: Making Tough Choices to Preserve Universal Mail Service.

Robinson, A., and K. Stanley. 2003. "Evaluating the Playing Field Facing Parcel Competitors in the United States." Association for Postal Commerce.

Robinson, A. 2003. "Competition within the United States Parcel Delivery Market." Association for Postal Commerce.

Ryan, S. 2004. "After Supreme Court Ruling, Where Won't the Post Office Compete Next?" Lexington Institute.

Schuyler, M. 2004. "A Checklist for US Postal Service Reform." Institute for Research on the Economics of Taxation.

Schuyler, M. 2004. "The Danger of Monopoly-Subsidized Pricing by the US Postal Service in Competitive Markets." Institute for Research on the Economics of Taxation.

Smith, F.W. 2004. Prepared Statement Before the Special Panel on Postal Reform and Oversight of the Committee on Government Reform,

United States Postal Service v. Flamingo Industries, 124 S. Ct. 1321 (2004).

United States Postal Service. 2002. Transformation Plan.

United States Postal Service. 2003. Brief for the Petitioner United States Postal Service in *United States Postal Service v. Flamingo Industries*, No. 02-1290.

United States Postal Service. 2003. Comprehensive Statement on Postal Operations.

Wachter, M.L., B.T. Hirsch, and J.W. Gillula. 2001. "Difficulties of Deregulation When Wage Costs are the Major Cost." In *Future Directions in Postal Reform,* edited by M.A. Crew and P.R. Kleindorfer. Boston, MA: Kluwer Academic Publishers.

White, J.P. and R. Janzen. 2000. "The Industrial Relations Implications of Privatization." *Relations Industrielles/Industrial Relations* 55(1).

Chapter 14

Selective Rate Discounts To Preserve First-Class Mail Volume*

David M. Levy
Sidley Austin Brown & Wood LLP

1. INTRODUCTION

This paper considers a paradox of postal ratemaking in the United States: the failure of the Postal Service to offer targeted rate reductions to stem the diversion of bill presentment and payment communications from First-Class Mail to the Internet. There is a growing consensus that electronic bill presentment and payment ("EBPP") threaten one of the largest and most profitable sources of First Class mail. The preference of consumers for EBPP is hardly unanimous, however, and the mails are likely to remain an accepted (or even preferred) bill paying medium for a high percentage of households for the foreseeable future. Hence, a large share of bill paying mail volume is still very much in play.

Regulators of other network industries such as transportation, energy and telecommunications have long allowed individual firms to meet analogous threats of intermodal competition with selective rate discounts. To date, however, the Postal Service has not proposed to offer volume-retention discounts for billing and bill payment mail. The Service's inaction appears to reflect a widely shared assumption in the postal community that volume-retention discounts constitute undue discrimination, or are otherwise

* The author and others at his law firm have represented a number of mailers and trade associations of mailers concerning the matters covered in this paper. The views offered here, however, are those of the author, not Sidley or its clients.

inconsistent with the Postal Service's common carrier status. This paper argues that volume-retention discounts of this kind, if reasonably justified by competitive threats, would in fact benefit all classes of mail, and comply with well-established legal norms for undue discrimination.

2. THE GROWING DIVERSION OF BILLS AND BILL PAYMENTS FROM THE MAIL TO THE INTERNET

The "oft-predicted" mass migration of EBPP from the mails to the Internet (Kane (2001); Plum (1997); Nikali (1995); Reisner (2000); Robinson (1980)) until recently has been more promise than reality in the United States. Ten years ago, for example, a consulting firm predicted that 13.8 million households would pay bills online by 2000. In fact, only 3.4 million people paid bills online by that date (USPS (2002), Ezell (2004)).

Since then, however, on-line bill paying has finally begun to achieve critical mass. By 2003, an estimated 25 million households paid utility and credit card bills by computer (Ezell (2004)). This year, approximately 25 percent of American households currently pay bills online each month (Park (2004), Walker (2004), President's Commission (2003)). According to one consulting firm, Jupiter Research, consumer adoption of online banking is increasing 14 percent each year (PR Newswire (2004)). Another consulting firm, TowerGroup, has estimated that adoption of Internet bill payments rose 26 percent in 2003 and 19 percent in 2002, and one-third of the largest banks and brokerage firms in the U.S. are reported to offer free Internet bill payment (Walker (2004)). Two consulting firms have projected that 73 million U.S. consumers are expected to pay bills on-line by four years from now (USPS (2002), Park (2004)).

Both supply and demand factors encourage the growth of EBPP. The President's Commission on the U.S. Postal Service has estimated that processing a digital payment over the Internet costs between one-third and one-half less than a check sent through the mail." (President's Commission, 7). EBPP can also increase the loyalty of banking customers; the time and effort invested by an account holder in setting up and automating his or her bill payment preferences and payees is a sunk investment that changing banks would require the consumer to duplicate from scratch (Gonsalves (2003)). Customers who pay bills on line are 75 percent less likely to change banks, according to Wells Fargo (Park (2004)). Customers who pay bills on line also tend to use more financial services, and generate more income from fees and loans, than the average customer (Ezell (2004), Walker (2004)). For these reasons, credit card issuers and other financial institutions are eliminating fees for the convenience of on-line bill paying, and even offer incentives to customers who pay bills through their website—"everything from cash to Caribbean cruise raffles" (President's Commission, 7).

Consumers' reasons for favoring e-bill paying, according to a Harris Interactive® survey sponsored by MasterCard International, include convenience, 24/7 access, saving money, saving time, and security (Business Wire (2004), President's Commission, 7).

The shift to EBPP poses a growing threat to mail volume and revenue. The volume of First-Class single-piece letters mailed in the United States fell from 54.3 billion pieces in 1998 to 49.3 billion in 2002. And the total volume of all First-Class Mail—which accounts for more than half of all USPS revenues—declined in 2002, for the first time in more than a quarter century (President's Commission). Like many other recent observers, the President's Commission on the USPS concluded in 2003 that "Electronic substitution is the primary reason long-term First-Class mail volumes are threatened. The initial rise of the Internet, e-mail, instant messaging and other communications trends siphoned away a large share of personal, one-to-one correspondence" (*id.*). Largely as a result of EBPP, the number of checks written annually is predicted to decline by about one quarter by 2007, to 30 billion (Park (2004), Cornwell (2004), Celent Communications (2002)). The decline in First-Class volume is expected to continue over the long term. (President's Commission (2002); US General Accounting Office (2003).

The threat of electronic diversion matters in two respects. First, it "poses a significant threat to Postal Service revenue since more than half of all First-Class mail is composed of communications from businesses and other organizations to households, primarily the invoices and payments now shifting on line" (President's Commission 2002). Second, the volumes at risk include some of the most profitable and highest margin mail carried by the Postal Service. Average contribution per piece of First Class letters in Fiscal Year 2001, according to the USPS, was $0.177—almost three times the average contribution per piece of Standard mail ($0.061) (USPS (2002), App. E-9).

The decline of First-Class Mail as a means of bill payment and presentation should not be exaggerated, however. First, the embrace of EBPP by consumers has been far from unanimous. Approximately three out of four U.S. consumers, or about 116 million adults, still pay their bills by check (Koprowski (2004), Rosato (2004)). Moreover, a recent poll indicates that 42 percent of Americans remain uninterested in paying their bills on-line over the next five years (President's Commission (2003)). And the consumers who remain wedded to traditional checks are disproportionately represented among demographic groups—older people, lower-income families, and households lacking Internet access—that are less open to EBPP than the earlier adapters were (Plum (1997), Ezell (2004)).

Second, consumers have been less willing to use the Internet for bill presentment than for bill payment. In 2001, for example, when 8.7 percent of U.S. consumers were reported to have paid at least one bill over the Internet, less than one percent of consumer and business-to-business bills in the U.S. were both presented and paid via the Internet (Stefanadis (2002)). Nearly half of consumers surveyed stated that they were "not at all" comfortable with receiving electronic bill statements (President's Commission).

In sum, consumer preference for EBPP appears to fall across a broad continuum, from early adapters (who may have abandoned traditional bill paying permanently) to late adapters (who may remain loyal to traditional means for the foreseeable future), with an intermediate group of consumers at the margin, whose rate of substitution may be affected by changes in the relative cost of payment media. This range of consumer preferences and demand is likely to persist for many years to come.

The attractiveness of EBPP varies for creditors and financial institutions as well. As several Postal Service managers involved in contract rate negotiations have noted, "the degree to which [EBPP] is a viable substitute for paper-based billing varies across industries. For example, utility bills may contain less complex customer information than credit card statements and may offer limited opportunities for the seller to sell additional services. For these reasons, the cost advantages of EBPP may be of greater importance to a utility such that marginal discounts may have no effect on the pace of electronic diversion." (Adra, Ayub, Crum and Plunkett (2004)).

3. THE OPTION OF SELECTIVE RATE DISCOUNTS TO PREVENT OR SLOW THE DIVERSION OF MAIL VOLUME TO THE INTERNET

The threat to the Postal Service from the Internet is neither unique nor unprecedented in regulated network industries. Railroads, for example, have in turn faced competitive threats from barges, trucking companies, and pipelines. Long distance wireline telephone carriers have faced competition from unaffiliated microwave and fiber-optic networks, and today confront a major threat from packet-switched telephony over the Internet. The unbundling of electric power generation from transmission and distribution has confronted power producers with similar challenges.

Regulated carriers have often responded to intermodal competition of this kind by offering targeted rate reductions to stem or limit the potential loss in contribution. For the high-margin First Class mail generated by the presentment and payment of bills, competitive responses of this kind would consist of rate reductions targeted at the specific subsets of First Class mail matter most vulnerable to intermodal diversion. These target rate reductions could be adopted either through narrowly defined "niche classifications" for the particular kinds of First-Class mail most susceptible to diversion, or through rate contracts (also known as "Negotiated Service Agreements" or "NSAs") that provided rate discounts to individual mailers in exchange for volume commitments. To date, however, the Postal Service has not proposed to use either alternative to meet competition from the Internet, and the Postal Rate Commission has not invited it to do so.

3.1 Discounts For Narrowly Tailored Classes of Service

Rate reductions tailored to meet intermodal competition for narrowly defined classes of service have long been accepted in other regulated network industries in the United States. Moreover, the courts have held for more than a century that the existence of competitive differences is an affirmative defense to claims that rate differentials constitute unjust discrimination or undue preference:

> The judicial acceptance of such price differentials [i.e., differentials based solely on competition] is longstanding. For nearly 100 years, for example, the courts have interpreted the antidiscrimination provisions of the Interstate Commerce Act to allow the [Interstate Commerce Commission] to approve differentials justified exclusively by competition. . . . Indeed, the Supreme Court has even struck down an ICC finding of unlawful discrimination where it appeared to be based on an absolute rule that competitive conditions could never justify a rate differential.

U.S. Court of Appeals (1987), 1011; U.S. Federal Energy Regulatory Commission (1992), pp. 65,024-27; U.S. District Court (1973), pp. 946-69.

Consistent with this principle, regulators for many decades have found that discount rates tailored to meet competition from other modes of transportation are not unduly discriminatory. In 1959, for example, the Interstate Commerce Commission upheld discount rates offered for the transportation of coal by railroad between narrowly defined points, in part to meet competition from other modes of transportation (U.S. Interstate Commerce Commission (1959)). Nine years later, the same agency upheld certain discount rates offered by certain railroads for hauling minimum annual volumes of coal from mines in the Appalachians (e.g., Kentucky and West Virginia) to ports on the Great Lakes. Finding that the discounts were justified by the threat that the railroads' largest existing customers would build a coal slurry pipeline, the ICC rejecting claims by shippers of smaller amounts of coal that the annual volume requirements were unduly discriminatory (U.S. Interstate Commerce Commission (1968)).

In 1992, an Administrative Law Judge of the Federal Energy Regulatory Commission found that a common carrier petroleum pipeline could reasonably establish a variety of annual volume discounts and geographically-limited discounts to meet the threat of intermodal competition—and that the threat that some of the largest customers of a petroleum pipeline might build their own competing pipelines or relocate their refinery capacity to existing competing pipelines (U.S. Federal Energy Regulatory Commission (1992), pp. 65,024-65,027.

By contrast, volume-retention discounts appear to be largely untried by the Postal Service. In general, the Service has proposed narrowly tailored discounts only to (1) encourage *additional* worksharing by mailers, or otherwise deaverage the rate structure to reflect existing intra-class cost differences more precisely[1]; (2) generate *additional* mail volume from existing services;[2] or (3) set rates and conditions for *new* services.[3] The author is unaware of any case in which the Postal Service has proposed, or the Commission has considered, rate reductions aimed specifically at preserving existing high-markup volumes from the Internet or other intermodal competitive threats.[4]

---

[1] *See, e.g.*, US PRC Docket No. MC2001-1, *Experimental Presorted Priority Mail Rate Categories*; Docket No. MC2002-3, *Experimental Periodicals Co-Palletization Dropship Discounts, 2002*; Docket No. MC2003-2, *Experimental Parcel Return Services*; Docket No. MC2004-1, *Experimental Periodicals Co-Palletization Dropship Discounts For High Editorial Publications, 2004.*

[2] *See* US PRC Docket No. MC2003-1, *Customized Market Mail Minor Classification Changes.*

[3] *See* US PRC Docket No. MC98-1, *Mailing Online Service*; Docket No. MC99-4, *Bulk Parcel Return Service Expedited Minor Classification Case*; Docket No. MC2002-1, *Classification and Fees for Confirm.*

[4] In four cases between 1988 and 1998, the Commission proposed (and the Governors of the Postal Service rejected) the creation of a "shell" classification (i.e., a separate subclass unaccompanied by any rate differentials) for Courtesy Envelope Mail ("CEM"), defined as single-piece, pre-addressed, prebarcoded First-Class letter envelopes provided by creditors to consumers for use in paying bills. Docket No. R87-1, *Postal Rate and Fee Changes, 1987*, PRC Op. & Rec. Decis. (March 4, 1998) ¶¶ 5034-5059; Docket No. R90-1, *Postal Rate and Fee Changes, 1990*, PRC Op. & Rec. Decis. (Jan. 4, 1991), ¶¶ 5161-5181; Docket No. MC95-1, *Mail Classification Schedule, 1995—Classification Reform I*, PRC Op. & Rec. Decis. (Jan. 26, 1996) ¶¶ 5075-5084; Docket No. R97-1, *Postal Rate and Fee Changes, 1997*, PRC Op. & Rec. Decis. (May 11, 1998) ¶¶ 5166-5199. The primary justifications offered for this proposal were fairness and cost recognition—i.e., that the

3.2 Rate Contracts ("Negotiated Service Agreements") With Individual Mailers

Contract rates extend the logic of rate differentiation even further. A postal rate contract, or Negotiated Service Agreement ("NSA"), is a "written contract, to be in effect for a defined period of time, between the Postal Service and a mailer, that provides for customer-specific rates or fees and/or terms in accordance with the terms and conditions of the contract." 39 C.F.R. § 3001.5(r). Unlike a niche classification, a rate contract or NSA is offered only to a mailer that has specifically entered into the contract.

For nearly a century after the enactment of the Interstate Commerce Act of 1887, the progenitor of common carrier regulation in the United States, rate contracts between regulated monopolies and individual ratepayers were generally thought to be unlawful, on the theory that customer-specific arrangements necessarily violated the duty of a common carrier or public utility to serve all customers without undue discrimination, and the related prohibition against rebates or discounts from tariff rates. U.S. Supreme Court (1908); U.S. Court of Appeals (1960); U.S. Court of Appeals (1984), 1316-17.

This view began to change in the late 1970s. A consensus evolved among regulators that contract rates were not unduly discriminatory if the carrier offering them made them available to all similarly situated ratepayers. U.S. Court of Appeals (1984). Courts and regulators began to uphold to contract rates and similar arrangements even without express statutory authorization. U.S. Interstate Commerce Commission (1978); U.S. Court of Appeals (1982, 1984). And legislators amended several regulatory statutes to provide express authority for contract rates. Interstate Commerce Act (1980), § 10713(j) (authorizing rate contracts for rail transportation).

Allowed to flourish, contract rates quickly became a dominant feature of ratesetting in other regulated network industries. In 1982, for example, only two years after Congress enacted an explicit statutory mechanism for review of contract rate proposals, approximately 2,000 railroad transportation contracts were on file with the Interstate Commerce Commission. U.S. Interstate Commerce Commission (1982). Today, more than 90 percent of all railroad traffic moves under contract rates and other non-tariff rates.[5]

---

cost savings available from pre-addressing and barcoding should be reflected in rate discounts for single-piece mail, not just bulk mailings. At least one advocate of the CEM proposal also asserted, however, that it could help the Postal Service reduce the risk of losing "household-to-business mail because of the availability of computer networks and telephones for delivery and paying bills." R87-1 Op. & Rec. Decis. (March 4, 1998) ¶ 5036 (quoting testimony of OCA witness Olson).

[5] By 1994, 88 percent of all railroad tonnage in the United States moved under contract rates, not tariff rates (Association of American Railroads (1994)).

Intermodal competition—the form of competition offered by the Internet to First-Class Mail—has become one of the most important justifications for rate contracts. In 1984, for example, the ICC and the U.S. Court of Appeals upheld a contract that offered reduced rates designed to meet rail and water competition for the shipment of certain products between Alaska and the lower 48 states. U.S. Court of Appeals (1984). Another court decision in 1993 upheld discounted contract rates negotiated by AT&T with large corporate customers for integrated service packages, to meet competition from unregulated services offered by competitors such as MCI and Sprint. U.S. Court of Appeals (1993).

In the postal arena, the traditional antipathy to contract ratemaking prevailed until recently. Uniform rate tariffs were widely believed to be the only lawful mechanism for setting rates and fees for regulated postal services in the United States. Contract rates, by contrast, were believed to violate the statutory bar against "undue or unreasonable discrimination among users of the mails." Postal Reorganization Act (1970), § 403(c). As the Postal Rate Commission explained in 1989, its "reluctance to pursue the concept of contract rates" stemmed from "substantial uncertainty" over the lawfulness of after-the-fact review of contracts, and the possibility that contract rates might cause unreasonable discrimination or an unfair allocation among mailers of the burden of covering the Postal Service's institutional costs (U.S. Postal Rate Commission (1989)).

In 1992, a joint task force of the Postal Service and the Commission urged renewed consideration of rate contracts, arguing that "negotiated agreements tailored to the particular circumstances" of one customer or a limited number of customers "might be more effective than the broad [rate] schedules in meeting what the particular facts require, so that the benefits can be shared between the participating customer and the postal system" (Joint Task Force (1992), 54).

In the same year, the Postal Service began a contract rate service for international mail. Under the service, dubbed International Customized Mail ("ICM"), qualifying international mailers were invited to negotiate individualized service agreements with the Postal Service governing the services provided and the rates of postage. To qualify for the service, a mailer was required to have the capacity to mail at least one million pounds of international mail, or pay at least two million dollars in international postage, each year. After the program took effect, UPS and other private competitors filed suit to block the ICM service. The competitors argued, among other things, that individually-negotiated rate and service contracts for large mailers violated the antidiscrimination provision of the Postal Reorganization Act. A federal district court, agreeing with the competitors, enjoined implementation of the program, in part on the ground that it discriminated illegally against small mailers. U.S. District Court (1994).

The Court of Appeals disagreed. On the discrimination issue, the court ruled that the volume and revenue minima were a reasonable way to permit the Postal Service "to compete more effectively for the business of large-volume mailers" in the fact of "increasing competition from . . . flexible rate structures and customer-specific service" offered by competing private couriers. U.S. Court of Appeals (1995), pp. 632-35. The court specifically limited its decision to the Postal Service's international services, however. The Postal Service's traditional status as a regulated monopoly carrier in the United States, the court suggested, might warrant a different outcome for domestic mail services. *Id.*, pp. 637-38. Accordingly, the lawfulness of domestic rate and service contracts remained unresolved.

The Commission and the Postal Service took no further action to establish contract ratemaking until 2001, when the Congressional conference committee on postal appropriations ordered both bodies to report on the scope of Postal Service's existing authority to "enter into negotiated service agreements with individual customers or groups of customers." U.S. Congress (2001), p. 59. In response, the Commission reported that postal rate contracts could be implemented under current law if three conditions were met: (1) the contract was reviewed before its implementation under the rate and classification review provisions of the Postal Reorganization Act; (2) the terms of the contract benefited mailers users as a whole, and satisfied the general ratemaking standards of the Act; and (3) the package of rates and services was offered "on the same terms to other potential users willing to meet the same conditions of service" (U.S. Postal Rate Commission (2002d)). The Postal Service, in its report to Congress, also concluded that postal rate contracts could be implemented under current law.

Later in 2002, the Postal Service filed a request with the Postal Rate Commission for approval of an NSA with Capital One Services, Inc., a major credit card issuer that was reputedly the largest single mailer of First-Class Mail in the United States. For the three-year term of the proposed NSA, Capital One agreed to: (1) update the addresses in its mailing lists more frequently than required by the Postal Service's existing address hygiene rules; and (2) waive physical return of First Class solicitation mail that is undeliverable as addressed. In exchange, the Postal Service agreed to provide discounts, ranging from three to six cents per piece, for First Class bulk volumes exceeding 1.225 billion pieces per year, the annual volume that Capital One was projected to mail without the discounts:

Table 1

Annual volume of First Class bulk presorted mail entered by Capital One (pieces)	Discount ($ per piece)
0 to 1,225,000,000	--
1,225,000,001 to 1,275,000,000	0.030
1,275,000,001 to 1,325,000,000	0.035
1,325,000,001 to 1,375,000,000	0.040
1,375,000,001 to 1,450,000,000	0.045
1,450,000,001 to 1,525,000,000	0.050
1,525,000,001 to 1,500,000,000	0.055
1,600,000,001 and above	0.050

The NSA thus had the dual purposes of encouraging Capital One (1) to engage in cost-saving practices not otherwise required by the Postal Service, and (2) to encourage Capital One to mail *additional* volumes of high-margin First Class mail (US Postal Rate Commission (2002b)).

On May 15, 2003, the Commission recommended approval of the proposed NSA. The Commission held that NSAs were authorized by Postal Reorganization Act, and did not violate the statutory prohibition against undue discrimination. The Commission limited the proposed NSA in one major respect, however. Finding that the Postal Service and Capital One had failed to offer a "plausible" estimate of the volume of First Class mail that Capital One would entered even without the discounts, the Commission imposed a limit of $40.6 million on the aggregate amount of discounts that Capital One could receive over the three-year life of the contract (US Postal Rate Commission (2003a)). The Governors of the Postal Service voted to implement the NSA on September 1, 2003.

In the wake of the *Capital One* case, the Commission established general rules in February 2004 to govern future NSA cases. The final rules spell out in detail the evidence that must be submitted in support of the agreement. The required data include, among other things, the complete terms of the NSA; its anticipated effect on the Postal Service's volumes, costs and revenues; and the impact of the NSA on competitors of the Postal Service and its NSA partner, and on mail users generally. More information is required to support a "baseline" NSA (a NSA of first impression) than an NSA that is "functionally equivalent" to an NSA previously approved by the Commission (US Postal Rate Commission (2004a)). The Commission also has stated its willingness to waive some of the information requirements on a showing that the information "is not available and cannot be made available without undue burden." *Id.*

Neither *Cap One* case nor the rules adopted in 2004 resolved whether the Postal Service could extend rate discounts to individual mailers solely to respond to competitive threats to existing mail volume. And the Commission has had no reason to consider the issue in any subsequent case: the only two NSA proposals submitted to the Commission for approval since the *Capital One* case are functionally equivalent agreements with other credit card issuers.

4. POLICY ISSUES RAISED BY SELECTIVE DISCOUNTING TO PRESERVE EXISTING MAIL VOLUME

Why has the Postal Service not sought to offer selective rate discounts to stem the loss of high margin First Class billing and payment mail to the Internet? And why has the Postal Rate Commission failed to encourage this strategy? The reason appears to be a widely held assumption in the postal community that volume retention discounts are virtually illegal *per se*. In 2002, for example, the Commission stated that negotiated rates, if "unaccompanied by a change in service conditions that provides cost justification," are a "problematical approach" (US Postal Rate Commission (2002d), 13).

The assumption, however, is at odds with regulatory precedent. As noted above in Section 3.1, other regulated utilities and common carriers in the United States have long been allowed to offer discounts to narrowly limited groups of customers to meet competition. And, as explained in section 3.2, courts and regulatory agencies have extended this principle during the past three decades by upholding rate discounts offered in contracts with individual ratepayers.[6]

There also appears to be no compelling economic argument against volume-retention discounts. Forbidding the Postal Service from offering discounts needed to retain high-markup First Class mail volume in the face of intermodal competition from the internet would result in the needless loss of the volume to the competing mode of communication; reduce the net contribution to the Postal Service's revenues available from the mail; and leave other mailers no better off, and at worst facing higher costs if the Postal Service raised its remaining rates to offset its reduction in total earnings.

---

[6] As Ware has noted, "Pricing flexibility, including the ability to offer volume discounts, is consistent with both antitrust principles and practice, which allow price differences across customers to meet competition and/or if costs differ among customers. Regulations has also permitted such pricing; for example, the FCC and state regulators have authorized many volume discounts and individual customer rates for telecommunications services." (Ware, 379).

The opponents of volume-retention discounts generally argue that the discounts would (1) unfairly burden other classes or subclasses of mail or (2) unduly discriminate against competing users of the same class of mail (i.e., First Class mail). For the reasons explained next, available regulatory mechanisms should be able to accommodate these concerns.

4.1 Whether Volume-Retention Discounts Would Unfairly Burden Other Classes Of Mail

Rate discounts for one kind of mail do not unfairly burden other classes or subclasses of mail if the net effect of the discounts is to reduce the contribution to total postal costs that the rest of the mail would otherwise be required to bear (US Postal Rate Commission (2003a), ¶ 2006. If volume-retention discounts allow the Postal Service to retain a net contribution to institutional costs that otherwise would be lost to intramodal or intermodal competition, the discounts "work to the mutual benefit of mail users and the postal system as a whole."

More generally, economic price discrimination can enhance overall economic efficiency. A large share of Postal Service costs are fixed (in postal parlance, are "institutional"): they do not change with the volume of output.[7] Hence, equating each rate to the "attributable" (roughly speaking, "variable" or "incremental" costs) of a service would not produce enough revenue to cover total system costs. To recover total costs, including institutional or fixed and common costs, the Postal Service must set at least some rates above attributable cost (Kahn (1970), I:136).

The necessary markups cannot be uniform. The varying levels of competition and elasticities of demand for postal services make fully distributed cost pricing unworkable. Where competition is strongest and demand most price-elastic, raising rates to fully distributed costs would simply drive away volume, forfeiting the contribution to institutional costs that this volume could make (Kahn (1970), I:155, 199). Because competition holds some rates below fully-distributed costs, other rates must be set above fully distributed costs if, total are to be recovered (Baumol and Bradford (1970), Scherer and Ross (1990), 496-499).

Second (and in any event), uniform markups would not serve the best interests of mailers, consumers and society as a whole. Ramsey pricing theory indicates that when a firm must set some prices above marginal cost to recover total costs, economic efficiency is maximized by charging the highest markups over marginal costs for the services whose demand is least "elastic" (sensitive to price). Prices that satisfy this rule (also known loosely

---

[7] Roughly 38 cents out of every dollar of total postal costs are institutional (Danner (1999)).

as the "inverse elasticity" rule) are called Ramsey prices (Crew and Kleindorfer (1992), 23-26, Ware, 382-84). Fully allocated cost prices differ from Ramsey prices except in the purely theoretical instance of a firm that faces identical elasticities of demand for all of its services.[8]

This is all fine in theory, the skeptic may reply, but these efficiencies will be realized in practice only if the rate discounts are reasonably calibrated to competitive alternatives and elasticities of demand. If the Postal Service simply gives away the store, the benefits of volume-retention discounts will be illusory.

First critics might argue that *any* volume-retention discounts for billing and bill payment mail would be ineffective and thus inherently wasteful: if these kinds of communication are going to migrate to the Internet in any event, the Postal Service would maximize the present value of the remaining contribution from this declining line of business by opting for a strategy of short-run profit maximization instead of sacrificing margins in a vain effort to stem the inevitable loss of business. As noted above in Section 2, however, the demise of First-Class mail as a medium of EBPP is hardly eminent. While consumers that have already adopted EBPP are unlikely to revert to payment by mail even if the Postal Service reduced the cost of postage to zero, a significant percentage of consumers—particularly older and poorer individuals—appear highly resistant to abandoning payment by mail for many years to come. Between those extremes, there appears to be a continuum of consumers whose demand for payment-by-mail is likely to be responsive to changes in its cost. For these reasons, the willingness of credit card issuers to make the initial fixed investment in establishing and marketing EBPP is also likely to be affected at the margin by the price of First-Class postage. Moreover, the high margins currently earned by the Postal Service on bill presentment and payment mail mean that even deeply discounted rates can still make a positive net contribution to the Postal Service fixed costs. Hence, to the extent that consumers perceive EBPP as a higher quality substitute for traditional means of bill payment, discounting to reduce loss of First-Class volume to EBPP should be a rational strategy for the Postal Service. *See* Scherer & Ross (1990), 363-64.

Second, critics might argue that, even if properly designed volume discounts could benefit the Postal Service in some circumstances, the Postal Service cannot be trusted to limit discounts to the optimal level for each

---

8 Kahn (1970), I:155; Braeutigam (1980). Ramsey pricing is more efficient than fully allocated cost pricing because Ramsey pricing comes closer to the efficiency of marginal cost pricing. When marginal cost pricing does not permit recovery of total costs, Ramsey prices are the next most efficient alternative, because they minimize the distortion of consumption patterns that results when prices exceed marginal cost. Scherer & Ross (1990), 498-99.

customer. As Panzar testified in the Capital One NSA case, the assumption that bilateral negotiations result in a rate schedule that makes all ratepayers better off holds only if the firm is a profit maximizer—and the Postal Service is not.[9]

The extent to which the Postal Service and other national postal enterprises actually behave as a profit-maximizers (or cost-minimizers) is a question beyond the scope of this paper. On the one hand, the Postal Service responds to the demands of a variety of interest groups, with a wide variety of goals for the Postal Service other than profit-maximization (Bradley, Colvin, Perkins (2004), 172-173). On the other hand, a financial death spiral could obviously have adverse consequences for Postal Service management. Moreover, to the extent that the Postal Service undergoes a period when its earnings fall chronically short of its regulatory break-even constraint (i.e., the constraint is non-binding), the Postal Service's incentives may be closer to those of an unconstrained profit-maximizer than to a rate-of-return regulated monopoly.[10]

The desirability of volume-retention discounts does not turn on the this issue, however. Under existing law, the Postal Rate Commission retains regulatory oversight of proposed NSAs and niche classifications. Hence, interested parties who believe that proposed discounts are unwarranted or excessive in light of market conditions are entitled to raise the issue on review of the proposed arrangement, and the Commission is entitled to adjudicate the issue based on the evidence submitted by all parties.

4.2 Whether Volume-Retention Discounts Would Discriminate Unduly Against Competing Users Of The Same Class Of Mail

A separate question is whether volume-retention discounts would discriminate unduly against other mailers within the *same* class of mail. The issue is particularly important because First Class mail is not just a consumer good, but an input used by many firms as an input of production. Many of those firms compete against one another in downstream markets. Volume-retention discounts, if offered to some of these firms but not others, obviously could distort the competitive performance of downstream markets.

The Commission has adopted two policies aimed at these concerns. First, it has announced a preference for offering rate discounts through niche

---

9 Panzar (2003), 5-6, 13, 20; *see also* US Postal Rate Commission (2003a), ¶ 5084 ("the Postal Service cannot be relied upon to negotiate NSAs that maximize the public benefits (represented by the added contribution to postal net revenue) to be derived from them").

10 For an explanation of how the Postal Service analyzes and negotiates proposed contract rates, see Adra, Ayub, Crum and Plunkett (2004).

classifications rather than mailer-specific NSAs, where possible. Niche classifications, unlike NSAs, are common carrier services that the Postal Service must make available to all mailers that tender the necessary mail volumes and comply with the other published terms and conditions of the rates (US Postal Rate Commission (2003a), ¶¶ 3034-3040). Second, the Commission has established rules requiring the Postal Service to offer the terms of a given NSA to similarly situated mailers by negotiating "functionally equivalent" NSAs with those mailers (*id.*, ¶¶ 7001-7026; US Postal Rate Commission (2004a).

A separate concern involves the concern that volume discounts would discriminate unfairly against smaller mailers. Panzar has argued that volume discounts, even though designed for large users, are "inherently nondiscriminatory" because "the same outlay schedule is available to all consumers" (Panzar (2003)). As he has acknowledged, however, this is a complete answer only when ratepayers do not compete against one another in downstream markets; when they do, volume discounts may disadvantage smaller mailers vis-à-vis larger mailers (*id.*).

A more complete answer must focus on the cost structure of the non-postal competitive threat. If the threat of electronic diversion varies with the size of the mailer (e.g., because there are scale economies associated with the establishment of an on-line site for bill presentment and payment), then it is difficult to argue that barring the postal service from offering discounts to meet this competitive threat will make smaller mailers better off. In this scenario, the source of their competitive disadvantage is their scale, not the Postal Service's rate structure. Conversely, if the threat of electronic diversion lacks significant scale economies, then a linear (i.e., non-volume based) discount structure may be a sufficient competitive response.

5. CONCLUSION

The growing competitive threat to the Postal Service's role as a medium for electronic bill presentment and payment ("EBPP") is similar to the competitive challenges that other regulated network industries—including the transportation, energy, and telecommunications industries—have faced from intermodal competition. Unlike other regulated industries, however, the Postal Service has not tried to meet this threat by offering targeted rate reductions aimed at stemming the loss of this high-margin business. The inaction appears to stem from the belief, widely shared in the postal community, that volume-retention discounts constitute undue discrimination, or are otherwise inconsistent with the Postal Service's common carrier status. This paper has argued that volume-retention discounts of this kind, if reasonably calibrated to the competitive threat from the Internet, would be consistent with established legal standards for price discrimination.

REFERENCES

Adra, M., A. Ayub, C. Crum, M. Plunkett. 2004. "Pricing Innovation for a Transitioning Postal Administration." In *Competitive Transformation of the Postal and Delivery Sector*, edited by M.A. Crew and P.R. Kleindorfer. Boston, MA: Kluwer Academic Publishers.

Baumol, W. J. Baumol & D. Bradford. 1970. "Optimal Departure from Marginal Cost Pricing," 60 *Amer. Econ. Review* 265 (June)

Bradley, M., J. Colvin, M. Perkins. 2004. "Testing for Anti-Competitive Behavior in Public Enterprises." In *Competitive Transformation of the Postal and Delivery Sector*, edited by M.A. Crew and P.R. Kleindorfer. Boston, MA: Kluwer Academic Publishers.

Braeutigam, R. 1980. "An Analysis of Fully Distributed Cost Pricing in Regulated Industries." *Bell J. of Econ.* 11: 182-96.

Business Wire. 2004. "MasterCard Research Reveals Consumers Looking to Online Bill Payment as a Tool for Financial Management," *Business Wire* (April 27, 2004)

Celent Communications. 2002. "Online Banking Adoption: Beyond the Tip of the Iceberg" (Nov. 14).

Cornwell, T. 2004. "Hello E-Pay Bye Snail Mail," *Mortgage Technology* (March 2004), vol. 11, no. 2.

Crew, M.A. and P. R. Kleindorfer. 1992. *The Economics of the Postal Service.* Boston, MA: Kluwer Academic Publishers.

Danner, C. 1999. "Postal Service and the Telecommunications Analogy." In *Emerging Competition in Postal and Delivery Services*, edited by M.A. Crew and P.R. Kleindorfer. Boston, MA: Kluwer Academic Publishers.

Ezell, H. 2004. "The new way to pay: Consumers warm up to handling monthly bills online," *Atlanta Journal-Constitution* (April 25, 2004), p. F4.

Gonsalves, A. 2003. "Online Bill Payments Are A Hit With Consumers." *InternetWeek* (Feb. 20, 2003).

Interstate Commerce Act. 1980. United States Code, Title 49, Section 10713(j).

Joint Task Force on Postal Ratemaking. 1992. *Postal Ratemaking in a Time of Change: A Report by the Joint Task Force on Postal Ratemaking* (June 1, 1992).

Kahn, A.E. 1970. *The Economics of Regulation.*

Kane, Allen R, David E. Treworgy, Edward L. Gamache, Ellen Y. Wong, 2001. "Assessment and Responses of Postal Sector Operators to Electronic Diversions." In *Postal and Delivery Services: Pricing, Productivity, Regulation and Strategy*, edited by M.A. Crew and P.R. Kleindorfer. Boston, MA: Kluwer Academic Publishers.

Koprowski, G. 2004. "The Web: Online bill-paying burgeoning," United Press International (April 7, 2004).

Nikali, H. 1995. "Replacement of Letter Mail by Electronic Communications in Different Customer Groups." In *Current Directions in Postal Reform*, edited by M.A. Crew and P.R. Kleindorfer. Boston, MA: Kluwer Academic Publishers.

Panzar, J. C. 2003. Testimony filed Jan. 16, 2003, in Docket No. MC2002-2, *Experimental Rate and Service Changes to Implement Negotiated Service Agreement with Capital One Services, Inc.*

Park, A. 2004. "Checks Check Out," *Business Week* (May 10, 2004), p. 84.

Plum, M. 1997. "The Challenge of Electronic Competition: Empirical Analysis of Substitution Effects on the Demand of Letter Services." In *Managing Change in the Postal and Delivery Industries*, edited by M.A. Crew and P.R. Kleindorfer. Boston, MA: Kluwer Academic Publishers.

Postal Reorganization Act. 1970. United States Code, Title 39, Section 403(c).

President's Commission on the United States Postal Service. 2003. *Embracing the Future: Making the Tough Choices to Preserve Universal Mail Service.*

PR Newswire. 2004. "Growth Propels Bank of America to 10 Million Subscriber Milestone; more than half of consumers who pay bills through financial institutions now use Bank of America," *PR Newswire* (April 21, 2004).

Reisner, R.A.F. 2000. "Strategy And The Posts: the Case Of The USPS." In *Current Directions in Postal Reform*, edited by M.A. Crew and P.R. Kleindorfer. Boston, MA: Kluwer Academic Publishers.

Robinson, K. 1980. "The Postal Service and Electronic Communications: Various Legal Issues and Sundry Open Questions." In *Perspectives on Postal Service Issues*, edited by R. Sherman. Washington: American Enterprise Institute, p. 162

Rosato, D. 2004. "Why Are You Still Writing Checks?" *Money* (Jan. 2004), p. 94.

Scherer, F.M. & D. Ross. 1990. *Industrial Market Structure and Economic Performance* 3rd edition.

Stefanadis, C. 2002. "Why Hasn't Electronic Bill Presentment and Payment Taken Off." *Federal Reserve Bank of New York Current Issues in Economics and Finance* 8(7): 2.

United States Congress. 2001. H.R. Conf. Rep. No. 107-323, 107th Cong., 1st Sess.

United States Court of Appeals. 1960. *Empire Petroleum Co. v. Sinclair Pipeline Co.*, 282 F.2d 913 (10th Circuit).

United States Court of Appeals. 1984. *Sea-Land Service, Inc. v. ICC*, 738 F.2d 1311 (D.C. Circuit).

United States Court of Appeals. 1982. *Burlington Northern Railroad Co. v. ICC*, 679 F.2d 934 (D.C. Circuit).

United States Court of Appeals. 1987. *Associated Gas Distributors v. Federal Energy Regulatory Commission*, 824 F.2d 981 (D.C. Circuit), *cert. denied*, 485 U.S. 1006 (1988).

United States Court of Appeals. 1993. *Competitive Telecommunications Ass'n v. FCC*, 998 F.2d 1058 (D.C. Circuit).

United States Court of Appeals. 1995. *UPS Worldwide Forwarding, Inc. v. USPS*, 66 F.3d 621 (3rd Circuit).

United States District Court. 1973. *National Gypsum Co. v. United States*, 353 F. Supp. 941, 946-49 (W.D.N.Y.).

United States District Court. 1994. *UPS Worldwide Forwarding, Inc. v. USPS*, 853 F. Supp. 800 (District of Delaware).

United States Federal Energy Regulatory Commission. 1992. *Williams Pipe Line Co.*, 58 FERC ¶ 63,004.

United States General Accounting Office. 2003. "Major Management Challenges and Program Risks: U.S. Postal Service," GAO-03-118, Jan. 2003.

United States Interstate Commerce Commission. 1959. *Coal from Kentucky*, 308 I.C.C. 99.

United States Interstate Commerce Commission. 1968. *Huron Portland Cement Co. v. Baltimore & Ohio Railroad Co.*, 332 I.C.C. 655.

United States Interstate Commerce Commission. 1978. *Railroad Contract Rates: Policy Statement*, 43 Federal Register 58,189.

United States Interstate Commerce Commission. 1982. *Railroad Transportation Contracts*, 367 I.C.C. 9.

United States Postal Rate Commission. 1989. Docket No. RM89-5, *Further Invitation for Comments*, 54 Fed. Reg. 47223 (1989).

United States Postal Rate Commission. 1987. Docket No. R87-1, *Postal Rate and Fee Changes, 1987.*

United States Postal Rate Commission. 1990. Docket No. R90-1, *Postal Rate and Fee Changes, 1990.*

United States Postal Rate Commission. 1995. Docket No. MC95-1, *Mail Classification Schedule, 1995—Classification Reform I.*

United States Postal Rate Commission. 1997. Docket No. R97-1, *Postal Rate and Fee Changes, 1997.*

United States Postal Rate Commission. 1998. Docket No. MC98-1, *Mailing Online Service*

United States Postal Rate Commission. 1999. Docket No. MC99-4, *Bulk Parcel Return Service Expedited Minor Classification Case*

United States Postal Rate Commission. 2001. Docket No. MC2001-1, *Experimental Presorted Priority Mail Rate Categories.*

United States Postal Rate Commission. 2002a. Docket No. MC2002-1, *Classification and Fees for Confirm.*

United States Postal Rate Commission. 2002b. Docket No. MC2002-2, *Experimental Rate and Service Changes to Implement Negotiated Service Agreement With Capital One.*

United States Postal Rate Commission. 2002c. Docket No. MC2002-3, *Experimental Periodicals Co-Palletization Dropship Discounts, 2002.*

United States Postal Rate Commission. 2002d. *Report to Congress: Authority of the United States Postal Service to Introduce New Products and Services and to Enter into Rate and Service Agreements With Individual Customers or Groups of Customers* (Feb. 11, 2002).

United States Postal Rate Commission. 2003a. Docket No. MC2002-2, *Capital One* Opinion & Recommended Decision (served May 15, 2003).

United States Postal Rate Commission. 2003b. Docket No. MC2003-1, *Customized Market Mail Minor Classification Changes.*

United States Postal Rate Commission. 2003c. Docket No. MC2003-2, *Experimental Parcel Return Services.*

United States Postal Rate Commission. 2004a. Docket No. RM2003-5, *Negotiated Service Agreements*, Order No. 1391, 69 Federal Register 7574 (Feb. 18, 2004).

United States Postal Rate Commission. 2004b. Docket No. MC2004-1, *Experimental Periodicals Co-Palletization Dropship Discounts For High Editorial Publications, 2004.*

United States Postal Service. 1992. Interim Rule, *International Customized Mail Service,* 57 Fed. Reg. 30651 (1992)

United States Postal Service. 1993. Final Rule, *International Customized Mail Service,* 58 Fed. Reg. 29778 (1993).

United States Postal Service. 2002. *Transformation Plan* (April 2002).

United States Supreme Court. 1908. *Armour Packing Co. v. United States*, 209 U.S. 56.

Walker, L. 2004. "The Check's No Longer in the Mail," Washington Post (March 18, 2004), p. E1.

Ware, Harold. 1997. "The Competition and Rate Restructuring for Postal Services." In *Managing Change in the Postal and Delivery Industries*, edited by M.A. Crew and P.R. Kleindorfer. Boston, MA: Kluwer Academic Publishers.

Chapter 15

Possible End Games in the European Postal Market

Qui Bone?

J. Strikwerda[1] and D. Rijnders[2]
University of Amsterdam[1] and *Nolan, Norton & Co*[2]

1. INTRODUCTION

The aim of the liberalization of the European postal markets, as laid down in the *European Postal Directive 2002,* is to achieve more competition in its postal markets. A competitive market will result in lower costs of resources used to deliver services, lower market prices, higher quality of services and thus an increase in overall value created. At first sight, the incorporation of state postal services, then the privatization of those corporations, and next the partial liberalization of postal markets, did have a tremendous beneficial effect on costs, quality of service, and the development of postal service firms like Deutsche Post in Germany and TPG Post in the Netherlands. This liberalization is aimed at introducing competition in local markets. New entrants in local markets may be new firms starting from scratch, e.g. Sandd in the Netherlands, or they may be a subsidiary of a postal firm having its home market in another country, e.g. TPGPost in the UK. This phenomenon of incumbents taking footholds in each other markets, adds a new dimension in the market dynamics of the European postal markets. These footholds are to be interpreted as a change from the competition *in* national postal markets to a competition *for* the European market. This change from competition in markets to competition for markets may have different effects for large and for small countries: the first having a natural advantage over the latter. Add to this that postal services, as part of the wider business of logistic services, by its very nature have **L**-curve relations between average costs and volume, as a result of which large companies have an advantage over smaller companies. The **L**-curve relations suggest that in the end the result of the liberalization of the European postal markets is not that the market structure will develop into a state of pure competition, that is, a large number of players, but that most likely the outcome will be that a few players dominate this market. The unfolding of this scenario is supported by the phenomenon of asymmetric liberalization, as this presently is the case in Europe. Even more, the process of liberalization of postal markets has entered a new phase in its development, in which some players to compete for the European postal market deliberately use asymmetric liberalization. To present our argument we summarize in Section 2 the main argument for liberalization and explain why the benefits of liberalization are not naturally distributed equally across countries and companies of different sizes. Section 3 briefly describes the current state of the postal liberalization process, showing the asymmetry between the member states. Section 4 explains the changing nature of the business of postal services and the strategies the key market players are pursuing. Section 5 introduces the concept of strategic supremacy, which we will subsequently use in section 6 to analyze the present situation in four major postal markets. In Section 7 we describe the new phase of development in European postal markets, suggesting that asymmetric liberalizations deliberately is used in strategies to compete for markets. In Section 8 we formulate several conclusions on the basis of the analysis presented.

2. THE TRUE NATURE OF FREE TRADE AND LIBERALIZATION[1]

The policy of privatization (this is, transferring ownership of state run postal services to private ownership, be it closely held or in public corporations) and liberalization (that is lifting regulatory restrictions and monopolies in postal services) is pursued to increase the general welfare in a country: lower consumer prices, higher economic growth, minimizing externalities with respect to the environment, etc. The results of the liberalization of markets in the western world after the Second World War by and large have proven the neo-classical economic theory to be true (Turner, 2001; Yergin & Stanislaw, 1998). Liberalization of markets may however also lead to counter-intuitive results: increasing prices and lower quality of services (as in the case of the liberalization of the Dutch taxi-

---

1 The title of this section is inspired by (Kay, 2003)

market and in the case of the Californian electricity market (Stiglitz, 2003)). In the case of the European postal markets it is assumed that the liberalization and integration of its markets will contribute to the growth of the European economy and thus its welfare. The Dutch Planning Agency estimates that achieving the single European market will increase the gross national income with 6.5% (Mooij & Tang, 2003:30). Traditional economic theory assumes that benefits of economic integration, through liberalization of trade, will equally benefit all economies involved.

This neo-classical theory comprises a number of assumptions on liberalization, which do not hold up for the liberalization of the European postal market. Traditional economic theory on free trade and integration of markets assumes that the process of liberalization in the individual markets is *symmetric and synchronous* and that *neither differences in scale nor the nature of technology* affects the distribution of the benefits of this liberalization and integration. Further, it is assumed that all economies involved have sufficient comparable advantages available to share equitable in the created additional welfare. The underlying assumption is that resources are not mobile, that is they cannot be removed from a country or specific region. This is true for land as a production factor, but land is of decreasing importance as a production factor. So it is for minerals and infrastructures like distribution of electricity and water. The assumption of non-mobility of production resources does not hold for capital, including physical capital nor knowledge. Some services may be immobile in geographic terms, e.g. the delivery of a letter at a specific address, but other services, e.g. call center and other back office activities are mobile, as is demonstrated in the case of off shore call centers.

As a result value chains can be redefined in mobile and immobile components, allowing firms more choice to optimize, across borders, their manufacturing and delivery processes. The mobility of production resources has two effects with respect to economic integration and free trade:

The combination of mobile production factors with free trade enables firms with a large domestic market to concentrate mobile production and back office activities in a single place, thus optimizing economies of scale. As a result these firms can serve small adjacent markets with limited additional investments and costs. The small country may enjoy lower prices, but it will suffer loss of jobs, these especially being the knowledge intensive jobs, thus suffering welfare effects;

Large companies with large home markets have an additional advantage, as their mobile production factors, such as capital, knowledge and infrastructure-type production capacity, enjoy increasing returns. While non-mobile production factors, such as land, small-scale production and non-knowledge intensive services are subject to the law of diminishing returns.

The danger becomes apparent that the attractive compensation for capital, knowledge and large-scale infrastructure-type production shifts to large countries, while the profits on non-mobile production factors flow towards these large countries through corporate holding relationships.[2]

According to the Stolper-Samuelson theorem, in the case of significant economies of scale, countries with abundant resources will benefit most of economic integration (Grieco & Ikenberry, 2003:47-49). In the case of increasing return industries, the largest, most powerful economies are the ones to gain the most with free trade and economic integration. The competitive advantage of countries or regions relates to the ability of locations (regions, countries, or sub regions) to offer the immobile assets necessary for the mobile assets of domestic and foreign firms to be used more efficiently – both to add value to those assets and to create (through innovation or tapping into indigenous capabilities) new assets (Dunning & Wymbs, 2001).

With the postal services business being scale intensive, partly subject to modularization and the European liberalization process being asymmetrical the question should be raised whether the current liberalization process in the postal markets will lead to an equitable distribution of welfare benefits between the six large countries and nineteen small countries. In Section 3 we will briefly address the current (asymmetrical) status of the liberalization process, while in Section 4 we will point out the relevance of economies of scale in postal operations and the potential for modularization and sharing of back-office functions within multi-business-multi-market firms.

3. THE ASYMMETRIC LIBERALIZATION IN EUROPEAN POSTAL MARKETS

The formal state of liberalization in Europe can be split between a group of pro-liberalization northern-European countries (United Kingdom, Germany, Sweden, Denmark, Finland and the Netherlands) and a group of southern member states (of which Belgium, France and Austria are the main exponents) where the national postal markets are still hardly or not accessible for third parties (Bot, 2003). Even in countries where the EU postal

---

[2] "The new trade theory incorporates sectors producing under increasing returns to scale in general- equilibrium models, and has shown that trade liberalization may lead IRS industries (industries that operate under increasing returns to scale) to flee countries with small home markets" (Kind, 2002). Illustrative to the argument is the statement made by the CEO of KPN, Ad Scheepbouwer, that KPN (Dutch Telecommunications Company) contemplates on redirecting its investments to foreign countries, Het Financieel Dagblad, 11-08-2003

directive is implemented correctly, practical entry barriers of a technical or economical nature remain. Differences in the degree of liberalization between postal markets result in asymmetrical competitive situations between European market players. Companies operating from a protected market have an advantage vis-à-vis firms operating from more liberalized markets, as the firm from the protected market can access the more liberalized markets, and thus attack de player in the liberalized home market, while the other way around is frustrated.

The resistance to further liberalization of the European postal markets is stronger than expected. A majority of the European Union governments refuses further liberalization. This resistance appears to be prompted by their fear for a further increase in unemployment in the current economic climate, but this may also be a cover for serving the interests of their national postal companies ambitions for the European market.

4. THE NATURE OF THE BUSINESS OF POSTAL SERVICES

To understand the dynamics of the European postal market and the structures that may develop at industry level, it is necessary to understand the context of the postal services. The nature of the business of postal services can be described with respect to (a) its market(s) and (b) its operational processes and (c) whether it being a stand-alone business or being part of a multi-business firm. Table 2 provides an overview of the activities of the four main European market players, Deutsche Post, La Poste, Royal Mail and TPG. This overview demonstrates that the portfolio of these players is no longer confined to postal services.

Mail is both part of the communications market and the logistics market. To its users mail is part of their total communication mix and budget. However, from a process perspective, the postal service most logically is to be defined as part of the market of logistic services. In the execution of postal services synergies can be realized by sharing certain (parts of) activities with other activities of the value chains of e.g. express, parcels and logistics. In addition to operating synergies, financial synergies may exist (internal financing) with unrelated activities, e.g. in the case of Deutsche Post with its financial services. Figure 1 provides an overview of such possible synergies.

Table 1: Overview of Total Business Portfolio's of Main European Postal Players[3]

		TPG		Deutsche Post World Net		Royal Mail Group		Group La Poste	
Activity		Revenues in EUR x M	% of total revenues*	Revenues in EUR x M	% of total revenues*	Revenues in EUR x M	% of total revenues*	Revenues in EUR x M	% of total revenues*
Mail	Reserved	*1,159*[1]	*10%*	*7,900*[2]	*20%*	*6,850*[3]	*54%*	*6,586*[4]	*38%*
	Open	*2,846*	*24%*	*5,005*	*13%*	*3,030*	*32%*	*3,667*	*21%*
	Total	4,005[5]	34%	**12,905**[6]	**32.8%**	**11,123**	**86%**	**10,253**	**59%**
Express[7]		**4,398**	**37%**	11,250	28.6%	1,687	13%	3,074	18%
Logistics		3,389	29%	9,152	23.3%	53	<1%	n/a	n/a
Financial Services		n/a	n/a	8,872	22.6%	n/a	n/a	4,005	23%
Total revenues		11,782		39,255[8]		12,940		17,332	

Figure 1: Potential synergy areas on a European scale

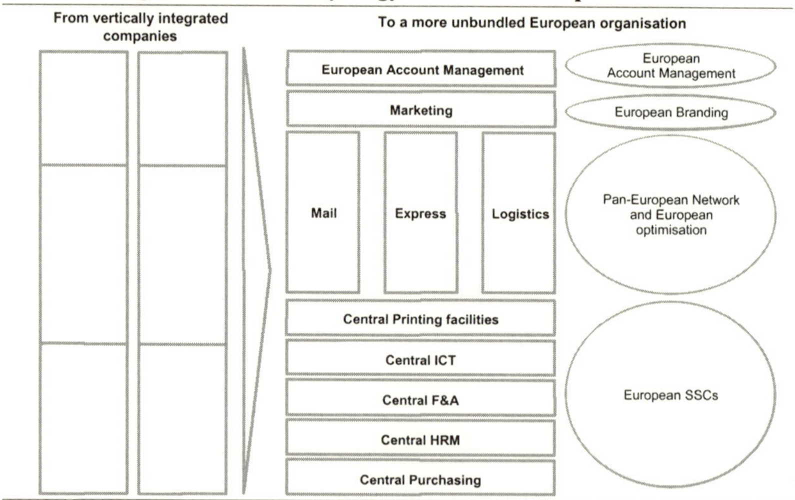

---

[3] Sources: Annual Reports 2002, TPG, DPWN, Royal Mail & La Poste. Notes: *) Due to differences in rounding up/down and inter-company revenues, the percentage of total revenues does not always add up to 100. 1) TPG Post Postal concession report 2002. 2) RegTP, Marktbeobachtungsdaten Postmarkt, Auszug aus dem Jahresbericht 2002 der Reg TP. 3) Royal Mail, Regulatory Financial Statements 2003. 4) Contrat de Performances et de Convergences entre La Poste et l'État 2003-2007. 5) Mail revenues include parcels for TPG Post. 6) Including revenues of Global Mail, which Deutsche Post records under Express. 7) Including parcel revenues for DPWN, Royal Mail and La Poste. 8) Total revenues of DPWN are € 42,179 million – € 2,924 million for other revenues / consolidation.

A process of unbundling of traditional vertically and functionally integrated value chains is progressing in today's economy (Evans & Wurster, 2000). The reason for this being that distinct parts of the value chain have different profitability levels as a result of differences in economies of scale and scope. Deutsche Post World Net is an example of a large, multi-product-multi- market corporation that is building its own group-wide infrastructures, to exploit economies of scale and scope and to exploit its accumulated knowledge under its STAR program[4]. These company-owned group-wide infrastructures are often called Shared Service Centers and can be used in back-, mid- and front-office processes to support market-oriented business units to enter new markets faster and cheaper than was previously possible[5]. Initially it was believed that synergies between mail, express and logistics were limited[6], now the assumption is justified that by implementing Shared Service Centers a great deal more synergies can be realized systematically (Strikwerda, 2003). To this has to be added that the value chain of postal delivery by technology and contracting can be perfectly unbundled in separate activities, each to be performed by separate, specialized firms coordinated through the market (see Strikwerda in Kok *et al.*). The consequences hereof are that (a) the dynamics in the competition in postal services no longer should be considered only through the lens of vertical integration, but should be considered as well through the lens of horizontal competing; (b) as this unbundling corresponds with that in other logistic services, exploiting synergies along functional specialized axis is possible; (c) competition in postal services will be from outside the traditional business borders of postal services. Especially in this process of unbundling players will try to compete through cost effective infrastructures. Given the cost-dynamics of these synergetic infrastructure activities, companies will pursue infrastructures on a pan-European or even global scale. The business units (being the commercial or market oriented activities) within such a group have a rather diverse optimal volume, varying from very small (Local postal delivery) to pan-European (European account management, logistics). The implication of the existence of large international groups, consisting of both Shared Service Centers and market oriented business units with strongly divergent optimal scales, is that these international players can serve local and national markets at lower costs, than their national or local counterparts. The former chasm between *local responsiveness* versus *global economies* is becoming smaller and is actually

4 Annual Report Deutsche Post World Net, 2002:12-17

5 From the perspective of an investor, respectively of the group holding, these business units have lower *entry* and *exit* costs

6 Statement made by the European Commission in Case No. IV/M.1168 DHL/Deutsche Post, cited in (RBB, 2003)

reversed to a logical and necessary combination, with the help of modern technology.

With physical mail volumes declining as a result of substitution by e-mail and other Internet message services, several former postal operators are expanding their portfolio of activities into other areas in order to pursue a sustainable corporate strategy. As Table 2 shows, most players have expanded into the related parcels, express and logistics markets, while some players are also (still) active in the market for financial services. With most companies being active in both protected and free markets, this raises the question how asymmetric liberalization may relate to or interfere with the expansion strategy of national postal service providers. As the de facto mail activities are not organized in single business firms and because synergies are to be exploited between postal services and other activities, the future competitive configuration of the European postal market cannot be analyzed at the level of the mail business. This argument is supported by the fact that it is not attractive to reinvest the free cash flows generated by the declining mail business, into the existing mail activities (apart from investments needed to increase efficiency and to broaden its geographical operations). It could be argued that the resulting cash flow should be handed over to the open capital market, which it will then reinvest in new opportunities. However, modern enterprises promise their stakeholders sustainability in order to maximize stakeholder value themselves, including shareholder value, and therefore opt to reinvest the free cash flow through their internal capital market into new opportunities.

5. THE CONCEPT OF STRATEGIC SUPREMACY

Which theoretical concepts are available to analyze, describe and predict a possible outcome in terms of market structure, number of players etc. for the European postal market? The traditional field of strategic management is restricted to the conduct-level of the SCP-paradigm, whilst the field of industrial organization is limited to pricing behavior. What needs to be acknowledged is that firms not only compete for customers or for market share, but also display conduct to push competitors from a market, pursue containment strategies, etc. (D'Aveni, 1994). In a way firms pursue power strategies in and for markets comparable with geo-political players in international relations (D'Aveni, 2001). In this paper we will use D'Aveni's concept of strategic supremacy to analyze and describe what will likely happen in the European postal market. D'Aveni's concept of strategic supremacy consists of three elements: the concept of spheres of interests, the concept of competitive pressure and the concept of competitive configuration.

Figure 2. D'Aveni's sphere of interests (D'Aveni, 2001:29-31).

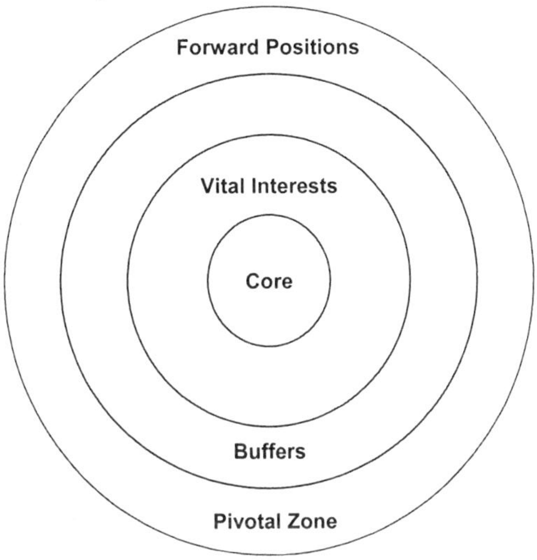

D'Aveni, see Figure 2, describes the activities of a firm in terms of core activities (those products, markets with respectively in which the firm generates its major cash flow, now and in the future), in vital interests (this sphere consists of products, brands, distribution etc. that contribute to the profitability of the core activities, through for example complementarity and its ability for attracting customers, although in themselves less profitable then the core activities), buffer activities (this consists of products or other activities that hinder competitors to attack core activities or vital interests), pivotal zone (products that reflect the future products and markets of the firm) and forward positions (products, positions in geo-market to attack specific competitors). This portfolio of activities, which D'Aveni defines as a sphere of interests, serves to optimize the company's power base as prerequisite to sustainable revenues and profit. Firms may use this labeling of their activities and especially that of their competitors to analyze the way they compete. By taking footholds in each other's markets, firms may signal their intentions and learn about response capacity of their competitors. In the next section we will use the concept of the sphere of interest to analyze the competition in the European postal markets.

The second element in the concept of strategic supremacy is *competitive pressure*. D'Aveni (2001:295) defines this operationally as:

$$M_{ba} = \sum_{i=1}^{n}\left[\left(\frac{S_{ai}}{S_a}\right)\times\left(\frac{S_{bi}}{S_i}\right)\right] \qquad (1)$$

In which:

M_{ba} = the magnitude of the pressure felt by the focal firm (*a*) from its overlaps with competitor (*b*);

S_{ai} = Euro (or unit) sales of focal firm (*a*) in the geo-product market *i*;

S_a = total euro (or unit) sales of focal firm (*a*) in all its geo-product markets;

S_{bi} = Euro (or unit) sales of competitor (*b*) in geo-product market *i*;

S_i = total dollar (or unit) sales of all competitors and the focal firm in geo-product market *i*;

i = a geo-product market among the *n* geo-product markets served by both focal firm (*a*) and competitor (*b*)

The first term in the equation, (S_{ai}/S_a), is a measure of the importance of the geo-product market *i* to the focal firm (*a*). The practical meaning of competitive pressure is whether one or more competitors of the focal firm have the ability to choke the (free) cash flow, which focal firm (*a*) enjoys from its activities in geo-product market *i*. This choking of the cash flow may be through price competition (above the line, below the line), forcing the focal firm to spend more on marketing, merchandising, product differentiation, etc. Reducing the cash flow of the focal firm (*a*), especially if the cash flow generated in market *i* is the main source of cash flow, may restrict the focal firm (*a*) in its resources and ability to expand to new markets, future sources of income and profit, or disable the focal firm to make investments in new products or technology. In the formula the sales volume of the focal firm is taken as proxy for the (free) cash flow, as many corporations do not publish the specific sources of their free cash flow explicitly. In other cases this source may be known to competitors, e.g. in the case of home markets, through disclosure or through business intelligence, and competitors may choose to, and often do, attack the focal firm in that geo-product market from which the focal firm generates most of its free cash flow. In the case of state monopolies, as for some parts of the postal market, competitors cannot attack the cash flow from those protected market segments for legal reasons. In the case of a monopoly no competitor exists and hence term (S_{bi}/S_i) is zero and thus M_{ba} is zero. In the case the focal firm has only one geo-product market: (S_{ai}/S_a) = 1. D'Aveni's formula then suggests that in this case the focal firm is more vulnerable for competition.

The total competitive pressure M_a on a focal firm (a) with m ($m<<\infty$) competitors S_j and active in a total of n markets labeled i is:

$$M_a = \sum_{j=1}^{m}\left(\sum_{i=1}^{n}\left[\left(\frac{S_{ai}}{S_a}\right)\times\left(\frac{S_{ji}}{S_i}\right)\right]\right) \tag{2}$$

In which S_{ji} is the Euro (or unit) sales of competitor (j) in geo-product market i.

In case of a single business firm the total competitive pressure is

$$M_a = \sum_{j=1}^{m}\left(\frac{S_{ji}}{S_i}\right) = 1 - \left(\frac{S_{ai}}{S_i}\right) \tag{3}$$

That is, the total competitive pressure on focal firm (a) is 1 minus its own market share.[7] In case of the focal firm (a) being a monopolist, the competitive pressure on (a) is zero. In case of infinite competitors (and focal firm (a)'s market share being very small) the total competitive pressure is 1, in this case of a pure market, assuming no friction etc., the marginal costs will equal marginal revenue and the profit will be zero (in this case however, the concept of strategic supremacy does not apply). In case that the focus firm has one competitor who is a near monopolist (as in some postal markets), and the focus firm is a single business firm with postal services only, the competitive pressure is equal to the market share of the incumbent player, e.g. 0.95 in case the incumbent player has a market share of 95%. In the following section we will apply D'Aveni's formula to the situation of some of the major European postal markets.

What is the importance of differences in the order of magnitude between companies market share within the same market, as is the case between the European postal markets where market shares differ in the order of magnitude of a factor $\approx$10, with the incumbent player holding a dominant market share ~ 95% in its home market? A numerical example illustrates.

[7] D'Aveni (2001:296) suggests that the pressure measures (M_{ba}) should be scaled such that their sum across all of a given focal firm's competitors will be equal to one. From the analysis given it follows that this scaling is not necessary and wrongly denies the role of the market share of the focal firm.

Table 2. Numerical example to calculate competitive pressure between companies in geo-markets of comparable sizes.

	Europe	USA	AP	Total
Firm A	240	25	35	300
Firm B	64	210	6	280
Firm C	16	15	109	140
Total	320	250	150	720

Table 3 shows revenues for Firms A, B, C in the indicated markets. In the example of Table 2 the competitive pressure of firm A on B is 0.25, and the pressure of B on A is 0.23, computed by applying formula (1). Suppose the USA market is much larger and the market shares of A and B in the USA are ~1%, the numerical example is given in Table 3.

Table 3. Numerical example to calculate competitive pressure between companies in geo-markets of strongly differing sizes.

	Europe	USA	AP	Total
Firm A	240	25	35	300
Firm B	64	2100	6	2170
Firm C	16	15	109	140
Total	320	2140	150	2610

In the example of Table 3 the competitive pressure of A on B is 0.03 and the pressure of B on A is 0.25, computed by applying formula (1). More in general, it can be argued that incumbents with large home markets naturally exert a higher competitive pressure on incumbents with smaller home markets.

The third element in D'Aveni's concept of strategic supremacy is the concept of competitive configuration. This concept describes what may happen in a market with multiple players that exert different competitive pressure on each other, be it in core markets or through pivotal and or forward positions. In general competitive configurations in mature markets, with entry barriers and transparency with respect to pricing and other competitive behavior, will tend to move to a balance of powers between a few players, in order to avoid destructive competition and protect profitability.

The current European postal market consists of six large countries and nineteen small(er) countries. It is doubtful if the corresponding situation of six large postal service providers and nineteen small postal service providers will automatically result in a stable competitive configuration, particularly in view of the fact that postal services in several cases is part of a larger (European) portfolio of activities. The question remains which stable competitive configuration may result from the liberalization process and along which paths the migration will move. This question will be dealt with in the next section.

6. THE COMPETITIVE CONFIGURATION IN SOME EUROPEAN POSTAL MARKETS

Our analysis takes TPG as the focal postal firm, and our analysis is concentrated on the four largest postal markets Germany, France, United Kingdom and the Netherlands, in part due to restrictions in time and budget and as this paper originates from a study performed for TPG Post on the question what the possible effects are of asymmetric liberalization of the European postal market on the Netherlands. The major players and their respective positions in these four markets are depicted in Table 4.

Table 4. Market shares of European postal firms in each other's mail markets[8]

Mail Market Share	Germany	France	UK	Netherlands
Deutsche Post	97%	-	License granted	2,5%
La Poste	0,5%	99%	-	0,1%
Royal Mail	-	0,2%	96%	1%
TPG	1%	0,1%	1%	95%
Total approximate market value	€ 10 b	€ 10 b	€ 9.5 b	€ 4 b

Table 4 shows that the incumbent firms are still the dominant players in their home market and Table 2 shows that Mail for most players is their core in terms of the sphere of interest. Using the spheres of interest, Table 4 suggests the pattern of footholds amongst the four players, as shown in Figure 3.

8 NNI analysis on the basis of the Annual Reports (2002) of the four companies and reports from the respective National Regulatory Agencies

Figure 3. The pattern of footholds in four postal markets in Europe

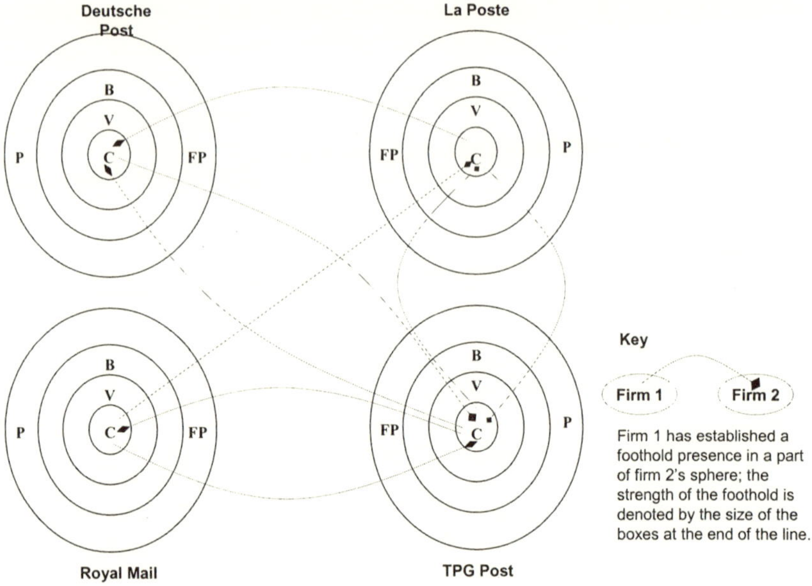

The pattern of footholds throws some light on a possible pattern of competitive configuration, e.g. that La Poste endures the least competition and TPG the most, but two elements need to be added to this analysis. The first is that significant differences exist in sizes of firms with respect to their postal services, as depicted in Figure 4.

Figure 4. Overview of mail-turnover for the largest European players

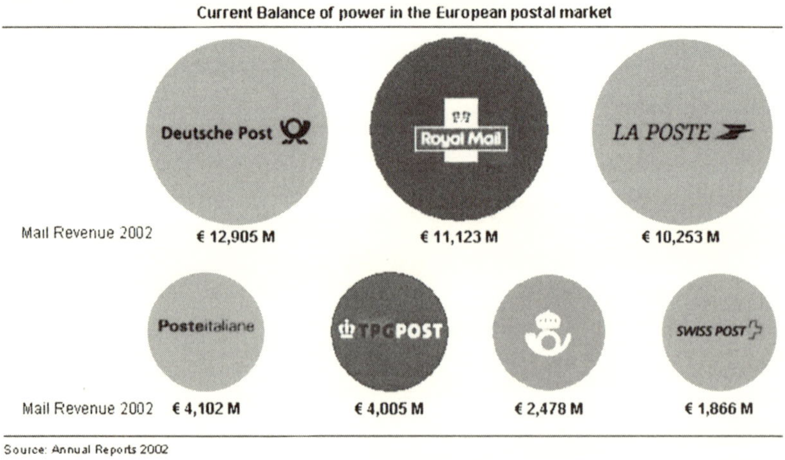

However, total competitive pressure is to be taken across all activities of these firms, e.g. including their express, logistics and financial services. Taken these into account, the power relations are suggested as in Figure 5.

Figure 5. The total turnover of the players in the postal market

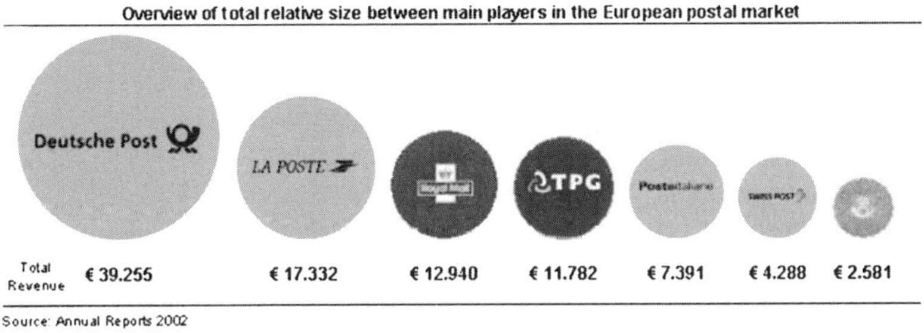

The second thing to be taken into account is that differences between the four countries exist with respect to liberalization. The Dutch market currently being ahead in liberalization, the UK market being opened up to a large extent in 2003 with full liberalization expected in 2007, the German market still relatively protected as a result of a complex license system and the French market in practice still being closed. The effect of this asymmetric liberalization is that the players from the more protected markets can access the more open markets of its competitors, draining its cash flows, while the opposite is not possible for the players from the more liberalized markets. Add to this that La Poste and Deutsche Post both have an additional protected source of cash flow in terms of their financial services activities (vital interest), leaving competitors only with the opportunity to attack the companies buffers in Express and Logistics. Taking this into account the pattern of footholds in Figure 3 needs to be redrawn as in Figure 6.

In the case of the US United Parcel Service (UPS) versus Deutsche Post, UPS charged Deutsche Post to use its profit (cash flow) generated in its monopoly activities in letters to subsidize its price competition on parcel express services in an attempt to push UPS from the market. The European Commission sentenced Deutsch Post with a fine of 24 million euro. In July 1999 the European Commission has started an inquiry whether Deutsche Post amongst others, uses its cash flow from protected core and vital interest activities to compete with other players in the postal and logistic markets (Miert, 2004). Also in the case of the Belgian Post the European Commission has ruled that it used cash flow from its protected core activities to compete with other players in either their core or forward positions. More in general we see that in the fight *for* the future European postal, express and logistics market, players use asymmetric liberalization to develop and play out a competitive game that can adequately be described by D'Aveni's concept of sphere of interests. The fact of asymmetric liberalization therefore results in asymmetric competition and asymmetric competitive pressure.

Figure 6. Deutsche Post and La Poste are able to attack Royal Mail and TPG from protected, walled sources of cash flow

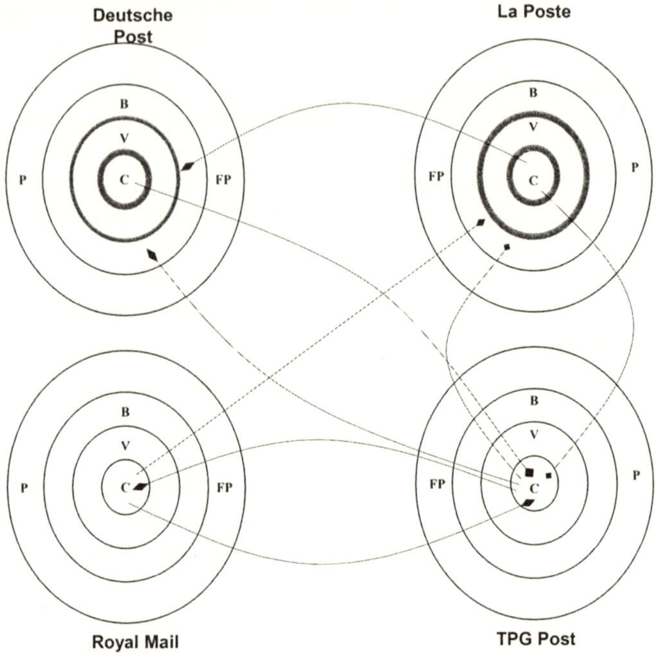

Calculating the competitive pressure for the four main European postal companies on the basis of their mail revenues in each other's markets provides the following result (see Figure 7).

Figure 7. Competitive pressure calculated for four players postal activities[9]

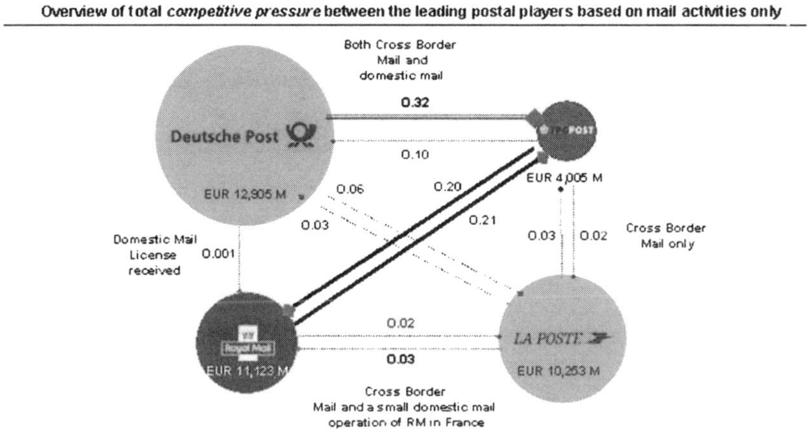

Symbols				
Pressure measures	0.01 - 0.10	0.11 - 0.29	0.30 - 0.40	≥ 0.40
Explanation	Toehold (Marginal Overlap)	Solid Foothold	Strong Foothold	Substantial Overlap (Clear Invasion)

Source: D'Aveni, 2001 and NNI Analysis

As was to be expected, on the basis of the size of its home market and its total portfolio, Deutsche Post exerts a significantly higher competitive pressure on TPG Post than vice versa. When, as in the case of TPG, that market generates a relatively high proportion of the total free cash flow of a company, the vulnerability of that firm for new entrants increases proportionally. In the case of TPG the mail activities make up 34,0 % of TPG's total revenues, but 66,7 % of its operational profit.

When taking all activities of the four players into account, an even more dramatic picture emerges with respect to the balance of powers, or lack thereof.

---

9 Source: calculations made by NNI, revenues based on the Annual Reports 2002 of the four companies, total market value figures for the respective markets are based on the reports of the respective National Regulatory Associations (OPTA, PostComm, RegTP and the performance-based contract between La Poste and the French Government). The calculated *competitive pressures* in this figure suggest a certain accuracy, which does not correspond to the accuracy of the sources used. Given the conceptual nature of this report, we forgo a formal error analysis. It is sufficient to note that between the highest calculated competitive pressure and the lowest competitive pressure there is a difference of a factor 10. As the competitive pressure analysis is used for strategic decisions, and not for say the determination of prices, this difference in magnitude is sufficient to draw conclusions.

Figure 8. Competitive pressure between the four main players based on their total portfolio, including mail, express, logistics and financial services[10]

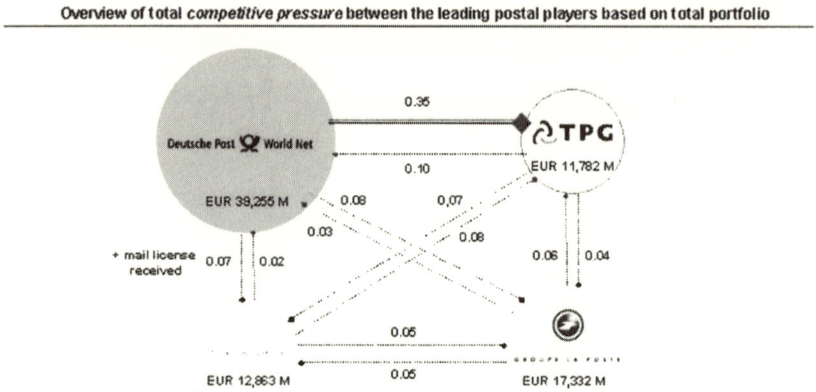

Symbols				
Pressure measures	0.01 - 0.10	0.11 - 0.29	0.30 - 0.40	≥ 0.40
Explanation	Toehold (Marginal Overlap)	Solid Foothold	Strong Foothold	Substantial Overlap (Clear Invasion)

Source: D'Aveni, 2001 and NNI Analysis

Clearly Deutsche Post is an unchallenged player in terms of competitive pressure. The next question is whether this system of market powers is stable or whether it may migrate to a different competitive configuration, assuming full liberalization of all of the European postal markets. First of all different stable competitive configurations exist, e.g. a small number of players of equal size and exerting more or less the same competitive pressure on each other. Another stable configuration may be one dominant, powerful player and a large number of small non-powerful players.

A number of additional questions have to be asked in studying the question what will be the end game in the European postal market. The first question obviously is whether there will be a truly pan-European demand for postal services in terms of decision-making, supply of post, negotiating power, etc. In 2004, approximately 90% of the postal deliveries are local-for-local and 10% is cross border. The structure of European market demand does not seem to be a driving factor for pan-European postal players.

Technology may be a driving factor, as infrastructures preferably should be pan-European to achieve lowest average costs. When restricted to (the declining market for) mail services only, this most likely is not a strong

[10] Source: see footnote 8

force. But the now wider portfolios of former incumbent postal operators can, as a result of the network character of its operations, its typical cost structure and cost dynamics, realize European economies of scale through proprietary infrastructures and shared service centers.

The ambition of several players to become a leading European mail, express and logistics company, is also a force that will shape the future competitive configuration. Deutsche Post, La Poste and TPG have all communicated their intentions to lead in the European postal consolidation process and have the cash flow to execute this strategy. Within these companies ambitions and strategy the current status and pace of liberalization in their home country has become an important 'asset' in their strategic arsenal. Deutsche Post and La Poste seem to have understood the value of this asset early on and have acted accordingly, towards their government. But with the legislative power increasingly moving to a European level, they will have to upgrade their negotiating power, e.g. with respect to mandatory service levels, from a national level up to the level of the European Commission. With the Express and Logistics activities gaining in importance in each of these players portfolio's, it is to be expected that it in several years time it will be the logic of the open, scale-intensive logistics market that will drive the future structure of the European market. With economies of scale being crucial for market success, we believe that the future stable competitive configuration will more likely consist of 2 or 3 powerful players with perhaps some small players (which will be contained by the larger powers in their possibility to expand), rather than the current combinations of six large and nineteen small(er) companies.

7. A NEW PHASE IN THE PROCESS OF LIBERALIZATION

The foregoing illustrates that the non-liberalization and especially the asymmetric liberalization is in the interest of a number of firms, as this may support their expansion strategy and their strategy to compete *for* the European postal market instead of just competing within their market. More in general it can be stated that the liberalization of the European markets has entered a new phase in its development.

This new phase in the process of liberalization in postal markets starts when postal services become part of a larger portfolio and cash flow from postal services needs to be used to build new activities to compensate for the (foreseeable) decline in the growth and profitability of postal services. Whereas first liberalization of postal markets was needed to improve the operations of postal services, now non-liberalization is in the interest of firms who want to expand. Competition shifts from competition *in* markets to competition *for* markets, as all players realize that growth within the European mail market can only come from entering foreign markets. In this new phase incumbents use asymmetric liberalization as an instrument in the power play for markets, in the run-up to full liberalization. Each of the players benefits from promoting liberalization within the EU, as this provides an opportunity for growth, but as soon as a time table is set, their interest is in not complying to the arrangements made as this will put them in an advantageous position vis-à-vis companies in countries that do implement further liberalization. Without a mechanism for reciprocity, companies and their national governments will retain an incentive not to comply with European legislation on further liberalization of the postal market.

National governments of smaller countries should become aware, that their countries will not naturally get an equitable share in the distribution of benefits from a liberalized and integrated European postal market. They may enjoy lower prices, but the prices to be paid for that will be loss of power to set service standards to suppliers and loss of high end knowledge work through the loss of head quarters (with a multiplier effect on supply firms). To ensure fair and constructive competition between postal operators on a European scale they should implement a reciprocity rule, allowing national governments to block foreign companies from entering (segments of) their national postal market, be it through their own start-up or through mergers and acquisitions, in case the home market of the entering firm is closed. And even then companies from small countries are at a disadvantage given the differences in size of their home markets with those like Germany, England and France. The national governments of small(er) countries should make a conscious assessment and subsequent decision on the potential position of their postal operators in a liberalized and integrated European market. If the decision turns out to be that the transport and logistics cluster within a country will not be capable of capturing a leading position in the future European market, the government should actively support and stimulate the innovative ability of its national economy to develop new sources of national income and welfare in order to be able to absorb the free-falling production factors that will be deployed within this cluster.

8. CONCLUSION

In this paper we asked ourselves a number of questions: who will benefit from the liberalization of the European postal market, what will the end game of the European postal market look like and how can smaller states secure an equitable share of the benefits given the current fact of asymmetrical liberalization and differences in sizes of home markets. We may assume, on the basis of the historical process of liberalization of markets, that in the long run the full liberalization of the European markets will positively contribute to the welfare of all member states. With economies of scale being so important for postal services, and its related markets of express and logistics, the companies with large home markets such as Deutsche Post and La Poste are in the advantage conform the Stolper-Samuelson theorem. We therefore believe that the future stable competitive configuration will more likely be one in which 2 or 3 powerful players lead the market, with perhaps some smaller players serving purely local markets (and which will be contained by the larger powers in their possibility to expand). The current practice of asymmetrical liberalization supports this development, as it limits the growth of postal operators from smaller companies, thereby deteriorating their future competitive position in a liberalized and integrated European postal market. To create a fair playing ground between larger and smaller countries, the European Commission should implement a –temporary- reciprocity rule, allowing national governments to block foreign companies operating from a non-liberalized home market, to enter (segments of) their national postal market, be it through an owned start-up or through mergers and acquisitions. However, in the end there needs to be a fully liberalized European postal market. The proposed reciprocity rule is a fair measure since companies from small countries are at a disadvantage, even in case of reciprocity, because of their small home markets. The rule should be used to allow the smaller member states to speed up the innovation in their economics in order to absorb the free-falling production factors in case their national postal and logistics clusters cannot compete in an integrated European market. Also, the European Commission needs to view the future development of the postal services no longer as a stand-alone business, but as an integral part of the business of logistic services, since the dynamics of that industry define the dynamics of the postal services.

REFERENCES

Baldwin, C.Y., and K.B. Clark. 2004. Modularity in the design of complex engineering systems: 36 p. Connecticut.

Besanko, D., D. Dranove, M. Shanley, & S. Schaefer. 2004. Economics of Strategy (Third edition). Hoboken, NJ: Wiley.

Bot, B. R. 2003. The True Face of Postal Liberalisation in the European Union: A Closer Look at the Liberalisation of the Eurpean Postal Market: 31 p. Brussel: Praaning Meines Consultancy.

D'Aveni, R. 1994. Hypercompetition: Managing the Dynamics of Strategic Maneuvering. New York: The Free Press.

D'Aveni, R. 2001. Strategic Supremacy: How Industry Leaders Create Growth, Wealth, and Power through Spheres of Influence. New York: The Free Press.

den Butter, F.A.G., et al., 2003. Netherlands as a Nation of Traders: The perspective of transaction costs: 269 p. The Hague: Dutch Scientific Council.

Grieco, J. M., and G. J. Ikenberry. 2003. State Power and World Markets: The International Political Economy. New York: W.W. Norton & Co.

Miert, K., van. 2004. Concurrentieregels en de praktijk van de post, Het Financieele Dagblad: 15. Amsterdam.

Chapter 16

Postal Liberalization in the EU
A Small Step in Weights, a Giant Leap for the Market

Mark van der Horst
UPS

1. INTRODUCTION

Postal Reform in the EU started in 1988. Its aim was to bring the postal and delivery market in line with the single European market, harmonizing the postal service whilst guaranteeing provision of universal postal service. The decision was made in 1997 to open the market in a gradual and controlled fashion.

Between 2005 and 2007 legislators and stakeholders will prepare the "decisive step". This step might be to reduce the 50 gram monopoly for domestic letter mail that will be in place as of 1/1/2006 to 0 gram. Although this looks like a small adjustment in weight, it is a significant change for the market. Not only will it effectively open up the major share of the letter mail market but – equally importantly – it will provide all parties involved with an opportunity to address the loose legislative and regulatory ends that were left in the previous rounds.

To do this in an effective way, all stakeholders and legislators should change their traditional view on the postal market and take the current market situation, including the structure of modernized postal operators, private competitors and (lack of) correct application of competition rules into account. The role of the regulator and the scope of universal service will have to be re-assessed. This paper seeks to provide input to this process.

In Section 2 – Gradual Opening - we will describe the steps taken to open the postal sector, the results of these steps and areas that need to be addressed such as price control and use of monopoly profits for acquisitions.

In Section 3 – Shifting Postal Paradigms – we will address the need for paradigm shifts with regards to 3 critical tenets of the postal sector: the social function of the postal operator, the scope of the universal service and the use of monopolies as funding mechanisms.

We will conclude by indicating that a proposal for further market opening in the postal sector will require all stakeholders to take today's market realities into account. We will require new legislation to call for full separation of commercial and public service aspects of the operators involved in the market.

2. GRADUAL OPENING

2.1 The starting point

The first initiatives taken to develop a framework for liberalization of the postal market in the European Union were taken pursuant to the Single European Act (1985) and looking ahead towards a single European market for services. The Commission took the first steps in drafting a Green Paper on Postal Liberalization in 1992 and invited the various stakeholders to provide their input and expertise to the consultation and drafting.

The challenges included overall harmonization of the universal postal service, provision of a coherent regulatory approach in the various member states and the introduction of a financing methodology to cover the cost of the universal service. The directive ensured that the broader delivery services market would be enjoying the full benefit from a single European market for delivery services. Hence competition had to be introduced and allowed for. Existing national monopolies for the postal sector had to be harmonized and ultimately reduced[1].

In addition to a guarantee to provide universal postal service and introduction of competition there was a third challenge. National postal operators (NPO), state owned and often part of the administration, had to rethink their role in a rapidly changing communications and delivery services market. Traditional operational postal processes were subject to innovation and the introduction of technology, the traditional mail market was facing competition from new communication techniques. New markets

---

[1] The Commission's 1992 Green Paper describes an equilibrium between harmonization and market opening as the "preferred scenario since it finds an appropriate balance" (page 237).

such as the national and European express and parcel delivery market were rapidly developing, providing growth opportunities for traditional postal operators as well as new private operators.

The development of a framework directive taking all these developments into account took 3 years (1992-1995) and was ultimately approved by the European Parliament and Council of Ministers in December 1997. The directive provided for harmonization of the postal monopoly for letter mail, both domestic and outbound cross border, at 350 gram or 5 x basic tariff. It set minimum requirements for the universal service and identifies the national authorities as being responsible to ensure provision of the universal service. It also provides for the introduction of a national regulatory body and an individual licensing regime for universal service providers. The directive also introduced a number of principles that are to be applied throughout the regulatory activity such as "tariffs to be geared to cost", "transparency of accounts", "size of the monopoly to be set to the extent necessary", "no re-monopolization allowed".[2]

Safeguards for competition in the sector were reinforced by the introduction of the Postal Notice (European Commission 1998) in 1998[3].

The directive also introduced the notion of a gradual and controlled opening of the market by setting a timeframe for further market opening and the obligation to reduce the monopoly further over time[4].

Indirectly the directive also provided for additional time for NPOs to realign their strategies and start restructuring programs. Some NPOs had started these processes already in the late 1980's and continued to make the necessary changes during the last decade. Others only started to face this challenge after the introduction of the directive, arguably losing precious time.

2.2 The second wave of market opening

In 2002 a second directive was approved, reducing the monopoly for domestic letter mail further to 100 grams or 3x basic tariff by 1/1/2003 and 50 grams or 2.5x basic tariff by 1/1/2006. The directive also provides for full liberalization of outbound cross border mail but at the same time allows for exemptions in this area if the necessity of the monopoly can be

---

2 Although the Directive introduces these concepts, it does not define the concepts to a degree that provides clarity upon enforcement. Enforcement of cost based pricing and reduction of monopolies have not taken place to the extent possible.

3 The postal notice clarifies that "subsidizing activities open to competition by allocating their cost to reserved areas is likely to distort competition in breach of article 86".

4 In article 7.3 of 97/67 it is stated that the Parliament and Council shall decide no later than 1/1/2000 on the further market opening, with effect on 1/1/2003.

demonstrated. This exemption has been used by countries such as Greece, Spain, Luxembourg, Italy, Portugal, Ireland, and France. More importantly, the directive also requires a "decisive step"[5] for further reduction of the letter mail monopoly, subject to a review of the impact of liberalization on the quality of universal service. The review and proposal will take place in 2006, envisaging the decisive step to take effect in 2009.

On May 1, 2004, 10 new Member States have entered the European Union. All these countries will have to modify national legislation to be compliant with the EU Acquis Communautaire, including the postal directives. Poland has negotiated an exception to this rule and will be allowed to maintain a domestic letter mail monopoly of 350 gram and 3 x basic tariff until 1/1/2006.

2.3 Small step, but important

The gradual and controlled opening of the postal sector will follow a weight and price reduction based market opening scheme. By reducing the weight threshold from 2 kg to 350 gram in 1999 and to 50 gram by 2006 certain portions of the letter mail market will open up to competition. As already indicated by CTCON (1998)[6] this process is not a linear process. The initial reduction to 350 gram opened up 3% of the market (in revenue). By 2006, when the weight threshold is reduced to 50 gram, 65.2% of the letter mail market will still be reserved. The value of the letter mail market is estimated at 54 billion Euro[7].

According to the CTcon study 53.2% of the letter mail market is located in the 0-20 gram segment (excluding direct mail). This explains why the reduction of the monopoly from 50 to 0 gram is significant with regard to the revenue base affected. It would, however, be a mistake to look at the impact of this reduction merely as a potential loss of volume, revenue and profit for the incumbent.

The gradual and controlled reduction of the domestic letter mail monopoly between 1999 and 2003 has already resulted in a number of market developments that help to appreciate the full and positive impact of this approach.

Whereas some originally feared for loss of jobs in the postal and delivery service sector as a result of market opening and – more importantly – the

---

5 The word "decisive" suggests that this decision will contain the end scenario for the liberalization debate.

6 Study on the weight and price limits of the reserved area in the postal sector, page 34, CT Con, November 1998

7 Report from the Commission to the European Parliament and the Council on the application of the Postal Directive 97/67/EC, Com (2002) 632 final, pages 51 and further.

innovation processes embraced by NPOs to prepare for competition, the sector has been able to increase employment overall by 4.7% between 1995-2000. This growth is mainly driven by the development of new activities and commercial service. It is however important to note that the NPOs have also been able to maintain employment levels throughout the period 1995-2000 (PLS Ramboll 2002).

Despite the original concern that volumes in the traditional letter mail market are declining, postal operators have embraced the opportunity to enter national postal markets outside their own national market. Private operators are also moving into the letter mail market. The UK has taken the lead in this area with 3 operators entering the market: UK Mail, TPG and Deutsche Post World Net. The UK example is even more interesting as the introduction of competition has been made possible as the result of a volume based market opening scheme that deviates from the EU based weight based market opening. Royal Mail is still playing a considerable role in the overall downstream access solution providing the sorting and ultimately delivery capabilities. The compensation charged to the other parties is part of a commercial agreement without direct involvement of the regulator. In the Netherlands we also see new private mail companies entering the letter mail market, focusing on printed materials and direct mail.[8]

2.4 Areas to monitor

In other markets we have seen a significant development of new services offered via the traditional NPOs retail network. These services include financial services, e-government services and other types of service provision to users and consumers.

The quality of the basic letter mail service has been carefully monitored and has improved. One area that does require further attention is the pricing of the universal service. Most countries have increased their postal tariffs for basic letter mail over time.

The basic stamp prices for delivery of domestic letter mail – a basic letter – vary considerably. Austria, Germany are at the high end with a price of 0.55 Euro. New Member States such as Malta and Slovenia are at the low end with a price of 0.16 Euro. Germany recently reduced its rate – as instructed by the regulator – by 0.01 Euro. Stamp prices – specifically those related to reserved services - do have a significant importance as they generate the profits used to fund the universal service obligation (USO).

Given the focus on the reduction of the size of the monopoly, it is also important to reflect on the legal conditions attached to the postal monopoly.

---

8 Excluding direct mail from the reserved area has provided for business opportunities in the Dutch letter mail market.

The monopoly thresholds as introduced by the directives set a maximum. The monopoly can be used as compensation in exchange for taking on the USO, provided that the USO carries a financial burden that cannot be covered by universal service revenues.

Both OPTA and NERA have argued that the profit levels achieved in the mail divisions of national incumbents such as Deutsche Post and TPG are however of such a nature that a monopoly is not required (OPTA 2002, NERA 2003, p 36). Their analysis also supports further lowering of stamp prices to avoid excessive profits. This observation is supported for Germany by the German Competition authority in a paper by its chairman Martin Hellwig (Monopol Kommission, 2003, p 124). In some cases of price increase, the alleged burden of universal service might be the driver of this increase. This process would benefit from strong regulatory involvement and transparency of accounts.

When reflecting on the impact on the next step of liberalization one should also take the transformation of NPOs into account. Through a number of acquisitions and joint ventures (often with majority share) postal operators have not only transformed themselves, they have also changed the European delivery market. A significant degree of consolidation has taken place over the years. This has resulted in a reduced number of delivery service operators that are not associated with NPOs.

Table 1: Estimated number and value of acquisitions/JVs 1997 - 2004

Operator	Estimated Number of Acquisitions/JVs	Estimated Value (Euro)
DPWN	> 80	> 10 billion
TPG	> 50	> 1.5 billion
Royal Mail	> 15	> 1 billion
La Poste	> 15	> 0.7 billion

Source: www.triangle.eu.com, annual reports, press reports, Commission website

The acquisitions are used to help provide additional sources of income and revenue in markets outside the traditional domestic letter mail market i.e. the collection, sorting, transportation and delivery of mail. One can distinguish acquisitions aimed at broadening the involvement in the overall mail services chain, including letter shop and database management services, international mail services complementing national mail services, financial services and expansion of delivery services and supply chain services.

DPWN has expanded its international express and logistics capabilities with the acquisitions of DHL, Danzas, Securicor, Trans-o-flex, VGL-Nedloydd, Ducros and other players. Its mail chain activities will benefit from acquisitions like Skymail in the US, Quickmail, Selectmail, Interlanden Speedmail (UK). Financial Services have been develop via the acquisition of

Postbank also generating additional funds for further acquisitions as a result of the recent IPO raising more than 2.5 billion Euro.

French La Poste has developed a European parcel delivery network via the acquisition of DPD and related companies such as Masterlink and Parceline. A similar approach has been used by Royal Mail through the acquisition of GLS – General Parcel. All these companies compete directly with other – private – operators in the international parcel delivery market.

The dominant role of state owned operators in the market and increasing trend of consolidation through state supported acquisitions has been identified as a threat[9] for the private transport and logistics sector and their users (HALTE 2004).

These acquisitions increase the complexity of the new entities and create additional challenges for the NRA to maintain insight in the financial structure and internal relationship between the various activities either being from a USO nature or being strictly commercial. This is also demonstrated by the ongoing legal dispute on the Chronopost case.[10]

These developments will require legislators, regulators and operators to change their traditional paradigms and move away from bundling/combining social/universal obligations with commercial/business objectives. To continue combining the two roles by one national incumbent would put too many restrictions on the development of a healthy and competitive market for delivery services and it will also blur the dividing line that needs to be respected when it comes to financing the social obligations.

The next round of debate will require a paradigm shift with regard to our postal thinking.

3. SHIFTING POSTAL PARADIGMS

What are the traditional paradigms that we need to shift? There are a 3 postal tenets that need to be critically examined in order to move the debate

---

9 In its report HALTE urges the European Commission to be more rigorous in implementing competition rules to avoid further consolidation of the market by state owned enterprises.

10 Judgment of the Court of Justice on July 3, 2003 in the Chronopost-UFEX case and of July 24, 2003 in the Altmark Case confirms this increasing complexity. For the meaning of the notion of State Aid in the present case the CFI refers to the Court of Justice judgment in Case C-39/94, SFEI vs La Poste point 62: *" the provision of logistical and commercial assistance by a public undertaking to its subsidiaries, which are governed by private law and carry on a activity open to free competition, is capable of constituting state aid within the meaning of article 87 of the Treaty if the remuneration received is less than which would have been demanded under normal market conditions"*. This requires detailed insight in the cost and compensation structure.

forward; the postal operator has to provide a social function ; the Universal Service should be allowed to evolve; and the fact that a monopoly is required to finance the burden of the USO.

3.1 The postal operator has a social function.

It is not the operator who has the social obligation or social function. As clearly indicated by the directives, the obligation for the provision of universal service is upon the Member State. It has often been argued that the postal service is embedded in the social fabric of a country. It is indeed hard to contradict that postal service has played and will continue to play an important role in the social and economical development of countries or markets. This does however not imply that we should continue to run them in their original fashion at all cost and taking the efficiencies embedded in the operations for granted.[11]

The debate on the role of public service has evolved significantly over the last years. The European Commission has contributed to this debate by issuing a green paper on Services of General Interest (European Commission 2003) and the European Parliament has developed a number of resolutions on this topic. All parties acknowledge the need for provision of basic service to citizens, including for postal services.

"Services of General Interest are at the core of the political debate. Indeed they touch upon the central question of the role public authorities play in the market economy, in ensuring, on the one hand, the smooth functioning of the market and compliance with the rules of the game by all actors and, on the other hand, safeguarding the general interest, in particular the satisfaction of citizens' essential needs and the preservation of public goods ***where the market fails***[12]*"*. (emphasis added)

It is important to note that it is suggested that exceptional action is only taken where the market fails. The high level of attention on this topic also confirms that NOT all services provided by a postal operator are services of general interest and could benefit from special regime with regard to funding. It is important to accept that NPOs have moved on from being "the mail man". The social aspects of the services should be clearly defined and separated from the corporate structure and development of the delivery

---

[11] In its 2002 decision to allow for aid to the Italian Post, the Commission referred to : "*This very high cost can be explained by a number of factors such as the historically low efficiency of the Italian postal operator, the reduced number of postal items per capita sent in Italy relative to the size of the network, and especially the very heavy burden imposed by the preferential tariff for the press and non-profit publications (which on its own represents between 1/3 and half of the total amount of net extra costs)*".

[12] European Commission, Green Paper on Services of General Interest, Com (2003) 270 final.

service multinational that might currently hold the national USO. A company that provides global logistics and financial services, invests in acquisitions across the border, participates in joint ventures in South American and Chinese markets can no longer be identified as the character played by Jacques Tati in Jour de Fete.

One should take other players into consideration for meeting certain parts of the universal service and not restrict the provision of these services to the traditional incumbent. This consideration should not be limited to other players in the same sector but expand into alternatives such as partnerships with existing retail network operators such as supermarkets and gas stations.

Further postal reform can take place provided that we shift the traditional paradigm and accept that the social aspects and role of postal services will be provided for in a way that they do not interfere with commercial developments and do not create competitive distortion. In addition to the sector specific rules provided for by the postal directives, the competition rules will continue to prevail[13].

3.2 Universal Service should be allowed to expand

The issue of a changing and expanding scope of universal service is closely related to the social role of the postal service. The current directives provide room for the scope of the universal service to change over time, to meet changing customer needs. The current directives also define minimum criteria for the universal service. It is up to the Member States to adapt these criteria to the requirements of the local markets.

Some countries (Belgium, Austria) have included the delivery of newspapers in the national USO. In the case of Austria, this particular obligation does create a financial burden requiring additional funding. Other countries refer to certain financial services such as pension payments as part of the USO.

To increase accessibility and availability of some services, NPO have introduced new innovative solutions in their retail outlets, making a wealth of services such as e-mail, e-government services, payment and cash collection services available to their visitors.

The variety of activities listed under the universal service and the difference in nature of the services – financial services being very different from delivery services, e-mail being different from traditional mail services – do create additional challenges for both service provider and regulator. In addition it could be argued that the inclusion of certain aspects of delivery services under the USO umbrella reduces the scope for the development of

---

[13] European Commission, DG Competition, State Aid Policy, Non Paper on Services of General Economic Interest and state aid, November 2002.

solution via competitive means, impacting service quality and pricing. Despite the objective - making certain basic services available to users – it will remain challenging to assess to what extent state funded e-mail services offered by a postal retail outlet distorts competition vis-à-vis e-mail services at home, offered by a commercial operator.

Competition can provide for many of the evolving needs in the market place, more specifically because newly arising needs provide a clear business potential whereas traditional mail services are provided in a market with strong existing players and have higher barriers to entry. The conditions to access the new markets should be non restrictive and open to all viable players. A continued development and expansion of the USO could hamper market dynamics.

A clear definition of a basic mail service would also provide for easier regulatory control by eliminating the broad variety of services that would need to be subject to controls. Initial fears that lack of development of the scope of the universal service would not allow postal operators to evolve seems to be misplaced given the high degree of innovation and investment already made in alternative services as reflected by the acquisitions and strategic developments.

The USO does not need to expand. New consumer needs will be catered for by commercial operators provided that operators are allowed to enter the market. The concept of an evolving USO does not provide the necessary incentives for commercial operators to do so. The situation would benefit from a well defined minimal postal service obligation for letter mail that can be regulated and surveyed by the NRA. This approach would also help to reduce the need for funding and allow for further reduction of the reserved area whereas ongoing change and expansion of the USO would only require permanent assessment of the cost of the services provided and the requirement to use monopoly proceeds.

3.3 A monopoly is required to fund the USO

This paradigm raises both legal and economic concerns. From a legal perspective the monopoly is not required to fund the USO but it can be used to the extent necessary to finance the burden of the USO[14]. There are alternatives to monopoly funding such as direct governments grants to cover the excess cost of the obligation that cannot be financed by the proceeds of

---

[14] Article 7 of EC Directive 97/67/EC clearly introduces a pre-condition for the use of monopoly and size of monopoly by stating "to the extent necessary". This should be used as the basis for making information of the burden of the USO and monopoly proceeds publicly available in order to demonstrate that the use of monopoly proceeds and the size of the monopoly are based on the cost of USO.

the USO. As indicated earlier, the monopoly is a source of financing received in exchange for a well defined service obligation.

The monopoly is an exception to the general competition rules that do not allow for monopolies and should be considered as one of tools allowed under article 86 of the EU treaties.

All 25 EU member states that allow for a reserved area have maximized the scope of the reserved area to its ultimate weight limits. This leads one to believe that the burden of the USO is of such a nature that significant funding is required. This approach is in contradiction with the observations made by NERA in 1998[15] and more recently in 2003 indicating that the USO should not create a significant burden and that current mail operations create healthy profit margins (NERA 2003).

Further reduction of the reserved area will require a fair and correct analysis of the cost of the universal service and of the profits generated by the postal monopoly. The cost of the USO – and the possible need for monopoly funding – is largely driven by the scope of the USO and the efficiency of the operations used to provide the USO. As indicated, the nature of the universal service (including newspaper delivery and financial services) drives the cost.

In a traditional postal operation, the relative cost of service and the processing of items are also likely to increase when volumes drop below 150-200 items per capita (Cohen, Waller, 2004). Whereas current justification of the use of the reserved area should be based on the current service obligations, considerations for reducing the scope of the reserved areas should be open to reducing the universal service requirement, such as the number of deliveries and collections per week.

3.3.1 Alternative ways of funding are problematical

The cost of the universal service should also take efficiency improvements into account and move away from accepting certain known practices. Although certain demographic and geographical aspects will always continue to play a significant role in the calculation of cost of the USO, other – culturally oriented aspects – should be evaluated in a stringent way. The cost of maintaining a fully owned retail network is considerable (NERA 2003) and should be evaluated. In recent years the European Commission has allowed for over 15 billion euro of State funding to cover inefficiencies, restructuring and other cases where tax money was used to compensate for the losses occurred by the NPO or fund innovation and modernization.

---

[15] NERA, Costing and Financing of the USOs in the Postal Sector in the European Union 1998.

Table 2: State Funding for NPOs

Member State	Date	Amount - Reason
Greece	11/11/2003	415 million Euro modernization of Greek postal infrastructure
Belgium	23/07/2003	297.5 million Euro capital injection and tax exemptions to compensate the cost of the services of general economic interest
Great Britain	27/05/2003	1.75 billion UKP compensation for rural delivery network 1.15 billion UKP loan for banking services at post office counters
Sweden	02/07/2002	44 million Euro cover expense of over-the-counter banking services
Italy	12/03/2002	9 billion Euro to cover "traditionally low efficiency"
Ireland	12/03/2002	12.7 million Euro for modernization of the nationwide postal network

Source: DG Comp website, various

Over 15 billion Euro of funding granted to national operators by their national government and approved by the Commission. Direct funding of universal service providers is an alternative, provided that a number of conditions are met. The recent Altmark case provides additional guidance on this issue.

3.3.2 Relevance of Altmark

The classification of state measures to finance or otherwise support the provision of Services of General Economic Interest (SGEI) as notifiable forms of state aid within the meaning of Article 87(1)EC has been clarified to a certain extent by the ECJ ruling in Case C-280/00 Altmark Trans (July 2003). In this case the Court rejected the so-called compensation approach to state measures which are designed to meet the financial burdens imposed on companies entrusted with the provisions of such services. This is a welcome development given the absence of a Community definition of the concept of an SGEI as well as the continued rights of Member States to define the nature and scope of such services, except in those few sectors where harmonization directives have been adopted. These include post, energy, telecommunications and transport. In these sectors, however, specific rules have been adopted to define the types of services which are recognized as SGEI or USOs. Any future Community initiatives on the financing of SGEI in general should not interfere with or otherwise affect the controlled market liberalization processes which must be accomplished under these sectoral Directives. If a clear division between these sector-specific measures and any general measures on the financing of SGEI is not maintained, this will undermine the creation of a 'level playing field which the former set of Directives seek to achieve and will only create unnecessary legal uncertainty for all involved.

With respect to general measures relating to the financing of SGEI outside theses specific sectors, the so-called Altmark criteria are to be welcomed. The ECJ has struck a fair compromise between the legitimate needs of Member States to ensure the provision of SGEI while at the same time ensuring that any such financial support will not distort competition through either over-compensation or unnecessary high levels of compensation to inefficient operators. At the same time the Altmark criteria are strict and they are cumulative. As a result there are likely to be numerous cases where financial support for an SGEI provider has not been awarded through a public tender or calculated on the basis of the ' most efficient operator test', as required by the Court in order to avoid the notification obligation under Article 88(3) EC. Indeed where the provider of the SGEI is an incumbent monopoly there can be little prospect, of or purpose in public tender procedures.

Thc Commission has indeed recognized the limited applicability of Altmark and has published a draft decision, exempting 'small-scale' State financing of public services altogether from the Treaty state aid notification requirements, and a draft Framework setting out the conditions under which 'large-scale' state aid measures can be considered compatible with the common market in accordance with Article 86(2). Neither measure is entirely satisfactory from a legal or economic point of view. A major objective should be to eliminate all risks of over-compensation which will inevitably provide a permanent source for unfair cross-subsidization from revenues earned in markets which are reserved to a public service provider into markets open to competition. Surprisingly hardly any reference to this objective is to be found in either the draft Framework or the draft Decision.

The draft decision will provide a straightforward exemption so that various forms of compensation for supposedly small scale public services will automatically be permitted provided that this does not exceed a yet to be defined ' *de mininimus*' threshold. The Commission justifies this approach because it assumes that smaller amounts of compensation to public service providers with a limited turnover will not affect the development of trade and competition. However the draft decision does not offer clear practical distinctions between those financial measures which are to be categorized as state aid and those which are only supposed to provide compensation. This may lead to unwanted confusion. A useful and straightforward way of mitigating this would be to expressly exclude all sectors subject to sector-specific Community rules on the provision of SGEI or USOs from the scope of the Draft Decision.

4. CONCLUSION

The debate preceding the development of a proposal for further postal reform should make a correct assessment of the situation in the market and specifically with regard to the role and development of the traditional postal operators entering new services and markets.

In addition to the continued provision of a broadly defined Universal Service, most operators have entered new activities and market and have gone through significant restructuring. This process has been to a large extent funded with government funding and proceeds from the reserved area.

The USO continues to be broadly defined and may be broader than what is efficient. It is not clear if markets have failed to provide solutions for some of the activities that are still being included in the local USOs. Nevertheless the assumed burden of the obligation is used to justify access to the maximum reserved area.

In some markets, private mail companies are entering the domestic letter mail market via licensing or by developing services that respect the reserved area. These developments indicate that there is room for commercial development, indicating market potential. It is however difficult for smaller operators to enter markets dominated by national incumbents.

NPOs have successfully acquired companies that provide services outside the scope of traditional postal services and are integrating these services, preparing for competition on a national, European and global level.

NPOs cannot have it all ways. They have been allowed to modernize and have expanded into commercial activities. At the same time they have enjoyed exclusive right to a significant portion of the letter mail market to compensate for the alleged burden of the USO. This privilege carries responsibilities including a requirement of greater accountability and transparency. Future abuse of the privilege can only be avoided by full separation between public service activities – there where the market fails to provide solutions – and commercial and competitive services. If this can be achieved with the next directive it would present a great leap forward for the market rather than a small step by reducing weight.

The development of a policy for further reform of the postal and delivery sector in the EU should take all these developments into account. Clear separation of commercial activities from public service activities seem required even more than before, given the high degree of restructuring and acquisition that has taken place in the sector.

REFERENCES

Cohen, Robert and John Waller. 2004. *The Role of Scale Economies in the Cost Behaviour of Posts*. WIK 8th Koenigswinter Seminar on regulation of Postal Markets, Bonn, 2004.

Commission of the European Communities. 1992. *Green Paper on the development of the single market for postal services* . CEC, Brussels 1992.

Commission of the European Communities. 1998. *Notice of the Commission on the application of the competition rules to the postal sector and on the assessment of certain State measures relating to postal service*. Official Journal of the European Communities, Brussels 1998.

Commission of the European Communities. 2002. *Report from the Commission to the European Parliament and the Council on the application of the Postal Directive 97/67/EC – Com (2002) 632 Final*. CEC, Brussels 2002.

Commission of the European Communities. 2003. *Green Paper on Services of General Interest – Com (2003) 270 Final*. CEC, Brussels 2003.

CT Con. 1998. *Study on the Weight and Price Limits of the Reserved Area in the Postal Sector*. CTCon, Brussels-Vallender 1998.

HALTE (Honorable Association de transporteurs et logisticiens europeens). 2004. *State and partly-state owned companies distort competition in the European freight forwarding and logistics market*. Paris, 2004.

M. Hellwig. 2003. *Telekommunikation und Post 2003: Wettbewerbsintensivierung in der Telekommunikation – Zementierung des Postmonopols*. Monopolkommission, Bonn 2003.

NERA. 1998. *Costing and Financing of the Universal Service Obligations of the Postal Sector in the European Union*. Final Report for EC DG XIII, London 1998.

NERA. 2003. *The Profitability of the Mail Division of Deutsche Post*. MMC – Marsh & McLennan Companies, London 2003.

OPTA. 2002. *Advies Tariefbeheersingssysteem Post*. NMA – Opta, Den Haag 2002.

PLS Ramboll. 2002. *Employment Trends in the EU Postal Sector – Final Report*. PLS Ramboll, Aarhus 2002.

Chapter 17

Paper or Electronic?

Preferred and Disfavored Reception Channels for Direct Marketing

Kari Elkelä
Finland Post Corp.

1. INTRODUCTION

Elkelä and Nikali (2003) recently estimated utility functions for messages received by customers. Their questionnaire contained questions about customer preferences for receiving messages. From responses, it was concluded that most persons who now receive over 30 messages a week and are threatened by a flood of messages would prefer to steer additional messages to their e-mail. Consumers who receive less than 30 messages a week prefer to use, in nearly equal proportions, letter, telephone and other reception channels for additional messages.

The responses to the questionnaire suggested further questions. Initially, it was planned that in order to better understand reception preferences, further research would separate messages according to their content. However, it was decided that the first area for analysis should be direct marketing, which is one of the biggest parts of the messaging business. New research focusing on consumer channel preferences for reception of addressed direct marketing was thus planned and executed (Elkelä 2003). That research is one of the main sources of this paper.

After this research was published late in 2003 in Finland, two other surveys on message reception channel preferences became available from the USA and Australia. In this paper results from these three studies are compared and combined.

The principle reason for interest in reception channel preferences is the rapid growth in the use of electronic communication channels and their continuously developing new features. During this era it is important to analyze not only in what way people are using the new channels, but also which factors affect their choice of communication channel. The aim of this paper is to outline the first stages in answering these important questions.

2. MAIN DATA SOURCES

This discourse is based on three principle data sources, which are from Finland, Australia and the USA. The most important source derives from the research "On paper or electronically" by Finland Post (Elkelä 2003). This study focused on addressed direct marketing, for which the channel alternatives examined were letter, phone call, text message and e-mail. Respondents were asked to state their reception channel preferences in different direct marketing situations. In addition to the preferred channel, disfavored reception channels for direct marketing were also determined. Circumstances of choice and changes between them were examined. The Finnish data was a representative sample of 1600 Finns over the age of 12. The data was collected in 2003 by TNS Gallup Finland using their weekly panel in which respondents answer using an Internet form or via an accessory connected to their TV set.

The second principle source is the survey "Reaching Consumers in the Information Age" (TNS Australia 2003) commissioned by Australian Post. This research provides the widest view of potential communication channels, because in it the respondents were able to choose their preferred alternatives from all targeted and mass communication channels. The object of the questions was to determine consumer channel preferences for receiving messages from organizations. The study provided excellent basic data with the help of which it was possible to estimate the figures for reception preferences for paper and addressed communication forms. The Australian data is a representative sample of 1000 Australians in the age group 18-60 years. In 2003, TNS Australia made 1000 telephone interviews with those persons mainly responsible for receiving and opening household mail.

The third main source is an American survey "Household Mail Preference Study" (Pitney Bowes 2001, 2003) which concentrates the preferences of consumers as to whether they wish to receive regular mail or e-mail. Because this study was conducted three times during the period 1999–2003, it also provides an opportunity to evaluate the development that has taken place over recent years. These studies utilized three representative samples of over 17 year-old Americans. ICR (International Communications

Research) made 1000 telephone interviews in 1999, another 1000 in 2001, and 750 in 2003.

Table 1 shows the most important reception channels for marketing communication and their basic properties. Some marketing communication means have been omitted from the table, such as personal selling and billboards. The table also shows the coverage of these channels in each of the three main data sources.

Table 1: Marketing communication – properties and analyses

Marketing channel	Targeted/ addressed	Mass media	Paper	Electronic	Survey data sources*
(Letter)mail, personally addressed	x		x		AFU
(Letter)mail, unaddressed		x	x		AU
Catalogues, personally addressed	x		x		A
Catalogues, unaddressed		x	x		A
Newspapers		x	x		A
Magazine		x	x		A
Telephone	x			x	AF
SMS	x			x	AF
Television		x		x	A
Radio		x		x	A
Websites		x		x	A
E-mail	x			x	AFU

*Survey data available from: A = Australia, F = Finland, U = USA

Marketing communication can be split into targeted communication, i.e., addressed communication, and the mass media. Personally addressed letter mail and catalogs are obviously targeted communication, as are also phone calls, text messages (also called SMS or short message services) and e-mail messages. Television and radio belong to the mass media. Newspapers and periodicals can also be regarded as the media, although they can be delivered to consumers addressed or personally, or as targeted groups. Also unaddressed catalogues and letters can be considered as part of the mass media, even though in this case delivery can be locally targeted. As far as the future is concerned, technological development appears to be making the boundary between targeted communication and the mass media more difficult than ever to delineate.

The division of marketing communication into electronic and paper forms is clear, because letters, catalogues and papers are easily identified as paper products. Correspondingly, all communication through telenetworks, broadcasting and Internet are electronic.

From the final column of table 1 it will be first observed that the research by Finland Post (F) focused on addressed direct marketing. However, addressed catalogues are not dealt with separately, since they are considered to be letter post. Second, the Australian survey (A) covers the whole spectrum of marketing communication channels. Third, it can be seen that the studies conducted by Pitney Bowes (U) in the USA concentrate on a simple dichotomy of regular mail and e-mail.

3. PREFERRED RECEPTION CHANNELS FOR MARKETING

3.1 The Effect of Message Content on Channel Preference

In the Australian survey "Reaching Consumers in the Information Age. How Australian consumers prefer organizations to communicate with them" (TNS Australia 2003) respondents were asked which reception channel they prefer in different marketing situations. Respondents usually chose at least one channel but some chose several channels because multiple answers were allowed. It was also possible to answer "none" or "don't know" and this alternative was usually chosen 10-20 percent of the time. For these reasons the total sum of revealed preferences can be above or below 100 percent. The percentages of preferred reception channels for different customer message contents can be seen in table 2.

Addressed letter mail is clearly the preferred reception channel for customer messages having diverse content. The letter is particularly popular in the case of those messages that are important to the recipient, such as loyalty customer communication and information for regular customers or letters to members. [1] In these cases almost all consumers chose one preferred delivery channel. So in fact there are very few multiple answers, and therefore the total revealed preference is about 100 percent.

[1] Loyalty customers are regular customers with special status. An example of such customers would be "frequent flyers." Often such customers are given a plastic card to be used when paying. Consequently, the seller gets all the data about the customer's purchases over time. Subsequently, the customer receives special offers, bonuses and other benefits, such as invitations to special events. Customers usually receive a monthly direct marketing letter and/or magazine, and these are at least partly based on the information about the customer's previous purchases. This material that the customer receives is termed here loyalty customer information.

Table 2: Preferred media for receiving marketing and promotional communications in Australia according to customer message contents

Preferred Reception Channel	Marketing Message Contents					
	Loyalty customer communication & info	Club/ membership newsletters	Invitations to special events/ sales	News and updates	Advertising and promotional material	New product announcements
Mail (personalised)	71%	62%	54%	46%	30%	26%
Mail (unaddressed)	2%	7%	12%	7%	16%	11%
Catalogues (personalised)	1%	1%	3%	2%	6%	4%
Catalogues (unaddressed)	1%	2%	6%	4%	15%	12%
Newspapers	3%	5%	9%	15%	16%	19%
Magazine	1%	2%	3%	3%	6%	10%
Television	3%	6%	16%	20%	29%	44%
Radio	1%	1%	4%	6%	7%	9%
Websites	1%	2%	1%	3%	3%	3%
E-mail	9%	12%	9%	13%	8%	8%
Other	6%	6%	6%	6%	6%	8%
Total revealed preferences	99%	106%	123%	125%	142%	154%
None or don't know	13%	12%	10%	8%	11%	6%

New product announcements are a different story. Customers prefer to view these on television. In this case addressed letter mail is the second most popular channel but consumers choose also newspapers, catalogs, unaddressed mail and many other channels so that the total revealed preference rises above 150 percent. Consumers clearly like multichannel reception of new product announcements.

Summing the entries for the first 6 rows of Table 2 and dividing by the Total Revealed Preference entry (the second last row of Table 2), we obtain an aggregate measure of the reception preference for paper communication for various customer messages. This is fairly large. It is greatest for loyalty customer communication (79%), club and membership newsletters (75%), and invitations to coming events (71%). Even for new product announcements, a majority of the respondents want to receive the information in paper form (53% by our aggregate measure). The strength of paper communication in customer messaging is mainly based on the great popularity of addressed letter communication.

Table 3: Address use preferences for receiving marketing and promotional communications in Australia according to marketing message contents

Preferred Reception Channel	Marketing Message Contents					
	Loyalty customer communication & info	Club/ membership newsletters	Invitations to special events/sales	News and updates	Advertising and promotional material	New product announcements
Postal address	73%	59%	46%	38%	25%	19%
E-mail address	9%	11%	7%	10%	6%	5%
Total address preference	82%	70%	53%	48%	31%	24%

In customer communication, clearly the popularity of addressing varies on both sides of the mean of 51% (the average of the entries in the last row of table 3). Addressed reception is considered more important for loyalty customer communication and letters to members. Conversely, in the case of new product announcements, advertisements and sales promotions, the majority of respondents favored unaddressed communication. For many, addressing involves a postal address. Averaging across the columns of Table 3, we see that only 8% prefer to receive marketing and promotional messages via e-mail.

3.2 The Effect of the Industry and Customer Relationship on Channel Preferences

The Australian research (TNS Australia 2003) discussed immediately above also measures the effect of the sender's industry on channel preferences. In table 4 there are three industries and in every industry consumers are divided into customers and non-customers. Customer relationship was determined by asking from respondents if they were or were not customers for certain types of organizations. This gives six classes or columns for which the channel preferences are given in table 4. The Table presents average channel preferences for every industry. In addition, several interesting channel preferences from the sub-branches of these industries should be noted.

For service sector customers addressed letter messaging is the most preferred way to receive messages. It is especially popular with the customers of banking and finance (66%), the utilities (65%) and telecommunications (54%). In these industries addressed letter mail is also the favorite of non-customers, although in their case its popularity is clearly of lesser significance. On the other hand, for restaurants, travel and real estate no media can be shown to be the most preferred, although in addition to addressed letter mail, unaddressed catalogs, newspapers and television are relatively popular channels of reception. A clearly preferred channel is lacking in these industries among both customers and non-customers.

Table 4: Preferred media for receiving advertising and promotional information in Australia according to industry – customers and non-customers

Preferred reception channel	Customer Relationship and Industry Sector					
	Service sector		Not-for-profit		Retail sector	
	Customer	Non-Customer	Supporter	Non-supporter	Customer	Non-Customer
Mail (personalised)	40%	23%	33%	18%	15%	9%
Mail (unaddressed)	12%	17%	17%	20%	17%	18%
Catalogues (personalised)	3%	2%	2%	2%	7%	6%
Catalogues (unaddressed)	11%	11%	6%	9%	36%	33%
Newspapers	12%	16%	11%	15%	14%	16%
Magazine	2%	3%	2%	1%	16%	3%
Television	11%	17%	12%	16%	3%	18%
Radio	3%	4%	5%	5%	4%	4%
Websites	2%	2%	1%	1%	1%	1%
E-mail	5%	3%	4%	2%	3%	1%
Other	7%	4%	8%	3%	3%	1%
Total revealed preferences	108%	102%	101%	92%	119%	110%
None or don't know	16%	20%	22%	25%	17%	17%

Consumers behave in a different way towards the retail sector. In particular, customers prefer that offers from department stores, supermarkets, hardware outlets and fashion stores be displayed in picture catalogs, which do not need to be addressed. This applies to both customers and non-customers of retail stores. An exception to this finding is auto manufacturers and dealers; their customers prefer to read automobile adverts in newspapers or see them on television.

From the total revealed preferences (the second last row of table 4) we can see that multichannel reception of marketing material is most popular in the retail sector and least popular in the not-for-profit sector, which includes clubs, the charities and political parties. In every sector customers are more inclined towards multichannel reception than non-customers.

Also, it is clear that paper communication has a firm status in all industries (table 5). It is favored by over 70 percent of customers and non-customers from each industry. The customers of retail stores, in particular, are more willing to receive paper communication. The type of marketing communication in paper form preferred from retail stores is primarily letter mail and catalogs. On the other hand, marketing messages on paper from the service sector and non-profit organizations would be preferred in the form of letter communication or newspaper advertisements.

Table 5: Proportional preferences for receiving advertising and promotional information in Australia according to industry and customer type (customers and non-customers)

Preferred Reception Channel	Customer Type and Industry Sector					
	Service sector		Not-for-profit		Retail sector	
	Customer	Non-Customer	Supporter	Non-Supporter	Customer	Non-Customer
Preference for Paper	74%	71%	71%	71%	88%	77%
Preference for Addressed Communications	44%	28%	39%	23%	20%	14%

The addressed reception of marketing communication is not considered a particularly important area of activity. In the service sector, preference for addressed reception by customers exceeds 50 percent only in banking, telecommunications and utilities companies. In the retail trade address use preference falls below 25 percent, regardless of the branch of activity and the type of customer relationship. Only 2 percent of customers and only 1 percent of non-customers want retail trade marketing sent through their e-mail addresses.

E-mail and the Internet have been available so long in developed countries that they are accepted channels for most consumers. This does not mean that they are favorite channels. Only a minority of consumers prefer to receive marketing material through them. Although changing to electronic communication does produce cost efficiencies in business-to-business communication, for the consumer, paper communication is often better than electronic in everyday situations. On the other hand, in the retail business consumers wish to respect the independence of the retailer. They consider it important that marketing material be available, but do not necessarily wish to surrender their own address to the retailer.

4. RECEPTION CHANNELS OF ADDRESSED DIRECT MARKETING

4.1 Preferred, Accepted and Disfavored Channels

The study by Finland Post (Elkelä 2003) focused on addressed direct marketing and examined the reception channel preferences for letter, phone call, text message and e-mail in different cases. As noted above, this study administered a survey to a representative sample of 1600 Finnish citizens above the age of 12. In the questionnaire, respondents revealed first their most preferred reception channel. It was also possible to answer, "don't know", as indeed some 14 percent of respondents did. After naming their "favorite" choice, they were asked to name from zero to four other reception channels they were not willing to use. We refer to these as "disfavored" channels. The rest of the channels that consumers did not designate as either "favorite" or "disfavored" are referred to as "accepted" channels.

The central part of the survey consisted of three pairs of cases, in which a comparison was made of the effect of the number of messages (few or many), frequency of messages (seldom or often) and the customer relationship (old or new). We will return to these separate cases later. First of all, we will take a general view of direct marketing reception preferences for the three ordinal preferences: preferred (favorite), accepted and disfavored.

Figure 1: Preferences for direct marketing reception channels in Finland

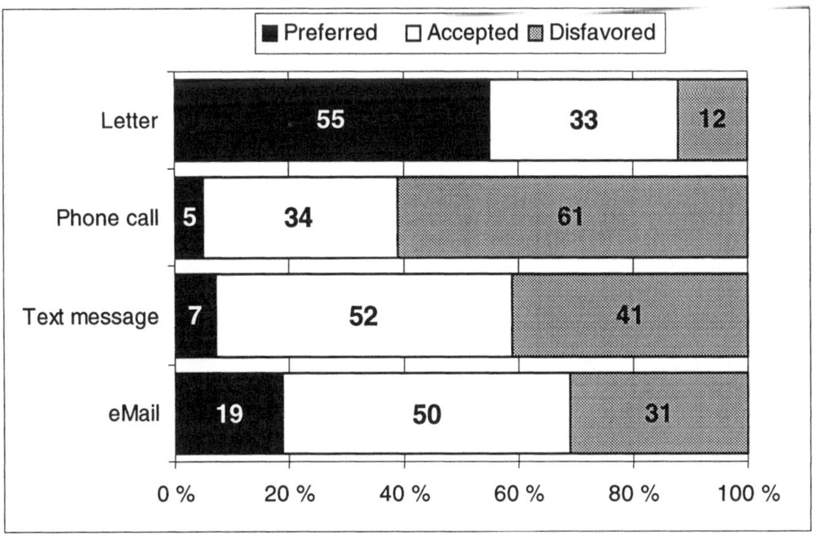

In general, letter communication is overwhelmingly the preferred reception channel for direct marketing. It was chosen by 55% of Finnish respondents (figure 1). In addition to extensive preference, there is very little disfavor, which bolsters the conclusion that there is widespread acceptance of marketing material via letter communication. The letter is disliked by only just over 10% of consumers and the percentage of disfavor remains roughly the same regardless of the recipient's age, profession, total amount of communication or Internet use. Advertising letters are not even disfavored by the most active e-mail users.

About one-fifth (19%) of Finns say that they would prefer to receive marketing via e-mail. Conversely, every third person (31%) is not willing to use e-mail as a marketing channel, and the reason is usually the lack of adequate e-mail access. The more elderly age groups, in particular, are unable to use e-mail. Nonetheless, e-mail is the second most accepted reception channel, not far behind letters. Therefore, while there is little enthusiasm for using e-mail to receive marketing information, neither is there antipathy.

The same cannot be said for the receipt of marketing via the telephone. Only 5% of respondents stated that the phone call is their preferred reception channel for direct marketing; and over 60% of consumers wanted no telemarketing at all. The popularity of text message advertising is almost as low (7 %), even though they are not disfavored to the same degree (41 %).

4.2 E-Mail Preferences at a Standstill

For the reception of addressed direct marketing consumers consider their choice as primarily between the letter and e-mail. Finnish consumers estimate that both channels offer marketing possibilities that do not present untimely intrusions and can be read regardless of time and place. Further, unnecessary letters and e-mails can be both easily recognized and destroyed.

While a letter is considered to have the advantage of greater security and hardware is not required for its reception, the strongest points about e-mail are its speed, the possibility of avoiding paper wastage and lack of restrictions on place of reception. Nevertheless, the speed of e-mail is relative; because many holders of an e-mail address only read their home e-mail once a week or once a month. In such cases, letter communication is for them undoubtedly a faster reception channel.

Channel preference studies conducted in both Australia and Finland show that letter communication is clearly a more desired marketing message reception channel than e-mail. This conclusion is also supported by American results from the survey "Household Mail Preference Study, Regular Mail vs. Electronic Mail" (Pitney Bowes 2001 and 2003), in which the questions were simple pairwise comparisons contrasting paper and electronic mail only. The added value of this study is that channel preferences were measured three times, in 1999, 2001 and 2003.

In the Pitney Bowes market surveys, the problem of channel preferences for new product announcements was resolved. Most surprising is their finding that channel preferences have not changed in recent years. The popularity of regular mail, i.e., letter mail, has remained at the same level of approximately 75% for the entire four-year period from 1999 to 2003. The Pitney Bowes studies estimate the popularity of e-mail at about 20% over the same period. What makes this result so surprising, taking into consideration advance expectations, is that during the same period e-mail penetration in the USA almost doubled, increasing from 34% to 62%.

Interestingly, similar result has been reported in the Finnish "Content Survey of Letter Communication" (Nikali and Heino 2003). The proportion of consumers who now receive an offers or advertisements by post but would prefer to receive them in an electronic form has remained at a level of 5–6% from 1999 to 2003 despite the increasing general use of e-mail. Furthermore, letter recipients' interest in transferring to e-mail actually fell slightly over the period under review.

The situation can be clarified if the Finnish users of e-mail are studied separately. In 1999, 21% of them would have preferred to receive through e-mail an offer or advertisement delivered by post, but in 2003 there were only 13% still favoring electronic reception. During the same period e-mail penetration at home had almost doubled from 20% to 36%. It seems clear that new e-mail users are less willing to use e-mail compared with experienced users. The letter, familiar and trustworthy, is still holding its place; reception channel preferences appear to change at a very slow pace.

However, some consumers have an active attitude towards e-mail, text messaging and the Internet. The existence of these digital message pioneers suggests possibilities of growth in the popularity of e-mail (Elkelä 2003). The members of this group are generally 20–34 year-olds. However, not even the members of this group disfavor letter communication, although they accept direct marketing by e-mail just as readily as the letter. In all other groups the letter is without doubt the most popular. Since e-mail reception preferences appear for the present to be at a standstill, the interesting question arises as to which factors would probably produce growth in the preferences for e-mail marketing and at what stage this would take place.

For the time being, the main impetus for transferring to electronic communication would seem to be more the rationalization efforts of companies sending mail than consumer reception preferences. This kind of rationalization in consumer marketing is not necessarily a sensible policy, since it is estimated (Pitney Bowes 2003) that, compared to the letter, e-mail is much more likely to be discarded without opening. Indeed, these estimates suggest that consumers that e-mail remains unopened more than four times as often as paper post. Further, in the course of two years the amount of respondents who apparently intend to discard their e-mails has risen from 66 percent to 75%.

It seems that in the background is the fact that recently e-mail has been clogged up with a deluge of uninteresting and untargeted advertising messages (also known as "spam"), while at the same time an increase has taken place in message viruses that has caused more harm still. An active e-mail user can have tens of junk mail messages dumped on her/him every day, perhaps even hundreds. It these cannot be eliminated through filtering programs, legislation or other means, e-mail will never become an efficient marketing channel.

4.3 Similar Letter Mail vs. E-mail Results from Different Countries

We have gone through Australian, Finnish and American studies on the reception channel preferences of marketing. The main difference between those three studies was the number of reception channel alternatives that respondents could choose in the questionnaire. The Australian study included more than ten channels for receiving marketing. Finnish research focused on four channels of addressed direct marketing. The American studies concentrated on comparisons between letter and e-mail.

Figure 2 presents the primary choice between letter and e-mail in these studies. In it, all other choices except letter and e-mail are incorporated in the class "neither". This class also includes those respondents who did not reveal their preferences. The data from Finland and the USA are clear because respondents could choose only one alternative. In the Australian study multiple answers were allowed, from which it follows that the sum of choices usually exceeds 100%. Nevertheless, the length of the Australian bars has been adjusted to 100% to allow a better comparison with Finland and the USA.

It can be ascertained from Figure 2 that first and foremost, letter mail is in all cases plainly more popular than e-mail. Second, it is evident that increasing the number of answer alternatives from which to choose most frequently reduces the chosen proportions of letter mail and e-mail. However, in the reception of loyalty customer communication and information, this does not have much effect, because in this case most people choose letter mail or e-mail regardless of what other alternatives are on offer.

For its part the difference in new product announcements is the clearest of all, because information concerning these is preferably desired through television or other mass media, and not so much by letter mail and e-mail. Thus, in such cases many consumers wish to take personal responsibility for receiving their marketing communications. In this case, the Australian survey gives clearly a more realistic picture than the simplified paired comparison of the US study, which did not encompass television or other media in the evaluation.

Figure 2: Reception channel preferences for letter mail and e-mail marketing in Australia, Finland and USA

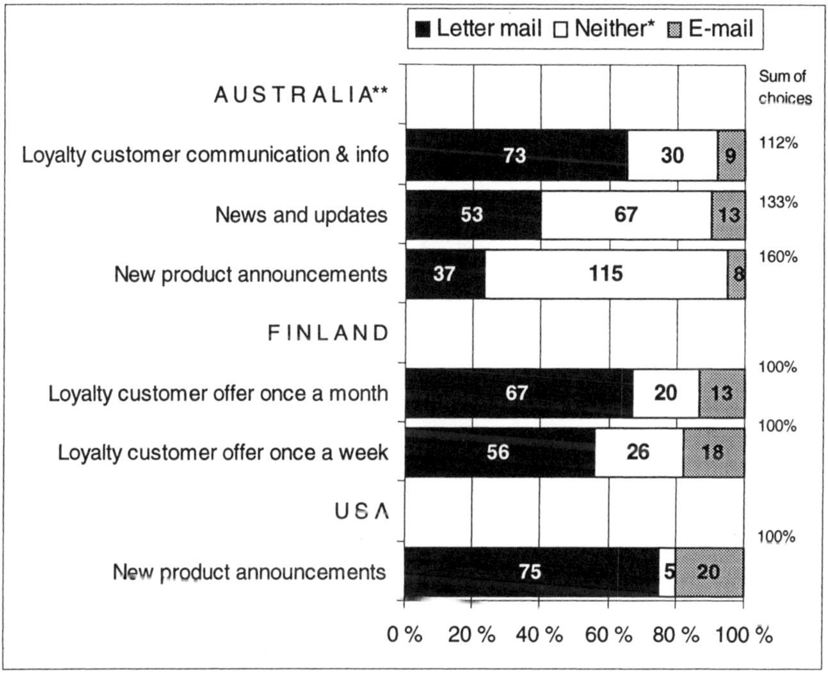

* Neither = AUSTRALIA: catalog, newspaper, magazine, phone, SMS, TV, radio, web, no answer; FINLAND: phone, SMS, no answer; USA: no answer. Multiple answers allowed only in Australia

** In Australian results the bar length was adjusted to 100 % but unadjusted preference values are presented

4.4 A Majority Opposes Telemarketing

Besides e-mail problems, the Americans have in recent years been debating the escalation of telemarketing. A study by the Auriemma Consulting Group (2001) in the USA asked about the most and least preferred credit card marketing channels. In this consumer survey the most popular was direct mail (32%), but mass media marketing almost reached the same level (30%), as did also different Internet marketing forms (24%). So there were no particular differences between preferred marketing channels. On the other hand, telemarketing was clearly the least preferred channel, with 59% of Americans not wanting to get credit card marketing through that channel.

The Pitney Bowes (2003) survey contained a question concerning through which channel consumers prefer least to receive new product announcements or product offerings from companies with which they currently do not do business. Respondents had the possibility to choose regular mail, e-mail or telephone. Again the least preferred channel turned out to be the telephone, disfavored by 60% of respondents. The unpopularity of paper mail and e-mail was on the same level: Both were disliked by 20% of respondents.

Both of the two results from the USA concerning the disfavor of phone calls are on the same level as in Finland where the average is 61% (Elkelä 2003). On the other hand, e-mail disfavor is greater in Finland (31%) and letter disfavor smaller (12%) compared to the Pitney Bowes (2003) results. A question concerning the disfavor of text messages as a means of receiving marketing communications was also asked in Finland and dislike proved to be substantial (41%). However, the results are not entirely comparable, since in the American survey the respondents were limited to the disfavor of one reception channel. On the other hand, in the Finnish survey it was possible to indicate the dislike of all other channels with the exception of that which had been chosen as the preferred channel in the previous question.

Telemarketing has started to irritate Americans and in the past few years many people have listed themselves on the "Do-not-call" register. Of the respondents to the Pitney Bowes survey 61% had already joined or intended to join. A comparable Robinson Register in Finland contains the names of 260,000 Finns that have prohibited marketing by telephone, which corresponds to approximately 5% of the adult population, and addressed direct marketing in paper form has been prohibited by 60,000 Finns, which is only 1% of the adult population.

In the Pitney Bowes study consumers were asked to compare the features for marketing by mail and telephone (figure 3). Respondents could choose between five features in determining which was better, mail or phone. It turned out that the best feature of advertising mail was that it could be retained and then read when most convenient to the recipient. Photos of offers sent by post can be examined at leisure, giving a better impression of the product features. An offer that arrives by post is experienced as more persuasive, encouraging one to respond.

Figure 3: Comparison of features of mail/phone marketing in the USA

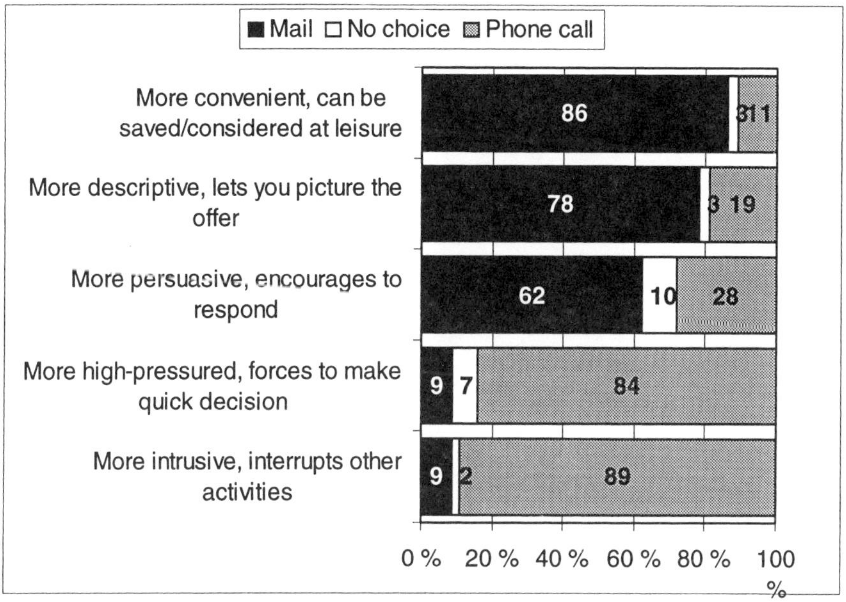

The sales telephone call is conspicuous for its negative features, which seem to defend paper communication even more than the positive features of paper communication itself. A phone call interrupts other activities and for this reason is regarded as more intrusive than a marketing message arriving by post. In the mind of the consumer a sales call forces one to make a quick decision. For these reasons it is experienced as much more high-pressured than marketing by mail. To some extent these reasons explain why in many surveys the majority of respondents disfavored telemarketing and considered it the most annoying marketing channel. Very often a marketing call comes just when more important things have to be done. From the salesperson's point of view the call may seem efficient, because at this stage the customer is often compelled to make a decision. Nevertheless, customers feel irritated that they are forced to face a well-prepared sales person when they are not themselves prepared, which puts them under pressure to make a quick decision. The resistance to selling by telephone appears at a time when the amount of communication is increasing at a fast rate. On the other hand, new forms of communication also offer new possibilities more exciting than before for the marketing community. Both courses of development increase the consumer's desire to control the flood of messages by allowing a choice of the most agreeable channels of reception.

5. DIVERSE RECEPTION SITUATIONS OF DIRECT MARKETING

5.1 The Effect of the Frequency of Messages

The final part of this paper will concentrate only on survey results obtained in Finland (Elkelä 2003). The purpose is to present some new insights missing from other studies.

The effect of the density of the number of messages received via direct marketing on channel choice was determined by comparing situations in which direct marketing messages connected with a particular subject area received was either "seldom" or "often". The respondent was first asked to select the preferred way of receiving a message in a situation in which (s)he gets a loyalty customer offer once a month from a company from which (s)he makes regular purchases. Second, the respondent was asked to state those possible ways of receiving a message, which would be disfavored in this situation. After that the same questions were presented in relation to a situation in which the recipient gets a loyalty customer offer once a week from a company from which (s)he makes regular purchases.

In figure 4 we can see four pairs of bars. Every pair presents preferences for one reception channel. The upper bar of any pair presents the normal situation, in which loyalty customer offers come monthly. On the other hand, the customer may receive an offer once a week; the preference for that possibility is shown by the lower bar of the pair presents the possibility of getting an offer from a company once a week. The main point is to see the effect of the frequency of messages and to compare a situation in which messages are received seldom to the situation when they are received often.

The letter is a particularly popular channel for receiving loyalty customer offers once a month from a company from which regular purchases are made (67%). The change from once a month to once a week of loyalty customer offers causes a drop of 10 percentage points in the desire to receive the offers as a letter communication and shifts interest to the other three channels. Of these the channel that has increased its percentage most is e-mail, but the text message and telephone also increased their percentage. Disfavor rises by a few percentage points for all channels.

As message density increases, letter communication is still to be regarded as clearly the best reception channel for loyalty customer offers (56%) and the telephone the worst (4%). For weekly offers the letter is chosen over three times as often as the second most popular channel, e-mail (18%). For the reception of often recurring loyalty customer offers the text message is also exceptionally popular (12%).

Figure 4: Preferred and disfavored reception channels in Finland for

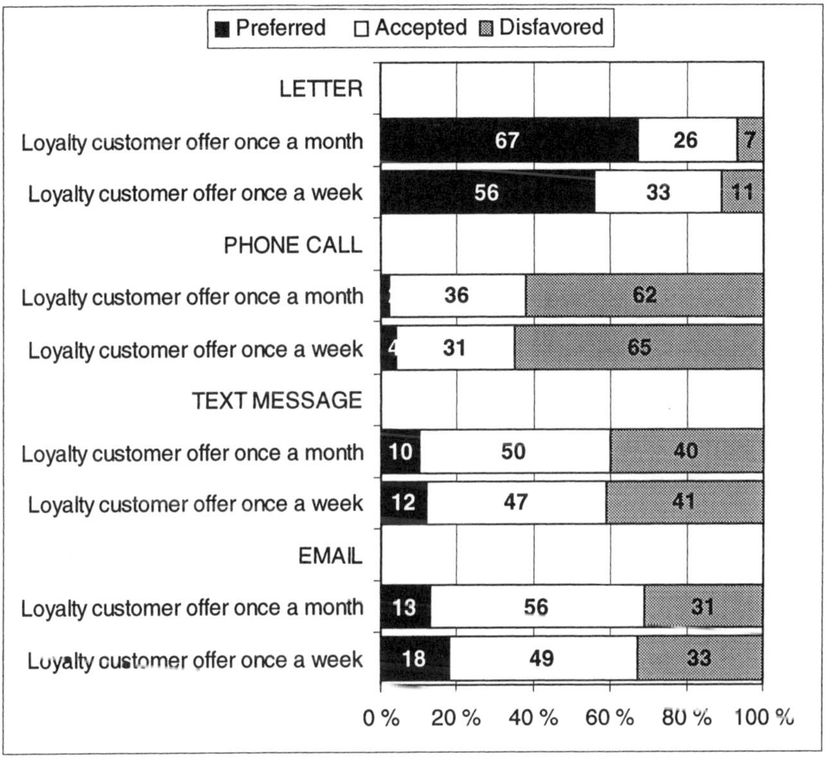

loyalty customer offers

The loyalty customer offers of frequently used companies are considered just as important whether they arrive monthly or weekly. Nevertheless, total disfavor of channels is 10 percentage points greater for weekly offers. When the message has meaning for oneself there is a desire to confirm it, but the growth in message density also increases the wish to eliminate undesired reception channels.

Table 6 presents data on the effect on reception preference of an increase in the frequency of Loyalty customer information. The data is displayed in a transition matrix. The matrix is able to show how many customers changed their reception preference from, say, letter to e-mail, when the direct marketing frequency increased from once a month, case (a), to once a week, case (b).

Therefore, the matrix shows the reception preferences for the media in cases (a) and (b). In each case, the sum of the figures in the row is the total reception preference for that medium in case (a); the sum for the column is the total preference in case (b). Clearly, the difference between those totals is the total change in preference for that medium. The terms on the diagonal show the number of respondents whose preference did not change. All percentages are presented as whole numbers. A missing number means that the percentage is below 0.5%.

Table 6: Transition matrix from monthly to weekly loyalty customer offer in Finland

Preferred Reception Channels		Case b) Loyalty customer offer once a week						Change from case a) to case b)		
		Letter	Phone call	SMS	E-mail	No answer	Total a)	Addition (%points)	Reduction (%points)	Net change (%points)
Case a) Loyalty customer offer once a month	Letter	53%	2%	4%	6%	2%	67%	3%	14%	-11%
	Phone call	%	2%	%	%	%	2%	2%	%	2%
	SMS	1%	%	7%	1%	%	10%	5%	3%	2%
	E-mail	1%	%	%	10%	%	13%	8%	3%	5%
	No answer	1%	%	%	1%	7%	9%	3%	2%	1%
	Total b)	56%	4%	12%	18%	10%	100%	21%	22%	

The terms in the row represent the respondents which moved from a specific preferred channel in case (a) to a different preferred channel in case (b). The terms in the column represent those respondents which moved into that specific channel in case (b) from another channel in case (a). For example, the "Letter" row shows that in case (a), 67% of respondents chose to receive it by letter. However, in case (b), many of the 67% switched their reception preference to other media. From the "Letter" row it can be seen that of that 67%, 53% still wanted to receive the communication by letter, but the remainder had switched to other media: telephone (2%), text message (4%) or e-mail (6%). However, in addition, as the "Letter" column shows, some who did not choose letter in case (a) changed their reception preference from other media to letter. The "letter" column shows that 1 percentage point from each of text message, e-mail, or no response previously now preferred to receive marketing information by letter.

In total, 56% of respondents in case (b) opted to receive marketing information by letter. That is a net change of -11% compared with case (a). Behind this is 3% addition and 14% reduction of letter choices between cases (a) and (b). The table shows that when marketing frequency increases, its reception by letter becomes less popular. Other media become more popular, the reception preference for e-mail rising the most (5%). However, letter (56%) remains by far the most popular means of receiving customer loyalty information, with e-mail a distant second (18%). Furthermore, as the figures in the diagonal show, most customers remain loyal in their choice of preferred means of reception. In spite of that it is important to notice that 21% of consumers have different preferred channels under the scenarios covered by cases (a) and (b) (where 21% is the sum of the absolute value of the entries in the last column).

5.2 The Effect of Product Familiarity and the Customer Relationship

The actual effect of product familiarity and the customer relationship on direct marketing channel choice was studied for the case of subscriptions. A respondent was first asked to choose the most acceptable way of receiving a personal offer for renewing an already existing subscription. In the second stage a request was made to state those possible ways of receiving a message, which were not acceptable at all in this case. After that the same questions were asked concerning a case in which the recipient gets an offer of a magazine that includes the subjects of that person's hobbies or work, and about which that person is now hearing for the first time (figure 5).

Figure 5: Preferred and disfavored reception channels in Finland for subscriptions

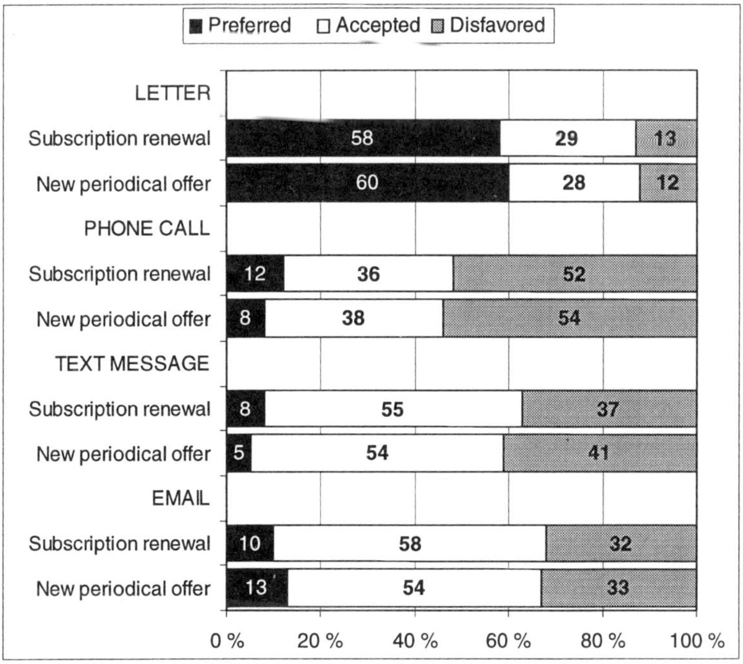

The attitude is almost the same towards subscription renewals and new periodicals. The letter is obviously the most popular means of reception. Evidently, the difference is small because in both cases it is a question of well-targeted direct marketing, for a type of product in which the customer is known to be interested. It would be a different matter if, for example, a magazine about cars were to be offered to a nature activist.

The popularity of the letter increases slightly as we move from the subscription renewal to the new magazine offer, on account of the increase of preference and the decrease of disfavor. Also, the popularity of e-mail is growing slightly, but then a polarization is taking place, because both the preference and disfavor percentages are increasing. In the case of new magazines, the telephone and text message are still less preferred and more disfavored channels.

The subscription for a periodical differs from other reception cases in that marketing by telephone is preferred by 8–12%. Consumers primarily make a choice between a letter and a phone call. Particularly in the case of subscription renewals do some choose the telephone, which is an easy and trouble-free way of confirming the uninterrupted arrival of a newspaper or magazine.

5.3 Marketing oversupply and other extreme cases

Further light can be shed on the reception channel preferences of direct marketing by looking at some extreme Finnish cases. There are at least two quite favorable cases for possible utilization of channel preference data. The total sum of revealed channel preferences is greatest in loyalty customer offers and the total sum of revealed disfavors is smallest for subscription renewal.

The reception of loyalty customer offers is considered so important that in this case there is added enthusiasm for making the right reception channel choice. Subscription renewals are so important that there is a desire to attend to the matter regardless of the channel used. There are even 12% who approve of the telephone, whereas in other cases the figure is only a few percent.

The clearest oversupply situation analyzed was the reception of 20 holiday offers a week, which really tries the patience of would-be recipients. This type of message deluge noticeably increases the number of disfavored reception channels and, on the other hand, it deflates enthusiasm to state the preferred channel. If the marketing messages flood in, there will be two clear changes, letter communication becomes less preferred and phone calls become still more disfavored.

In finding themselves in the middle of such a flood of messages many of those persons that are best prepared to receive messages frequently change to e-mail for a more satisfying reception channel even when they have under normal circumstances preferred the letter. They have thus prepared themselves for implementing a clear survival strategy aimed at extricating themselves from the problem. On the other hand, of those not so well prepared for dealing with messages, many become passive, i.e., make no choice of preferred channel, even though in normal direct marketing reception situations they generally choose the letter. So it is also a precondition for the survival of the popularity of letter communication that the number of dispatched messages for reception remains at a reasonable level.

The proportion of those changing channel preferences in different direct marketing cases is greatest when comparing an offer for the renewal of a magazine subscription case to the case of 20 holiday trip offers a week. In comparison of these two cases it was found that every second consumer shifts the preferred reception channel. This also clearly shows that general direct marketing reception channel preferences do not exist; rather, even individual consumer preferences vary considerably according to the reception situation. This makes the utilizing of channel preference data more challenging.

6. SUMMARY AND CONCLUSIONS

This discourse interpreted data collected from Australia, Finland and the USA and found many similarities between those studies. The paper has attempted to elucidate the picture concerning consumers' marketing channel preferences and the factors affecting them. The main findings can be summarized as follows.

The results show that usually a majority of consumers prefer letter mail when receiving marketing communication. Additionally, those who disfavor the letter account for about 10%. Thus, the letter is a very widely accepted marketing channel. Preferences for receiving marketing communication as e-mail usually vary from 10 to 20%, while around 30% disfavor e-mail. A clear majority of consumers also seem to accept e-mail marketing.

Since e-mail reception preferences appear for the present to be stable, the interesting question arises as to which factors would probably produce growth in the will to not only accept but also prefer e-mail marketing, and at which stage this would take place. The group of digital message pioneers, who prefer to receive mainly electronic messaging, is small today but when will it become a majority?

On the other hand, many consumers seem to want still more control over the reception of direct marketing. So it will become more and more important to receive messages through channels which are easy, acceptable and do not annoy. In the future the precondition for effective marketing seems to be based even more on knowing and respecting the channel preferences of recipients.

If we are to understand and utilize the knowledge of preferred, accepted and disfavored reception channels, further research and modeling of influencing mechanisms will nevertheless be required. For the time being the popularity of paper-based marketing communications has remained somewhat stable, even though there are many electronic alternatives on offer. A particularly important subject for future research would be to delineate those factors that could possibly trigger a change in this situation.

REFERENCES

Auriemma Consulting Group. 2001. *Marketing Vehicles Preferred by US Consumers.* (eMarketer 2003-09-05 presents Auriemma Consulting Group study from the year 2001) www.emarketer.com

Elkelä, Kari, and Heikki Nikali. 2003 *Viestitulvan vastaanotto.* Helsinki: Suomen Posti Oyj. Tutkimuksia 23/2003

Elkelä, Kari. 2003 *Paperilla vai sähköisesti? Osoitteellisen suoran halutut ja torjutut vastaanottokanavat.* (On paper or electronically? Desired and undesired reception channels for direct marketing) Helsinki: Suomen Posti Oyj. Tutkimuksia 28/2003

Nikali, Heikki. 1998. *The substitution of letter mail in targeted communication.* Helsinki: Finland Post Ltd. Quality- and business development studies 27/1998.

Nikali, Heikki, and Aulikki Heino,. 2003. *Kirjeliikenteen sisältötutkimus. Vuoden 2003 loppuraportti.* (Content Survey of Letter Communication) Helsinki: Suomen Posti Oyj. Tutkimuksia 31/2003.

Pitney Bowes. 2001. *Household Mail Preference Study. Regular Mail vs. Electronic Mail.*

Pitney Bowes. 2003. *Household Mail Preference Study. Regular Mail vs. Electronic Mail.*

TNS Australia. 2003. Reaching consumers in the information age. How Australian consumers prefer organisations to communicate with them (Commissioned by Australian Post).

Chapter 18

The Role of Pilot Projects in Facilitating Changes in Work Organization in the Postal Sector Canadian Case Study

Lynn Bue and Geoff Bickerton
Canadian Union of Postal Workers

1. INTRODUCTION

Throughout the world postal administrations and postal unions are coming under intense pressure as they try to cope with the economic, technological and political changes that are revolutionizing the communications industry. Email, the Internet, and electronic fund transfers pose enormous challenges to an industry whose culture remains heavily shaped by the security of public ownership, legislative monopolies, and ever increasing mail volumes and delivery points of call. The prospects of deregulation and privatization place further pressures on the postal sector. Increasingly private sector competitors demand open markets and challenge the legitimacy of publicly owned postal services.

As a result of these developments, tranquility and stability have been replaced with insecurity and doubt. Never before have postal services been subjected to so many conflicting pressures to change. Postal administrations are being required to simultaneously reduce costs and improve services. The pressures on labor are especially acute, and unions that represent the millions of postal workers worldwide must deal with demands for improved working conditions and increased wages and benefits. This process is complex under the best of circumstances, as integrated, nation-wide production processes have standardized work rules and practices that are embodied in collective agreements. Typically labour agreements are nation-wide covering many operations and extend for several years. There is a strong tendency to maintain the *status quo*.

Introducing change would be difficult even if management and labour had the same objectives. However this is not the case. Managers often perceive work rules designed to protect health and safety as unnecessary impediments to productivity improvements. Proposals from either party are usually greeted by the other with a healthy dose of skepticism. There is a tendency of both sides to over-exaggerate the negative consequences of proposals made by the other.

In democratic societies, with a balance of rights and powers between labour and capital, it is unlikely that significant changes in the work process can be introduced without conflict unless both management and workers see benefits for themselves.[1] Is this possible? In such a labour intensive industry as the postal sector, is it possible to improve health and safety provisions at the same time as introducing new measures to improve productivity? Is it possible to reduce unit labour costs while expanding opportunities for full-time employment?

These are some of the questions that faced the management of Canada Post Corporation (CPC) and the leadership of the Canadian Union of Postal Workers (CUPW) as they negotiated a new collective bargaining agreement in 2000. Realizing they could not reach an agreement on the fundamental issues of work rules, workload, and contracting in, the parties agreed to establish a joint process to test the proposals of both parties and then evaluate the consequences. In 2003 the parties reached a collective agreement including significant changes in the work rules and work methods of letter carriers and in the processing and delivery of parcels.

This paper describes the joint process that was undertaken to achieve the collective agreement and some of the accomplishments included therein. As we note, the knowledge gained by the joint process of experimentation played a major role in shaping the proposals and responses of the parties in the 2003 negotiations and led to the successful resolution of many contentious issues.

2. BACKGROUND TO THE 2003 NEGOTIATIONS

In many ways the 2003 collective bargaining negotiations were an extension of the failed negotiations of 1997. In that year the parties had

---

1 A few years ago this looked quite a daunting prospect as noted in Clark and Bickerton (2002), which provides an evaluation of Canada Post's performance and labor relations.

entered that round of bargaining with diametrically opposed objectives. Canada Post was determined to cut the labour costs of the letter carriers and truck drivers by $200 million. This would represent a reduction of approximately 4,000 jobs or 20 per cent of the full-time external work force. CUPW entered negotiations determined to address the serious workload issues that it believed had contributed to a 35% rise in injuries during the previous two years.

To achieve significant staff reductions management tabled numerous demands designed to reduce what it considered to be "unproductive time". The proposals included a requirement for letter carriers to eat their meals on the route instead of returning to their facilities for lunch, more use of private vehicles, greater management ability to adjust work standards, reduced use of public transport, more flexibility in providing replacement for absences and a change in the timing of the lunch period which would enable letter carriers to take their lunch break prior to leaving the office.

To address health and safety issues the union demanded the right for letter carriers to use carts, a reduction in the maximum weight limit, the re-inclusion of unaddressed ad mail into the work measurement system, and a process whereby mutual agreement was required prior to any change in the evaluated work standards. The union also demanded that parcel delivery work contracted out in 1989 should be re-integrated into postal operations.

The parties also had disputes on several other issues including benefits, wages, staffing, and job security. The negotiations did not succeed and a national postal strike commenced in mid November 1997. In early December 1997, after two weeks of strike action, the federal government intervened. The back to work legislation provided for a government appointed arbitrator who would decide on all of the issues in dispute with the exception of wages, which were stipulated in the legislation.

The legislation required the arbitrator to render his award within three months of his appointment. However the complexity of the issues resulted in the hearings lasting almost two years. This meant that the decisions of the arbitrator concerning work methods and work rules could not be effectively implemented prior to the expiry of the three-year agreement when they would once again be up for re-negotiation. Confronted with a situation in which the arbitrator's decision would not likely resolve anything and more likely only lead to further conflict, the parties returned to the bargaining table in late 1999 to once again try and negotiate a settlement.

These negotiations were successful on many important issues such as job security, wages, health benefits, staffing, and pensions. However the parties were unable to resolve the above-mentioned central issues of workload, work process and the use of contract workers in the parcel delivery work.

3. A PROCESS TO TEST PROPOSALS

During the proceedings before the arbitrator, the union argued he should not impose any major change in working conditions unless he was confident there would be no unforeseen negative consequences for the workers. The Union argued that any major change that might increase workload should be tested in the real world prior to its introduction on a nation-wide basis. The union believed that a process for testing its proposals was necessary, as management tended to overestimate the costs of the union's proposals. Eventually both parties recognized that negotiating significant changes in work rules and working conditions would only be possible if they had a shared perspective of the costs and benefits of the proposals and their implications for jobs and health and safety.

To overcome the impasse the parties agreed to a process to test the ideas of both parties prior to negotiating implementation. The purpose was to "review the collection and delivery systems currently in place and develop a new collection and delivery operating model designed to meet the needs of the employees, the Corporation, and the customers".[2] The agreement required the parties to establish pilot projects to test new collection and delivery models. The provision, identified as Appendix AA in the collective agreement, (and referred to as the AA process in this paper,) permitted the parties to temporarily change provisions in the collective agreement to carry out the pilot projects and permanently introduce new conditions of employment after the completion of the pilot.

To develop and implement these projects a joint committee (the Appendix AA Committee) was established. At the outset it was agreed that the AA Committee would have to have significant resources and possess the power and credibility required to obtain the active participation and support of local management and union representatives for the pilot projects. The agreement called for a working committee, involving four experienced and knowledgeable representatives of each party working full-time on the project, and a national steering committee comprised of two union national vice-presidents and two senior corporate representatives. All expenses of the national committees and any local committees were paid by management. This included paying the wages of local several union representatives who were booked off for many months to work full-time on pilot projects. Additionally the agreement provided for the union to receive funding of $100,000.00 to be used to support its efforts. The financial support was extremely important enhancing the effectiveness of the union representatives

---

[2] Agreement Between Canada Post Corporation and the Canadian Union of Postal Workers. January 2000; Appendix AA. For the terms of the agreement go to: <http://www.cupw.ca/pdfs/eng/cpc-cupw2000.pdf>

to fully participate in the various initiatives. It permitted the union to provide necessary office and secretarial support and helped defray travel costs for union representatives and other employees.

Although Canada Post provided the funding, all decision-making required mutual agreement of both parties. By definition, the pilot projects required changes to the terms and conditions of the existing collective agreement. Since the consent of both union and management was required to amend the contract, both parties had an effective veto over the process, including the number and location of pilot projects, the issues that would be tested, and the means by which they would be evaluated.

There was an ambitious 14-month timeline included in the terms of the agreement requiring the review process to begin on February 17, 2000, and the implementation of the new operating model to be completed by April 21, 2001, well in advance of the expiry of the collective agreement on January 31, 2003. This timetable was never met.[3]

The agreement also provided for the Committee to jointly evaluate the results or any pilot project or test. The parties agreed that in order for any joint evaluation process to be credible both parties would require access to the same information sources. Both parties would identify the elements to be evaluated and would jointly develop the methodology and assumptions to be used in the evaluation process. It was agreed to evaluate the impact on employees, health and safety, corporate finances, and customer service. It was also agreed that only the parties would have access to any commercially sensitive information generated through the process. Since the purpose was to facilitate future collective bargaining negotiations it was agreed that data gathered during the process could be used in the next round of bargaining.

Both parties devoted significant resources to the evaluation process. Beginning in October 2001 senior representatives from the Corporation and the union began to establish the methodology for the evaluation process. From the very beginning of the Appendix AA process it was understood that the evaluation of the process was as important as the actual development and implementation of the pilot projects themselves.

3.1 Phase One: Analyzing the Environment

The first decision of the Committee was to permit each party to present its perspectives on the past and current situation of Canada Post. As the employer representatives were drawn primarily from engineering, operations, and marketing it was necessary for them to become more aware of labour relations issues and practices. In addition to meeting with

---

3 For information on all of the projects and developments of the Appendix AA process go to the information bulletins section at the CUPW website <http://www.cupw.ca>

representatives of large volume mailers the parties invited outside experts, such as the Conference Board of Canada and the Institute of the Future, to provide information on the market situation, employees demographics, and future prospects of postal operations. Representatives from the Canadian Auto Workers and the National Association of Letter Carriers (USA) also made presentations on labour relations issues.

During this information-gathering phase the parties discussed the type of initiatives that could be taken under the AA process. Agreement was reached on several separate initiatives including the testing of a new A62 letter carrier case, the examination of different ways of calculating parcel delivery rates, a test of the City Mail Volume Index involving actual mail volumes received in the postal depot, the development of new software and training of union and management in the application of the collective agreement concerning staffing relief employees to replace absences, and the development of two research studies to examine the source of injuries and how they might be reduced. Each of these projects was designed to assist the parties to address long-standing issues in dispute and facilitate the next round of bargaining.

3.2 Phase Two: The Pilot Projects

The most significant work of the AA committee was the development and implementation of three major pilot projects, involving significant changes in the work process and work rules in collection and delivery functions. These pilot projects were conducted in Winnipeg, Manitoba, Kelowna, British Columbia, and Burlington, Ontario. Each of the pilot projects involved several stages including, negotiation and agreement between the parties, planning and consultation with local management, the local union and employees, restructuring of work, implementation and adjustment, stabilization, and evaluation. It was planned that the evaluation would compare a one-year stabilized pilot project with a similar baseline period. However all pilot projects required significant modifications in the planned timeframes for introduction and evaluation.

In all locations the parties included numerous proposals from both union and management. This was necessary to win the acceptance of the local employees and management to participate in the pilot projects. The simultaneous introduction of many changes, some perceived as positive and others as negative, created difficulties. It was difficult to evaluate the impact of any single initiative independently due to the integration of the production process and the inter-relationship between various initiatives.

The introduction of the pilot projects proved to be more difficult than planned. The original timetable called for completion and evaluation of the pilot projects at a time that would permit implementation of the new operating model to be completed by April 21, 2001. Instead, the pilot projects did not get off the ground until after this date. This delay meant that they could not be evaluated prior to the start of collective bargaining in November 2002. However the experience obtained in the pilot projects enabled the parties to reach a new collective agreement in 2003.

3.3 The Burlington Project

The Burlington pilot project was conducted in one letter carrier depot involving 33 letter carriers and 5 postal clerks. Management proposals included a 4:00 a.m. or 5:00 a.m. start time enabling delivery prior to 1:00 p.m. A number of additional part-time, delivery-only routes were created to add sortation time to the full-time staff, thereby reducing their on-street delivery time. This re-balancing of inside and outside duties allowed all the full-time letter carriers to have their meal break prior to leaving the station, thereby eliminating the travel time associated with the return to the facility at lunch. This model also involved the separate sequencing of mail by letter carriers from what they actually delivered, so that the inside sort and preparation duties were spread over all the carriers in the depot with the exception of the part-timers who started and ended on their route. A new method of "staffing to workload" involved a distinct staffing pattern for Monday, the heaviest day of the week for volumes, and a Tuesday-Friday scenario. On Mondays, and on other heavy volume days, part-time employees were extended to eight hours to assist in the sortation of mail. On the Tuesday-Friday scenario several part-time employees were scheduled to start and end their workday on route without reporting to the facility. The pilot also included the testing of delivery of larger sizes of householders that were not normally permitted under the collective agreement.

Several union proposals were also tested in Burlington. Employees were provided extra time to sort and prepare unaddressed admail. Contracted mail delivery in suburban areas was brought in-house. Instead of taxis, Canada Post employees performed the conveyance of letter carriers to their routes. Some residential delivery points that had been receiving community mailbox service were converted to door-to-door delivery by letter carrier. Since Canadian letter carriers go home upon completion of their route there is a tendency to take short cuts and work very fast. To reduce the incentive to work at an unsafe pace, letter carriers were required to punch-out after eight hours work instead of being permitted to leave early. Carts were made available to all letter carriers upon request.

3.4 The Kelowna Project

This pilot project involved changes in the organization of work of 108 letter carriers working out of the two facilities in Kelowna. It involved testing several initiatives proposed by the union including greater motorization of letter carriers. This involved a "buddy system" with two letter carriers attached to most vehicles. Several pieces of work were contracted-in including parcel delivery, street letterbox clearances, relay box deliveries and pick-ups from customers. A letter carrier "customer contact" program was tested in which letter carriers received incentives to sign up customers to Canada Post products and generate sales leads. As in Burlington the parties agreed to test the "eight hour day" concept requiring letter carriers to punch-out at a time clock at the end of their working day and the impact of making carts available to letter carriers.

Employer proposals tested in Kelowna included a distinct staffing model to deal with Monday volumes, meal on route for motorized workers, and the introduction of a system of parcel load leveling.

3.5 The Winnipeg Project

This pilot project dealt with parcel delivery. The parties agreed to contract-in the delivery of expedited parcels using a new work process and new work rules. This work had originally been contracted out as part of a national program in 1989. Contracting in this work effectively doubled the number of parcels delivered by Canada Post employees. Drivers were structured to take their meal in their delivery area instead of returning to a corporate facility and to pick up parcels from customers at the end of the day. In order to reduce unproductive time, the delivery area for each route was adjusted daily, based on the number of stops and the available delivery capacity. Also, the weekly work schedule was adjusted to provide longer hours of work on Mondays. Weekend delivery was introduced to meet customer demand and reduce the volumes for Monday delivery.

There were also two additional features that were common to all three pilot projects. In each project the union agreed to the creation of "composite positions", which integrated work traditionally included in either the internal or external job classifications. In Winnipeg, these workers sorted sequenced and loaded parcels so that drivers could arrive to a pre-loaded vehicle. In Kelowna, composite workers performed inside duties and also performed some pick-up and delivery functions. In Burlington the composites performed the work of postal clerks and letter carrier assistants. Also, in all of the pilots, it was agreed to maximize the use of full-time staff and guarantee all part-time employees a minimum of 20 hours work per week.

The parties signed a memorandum of agreement to amend the collective agreement and establish the new work rules for the pilots.

3.6 Joint Evaluation

When the parties began negotiations for a new collective agreement in November 2002, the evaluation of the pilot projects was far from complete. However, the members of the national and local working committees had been gathering data continuously from the beginning of the process. As a result, both parties had gained a significant appreciation of the impact of most of the initiatives on the four criteria of health and safety, impact on employees, service performance and finances.

From the beginning the parties attempted to establish an evaluation process that would be seen as credible, transparent and accurate. To examine the health and safety impact the parties decided to examine the injury experience, absenteeism, and answers to the employee questionnaires and focus groups. With respect to employee impact it was agreed to examine grievances, turnover and transfer applications, and training. It was also agreed to use surveys and focus groups to capture the experience of employees on all aspects of the pilot projects. Concerning customer impact the parties reviewed various measures of service performance including the rate of on time deliveries, returns and missed deliveries, customer complaints, sales revenues, and customer interviews and surveys.

The evaluation of cost and revenues included examination of hours paid by classification and type, benefit costs including paid leaves, householder allowances, vehicles, conveyance, real estate, contractor costs, volumes, revenues, absenteeism, grievances, uniforms, points of call by delivery agent, number of stops, and structured minutes of work. The parties used corporate data that already existed at the local and national levels and agreed to conduct special investigations needed to capture data not normally tracked through corporate information systems. The parties also agreed to examine the degree of managerial compliance to agreed upon work processes to ensure that results were attributable to the model and not to any incorrect managerial practices that might result from local management's resistance to the changes.

The parties recognized that some factors were impossible to accurately evaluate and that the absence of accurate data for some items might undermine the validity of the exercise. They also recognized the difficulties of evaluating several complex changes where various elements interact with each other and with other factors that are unrelated to the projects. To promote transparency it was decided to identify these issues as being subject to interpretation.

Several issues defined as areas subject to interpretation related to difficulties in obtaining baseline data. In some instances, such as service performance in Burlington, the Corporation did not keep separate statistics for delivery performance in that geographic area prior to the project. This is significant when evaluating a project in which the early start time may adversely affect delivery performance. For conveyance costs, the actual baseline costs differed significantly from the structured cost, undermining the usefulness of structure-to-structure comparisons. Likewise the uneven adherence to work rules undermined the credibility of the results. Inadequate reporting systems for contractor parcel volumes in the base year impacted on the accuracy of cost and productivity comparisons. The short evaluation period, undermined the usefulness of accident and absenteeism data.

The cooperative approach to the evaluation process was not without its problems. Impatient with the slow process of implementing the pilot projects the Corporation conducted its own preliminary assessment of a structure-to-structure cost analysis for each pilot project and presented these to the Union in July 2002. This data had been worked on by the Corporation without input or verification by the Union. It did not correspond to the actual experience of the pilot projects and was heavily biased by the inclusion of many one-time costs associated with the introduction of the pilot projects. Many costs not associated with the pilot projects were also included in this preliminary assessment.

After very strong objections by the union it was agreed that this document did not constitute a substitute for a proper evaluation of the actual pilot projects which would be jointly conducted comparing a period of time following the "stabilization date" with an equivalent base year period. Unfortunately the erroneous conclusions contained in this preliminary assessment concerning the cost of contracting in the processing and delivery of parcels in Winnipeg continued to be used as a reference point by some senior managers and negatively influenced managements negotiating strategy. To facilitate the collective bargaining negotiations on the union's demand to contract-in parcel delivery it was necessary for representatives of both parties to travel to Winnipeg in April and May of 2003, during the final stages of negotiations, to conduct a preliminary cost comparison so that management would have a more realistic assessment of the actual costs of contracting in the parcel work. The results of this analysis were far more favorable with respect to the financial feasibility of contracting in the work.

4. THE 2003 NEGOTIATIONS

Both parties entered negotiations with agreement on many major issues facing the Canadian postal service. There was agreement that volume of lettermail was threatened as a result of electronic diversion, although CPC believed this to be more of an imminent threat then did the union.[4]

Both parties also agreed that the injury rate of external workers was a major problem. . In the previous year fully 19% of full-time letter carriers had been injured on the job with 57% of these injuries being classified as disabling injuries. CUPW believed that this problem was related to increased workload while management emphasized the impact of weather and poor performance of local health and safety committees.

Both parties recognized the strategic need for Canada Post to expand its parcel business although there was no agreement on whether the work should be out-sourced or performed in-house.

Both parties agreed with the need for CPC to remain financially self-reliant, although the union maintained that there was no legislative requirement for CPC to continue to contribute significant dividends to the federal government. In the five years between 1997 and 2002 Canada Post had paid over $466 million in dividends and income tax to the federal government. The union also objected to the CPC policy framework, which limited rate increases for products covered by the exclusive privilege to an amount that is two-thirds the overall national rate of inflation.[5]

Both parties also recognized the threat posed by the United Parcel Service (UPS) dispute with the Government of Canada claiming that Canada Post was engaging in cross subsidization of its parcel service and unfair competitive practices that is currently the subject of arbitration under the provision of the North American Free Trade Agreement. Despite this consensus on many aspects of the economic and political environment facing the postal service there was no shortage of issues in dispute between the parties as they entered the 2003 negotiations. In addition to their differences on issues such as contracting in of parcel delivery, the hours of work for motorized employees, and letter carrier work rules, the parties had major differences with respect to wages, benefit plans, staffing of retail offices, pensions, the employment status of rural and suburban mail carriers and the rights of temporary workers.

The collective bargaining negotiations that began in November 2002 were heavily influenced by the experience of the parties during the two years of the operation of the Appendix AA Committee. The members of the local

---

4 Canada Post Corporation, Annual Reports 2000,2001, and 2002. For information on mail volumes go to <http://www.canadapost.ca/segment-e.asp>

5 Canada Post Five Year Plan, 2003-2007.

and national Appendix AA Committees served as advisors to their respective negotiating committees and were often directly involved in the negotiations process. On the union side, the working committee members of the AA Committee constituted most of the membership of the union's sub committees on parcel delivery and letter carrier work process.

The experience of the pilot projects directly influenced the proposals that ended up on the bargaining table. It is likely the negative experiences encountered with some of the initiatives in the pilot projects were a factor in the decision not to pursue the issue in negotiations. Examples of issues tried in pilot projects and not pursued in bargaining included a distinct "staffing to workload" model to deal with Monday volumes, delivery-only routes for part-time letter carriers, a 4:00 a.m. or 5:00 a.m. start time, and the requirement for letter carriers to punch out after eight hours of work instead of going home when they finish.

4.1 Parcels

Most of the initiatives tried in the Appendix AA pilot projects did get to the bargaining table. Virtually all aspects of the Winnipeg pilot project on parcel delivery made it to the bargaining table and very many aspects of the pilot ended up being incorporated into the collective agreement. The union demanded that expedited parcels be contracted-in in all locations where they were still outsourced. The union proposed a minimum of 20 hours per week for part-time employees and a staffing model that would maximize the use of full-time employees.

The employer demanded their proposals that were being tested in Winnipeg such as:

1. A new classification of employees, composites, to sort and sequence the parcels;
2. Drivers to take their meal in their delivery area instead of returning to a corporate facility;
3. Structured pick ups from customers at the end of the day;
4. Daily adjustment of the delivery area for each route based on the number of stops and the available delivery capacity;
5. The ability to adjust the weekly work schedule to provide longer hours of work on Mondays.

In addition to of the changes that were part of the Winnipeg pilot project, Canada Post proposed the elimination of the one half-hour paid meal period for all Mail Service Couriers (parcel delivery drivers) and instead substituted a 3% wage increase. The Corporation also made proposals that would have made it easier to contract out parcel delivery work.

4.2 Letter Carriers

With respect to the letter carrier model, many of CPC's original bargaining proposals were contrary to the spirit and objectives of the initiatives being tested in Burlington and Kelowna. Instead of promoting greater motorization through corporate vehicles, as was the case in the Kelowna pilot, CPC proposed greater use of private cars. Instead of looking towards reducing the delivery hours for letter carriers, as was the case in Burlington, CPC proposed longer continuous hours of delivery. Altogether management's proposals would have eliminated hundreds of letter carrier positions and increased the workload on letter carriers.

CPC's demands with respect to letter carriers included:

1. Motorized letter carriers and their buddies to be required to take their meal on route;
2. Early starts to be permitted;
3. Routes to be structured so that letter carriers could be required to deliver for 5 continuous hours;
4. Change public transportation routes to taxi or private vehicle routes;
5. Various new incentives for employees to use their private cars and take out their own bundles.
6. Conversion of all postal clerk positions, letter carrier assistants and night routers into one new function called Delivery Support with no guarantee to maintain or create full-time positions.
7. Increase the maximum size and weight of householders and reduce the number of days for delivery of samples.

The union's proposals focused on health and safety concerns and the need to ensure that changes to the work measurement system were negotiated. Specific proposals included greater rotation of duties, access to carts for letter carriers, reduced maximum weight limits, training for health and safety committee members, expansion of door to door delivery by letter carriers, improvements in the barchart system for the replacements of absences, the installation of a City Mail Volume Index based on actual counts of mail, the reinstatement of householder time values in determining the workload of letter carriers, increased union involvement in the restructuring process, in-house conveyance of letter carriers to their routes, no compulsory overtime, and an end to the use of private vehicles. The union also proposed the establishment of composite positions to combine the work of various classifications to permit more full-time jobs.

5. A COLLECTIVE AGREEMENT

The 2003 negotiations ended with a negotiated collective agreement, reached in July 2003 after 9 months of bargaining. It involved 66 major changes to the collective agreement.[6] The most significant breakthrough was the conversion of 6,000 rural and suburban mail carriers from contractor status to employee status and covering these employees under a separate collective agreement.[7] Other important changes included the termination of severance pay, a wage increase of 12.5% over four years, reduction of the maximum weight limit for lifting, and significant improvements concerning training of health and safety activists and human rights protections. The new collective agreement also contained many significant changes in work rules and the work process associated with parcel and letter carrier delivery. These changes were a direct result of the experience obtained by the parties through their involvement with Appendix AA.

5.1 Contracting-In Parcel Delivery with a New Model

The agreement included the contracting-in of the delivery of expedited parcels and the introduction of a new parcel delivery model in all cities with mail service courier delivery. The union saw this as a major victory, both protecting the current parcel processing and delivery positions and generating hundreds of new jobs in a vital product line.

The delivery of expedited parcels was originally contracted out in 1989, eliminating hundreds of jobs, and leaving Canada Post with an incoherent operation incapable of making use of CPC's large economies of scale. CPC was left to deliver "regular parcels" with service standards of four to eleven days and next day Priority Parcels while expedited parcels with a one or two-day delivery standard were given to contractors for delivery. It was the union's belief that this inefficient operation could not continue given the increasing competition within the industry. The union opted to push for contracting in the parcel delivery recognizing that this would require operational and work rule changes.

In the pilot project in Winnipeg the parties had introduced new means of organizing delivery routes by delivery areas or loops and several new work rules. (see above) The final agreement strongly resembled the conditions set out in the Winnipeg pilot project. It involved a commitment of the corporation to invest $50 million in the parcel processing and delivery

---

6 For details of the 2003 collective agreement covering urban operations go to <http://www.cupw.ca/pages/document_eng.php?Doc_ID=478>

7 For details of the 2003 collective agreement covering rural operations go to <http://www.cupw.ca/pages/document_eng.php?Doc_ID=481>

infrastructure and to contract in all the Expedited/Xpresspost pick-ups and delivery work.

In order to balance the employer's desire for greater flexibility and the union's requirement to maximize full-time jobs the parties agreed to create flex part-time Mail Service Courier routes which may be scheduled for a minimum of 4 hours per day, 20 hours a week. The number of flex part-timers will be limited to one per loop or combination of loops with seven or eight full-time routes. On high volume days the flex part-timers are required to work up to eight hours a day to help clear the excess parcels.

The agreement allows the corporation to schedule workdays up to 10 hours within a 40-hour week. The paid meal period was maintained. There is a national joint union-management steering committee to oversee the implementation of the parcel model and local committees to operate at the local level. The union is guaranteed independent financial resources to book off union representatives as required.

In keeping with the practice of the Winnipeg model mail service couriers will take meal break on their routes. The employee will determine their meal location and three minutes of structured time will be allocated as travel time. As part of the New Parcel Delivery Model, all part-time mail service courier assignments created within the model will be structured for at least 20 hours per week, except for weekend-only assignments.

The agreement prohibits the employer from making unilateral changes to the Mail Service Courier Workload Structuring System that would impact on the workload of employees and provides for an improvement of union observer rights in the case of restructuring of mail service courier routes.

5.2 Changes To Letter Carrier Delivery

The collective agreement included several major changes to the work rules concerning letter carrier delivery. The agreement permits non motorized letter carriers, whose routes are structured so that they return to the facility to have their meal, to choose not to return and to take their meal elsewhere. Both parties saw this as a very significant change. Previously letter carriers had been required to return to the facility. The implementation of this rule had caused conflict at the workplace and between the union and management. The productivity of any letter carrier that chooses not to return to the installation for lunch will not be used for comparison purposes with other letter carriers. These routes continue to be structured including travel time to and from the facility at lunch. Although this change did not impact upon the work content of letter carrier routes it was opposed by many employees because they believed that many letter carriers would not stop for lunch as required by the collective agreement. This might result in greater fatigue and potentially result in increased injuries.

The most significant increase in productivity will result from the agreement to allow Canada Post to structure motorized routes and "buddies" to have their meal at a designated spot on their route as opposed to structuring their routes to include travel time to and from their home depot. The designated meal location must meet hygiene standards and letter carriers are entitled to a daily beverage allowance if required to make a purchase. Time to and from their “on-route” meal locations, and for parking, will be built into the route. This is a considerable benefit for management as it will reduce lunch travel time for these employees by an average of 10 minutes and correspondingly increase their productive time.

The charts concerning weight and size of householders were simplified. Employees are not required to carry oversize householders unless there is agreement from the appropriate level of the union.

The employer continues to be prohibited from unilaterally making changes in the work measurement manuals. There were improvements in the rules governing paid union observers during the structuring of routes. Proper mail redirection time values in all walks will be implemented prior to the end of the collective agreement. The parties also agreed to jointly develop a new time value for the mail mobile stop and adopted a new interim value.

To eliminate compulsory overtime for letter carriers management will solicit volunteers. Local management will analyze routes that require regular overtime and eliminate the source of the problems. The mileage allowance was increased for employees choosing to take their private vehicles but additional incentives for private vehicles and taking out relays were not part of the agreement.

Several other proposals of the parties were not included in the new collective agreement. Maximum time for continuous delivery was not increased to five hours. The requirement to begin work at the official start time remains. Management’s proposal to convert public transportation routes to either taxi or private vehicle routes was rejected. There was no guarantee employees would have access to carts. Although both parties entered the negotiations with proposals to negotiate “composite” positions combining job classifications there was no agreement that these employees would be full-time or part-time so the issue remains status quo.

5.3 The Influence of the AA Process and the 2003 Negotiations

The parties could not have achieved a negotiated collective agreement without resolving the issues concerning parcel delivery and the letter carrier work rules. The Appendix AA process was instrumental in enabling the parties to do so without a strike.

This is especially true concerning the issue of the contracting in parcel delivery and the new parcel model of operation. It is impossible to conceive how this would have occurred in the absence of the Winnipeg pilot project. Originally Canada Post Corporation believed that it would not be cost effective to contract-in the parcel delivery unless there was also additional cost savings in the form of the elimination of the paid meal period. This was based on their initial and very faulty structure-to-structure cost analysis. The interim costing exercise conducted by the parties in April and May 2003 enabled Canada Post to reconsider this position. This costing exercise was only possible due to the operational knowledge of the members of the local joint committee. They identified many serious problems with the initial baseline costing that resulted from inadequate records keeping and improper interpretation of data taken from the time and attendance systems.

Prior to the 2003 negotiations the union strongly objected to several items such as the 10-hour maximum day schedule and the taking of the meal on route. However witnessing the actual impact of these changes enabled the union to modify its position.

The conflict between the employer's demands for flexibility and the unions need for the maximization of full-time employment has been a source of many disputes between the parties. This was resolved through the agreement to create flex part-time routes. This solution was based on expertise developed through experience in the Winnipeg pilot project.

The parties experience in the Appendix AA Committee was also instrumental in creating conditions that allowed the successful negotiations of new work rules for letter carrier delivery. In the Appendix AA process the union had become aware that some of the employers proposals did not pose as much of a threat as it had previously believed. This was certainly the case of the employers demand to have the meal on route for motorized carriers. The pilot project process enabled the union to evaluate the actual staffing implications of introducing this work rule change and consult with the membership as to the impact on their working conditions.

The pilot projects also enabled management to gain a fuller perspective of the work content of letter carrier jobs and the relationship between workload and injuries. This may account for CPC's decision to drop several demands to extend delivery time and increase workload and instead focus on proposals to reduce other costs such as transportation.

Through the conceptualization and implementation of the pilot projects both union and management representatives were completely clear about promoting their own self-interest. This articulation of self-interest enabled the parties to reach the compromises required to obtain the necessary support of both local union and management representatives. The process also encouraged both parties to seek solutions that enable both parties to meet their objectives. Perhaps this is just good collective bargaining practice. And sometimes this is not possible and industrial conflict is necessary to provide an incentive to force a compromise. However in the Canadian post office the history of government-imposed contracts had frequently served to absolve both parties of the responsibility to make the necessary compromises to reach voluntary collective agreements. The experience of this process greatly assisted the parties in all aspects of the negotiations.

Likewise other initiatives of the Appendix AA process, such as the testing of a new City Mail Volume Index, the testing of the A62 letter carrier case, and the development of new software to facilitate the barchart process of determining relief staff addressed longstanding grievances of the union which had been the subject of numerous disputes.

5.4 Continuing the AA Process

The value that CUPW and Canada Post Corporation now place on joint testing of initiatives prior to their implementation is illustrated by the fact that the 2003 agreement contains a provision for the continuation of the Appendix AA process, in somewhat of an abridged form.

The Appendix AA process will be continued to oversee several important initiatives, which remain incomplete from the negotiations including:

1. A pilot project to test new product specifications and delivery methods for unaddressed householders;
2. Determination of standards for the new A62 letter carrier workstations. This will involve observing and videotaping the work of 150 letter carriers to establish the frequencies of various work related movement to develop proper time values for the letter carrier work involving the new sortation case;
3. A statistical analysis of factors related to letter carrier injuries;
4. A study of the physiological, physical, and mental effects of letter carriers' workload.

The new provisions governing the Appendix AA process do not include requirements with a fixed number of permanent representatives on the working committee. Both parties will determine the necessary resources depending on the requirements of the initiatives and pilot projects agreed to during the collective agreement. The collective agreement provides for a national committee and CPC will be required to pay for the salaries, expenses, and benefits of the members of any joint work groups established to oversee projects. Both parties shall appoint their own representatives and both parties will be required to bear the expenses of any experts who are not jointly selected. However the union will be provided with $100,000 to pay for expenses directly connected to activities relating to the process.

The contract provisions permit the parties to amend the collective agreement in order to engage in pilot projects and may make these changes permanent. All decisions must be taken by consensus.

6. CONCLUSION

A process that permits labour and management to test new work methods and new work rules can facilitate the introduction of changes and assist parties in resolving longstanding disputes.

The process must be truly jointly controlled with both parties having equal rights and input into all decisions. The process designed by the Canadian Union of Postal Workers and Canada Post Corporation was successful due to a number of factors:

1. Clear identification of objectives and self-interest of each party;
2. Collective agreement protection for new work rules;
3. Separate and independent communications to employees;
4. Mutual veto power over decisions;
5. Significant and independent resources for both parties at the local and national levels including funding for the union;
6. Direct access to decision makers;
7. Use of independent surveys and focus groups;
8. Joint development and implementation of the evaluation process;
9. Access to all relevant information;
10. Independence of the process from other areas of conflict.

The success of the Appendix AA process was due to the acknowledgement of both union and management that there is a need to improve working conditions with respect to health and safety while enhancing the quality of services and addressing the realities of increased competition and the threats posed by deregulation and privatization. This progress is a significant especially given the poor labor relations[8] that existed for many years. Continuation of this approach promises further progress.

[8] Bickerton and Clark (2002, 297) use this phrase only recently "Overwhelmingly, the problems of poor labor relations and inadequate service to the public are the result of government inspired policies…"

REFERENCES

Clark, Dale, and Geoff Bickerton. 2002. "Evaluation of a Public Post Office: A Canadian Experience." In *Postal and Delivery Services: Pricing, Productivity, Regulation and Strategy,* edited by M.A. Crew, and P.R. Kleindorfer. Boston, MA: Kluwer Academic Publishers.

Bickerton, Geoff. 2003. "Evaluation Productivity Improvement Initiatives, A Joint Union Management Approach". Paper presented to the Rutgers University 11th Conference on Postal and Delivery Economics, Toledo, Spain, June 2003

Panitch, Leo, and Donald Swartz. 2003. From Consent to Coercion, Aurora, Ontario: Garamond Press

Vegliante, Anthony, John Mularski, James Sauber, David Treworgy, and Jarret Jackson 2003. "Enhancing Postal Performance Through Customer Connect." In *Toward a Competitive Transformation of the Postal Delivery Sector: Regulation, Pricing and Strategy,* edited by M.A. Crew, and P.R. Kleindorfer. Boston, MA: Kluwer Academic Publishers.

Chapter 19

Power and Discretion in Independent Regulation

The Case of Portuguese Communications Markets[*]

João Confraria
Catholic University of Portugal

1. INTRODUCTION

Since the early stages of communications liberalization in the European Union (EU), regulatory independence has been based on the separation of the regulatory authority from communications organizations. In Portugal, the distinction and separation between the regulatory functions of the state and the state-owned communications operators were implemented in 1989. Subsequently, the concept of regulatory independence changed, to mean increasingly independence from the government and not merely independence from operators. This process of change is discussed in section 2 of this paper. Section 3 explores the sources of increasing regulatory discretion arising in this framework; while section 4 considers issues of accountability related to this greater discretion. The benefits and costs of the current institutional arrangements in Portuguese communications markets are discussed in section 5. It is argued that the current institutional design may have some cost advantages, even if it may lead to substantial discretion in regulatory behavior. It remains to be seen how the current institutions will adapt to both EU and domestic political and regulatory pressures. Section 6 presents conclusions.

---

[*] From 1996 to 2002, the author was member of the board of the Portuguese national regulatory authority for communications, Instituto das Comunicações de Portugal – Autoridade Nacional de Comunicações.

2. THE NATIONAL REGULATORY AUTHORITY AND THE EVOLUTION OF INDEPENDENT REGULATORY POWERS

2.1 Conditions of regulatory independence

The European Union first called for independent national regulatory authorities in EU countries in 1990. Directive 90/388/EEC, on competition in the markets for telecommunications services, stated that member states should ensure that from 1 July 1991, the granting of operating licenses, the control of type approval and mandatory specifications, and the allocation of frequencies and surveillance of usage conditions would be carried out by a body independent of telecommunications organizations. This concept of independence was extended during the nineties to the telecommunications networks and services markets and is currently enshrined in Directive 2002/21/EC, the Framework Directive. Member states shall guarantee the independence of national regulatory authorities by ensuring that they are legally distinct from and functionally independent of all organizations providing electronic communications networks, equipment or services. Moreover, member states that retain ownership or control of organizations providing electronic communications networks or services shall ensure effective structural separation of the regulatory function from activities associated with ownership or control. In postal markets, a similar concept of independence has been in place since 1997, according to Directive 97/67/EC on the internal market for postal services.

In Portugal, the separation of the policy and regulatory functions of the state from state-owned communications operators has been under discussion since the early 1980s. An organization known as the Instituto das Comunicações de Portugal (ICP) was nominally created in 1981. Its role was to advise the government on communications policies, one that was formerly performed by the state-owned communications operators.[1] However, in fact, the full operationalization of the ICP was delayed significantly, mainly because of opposition from state-owned operators, who faced the prospect of a reduction in their power to influence government policy. The civil service was another likely source of opposition: The ICP was not going to be part of the traditional civil service framework, enjoying greater administrative and financial autonomy; thus it was almost inevitable that a bureaucratic rivalry between the existing state sector and this new entrant into it would develop.

[1] Decree-Law 188/81.

In 1989, the ICP was finally born.[2] The ICP brought a structural separation, at the governmental level, of the regulatory function from activities associated with ownership or control. This separation was considered effective, as long as the Ministry in charge of communications supervised the ICP and the Ministry of Finance performed the state activities associated with ownership. The new organization also received independent powers from the government in specific areas, such as approval of equipment, management of radio electrical spectrum, including licensing of radio equipment, and licensing of telecommunications service providers. Independence meant, in these cases, that decisions of the Board of the ICP were not submitted for governmental approval, and increasingly, that interested parties should appeal against these decisions to the courts, not to the government.

So, in sum, it can be argued that, after 1989, the ICP formally complied with the conditions of independence from the communications organizations as required in Directive 90/388/EEC. At the same time, independence from the government was also established within well-defined boundaries.

The idea of regulatory independence evolved during the 1990s. In industry meetings and in the press, some entrants into Portuguese telecommunications markets expressed concern about the effectiveness of the structural separation of the regulatory and shareholder functions at the governmental level. At the same time, the privatization of the former telecommunication monopolistic operator was progressing, so that by the end of the 1990s the state retained only a minority stake. Arguably, the entrants had a critical position against regulation and the policy being pursued by the Ministry in charge of communications, and not only an argument about the effectiveness of the separation of powers between different ministries. The domestic debate on independence was helped by the widespread lack of domestic confidence in traditional state bureaucracies and, probably, also in politicians in general. Although this public skepticism about politicians was not specifically related to communications markets it lent support to the idea that any system of regulation deemed credible had to be seen to be completely independent from the government.

During the 1990s, with the transposition of EU ONP Directives into domestic law, the ICP was granted new powers independent from the government, covering (eventually) every major area of communications markets. By 2001, it was stated in the new statutes of the ICP that the members of the Board were independent in the exercise of their functions, and were not subject to (governmental) instructions or specific guidelines.[3]

---

[2] Decree-Law 283/89.

[3] Decree-Law 309/2001.

At the same time, other measures were taken in order to reinforce this notion of independence. Initially, according to the ICP statutes of 1989, the members of the board were nominated by the government and had a three-year renewable term.[4] Members had the status of public managers with salaries and benefits similar to the members of the boards of state firms. That also meant that there was a formal possibility of dismissal for political reasons. Recently, according to the 2001 statutes, members of the board are still nominated by the government, but for a five-year, non-renewable term. There are stronger restrictions on dismissal and a more flexible remuneration system.[5] There are also some restrictions on hiring: Members of the board or directors of communications companies are not eligible for the board of the regulatory authority. Moreover, after their five-year term, members of the board may apply for a financial compensation at the end of their term and they cannot work for communications companies for two years. [6]

However these were mainly formal changes. Another major force behind the development of regulatory independence from the government has been the degree of autonomy and flexibility in financial and administrative affairs awarded to the ICP since 1989. Concerning labor contracts, investments and contracts with suppliers, the ICP enjoys a greater flexibility than the civil service. This is a requisite for regulatory independence from the government; but it also might increase organizational efficiency.[7] More significantly, since its inception, the ICP has been awarded its own sources of revenues. They include fees on spectrum usage, licensing fees, and fines and fees related to the approval of terminal and radio equipment. Since then, usually on an annual basis, the ICP has had to propose a value of these fees to the government, on which the government adjudicates. However, having its own revenues means that the invoices are sent by the ICP, the money is paid directly to the ICP and the ICP shall take legal action in case of non-payment. These revenues have been managed according to the contemporary legal framework, which has always been focused on budgets and plans approved by the government on an annual basis.

The extraordinary development of mobile telephony led to a substantial increase in revenues arising from fees on spectrum usage by mobile operators. From 1994 to 2002, revenues to the ICP increased from about €18 million to €70 million (current prices and 2002 exchange rates). This was

---

4 Decree-Law 283/89.

5 Decree-Law 309/2001.

6 Under the new 2001 statutes, the ICP was officially renamed as the Instituto das Comunicações de Portugal – Autoridade Nacional de Comunicações (ICP - Anacom). In this paper, the name ICP-Anacom is used when there is a reference to a period after the new statutes. Otherwise, the agency is designated by ICP.

7 In this sense, it may be argued that the creation of the ICP was also a trial run for eventual changes in the civil service, which were under discussion in the late 1980s.

basically a result of the increase in the value of fees from spectrum usage. It happened notwithstanding successive cuts in fees on mobile spectrum usage proposed by the ICP and accepted by the government in the second half of the 1990s. Not surprisingly, for the ICP and the industry, there was a succession of persistent and increasing surpluses, from about €2 million in 1994 to €33 million in 2002. These financial surpluses were allocated according to guidelines and rules set by the Ministry of Finance. As should be expected, most of the accumulated surpluses went straight to the State Treasury. In some cases, smaller amounts were allocated to specific government projects related to the development of the information society, under guidelines set by the Ministries of Finance and those in charge of communications and the information society.

Ultimately, having its own revenues meant that the ICP did not have to bargain for a share of the state budget in the annual budget-making process. Consequently, the government had less scope to impose controls on the agency through budgetary means. Arbitrary cuts in the proposed budget might be seen as a reduction of regulatory independence, contradicting publicly stated policy objectives. This was perhaps the most interesting implication of this arrangement, at least concerning regulatory independence. In 1998, the ICP budget became part of the state budget, but this did not imply meaningful changes in relations with the government. The main point was that as part of the state budget, the agency's budget was also to be approved by Parliament.

2.2 Independence from the government: telecommunications

In the years after the creation of the ICP, the development of regulatory independence in Portuguese telecommunications markets was related to the extension of regulatory powers independent from the government.

As mentioned above, by 1989, the ICP was awarded some powers independent from the government on a well-defined set of issues, related to the approval of equipment, spectrum management and the licensing of new service providers. Licensing powers were extended, in 1990, to include the power to supervise compliance with the licenses, and to fine or to revoke licenses in cases of non-compliance. Markets to be included under these regulatory functions were CATV, mobile telephony and paging (since 1991), trunking and data services (since 1992), and satellites and voice services to closed user groups (since 1996). ICP powers also included the punishment of anti-competitive behavior by incumbent monopolists, or by new firms controlled by them, licensed to operate in liberalized areas.[8] With the development of the legal framework for liberalized markets, the ICP acquired additional powers to regulate contracts between each operator or service provider and final consumers. Licensing powers were clarified and enhanced in 1998.[9]

In the leased lines markets, the ICP could intervene independently via the power to approve contracts to supply leased lines, including the conditions for interruption or termination of supply; this was in addition to the (by then) usual power of supervising and fining in cases of non-compliance.[10] These rules were supposed to give the ICP some power to protect service providers entering liberalized telecommunications markets against eventual anti-competitive behavior of the monopolistic supplier of leased lines. Clearly, the first regulatory powers of the ICP independent from the government were concerned with liberalized markets. In a sense, these powers were remarkable, as they were among the first important cases of independent power for regulating behavior in communications markets where there were firms still enjoying exclusive rights.

Price regulation of services under exclusive rights was initially put into a different framework. Until 1992, the government set the prices of some services, considered essential, and set the rules for the determination of the other prices, allowing the operators some flexibility. In 1992 this system was changed. Price regulation of services provided under exclusive rights was based on an agreement between the operator, the ICP and the competition authority. This agreement was subject to approval by the members of government in charge of communications and competition policy.[11] Telecommunication services covered by this framework included fixed voice telephony and leased lines. Regarding interconnection, in case the operators (mainly fixed and mobile) could not agree, the ICP had the right to intervene, setting interconnection prices, after consultation with the competition authority.

In 1995, the ICP's role was augmented by the concession contract agreed between the government and Portugal Telecom S.A (PT), by then the fixed network operator enjoying exclusive rights.[12] The ICP was given a major role monitoring the compliance of PT with this contract and imposing fines in cases of non-compliance. The ICP might also impose price reductions up

[8] For CATV see Decree-Law 292/91, later revised by Decree-Law 241/97, and for satellites, Decree-Law 120/96. For the other services see Decree-Law 346/90.

[9] Decree-Law 381-A/98.

[10] Decree-Law 198/94.

[11] Decree-Law 207/92.

[12] See Decree-Law 40/95. This contract set the conditions of operation of Portugal Telecom as a monopolistic operator and defined a framework for regulatory change with the liberalization process.

to a ceiling set by law if the PT failed to comply with quality-of-service objectives. Moreover, the ICP was given the power to set the basic framework for cost accounting and to ask PT for detailed financial and technical data.

The development of the process of liberalization at the EU level during the 1990s was used to confirm and enhance the powers given to the ICP in the regulation of PT. In 1997, in fixed voice telephony services, the ICP received additional independent powers to supervise PT's relationships with consumers.[13] A similar role was already played by the agency in liberalized markets. A major landmark in the development of independent price regulation was the interconnection law, also published in 1998.[14] The ICP was given the power to set interconnection prices and to intervene in interconnection agreements – as well as the power to define the entities that might be subject to price regulation in interconnection. In 1999, the ICP obtained independent powers of price regulation in leased lines and in voice telephony[15], extended in 2000 to local loop unbundling[16]. A framework based on agreements between the ICP, the competition authority and the operator, and approved by the government, was maintained for some services provided under universal service obligations.[17]

Further changes followed European and domestic policy developments. The legal framework set by the new EU Directives, arising from the 1999 Review, reinforced the powers of the ICP in price regulation, notwithstanding the adjustments in the concession contract made necessary by the liberalization process. This was mainly the result of the greater flexibility awarded to national regulatory authorities to choose the best regulatory instruments for each situation. The scope for regulatory intervention also increased concerning the regulation of access: One-way access and two-way accesses in mobile markets, one-way access for broadband service providers and conditional access in digital television are markets where the ICP's power to intervene was given a stronger legal basis than previously.

Several extensions of regulation independent from the government were related to particular conditions in other markets, sometimes loosely related to

---

13 Decree-Law 240/97.

14 Decree-Law 415/98. This law transposed Directive 97/33/EC, also known as Interconnection Directive.

15 Concerning leased lines; see Decree-Law 290-A/99, transposing Directive 97/51/EC. Previously, there was already some independence from the government. According to the Concession Contract, whenever a service was liberalized, price regulation would be based on an agreement between the ICP and the operator. The new rules for voice telephony were included in Decree-Law 474/99, transposing Directive 98/10/EC.

16 Rule (EC) 2887/2000, of European Parliament and Council.

17 Decree-Law 458/99.

the core telecommunications markets. This was the case of markets for electronic and telecommunications equipments, home networks and audio text services.

In 1992, the ICP had been designated as the agency in charge of monitoring the implementation of electromagnetic compatibility rules, including the power to impose fines in cases of non-compliance.[18] These functions were, in a sense, a by-product of the traditional role of spectrum management and regulation of terminal and radio equipment markets, a role inherited by the ICP from the former postal and telecommunications state organization, CTT – Correios e Telecomunicações de Portugal E.P. These powers of intervention were basically maintained after the review of the legal framework in 2000.[19] Also in 2000, a new domestic legal framework for home networking gave increased powers to the ICP, related not only to the need to protect competition, but also to the pursuit of the technological development of domestic networks.[20] Until then, the regulator was basically in charge of implementing a framework designed by CTT in the late 1980s.

Audio text services were a different case. Audio text was used to offer adult services. There were also several cases of consumer fraud. The law tried to provide for some protection of consumers' interests, increasing publicly available information about the content and the price of these services, and this led, since 1991, to some involvement of the ICP in content regulation. Currently, numbers are allocated by the ICP to audio text service providers according to the nature of the service provided. The ICP can also monitor the effective use of allocated numbers according to the service provided and impose fines or revoke authorizations in case of non-compliance[21].

2.3 Postal services

The role of the ICP in postal markets has been more limited than in telecommunications. Nevertheless, since 1989, the agency has had an advisory role on postal policy, and has been one of the parties to the price and quality service agreement that was the core of regulation in postal markets. As in telecommunications markets, this agreement involved the competition authority and had to be approved by the members of

---

[18] Decree-Law 74/92 and Administrative Rule 767-A/93.

[19] Decree-Law 192/2000, for terminal telecommunications equipment and Decree-Law 151-A/2000 for licensing radio communications stations and equipment.

[20] Decree-Law 159/2000.

[21] Decree-Law 177/99.

government in charge of communications and competition policy.[22] A further but minor regulatory role concerned the definition of conditions for installation of residential mailboxes.[23] Moreover, the role of the ICP in postal markets was enhanced by the end of the decade. As in telecommunications, this process is associated with European liberalization as well as with domestic political reasons.

In 1999, a new law on postal services and a concession contract signed between the government and the postal operator, CTT – Correios de Portugal S.A. – gave the ICP a role in postal markets similar to the role it had in telecommunications markets before 1999. The ICP has, in some cases, an even higher degree of independence from the government. For services included under universal service, price regulation is based on an agreement between the operator, the ICP and the competition authority. Quality of service regulation is set by an agreement between the ICP and the postal operator, to be achieved simultaneously with the agreement on prices; and the ICP may impose price reductions if the postal operator does not comply with quality of service objectives. The ICP also has the right to forbid changes in working hours, and the creation or closure of postal establishments. However, in one significant case, the independent role of the regulator was diminished. Although it retained the power of monitoring compliance of CTT through the concession contract, it only received the role of proposing fines to the government in cases of non-compliance. The final decision on fines belongs to the member of government in charge of communications policy.[24] Finally, in 2001, according to the legal framework for postal operators in the liberalized areas, the ICP was given the power to license postal operators, to supervise compliance with the licenses and to impose fines in cases of non-compliance.[25]

3. SOURCES OF REGULATORY DISCRETION

In the use of their own powers of decision, regulatory agencies are supposed to pursue public interest objectives clearly defined by law. According to a popular view, the government sets political objectives, and the mainly technical issue of implementing these objectives is left to agencies independent of the conflicts and ambiguities that affect daily

---

22 The framework for price regulation of postal services was similar to the one in place for telecommunications until 1998. See Decree-Law 207/92.

23 Regulatory Decree 8/90.

24 Law 102/99 sets the essential framework of postal services. For the concession contract see Decree-Law 448/99.

25 Decree-Law 150/2001.

politics.[26] In this simple setting there is almost no regulatory discretion; accountability is related simply to the degree to which the objectives assigned to the agency are implemented (within its imposed cost constraints). In reality, though, it is unlikely that this vision of regulatory practice was ever achieved in communications markets. Rather, in general, the delegation of authority to the agency by the executive or legislature gives it discretion; this was certainly the case in Portugal.

It should be said, first, that there may be scope for regulatory discretion even when the regulator's objectives are clearly stated in law. For instance, there are no major ambiguities in the implementation of objectives, as in the licensing of radio communications equipment according to known technical specifications or supervising electrical and electronic equipment markets for the purpose of ensuring compliance with known technical requirements. Nevertheless, most of the activities of the agency pursuing those objectives are costly, and the effectiveness of the agency depends on the budget allocated internally to each activity. Usually, even if the government or the parliament have a say on the global budget, it is unlikely that this will significantly reduce the agency discretion on the detailed composition of its expenditures and investments.

In some cases, the scope of action of an independent agency may even fall into the realm of economic policy. For instance, setting technical requirements for home networks involves the definition of a given technological level to be achieved at every home in the country. It affects the families using the homes built according to such requirements, and the firms and employees in the home networking business. That is, a whole industry may be changed by new technical requirements. Eventually, monitoring compliance with technical requirements may also have policy dimensions. Fewer resources allocated to monitoring electronic equipment markets might allow cheap imports that do not meet technical standards requirements to enter the domestic market. Similarly, when the agency has several objectives to pursue simultaneously over a given period, it often has the discretion, given its budget constraint, to construct its own hierarchy of objectives.

A choice between objectives may also be imposed whenever there is some inconsistency between objectives assigned by law to the regulatory agency. For instance, the promotion of investment in new networks and the promotion of access to incumbent networks, or network elements, may be

---

[26] "But why should regulators be political at all? Once the broad legislation is in place, the job of detailed day-to-day regulation, which is both highly complex and technically demanding, is best done wholly free of political interference. A good analogy is with central banking: within a broadly agreed political framework, it works best when the detailed decisions on monetary policy are taken independent of any outside political pressures"(The Economist, July 24th 2003).

inconsistent objectives. However they are arguably two of the most important objectives of economic regulation in communications markets.

It also seems possible to suggest that in communications markets, the definition of objectives to be pursued often involves a substantial amount of ambiguity. In price regulation, for instance, the principle of cost orientation of prices in postal and telecommunications markets is subject to some ambiguity concerning the definition of the relevant cost concepts and the speed of adjustment of prices to costs. In interconnection and access prices, the regulator is often allowed or encouraged by law to take into consideration efficiency issues, something that also involves a considerable amount of ambiguity. More recently, one of the main objectives of regulation has been the promotion of competition. However, the relevant concept of competition is not obvious. For instance, which concept of competition are the regulatory authorities expected to pursue? Should regulators adopt a structural concept based on observed market concentration; or should they emphasize behavior and performance in their appraisal of competitive conditions?

After the definition of objectives, another possible source of discretion is the choice of instruments to be used, given expected causal relationships between instruments and objectives. Certainly, the scope of legal instruments available to national regulatory authorities to achieve a given objective has increased in telecommunications markets. The Framework Directive puts a strong emphasis on the principle of proportionality in regulatory action. The Interconnection and Access Directive states that for operators with significant market power, national regulatory authorities will be able to impose, as appropriate, obligations of transparency, non discrimination, accounting separation, access and use of specific network facilities or price control and cost accounting.[27]

Ultimately, regulatory agencies are bureaucracies. One natural assumption for bureaucratic behavior may be the pursuit of power, as the pursuit of profit is assumed to be the objective of 'economic man'.[28] Moreover, as monopolists in a market, bureaucracies are sources of inefficiencies, resulting from reduced effort in the pursuit of objectives or lack of cost-minimization procedures. In an independent regulatory agency these features of bureaucratic behavior may well interact with different forms of political behavior, as long as the agency has some discretion in offering or withdrawing regulation.

In this framework, asymmetry of information and uncertainty may well play an additional role in the development of regulatory discretion. Uncertainty and asymmetries of information are often recognized as sources

---

27 Directives 2002/21/EC and 2002/19/EC.

28 Mueller (2003, 359-361).

of political power. According to a generally accepted idea, the possession of superior information is a source of power. In regulation, it is not obvious that the regulators always have better information than regulated firms or, eventually, consumers' associations. Indeed, the opposite may well happen and a common assumption is that firms have better information about market conditions than the regulator. If true, this may be a check on regulatory power. It is clear that it may also be a source of error in regulation – but errors in regulation may also be a source of checks on regulatory power, as long as the agency becomes subject to greater scrutiny from the interested parties and to critical appraisals from the press.

However, in a different sense, it can be suggested that a regulatory agency may use lack of information and increasing uncertainty to maintain or increase power and discretion. This follows because, in regulatory practice, imperfect information and asymmetries of information are part of the initial problem, but they are not a "state of nature." Action can be undertaken to reduce uncertainty and asymmetries of information; and it may not always be in the interests of the agency to allocate resources to these activities. In principle, this is a matter of cost-benefit analysis.

It is reasonable to assume that reducing uncertainty and knowing more about a given market situation brings benefits to the agency. However, acquiring incremental knowledge imposes costs on the regulatory agency and these costs depend on the scope for bureaucratic behavior at the agency. Beyond the obvious financial costs of the resources employed in the acquisition of knowledge, the agency bears some disutility from effort. It is clear that the opportunity cost to the regulatory bureaucracy of an activity intended to reduce uncertainty about a given market situation is higher than in an organization strictly focused on the pursuit of the "public interest." This suggests that bureaucratic behavior leads to sub-optimal investments in knowledge; but it is not necessarily the end of the story. It is noteworthy that, in fact, acquiring information and knowledge about an uncertain situation usually means that uncertainty is reduced concerning the analysis of that situation. If so, it may be possible to make a reappraisal of the costs and benefits to the market of a given set of regulatory options. It may well happen that this process leads to shedding additional light on the costs that some regulatory options may impose on the market. In the end, some of the options initially considered no longer look acceptable. However, these options might have been the preferred options of the regulatory agency, because they might have involved increasing power, or they might have been related to the supply or withdrawal of regulation as responses to private actions. Without additional information these options might have been defended according to some rhetoric of the public interest and might have been followed by the agency. The availability of information about the potential consequences of regulatory actions may make impossible a credible defense of actions that could be defended with less information. As long as the information is available, the regulator must use it. In practice, it does not seem reasonable to discard available information. That would obviously compromise the credibility of the regulator. Such behavior might also be illegal. The legal framework for regulatory procedures usually implies that the agency cannot ignore information directly available. In the end, additional information may reduce the scope for discretionary regulatory behavior.

At the margin, an investment in knowledge may have negative benefits for the regulatory agency if the eventual benefits of this investment are outweighed by increasing effort, and by highlighting the social costs of regulatory options. Because of this, before any investment in acquisition of information and knowledge, the bureaucrats-regulators must decide if they want to know what will become known if the investment is made. This decision may well be an important source of regulatory discretion.[29]

It seems possible to argue that private parties negatively affected by regulatory behavior have the incentives to provide the agency with free information that may deter effectively the exercise of regulatory discretion. This is certainly an interesting possibility, but some qualifications and doubts should be considered. Private parties are also affected by imperfect information about market outcomes and may not be able to provide credible information about them. They also have imperfect information about the regulator. In particular, they do not know what the regulator knows; they do not know what information to supply. In this case, to supply substantial amounts of information is an option, but it is not necessarily the best option. Interested parties may be willing to provide information about the impact of regulatory action on their own surpluses, namely if this impact is negative. But this possibility should not be taken for granted. Private parties might be involved simultaneously in several regulatory processes, and supplying detailed information in one of them may jeopardize their position in the others. Or, as a rule of thumb for regulatory interaction, private parties may never reveal very much to the regulatory agency about their own surpluses, positive or negative. This happens because they may believe that over time, the possession of superior information is an important source of advantage in dealing with the regulator. It may well be important for them that the regulator does not know what type of knowledge they have – and revealing that knowledge in a given situation might have negative effects in future interactions with the regulator. Finally, firms may simply not trust the

29 The opposite may also happen. Investing in the acquisition of information on uncertain market situations may allow the regulatory agency to present a credible defense of a decision that may be essentially a response to private interests.

regulator for the purposes of supplying sensitive data. For instance, they may assume that competitors will offer jobs to people from the regulatory agency dealing with such data. Currently, only members of the board face restrictions moving to private employment when leaving the agency.

4. ACCOUNTABILITY

The arguments in the previous section suggest that independent regulatory behavior may be subject to some of the limitations usually associated with bureaucratic behavior. Accordingly, the design of accountability rules facing the independent regulator is crucial in communications regulation. Accountability rules governing Portuguese communications markets involve the rules covering relations between the ICP and the internal judicial, legislative and executive powers, as well as the relations with the industry and consumer groups. Moreover, in the EU institutional arrangements, the European Commission also has considerable power to supervise national regulatory authorities in communications markets.

First, it should be noted that the parties subject to ICP decisions have always had a right of appeal in the general framework of the regulatory process in Portugal. The court of appeal is usually an administrative court.[30] This often implies that the main issue at stake in court is the compliance of a decision with the procedural rules set for the regulatory process. The content of that decision, its consequences to firms, consumers and markets, often play a minor role or no role at all. Recently, a major step was taken to improve on this in telecommunications markets. According to Directive 2002/21/EC, member states shall ensure the right of appeal to a court having the necessary technical and specialized knowledge, making sure that the technical merits of each case are given due appreciation. This principle may become one important source of accountability in independent regulation in internal telecommunications markets.

Concerning the relationship with the government, it is striking that, from 1989 to the late 1990s, the government retained important formal powers of control in price and quality of service regulation of telecommunications and postal operators enjoying exclusive rights and with universal service obligations. This happened even after the formal involvement of the ICP in

---

[30] PT and CTT also have the possibility of settling some disputes with ICP, arising in the specific framework of their concession contracts, through a court of arbitration. This court is made up of three members, one being appointed by each of the parties and the third being chosen by the arbitrators selected by the parties. This process of settling disputes has been used very rarely, basically in cases of fines imposed under the concession contract.

the regulatory process in 1992. However, the government role has been an increasingly limited one. In practice, it would be difficult for the government to take a very active role in supervising the ICP. There was no bureaucracy inside the civil service to monitor the communications industry and to provide the government with technical analysis independent from the regulatory agency. The ICP had the statutory role of advisor to the government on communications policy, and successive governments have chosen not to have a civil service bureaucracy monitoring the communications industry. They relied on ICP advice and, eventually, also on independent work from advisors and aides appointed on an individual basis by each member of government.

In 1996 some major steps were taken to improve accountability in regulation and in policy advice. The statutes of the ICP were changed to give a greater role to an advisory council.[31] This council was first formed at the same time as the ICP, in 1989. At that time it comprised mainly representatives of different ministries and operators enjoying exclusive rights. Its main functions were to give advice on the financial and activity reports of ICP, and to advise the board of the ICP, as long as the board found such advice useful.

In 1996, the council was enlarged to include representatives of all operators and service providers, with a bias favoring the inclusion of entrants not related to PT and CTT. Consumers' associations were also represented. At the same time, the functions of this council were enhanced. It was given an advisory role in the definition of patterns of quality of service to be imposed in communications markets, and in the definition of global policies for communications and economic and social development. Even more significantly, the council was given the right to be asked, either by the board of the ICP or by the government, to give its advice on any other subject.

These moves improved the government access to sources of advice other than the regulatory agency and so increased government supervision of the ICP. They also improved accountability with the industry and with consumers' associations. The role of consumers' associations was further reinforced in 1996, in the framework of new consumer laws. Consumers' associations received the right to participate in the regulatory process and to ask, at any moment, for information on the economic and legal basis of regulated prices. This was to happen mainly in telecommunications markets, but in practice consumers' associations also became directly involved in the regulatory process in the postal markets.[32]

On a more formal level, in 1998, another change in the statutes, mainly symbolic in practice, concerned financial accountability. The ICP

---

[31] Decree-Law 95/96.

[32] Laws 23/96 and 24/96.

maintained financial and administrative autonomy, but the ICP budget became part of the state budget. Significantly, this change implied increasing accountability to Parliament.

Further changes occurred by 2002, under the new ICP-Anacom statutes, and in 2004, with the transposition to domestic law of the EU Directives on electronic communications networks and services. The new institutional arrangements are likely to provide checks on regulatory power from several different sources. The first one is the reinforcement of the right of appeal at the national level, to include, as mentioned, the analysis of the technical merit of regulatory decisions in telecommunications markets.

Second, the design of institutional relationships with Parliament was improved, as ICP-Anacom also became more accountable to it. A provision in the new statutes gives ICP-Anacom an advisory role to the government and to the parliament. The authority must also present an annual report on regulatory activities to the government and to the parliament.

A third significant development in the new regulatory framework in telecommunications and of the new ICP-Anacom statutes is the new focus on public consultation. As a general rule, any decision by ICP-Anacom with a significant impact on relevant postal and telecommunications markets must be preceded by a consultation of the draft decision with the interested parties.[33] The interested parties may be an extremely large group – the government, the European Commission, firms, consumers and national regulatory authorities in other member countries.

Finally, in telecommunications markets, in several cases explicitly mentioned in the Framework Directive and in the Access Directive, related generally to the development of the single market, the draft decision shall be made accessible for comments to the Commission and national regulatory authorities in other member states. Moreover, the Commission may require the withdrawal of the decision in any of the following cases: when the intended measure aims at defining a relevant market that differs from those defined in the Commission recommendation on relevant markets; or when deciding whether or not to designate an undertaking as having significant market power; and when it would affect trade between member states.[34]

These provisions grant the Commission the power to impose an *ex ante* reversal of decisions of national authorities in two core areas: First, economic regulation related to the definition of relevant markets; and second, the identification of operators with significant market power. Moreover, the general consultation procedure with the Commission and other national regulatory authorities also suggests the possibility of *ex ante* reversal or change of draft decisions of national authorities through some

---

[33] See Directive 2002/21/CE and Law 5/2004.

[34] Directive 2002/21/CE.

kind of peer advice or peer pressure. National regulatory authorities may find themselves in publicly odd situations if, in the framework of these consultation procedures, it becomes obvious that most of the EU national authorities are against their draft decisions under consultation. At the same time, to reinforce the cooperation between the European Commission and the national regulatory authorities, the European Regulatory Group was created.[35] This group includes the national regulators and the European Commission and it may also contribute to the increasing accountability of each national regulator to the Commission and, eventually, to the other national regulators.

In general, it seems that recent developments in the Portuguese institutional arrangements give a greater role to EU institutions for checks on domestic regulatory discretion, at least in the area of telecommunications regulation.

At the national level, the recent developments may lead to some ambiguity. In the case of consumers and the industry, much depends on the details of the implementation of the consultation procedures generally set in law. With regard to the government, much depends on the degree of trust that develops between the government and the regulatory agency at the political level. In many areas related to policy advice, the agency is not supposed to be independent from the government. More generally, it remains to be seen if Parliament, the government and private, interested parties are able to supervise regulatory discretion. This is a very practical point but essential for the effectiveness of the domestic institutional framework. Another major question is related to the role of the advisory council. Formally, this council was restructured to make it more representative of the changing communications industries. However, from 2002 and 2004 the government failed to obtain nominations to the council. It seems that, during this period, the government believed that the new regulatory frameworks provided adequate checks on regulatory discretion.

5. ARE THESE ARRANGEMENTS EFFICIENT?

The control of the direct financial costs of regulation is likely to have been a persistent objective in the evolution of the Portuguese regulatory framework. As mentioned above, in 1989 there was a political option of not developing a bureaucracy within the ministry and the civil service to support political decision-making in communications.

---

[35] Decision 2002/627/CE.

The reasons for this political option may be related to some lack of trust in the efficiency of traditional state bureaucracies. In communications, the Portuguese government really tried to create a new bureaucracy, subject to rules governing employment and expenditure that were closer to the rules governing state-owned firms than to the rules governing traditional state bureaucracies. At the same time, the government maintained some control on the agency's costs through the budget approval process, regular audits and the imposition of specific rules. The most obvious of these rules has been a cap on labor costs, imposed on an annual basis and related to the changes in labor costs in the civil service. These arrangements also avoided potential (and traditional) costly conflicts between different state agencies acting in the same sectors and in conflicting areas of supervision. Such conflicts are likely to be the source of additional uncertainty in the markets, imposing additional burdens on firms and consumers.

One possible shortcoming of this framework was a decrease in the government's ability to supervise the regulator. Two features of the Portuguese regulatory framework may be seen as addressing this issue. First, the agreement on price regulation of services provided under exclusive rights can be seen as an inexpensive way to limit regulatory discretion. It may seem somewhat awkward since a specific regulation depended on the agreement of the regulated entity. But in the end the final decision belonged to members of government that could always hear all the interested parties – and the regulated entities were, for most of the time, state-owned firms, or at least firms controlled by the state. Second, the role given to the advisory council and the direct relationship that was allowed between the advisory council and the government may also be seen as a cost effective way to get "insider" and specialized knowledge to monitor the regulatory agency and to get additional advice on communications policies, until the end of 2001, without additional financial or political costs.[36]

A cost effectiveness argument may also be presented concerning one of the most contentious issues of the new regulatory framework: The possibility of *ex ante* reversal of the decisions by the European Commission. It would certainly be costly for the Commission to promote an *ex post* reversal of a decision of a national regulatory authority. It would also be costly for the national regulatory authority to defend it in the courts. The expected cost savings resulting from *ex ante* reversal of national decisions are probably higher than the additional expected costs of analysis and treatment of information arising from the consultation procedures at the EU level. Moreover, the approach followed in the Directives brings greater certainty to

---

[36] McCubbins and Schwartz (1984) noted that the participation of interest groups in the regulatory process contributed to the supervision of the regulator. The advisory council can be seen as an inexpensive framework to implement this kind of supervision.

each national market and, as this procedure is aimed at the development of the single market, it seems likely that an increasingly common regulatory framework in the EU will decrease the costs of doing business in different EU countries.

Another issue relates to the efficiency of arrangements increasing the discretionary power of the agency. It was noted above that the scope for discretionary behavior has increased by the lack of detail in the definition of objectives and instruments of regulation. However, this may be an efficient way to deal with the complex decision-making process at the EU level. Greater detail in the Directives would probably impose very high costs in the EU legislative process. Whenever it is not possible to achieve greater detail because of differences between member states or between member states and the European Commission, the necessary level of detail will have to be achieved in regulatory practice. The consultation procedures set in the Framework Directive give a clear role to the European Commission in this process. It remains to be seen to what extent differences in national positions that prevailed in the political process and blocked agreements on more detailed laws will reappear in the daily business of implementing the Directives.

It can be also argued that setting general principles in law is not necessarily the result of political deadlocks. General principles may be simply the best technical option. Conditions prevailing in each national market, technological change, and/or changes in preferences, may suggest that a detailed legislative approach might lead to excessive rigidity in regulation. If so, there is a trade-off between increased flexibility for regulatory action and the control of discretionary behavior. At some point, it may be possible that less flexibility and more detailed rules may be welfare improving, even if these rules are not first best rules.[37]

6. CONCLUDING REMARKS

The institutional arrangements for regulatory independence implemented in Portuguese communications markets are relatively inexpensive from the point of view of the state budget, and, at least in some cases, it seems possible to find a rationale for them on efficiency grounds. However they may be potentially unstable. The advisory role to the government is not necessarily consistent with the pursuit of independent regulation. A government can always claim the right to choose its own advisors, at least in

[37] Laffont (2000) argued that constitutional constraints on regulation can improve expected welfare because they dominate alternative rules that open up too large opportunities for political discrimination.

the traditional Portuguese political framework. For instance, the current arrangements may lead to weaker regulation if it is felt that there is no political trust between the regulator and the government. However, it remains to be seen what might happen in such a case, as the regulator has effective powers wholly independent from the government. In the same sense, the co-existence of agencies, like ICP-Anacom, with traditional civil service bureaucracies, suggests additional analysis of the consistency of different institutional arrangements in the state sector.

Possibilities of discretionary behavior were highlighted in the previous sections. They seem to be strong enough to suggest that the decision-making process inside regulatory bureaucracies is an interesting area for additional research. On the other hand, the potential roles to be played by Parliament and by the European Commission, as checks on regulatory discretion, seem to be of particular relevance. Future work should provide new insights about the effectiveness of the new framework in place in increasing accountability in Portuguese communications markets.

REFERENCES

Laffont, J. -J. 2000. *Incentives and Political Economy.* Oxford: Oxford University Press.

McCubbins, M.D. and Schwartz, T. 1984. "Congressional Oversight Overlooked: Police Patrol vs. Fire Alarms." *American Journal of Political Science* 28: 165-79.

Mueller, D.C. 2003. *Public Choice.* Cambridge: Cambridge University Press.

Chapter 20

United States Postal Service Office of Inspector General

Developing Best Practices for a Postal Watchdog

David C. Williams and Thomas M. Sharkey
United States Postal Service Office of Inspector General

1. INTRODUCTION

This conference has focused in the past on postal economics relating to price and market regulatory issues such as controlling monopoly power and increasing competition in postal markets. This paper shifts that focus toward "oversight" of postal operators. Oversight ranges from informal oversight such as media coverage of the postal operator, to formal oversight such as that performed by the United States (U.S.) Postal Service Office of Inspector General (OIG), to include audits and investigations relating to the programs and operations of the postal operator. Oversight fosters good program management increasing the efficiency and quality of postal services, a goal all postal economists can embrace.

We appreciate the view that the market forces of competition can compel operators to be more efficient and ultimately lower prices and improve service; however, significant competition has not yet emerged in postal letter markets. We argue that in the meantime, traditional oversight of the posts still plays an important role. National governments would be wise to focus on oversight as they strive to maintain the quality and affordability of postal services for their citizens. Given that the postal service is an egalitarian element of a nation's character, national governments may never entirely relinquish control of their postal service.

We discuss the role and value of oversight organizations, outline the attributes of oversight, and identify organization types noting their strengths and liabilities. We review postal oversight in the U.S. and articulate how oversight responsibility is shared and coordinated among government entities. We discuss the strengths, liabilities, and value of postal oversight using the Inspector General (IG) model in the U.S. We summarize a survey of postal oversight activities and governance in selected countries, and propose three generalized models of postal oversight as a framework for discussion. Finally, we suggest key factors to effective oversight.

2. ROLE AND VALUE OF OVERSIGHT ORGANIZATIONS

To be a force of positive change, oversight must be neutral, objective, and credible, not simply negative criticism. Oversight of governmental entities is intended to gain efficiency and effectiveness in agency operations. In the case of the post, it is primarily concerned with the delivery of goods and services to the taxpayer or the ratepayer via performance and financial statement audits. Oversight identifies gaps in program delivery and recommends ways for an agency to execute corrective action and foster transparency. In the form of investigations into criminal, civil and administrative allegations of wrongdoing, oversight ensures the integrity of financial transactions and diminishes the exposure of governmental programs to fraud, abuse, and misconduct. Where there is competition, oversight assures a level playing field and fairness to private sector competitors. Additionally, governmental oversight bodies provide a voice for the public, as special interests can ably articulate their own concerns.

Postal economists may ask whether there is a positive return on the postal ratepayer's investment in oversight. Recognizing this concern, the OIG calculates the return on investment by estimating monetary benefits of audit recommendations to show management how implementing these recommendations can help improve their bottom line, and by identifying the amount of fines, judgments, and restitutions resulting from investigations. The OIG is required to report semiannually the amount of these monetary benefits to Congress and the Governors of the Postal Service. The OIG relies on staff such as statisticians, cost/benefit analysts, economists, engineers, subject matter experts, and computer assisted audit technical support to assist in developing the monetary impact of audited areas. This process then undergoes a quality control review by a designated in-house expert.

Additionally, there are nonmonetary benefits that increase the value of an oversight organization, such as the deterrence of fraud, waste, or misconduct; assuring a level playing field for competitors; and the efficiency gains from certain recommendations (i.e., process improvement) that may be quantified later. Further, oversight organizations provide an invaluable service when management corruption is suspected because the oversight function provides an avenue to either go in and remove the cloud of suspicion or allow corrective action, as warranted, thereby strengthening the integrity of the management and operations of an organization.

In identifying the amount of monetary benefits, auditors use the evidence gathered during fieldwork and are encouraged to obtain postal management's agreement as to the potential savings that can be reasonably determined and supported. Savings can be identified as a one-time occurrence or recurring, and are linked to recommendations such as, reduce staffing or terminate contract routes to save money over a period of time without detracting from service delivery. To estimate savings, the OIG uses the current period (starting from the issuance of the audit report through the end of the current year) and projects to the next fiscal year, or the remaining term of the contract, lease, Decision Analysis Report (typically 10 years cash flow), or other period used by the Postal Service. The amount of savings is offset by the cost of implementing the recommendation; for example, the termination cost or the cost to set up a monitoring group. When choosing between two or more equally reasonable assumptions or methods of estimation, the one that yields the least amount is reported.

Since 2003, the IG Act requires the establishment of a peer review process to ensure that "adequate internal safeguards and management procedures continue to exist within OIGs" (Quality Standards, 2003). In that way, the exercise of law enforcement powers by each OIG is reviewed periodically by another OIG or by a committee of Inspectors General. This process examines whether OIG investigative programs have adequate internal safeguards and management procedures, fosters high quality investigations and investigative processes, ensures that the highest levels of professionalism are maintained, and promotes consistency in investigative standards and practices within the IG investigative community.

3. ATTRIBUTES OF OVERSIGHT & TYPES OF OVERSIGHT ORGANIZATIONS

Oversight has both strengths and liabilities depending upon how the oversight function is managed and balanced with other oversight entities.

Basic questions to ascertain the desired strengths of oversight include: Is the work credible, objective, compelling, comprehensive, independent, and transparent? Is the area examined at a high level of discourse to focus management attention? Is the venue energized for change? Does the oversight organization possess in-depth program knowledge? Is there effective follow up?

Basic questions to ascertain the liabilities associated with oversight include: Is the oversight burdensome on the operator, expensive to conduct, distracting to the operator's leadership agenda or, in a worst case, disruptive (i.e. investigators descend on an office and operations are hindered)? These are liabilities to be guarded against or mitigated.

Against this perspective, we consider the strengths and liabilities of types of organizations that conduct oversight below.

3.1 Postal Regulator

In general, a postal regulator is not charged with direct oversight of the efficiency, effectiveness, and integrity of postal programs. However, many regulators can indirectly compel efficiencies by setting price caps that attempt to mimic the efficiencies of a competitive market. Most postal regulators do not look at criminal activity and few have the power to force disclosure of information or order sanctions against the operator. Some regulators have found this to be a major handicap. Regulators oversee and review limited but vitally important areas such as prices, service quality, and entry requirements. As a result, regulators often develop in-depth knowledge of postal operations, and credible, objective and compelling evidence to support their work. But postal operators may find the information demands of the regulator to be burdensome and intrusive. The establishment of dedicated national postal regulators in the European Union has energized the sharing of best practices and may enhance the price and quality of postal services.

3.2 Special Commissions

Special commissions can be an effective tool in that they are high profile, facilitate high-level discourse, are charged with making recommendations generally unencumbered by preconceived notions, and, if properly constructed, are objective and fair. On the other hand, there are liabilities to the special commission approach. As they go out of existence there is no guarantee that there will be action and follow up to their recommendations, particularly if they lack allies to support their recommendations. Special commissions, although confronting complex issues and organizations, may lack in-depth knowledge while challenged to develop sophisticated assessments of postal programs.

In U.S. postal history, the 1968 *Report of the President's Commission on Postal Organization* (a.k.a. Kappel Commission Report) laid the foundation for transforming the Post Office Department into a "modern day" Postal Service. However, that was 36 years ago and many believe the business model of the Postal Service is broken. To address this issue, the President established a special commission in 2002, resulting in a President's Commission Report on the U.S. Postal Service in 2003. Congress is holding hearings on the Commission's recommendations and may use them as a basis for reform legislation (House Committee, Feb. 11 & Mar. 4, 1999).

3.3 Congressional (Parliamentary) Hearings & Legislation

Congressional hearings by oversight committees are powerful in that they are high profile, enable high-level discourse at a rapid pace, and give voice to constituents and allies. However, some find that the issues addressed in hearings get a superficial treatment; that is, the examination is wide but not very deep due to time constraints. There is generally little follow-up on issues and there is a perception that committees work behind closed doors where the decision making process is not transparent. Finally, hearings often breed confrontation, rather than consensus, among opposing parties.

When all else fails, Congress will introduce legislation to directly address an oversight issue or to enhance the role and funding of responsible oversight organizations to audit or investigate issues of concern. The major strength of congressional legislation is that the law forces compliance. However, Congress may focus on other issues and may not stick with the issue to ascertain that the new legal requirement is being met by the agency. Congress may not have the resources to verify that desired laws are properly reflected in regulations and that such regulations are being followed.

3.4 Internal Auditor

Internal audits are narrow in scope and focus management attention to critical operational issues. The strength of this type of audit is that subject matter experts conduct it. Possible liabilities include that the internal auditor's work is not transparent and may lack credibility, and may be reluctant to report out unfavorable findings to management.

3.5 Inspector General

IGs conduct audits and investigations. Well-trained auditors and evaluators who work with issue areas on a regular basis can become subject matter experts with insider expertise. Auditors make recommendations to management based on sound, thorough and defendable analyses that can reap significant gains in efficiency and effectiveness. IGs also conduct independent investigations of suspected criminal, civil, and administrative wrongdoing, which may be high profile and serve as a warning to other wrongdoers. Formal investigations, which lead to administrative or judicial action, adhere to strict standards of fairness, objectivity and professionalism, and result in strong action to remedy the situation and punish the guilty. When closely allied with the judicial system, independent investigations can be a powerful tool for maintaining the integrity of postal operations. However, IG's work may have liabilities if not properly managed. Some comprehensive and sophisticated audits can take a long time. Also, IGs cannot compel the agency to implement audit recommendations. Unlike the glare of spotlights when Commissions, Congress and the media examine issues, auditors tend to work under the gentle glow of an office lamp. As such, their work may need a champion. Additionally, investigations have inherent liabilities that must be recognized. For example, a particular allegation or case can be unique and not reflect a pattern of systemic criminal activity. As such, the result is narrow and dividends may be small. These liabilities can be remedied by determining the root cause or system failure that exposed the agency to waste, fraud or misconduct.

3.6 Outside Law Enforcement

Using outside law enforcement authorities, which appears to be a common practice in the posts, are, or can be perceived, as fair and objective since they lack bias toward protecting the interests of the agency. However, when investigating criminal activity associated with the mail, outside law enforcement authorities may not have specialized postal knowledge, may have a steep learning curve, may be narrowly focused on the specific criminal activity of the allegation, and may be slow in bringing a case to justice. Often outside investigators do not identify recommendations for management to implement to prevent that type of criminal activity from reoccurring. Investigators may not look at systemic problems and instead focus on the case at hand.

3.7 Media (Press), Interest Groups, Consultants & Consumer Advocates

The media play an important, albeit less formal, role in oversight. Media coverage of postal operator issues is high profile and there are communities of common allies on many postal issues. However, the media may lack objectivity in the rush to make headlines and fit complicated issues into limited airtime and newsprint. Unless the media has reporters regularly on the postal beat, stories may not have contextual richness. Reporters, if not vigilant, are also vulnerable to taking on special interest agendas.

Table 1: Matrix of strengths and liabilities of oversight organizations

		TYPES OF OVERSIGHT ORGANIZATIONS										
		Regulator	Special Commissions	Congressional Hearings	Congressional Legislation	Internal Auditor	Inspector General	Outside Law Enforcement	Media (Press)	Interest Groups	Experts	Consumer Advocates
STRENGTHS	Credible	H	H	M	H	L	H	H	M	M	H	H
	Objective	H	M	L	M	M	H	H	M	L	M	H
	Compelling	H	M	H	H	L	H	H	L	M	M	M
	High level of discourse	M.	H	H	H	L	M	L	L	M	H	L
	Comprehensive	M	M	L	M	H	H	L	L	L	M	L
	Energized for change	M	M	H	H	L	M	M	H	L	H	M
	In-depth knowledge	H	L	M	M	H	H	L	L	H	M	H
	Independent	M	H	M	M	L	H	H	M	L	M	H
	Transparent	M	M	M	M	L	H	L	M	L	L	M
	Effective follow up	M	L	L	L	H	H	L	L	L	L	L
LIABILITIES	Disruptive	L	L	M	L	L	M	H	M	L	L	L
	Burdensome	H	M	M	M	M	M	M	L	L	M	L
	Intrusive	M	M	M	M	M	M	H	L	L	H	H

Qualities rated H – high, M – medium, L – low.Interest groups, including government watchdogs, have an important voice in oversight of the post. Despite the image of interest groups fighting to get a bigger piece of the postal pie, most postal interest groups have more in common than they have differences. On many issues, such as the efficiency and effectiveness of postal operations, they are strong natural allies to oversight organizations. Interest groups have specialized knowledge of programs that affect them. However, interest groups also have the strongest agendas which can drown out the voice of underrepresented customers, are not always objective (as one would expect), and can be confrontational.

Experts offer detailed knowledge and experience from other posts and industries, which internal auditors often lack. Experts have high credibility and, in most cases, are energized for change. However, their recommendations lack transparency and may lack follow-up. In many cases, government salary constraints or budgets make experts unaffordable, so expert consultants are usually employed by special interests. From an oversight perspective, expert consultant analyses and recommendations need to be viewed with this in mind – they may not be independent and objective. Private sector consumer advocates seek to eliminate waste and inefficiency in government through nonpartisan public education programs and lobbying activities. Government consumer advocates represent the interests of the general public. They have in-depth knowledge and, if properly managed, can be independent, credible and objective; however, their recommendations can be found to be intrusive and may lack effective follow-up.

4. POSTAL OVERSIGHT IN THE UNITED STATES

4.1 Postal Regulation and Oversight in the U.S.

We begin by describing the mission and responsibility of the OIG. We then describe the role, mission, authorities and reporting relationships of entities within the U.S. that provide regulation and oversight of the Postal Service. Such entities include Congress, the Postal Rate Commission (PRC), the Board of Governors and its committees, and the General Accounting Office (GAO). In this way a picture of the oversight model comes into focus.

The U.S. has a tradition of strong regulation of public and private monopolies. Under rate-of-return regulation, the regulator closely examines the monopoly's revenue requirement request and has the authority to lower the request based on efficiency considerations. Additionally, regulators set prices and guarantee universal service. The *Postal Reorganization Act* in 1970 (the Act), created the current U.S. Postal Service, redefining the organization and oversight of what had been the Post Office Department. The Postal Service retained its status as a government agency, but the Act established a Board of Governors to manage the postal business, and the PRC to recommend rates, which resulted in a less-regulated post. The PRC has statutory authority to recommend price changes to the postal Governors but does not consider the efficiency of postal operations and does not guarantee universal postal services. While the Postal Service was designed to operate in a business-like manner, its statutory break-even mandate provides no explicit incentives for postal management to be efficient.

In 1996, Congress filled this void and returned, in part, to the traditional regulatory model by creating an OIG to help improve the efficiency of the Postal Service as well as to ensure data accuracy, program compliance with laws, and to investigate allegations of misconduct. Although the OIG does not have the power to deny the Postal Service its revenue requests to the PRC, it nonetheless affects the process by bringing to light apparent inefficiencies in postal operations. Without hampering the Postal Service's ability to manage its business, Congress, supported by GAO, the PRC and the OIG, strive for good working relationships and an understanding of the division of oversight responsibilities. Along with the other postal oversight groups described below, they provide comprehensive but sometimes burdensome oversight of the Postal Service. Although the sharing of postal oversight among different organizations in the U.S. is complex, it works reasonably well. We share our perspective with the hope of improving postal oversight in other countries that may not have the same regulatory tradition but may benefit from our experience.

4.2 Postal Service Office of Inspector General (OIG)

OIG authority is established under the *Inspector General Act* (IG Act) of 1978, which was extended to the USPS OIG in 1996. The IG Act provides statutory responsibility to protect the integrity of Postal Service programs and operations, and to ensure that the mail service is administered with maximum efficiency. The OIG fulfills these responsibilities by completing required audits of the Postal Service's financial statements, assessing the adequacy of internal control systems, identifying opportunities for improvement, and conducting investigations, as appropriate. Unlike most OIGs, the Postal Service OIG is not funded by taxpayers from the general treasury, but is funded by ratepayers from postal revenues. The Postal Service IG does not report to the Postmaster General (PMG) but rather to the Governors of the Postal Service. The Inspector General also reports to Congress. This dual reporting responsibility strengthens the independence and transparency of the OIG.

The OIG has a budget of $123.4 million and an authorized staff of 825 auditors and investigators who face unique challenges given the size, scope and nature of postal operations. The Postal Service has been operational since 1775, and is deemed to be an independent federal agency serving 141 million homes and businesses every day. The Postal Service is the only service provider to deliver to every address in the nation. The Postal Service receives no taxpayer dollars for routine operations, but derives its operating revenues solely from the sale of postage, products and services. The Postal Service has annual revenues of more than $68.5 billion, and delivers more than 46 percent of the world's mail volume—some 202 billion letters, advertisements, periodicals and packages a year— serving seven million customers each day at its 38,000 retail locations nationwide.

4.3 Postal Service Postal Inspection Service

The Postal Service was not one of the federal entities covered by the Inspector General Act of 1978 that established IG's in the federal government. In 1988, Congress amended the Act, designating the Postal Service's Chief Postal Inspector to serve as inspector general. The Chief Postal Inspector was still appointed by, and reported to, the Postmaster General. In the 1990's, Congress became concerned over Inspection Service abuse of power, and the IS's lack of oversight and independence from management under this hybrid arrangement. In 1996, to address these concerns Congress amended the 1978 Act to create an independent postal inspector general.

The OIG took over all audit work from the Inspection Service. The Postal Inspection Service now investigates crimes including mail fraud, mail theft, transmission of prohibited mailings (controlled substances, poisons, explosives, and weapons), threats against and assaults on employees, robbery, burglary, and destruction of postal facilities, extortion through the mail, and mailing of child pornography and other sexually oriented material. The Postal Inspection Service commits significant resources to investigating and preventing mail theft.

The OIG is responsible for investigating theft, fraud, and misconduct by Postal Service officers or employees, and entities or individuals doing business with the Postal Service. The OIG provides oversight of the Postal Inspection Service's activities and informs the Governors, postal management, and Congress about problems, abuses and deficiencies relating to Postal Service programs and operations.

4.4 The U.S. Congress

The principal oversight committees for the U.S. Postal Service are the House Committee on Government Reform and the Senate Governmental Affairs Committee. The committees are required to review and study, on a continuing basis, the application, administration, execution, and effectiveness of the laws dealing with the subject matter over which the committee has jurisdiction, and the organization and operation of federal agencies and entities having responsibility for the administration and evaluation of those laws. The purpose of the review and study is to determine whether laws and the programs created by Congress are being implemented and carried out in accordance with the intent of Congress and whether those programs should be continued, curtailed, or eliminated. In addition, each committee having oversight responsibilities is required to review and study any conditions or circumstances that may indicate the necessity or desirability of enacting new or additional legislation within the jurisdiction of that committee (Johnson, 2003).

4.5 The Postal Rate Commission (PRC)

The PRC is an independent regulatory agency composed of five Commissioners each appointed to a 6-year term of office by the President and confirmed by the Senate. The President designates one commissioner as chairman. The Commission's staff is organized into four offices: Rates, Analysis and Planning; General Counsel; Commission Secretary; and, Consumer Advocate. The Commission reviews Postal Service requests for new domestic mail rates, fees, and mail classifications. It then makes recommendations to the Governors of the Postal Service after reviewing the request in public proceedings. In general, the most active participants in proceedings before the Commission are persons and organizations whose livelihood is directly affected by the Postal Service. Such participants include individuals, businesses, and associations whose members depend heavily on postal services, or are competitors of the Postal Service.

The Office of the Consumer Advocate (OCA) is a component of the PRC and deals primarily with postal rates and mail classifications in cases before the PRC. OCA's mission is to be a vigorous, responsive, and effective advocate for reasonable and equitable treatment of the general public in proceedings before the PRC. The OCA strives to assure that postal rate increases are fair to the general public.

4.6 Board of Governors & Its Committees

The Board includes nine Governors who are appointed by the President with the advice and consent of the Senate to serve a 9-year term. The nine Governors select the PMG, who becomes a member of the Board, and those 10 select the Deputy PMG, who also serves on the Board. The PMG serves at the pleasure of the Governors for an indefinite term. The Deputy PMG serves at the pleasure of the Governors and the PMG. The Governors are chosen to represent the public interest and cannot be representatives of special interests. Not more than five of the nine may belong to the same political party. The entire Board determines the dates on which new rates and classification adjustments become effective. The Board directs the exercise of the powers of the Postal Service, directs and controls its expenditures, reviews its practices, conducts long-range planning, and sets policies on all postal matters. The Board takes up matters such as service standards, capital investments and facilities projects exceeding $10 million.

It also approves officer compensation. There are three standing committees: Audit and Finance, Capital Projects, and Strategic Planning.

4.7 The General Accounting Office (GAO)

Congress asks GAO to study the programs and expenditures of the federal government, including the Postal Service. GAO, commonly called the investigative arm of Congress or the congressional watchdog, is independent and nonpartisan. It advises Congress and the heads of executive agencies about ways to make government more effective. When GAO reports its findings to Congress, it recommends actions and issues legal opinions. Its work leads to laws and acts that improve government operations, and save billions of dollars.

5. INSPECTOR GENERAL MODEL

In the U.S., an OIG has administrative authority to: (1) receive full access to all records and materials available to the agency; (2) determine which audits, investigations, inspections, and reviews are necessary and issue reports; (3) issue subpoenas for non-federal records; (4) report directly to the head of the agency; (5) receive employee and other complaints, (6) protect confidential sources, and when necessary, (7) refer matter to the U.S. Attorney General. In addition, OIGs are authorized to hire employees, experts, and consultants; procure necessary equipment and services; and obtain assistance from other agencies, including federal, state, and local governments.

The IG model has stood the test of time. For over 25 years, federal IGs have had a profound impact on government operations via audits, investigations and evaluations identifying billions of dollars in potential savings and questioned costs that may violate law, regulation, or contract (House Committee, Oct.8, 2003). OIG investigations lead to thousands of prosecutions or other actions, as well as billions of dollars in potential recoveries. Further, auditors and investigators have different approaches to gathering, analyzing, and presenting evidence, which leads to superior findings when the two groups work together. Also, IGs' work is transparent as the IG Act requires IGs to publish semiannual reports to Congress.

The dual reporting of IGs to Congress and to their respective agency heads further enhances their independence, which is a fundamental aspect of the strength of the IG model. Further, IGs cannot be prevented from doing, conducting, or completing audits and investigations. Although, IGs have been accused of buckling to political or agency pressure, such cases are rare and usually exposed by "good government" watchdogs in the U.S., who not only keep watchful eyes on agency activity, but also carefully scrutinize IGs.

IGs report on vital issues and make judgments about agency successes and failures. If the work is good, it is more than the sum of its parts. IGs enter disputes, and sometimes the weight of IG findings is determinative. IGs inform debates with rich, useful data that is objective and compelling. IGs validate claims of performance, financial achievement, and progress on initiatives, restore confidence where charges of scandal have disabled programs, establish innocence and remove clouds of doubt over individuals, offices and corporations. IGs also ascertain guilt and permit a program to move forward after corrective actions have occurred. IGs are called upon to be barriers to initiatives that are poorly thought out and heading for disaster.

The IG model includes many techniques that are useful for oversight organizations. Of these, best practices include aligning the organization, communicating the report, and being accountable for performance.

One best practice is to have offices within the oversight organization aligned for the single purpose of their mission, which permits higher production rates, quality products, and gives field offices and staff greater autonomy with less organizational risk. Aligned offices allow employees to understand what their role is in achieving the IG's mission, and that of their team, their office, their function, and their senior leaders. Every element of the organization should strictly align to the overarching strategy and performance metrics. Teams then know exactly what is expected of them in terms of production and what resources they have to meet their goals.

Another best practice is to effectively communicate report findings by: (1) preparing concise, objective reports; (2) removing redundancies; (3) including executive summaries; (4) utilizing new report writing features such as PowerPoint and reports with embedded video; and (5) expanding product lines to include testimony, conferences, and working groups.

An important best practice is the performance measure process, which makes an organization accountable for results (Bryson, 1995). This process is based on the *Government Performance and Results Act* of 1993 (GPRA), which requires federal agencies to have strategic and annual performance plans. GAO has found that agency strategic and annual performance plans have improved over initial efforts, and that management reforms based on GPRA have begun to demonstrate slow and sustainable improvements (GAO-04-38). GPRA provides a statutory framework by which federal managers can adopt a strategic focus to link resources with results, improve the efficiency of their organization, and ultimately reduce the cost of government (Gruber, 2004). Examples of OIG performance measures that can serve as a best practice resource for other postal industry watchdogs include the timeliness and cost of audits and investigations, the number of audits and the significance of findings and monetary benefits; and the number of investigative cases and the resulting amount of fines, judgments, and restitutions.

The IG model also has liabilities, which can generally be addressed with improved management of the quality, timeliness and sophistication of audits and investigations. IGs need to be sensitive and address the following reoccurring criticisms: IGs are (1) too slow-moving to aid agencies responding to emergencies or urgent initiatives; (2) non-inclusive even when subject matters experts are readily available; (3) a distraction to leaders, who have limited amounts of time and energy for change initiatives; (4) irrelevant because they use cut and paste formulistic recommendations that do not address root causes of the problems; and (5) attention seekers that write sensationalized reports. Further, the dual reporting requirement for IGs raises the fear that individuals may question the loyalty of the IG and then compromise the information that they disclose. Sometimes IGs abuse their independence if their actions are unchecked. These are powerful criticisms; but the model is hardly broken.

To address these liabilities and improve the value of oversight work, it is best to create teams that are aligned with the postal operator and focus on evaluating business unit operations. Best practices for audit directors include: (1) understanding how Postal Service programs are performing, determining whether it is succeeding, and developing and articulating a "big picture" for the issue area; (2) conducting gap analyses and filling gaps with the Postal Service's planned corrective initiatives; and (3) monitoring whether initiatives are project-managed, on time, and on budget.

Additionally, it is helpful to identify Postal Service, congressional, and stakeholder counterparts to meet with regularly to get feedback on performance and to plan work. These meetings require a standard agenda to cover reviews of ongoing work, requests from other stakeholders, finished work with recommendations for signature, and future job possibilities. Engagement letters flow from agreements made during these meetings that have specific delivery dates, and an agreed upon scope and methodology. Further, having a strategy for releasing reports to maximize outcomes by assessing what Postal Service managers are focusing on, and identifying events that energize change such as legislation or oversight hearings, pressure from the PMG, and criticism from stakeholders is also helpful.

6. COMPARISON OF OTHER MODELS OF OVERSIGHT

Throughout the industrialized world, there are a variety of entities that regulate, audit, investigate and/or provide advisory opinions to governments about postal operators. Table 2 summarizes the role, authorities, and reporting relationships of entities that are charged with oversight or regulatory responsibilities based on a survey of selected countries. The legal status of public postal operators ranges from traditional federal entities, government owned corporatized enterprises, and operators that purport to be private with a government granted monopoly. As such, the form of oversight varies and appears to be related to the extent to which the post is corporatized. We offer three generalized models of oversight as a framework for further discussion.

The traditional model: The traditional model has many governmental entities that focus on specialized areas of oversight. These entities can include an internal auditor, an independent (of management) auditor, an external auditor, an internal investigator, and an independent investigator. The U.S. Postal Service, a traditional federal entity, with limited freedoms to operate in a business-like manner, typifies this model.

The hybrid model: The hybrid model has some governmental entities that focus on specialized areas of oversight, particularly focusing on the post's public performance at a high level (not individual programs), and the impact of the post's performance on competition. Royal Mail, a partially liberalized, government-owned corporatized post, typifies this model.

The corporatized model: The corporatized model may have a limited internal auditor or only have an external financial auditor who does not audit operations and does not make recommendations to improve performance. Violations of law are reported to the police like any other business company. The Sweden Post, a fully liberalized, government-owned corporatized post that faces competition in the letter market, typifies this model.

Oversight in a Changing World: Even with full liberalization and increased competition, governments still have a compelling interest in protecting and guaranteeing postal service for the public. Effective oversight to enforce regulations and to verify that obligations are met will continue to be important, particularly those related to universal service, quality of service, anti-trust enforcement, compliance with access requirements and price caps, corporate internal security, and the sanctity and security of the mail.

Table 2: Matrix comparing other models of oversight

	COUNTRIES								
	US	France	Switzerland	Italy	Ireland	Germany	UK	Finland	Sweden
Oversight Model	Traditional----------------→Hybrid------------------------→Corporatized								
Liberalization	No	Partial	Partial	Partial	Partial	Partial	Partial (Fully from 2007)	Fully	Fully
External Auditor	Fin. Only	Yes	Yes	Yes	Yes	Fin. Only	Yes	Fin. Only	KPMG
Independent Gov't Auditor	OIG Fin. & Programs	Yes	No	Corte dei Conti	No	No	No	No	National Audit Office
Internal Auditor	Yes	No	Yes	Yes	Yes	No	Yes	Fin. Stmts. internal controls	Fin. Stmts. Internal controls
Consumer Advocate(s)	OCA	Ombudsman ARCEP (draft postal law)	PostReg	None for postal matters	AP Ombudsman	RegTP	Postwatch	Six orgs. special roles	None for postal matters
Regulator(s)	PRC – Price & service	No nat'l regulator, DIGITIP, MINEFI ARCEP (draft postal law)	PostReg	Ministry of Comm.	ComReg	RegTP	Postcomm	FICORA	National Post & Telecom
Parliamentary/ Congressional	2 oversight, reform leg, GAO	Yes	Postal Act of 1997 and 2000	Yes	Review legs and regs, enacts	Postal Act of 1997	Yes, Trade & Industry Select Committee	Parliamentary ombudsman	Parliament
Ministry / Cabinet	Treasury – Debt Mgmt.	MINEFI	UVEK	Yes	DCMNR	Ministry of Economics & Labor	Dept. of Trade & Industry	Ministry of Transport & Comm.	Ministry of Industry, Employment &Comm.
Investigator – Internal Crimes	OIG	court	Police, PostReg	Police	Police	Police	Internal Security Service	Police	Police
Investigator-External Crimes	OIG, Inspection Service	court	Police, Court	Police	Police	Police	Police	Police	Police

Note: See glossary at the end of the paper for acronyms and abbreviations.

7. CONCLUSION

Postal oversight ensures the efficiency and integrity of postal programs, which may be accomplished with complementary postal watchdogs; however, it is best to avoid redundancies in oversight functions unless there is a compelling reason. Intended redundancies in oversight roles allow for checks and balances in the process. In countries with few oversight organizations, it is important to assure that there is adequate coverage of oversight functions. When designing comprehensive oversight programs, governments would want as many strengths contained in the oversight process as possible, exploiting the positive and mitigating the possible negative aspects of oversight. To be effective at facilitating continuous improvement via oversight, postal watchdogs need to be mindful of their role in the oversight process, demonstrate their value to the postal operator, and have mechanisms in place to improve the quality of their own programs.

Traditional oversight of government-owned postal monopolies is valuable. Anticipating competition in postal markets, governments may have prematurely moved toward a private sector model. We recommend that postal organizations reconsider and adopt some of the traditional best practices of postal watchdogs. In this way, governments can improve the affordability and quality of postal services, a goal everyone, especially economists, can embrace.

GLOSSARY OF ACRONYMS AND ABBREVIATIONS

admin.:	administrative
AP:	An Post
ARCEP:	Autorité de Régulation des Communications Electroniques et des Postes – Postal and Electronic Communications Regulatory Body, as foreseen in the draft postal law currently processed at the French Parliament
Comm.(s):	communication(s)
ComReg:	Commission for Communications Regulation
DCMNR:	Minister for Communications, Marine and Natural Resources
DETEC:	Departement Federal de l'Environnement, des Transports, de l'Energie et de la Communication – also known as UVEK
FICORA:	Finnish Communications Regulatory Authority
fin.:	financial
GAO:	General Accounting Office
legs and regs:	legislation and regulation
mgmt.	management
MINEFI:	Ministry of the Economy, Finance and Industry. The present postal regulator is its department responsible for industry, IT and post, DIGITIP.
OCA:	Office of the Consumer Advocate
OIG:	Office of Inspector General
orgs.:	organizations
Postcomm:	Postal Services Commission
PostReg:	In Switzerland, PostReg acts as an independent body for regulatory tasks and is affiliated to the General Secretariat of DETEC for administrative purposes
Postwatch:	Consumer organization acting as the voice of the consumer in all postal service matters in the UK
PRC:	Postal Rate Commission

RegTP:	Regulierungsbehörde für Telekommunikation und Post
stmts.:	statements
UK:	United Kingdom
U.S.:	United States
UVEK:	Eidgenossisches Departement für Umwelt, Verkehr, Energie, und Kommunikation - Federal Department for Environment, Transport, and Energy – also known as DETEC

REFERENCES

Bryson, John M. 1995. Strategic Planning for Public and Nonprofit Organizations: A Guide to Strengthening and Sustaining Organizational Achievement. San Francisco: Jossey-Bass.

Campbell, Robert M. 2002. The Politics of Postal Transformation: Modernizing Postal Systems in the Electronic and Global World. Montreal: McGill-Queen's University Press.

Cohen, Robert et al. Postal Regulation and Worksharing in the US. Washington, DC: n.p., 2004.

European Commission Directives on Community postal services.

General Accounting Office. 2002. Inspectors General: Office Consolidation and Related Issues U.S. GAO-02-575. Washington, DC: August.

General Accounting Office. 2003. Government Accounting Standards. Revised. GAO-03-673G. Washington, DC: June.

General Accounting Office. 2004. Results-Oriented Government: GPRA Has Established a Solid Foundation for Achieving Greater Results. GAO-04-38. Washington, DC: March 10.

Government Performance and Results Act of 1993. January 5, 1993.

Gruber, Amelia. 2004. "Daily Briefing Lawmakers call for five-year program reviews." GovExec.com, February 24.

House Committee on Government Reform, To Modernize the Postal Laws of the United States: Hearings on H. R. 22, 106th Cong., 1st session, February 11 and March 4, 1999. The Postal Modernization Act of 1999.

House Committee on Government Reform, 25th Anniversary of the Inspector General Act of 1978: Where Do We Go From Here?: Hearings on P.L. 95-452, 108th Cong., October 8, 2003.

Inspector General Act of 1978. 5 USCA Appx § 1 (2001). § 1 Government Operations and Employees.

Johnson, Charles W. 2003. Parliamentarian, How Our Laws Are Made, U.S. House of Representatives, H. Doc. 108-93, p.19.

Journal of Public Inquiry: A publication of the Inspectors General of the United States. Washington, DC.

Postal Service Office of Inspector General. 2002. Audit of the Postal Service's Transformation Plan, OE-MA-03-001. Arlington, VA: October 29.

Postal Service Office of Inspector General. 2002. Audit of the Transformation Plan. Letter to the Governors, Arlington, VA: April 30.

Postal Service Office of Inspector General. 2002. Five-Year Strategic Plan: FY 2004-2008, Arlington, VA: September 30.

Postal Service Office of Inspector General. 2004. Summary of the Commission's Recommendations, February 13.

Postal Service Transformation Plan. 2002. Washington, DC: April.
Postal Service Transformation Plan. 2003. Progress Report, Washington, DC: November.
Postal Services Commission - Postcomm / Consumer Council for Postal Services – Postwatch: Memorandum of Understanding. April 30, 2002.
President's Commission on the United States Postal Service. Embracing the Future, Making the Tough Choices to Preserve Universal Mail Service. Washington, DC: July 31, 2003.
Public Law 95-452, § 1, Oct. 12, 1978, 92 Stat. 1101, as amended. Inspector General Act of 1978.
Public Law 91-375, 39 U.S.C., The Postal Reorganization Act, August 12, 1970.
Quality Standards for Federal Offices of Inspector General: President's Council on Integrity and Efficiency/Executive Council on Integrity and Efficiency. Washington, DC: October 2003.
Study of the Impact of Certain Aspects of the Application of the Directive 97/67/EC on the Postal Service.
UK Government Resources and Accounts Act 2000 relating to Comptroller and Auditor General (C&AG) the statutory audit authority.